Hell Hath No Fury

THE ANCHOR YALE BIBLE REFERENCE LIBRARY

Hell Hath No Fury

Gender, Disability, and the Invention of Damned Bodies in Early Christian Literature

MEGHAN R. HENNING

YALE

AYBRL

Yale

UNIVERSITY

PRESS

NEW HAVEN

AND

LONDON

Yale University Press books may be purchased in quantity for educational, business, or promotional use. For information, please email sales.press@yale.edu (U.S. office) or sales@yaleup.co.uk (U.K. office).

Set in Adobe Caslon type by Newgen North America, Austin, Texas.
Printed in the United States of America.

Library of Congress Control Number: 2020951714
ISBN 978-0-300-22311-8 (hardcover : alk. paper)

A catalogue record for this book is available from the British Library.

This paper meets the requirements of ANSI/NISO Z39.48-1992 (Permanence of Paper).

10 9 8 7 6 5 4 3 2 1

For Doug

Contents

Acknowledgments

There are a number of people who have graciously supported my work on this project whom I would like to thank. I am tremendously grateful to John J. Collins and the Yale Anchor Bible Editorial Board for their support of this project from start to finish. Jennifer Banks, Heather Gold, Ann-Marie Imbornoni, and Abbie Storch at Yale University Press provided guidance and editorial expertise with an extra measure of care in the many stages of the editing and production process. Lys Weiss was a phenomenal copyeditor, unparalleled in her attention to detail. My research for this project was supported by several generous grants from the University of Dayton Research Council. My research for this project was also enriched through conversations facilitated by the Centre of Advanced Studies: Beyond Canon, University of Regensburg and its Fellows. This work draws upon a few previously published articles, all of which have been indicated in the notes. I do not reproduce the arguments, but I am grateful to Oxford University Press, Peeters, and Mohr Siebeck for permission to use small portions of these articles.

This project is one that would not have been completed without well-timed teaching releases and paid maternity leave. With this in mind, I thank my department chair, Daniel Speed Thompson; Dean Jason Pierce; Associate Provost Carolyn Roecker Phelps; and Provost Paul Benson, at the University of Dayton, for creating an academic culture in which the research of female faculty is supported and prioritized. The University of Dayton Library and the Marian Library faculty have kept me in books, articles, and critical editions all in good cheer, and I especially want to thank Jason Bourgeois, Fred Jenkins, and Stephanie Shreffler for their library assistance. My colleagues in the Department of Religious Studies have welcomed me to their intellectual family—I am very lucky to have found my way home to you all.

I am grateful to the many colleagues and friends who shared their work with me prior to publication, read portions of this book before it was published, provided feedback on presentations, or simply thought of me every time they came across a reference to worms or mire in the ancient world: Dustin Atlas, Richard Bauckham, Eric Beck, Sarah Bond, Adam Booth, Jan Bremmer, Silviu Bunta, Tony Burke, Adela Yarbro Collins, Chris de Wet, Jörg Frey, Kathleen Gallagher Elkins, Carl Holladay, Joe Kozar, Christine Luckritz Marquis, Heidi Marx, Candida R. Moss, Alexander Perkins, Michael Sommer, Robert von Thaden, Jr., Kristi Upson-Saia, Stephen Young, and Jonathan Zecher. I owe a debt of gratitude to scholars who read the entirety of this manuscript at critical moments and offered their feedback, especially the anonymous readers at Yale University Press, and also Adele Reinhartz, John Penniman, and Tobias Nicklas. Finally, I am grateful to Travis Ables for his editorial work on this book.

To Susan Ackerman I owe special thanks, for giving this book such a wonderful title—one that makes me smile and think of you often. I am so thankful for your generosity on that flight to Amsterdam for the International SBL conference, offering conversation and mentorship to a then very nervous doctoral student.

Several graduate students at the University of Dayton have played a role in the completion of this manuscript, including Drew Courter, Patrick Fitzgerald, Scott Howland, Shelby Mongan, Kathy Stout, Ellie Vela, and Rachel Williams. You have each made a mark on my life, and I treasure getting to learn alongside you. I gained new energy for revising this manuscript from conversations with Gillian Cooley, Ashley Klesken, and Nancy Romer, the students of the Beyond the Normate Hermeneutic Doctoral Seminar—your deep engagement with the material was an extraordinary gift.

I am tremendously lucky to have friends both near and far who have not only endured years of hell talk, but also sustain the day-to-day role of the teacher-scholar in big and small ways: Dustin Atlas, Jennifer Barry, Jana Bennett, Nikki Bennett, Sarah Bond, Laura Collier, David Darrow, Neomi De Anda, Michelle Hayford, Miriamne Krummel, Christine Luckritz Marquis, Kelly Murphy, Michelle Pautz, Leslie Picca, Gilberto Ruiz, Christopher Skinner, Shively Smith, Shannon Toll, Joe Valenzano, Kelly Vibber, and Jessica Williams.

Without our family's village of childcare professionals nothing we do, least of all this book, would be possible. Thank you to Liz Abbott, Mikaela Dean, Judi Gaines, Amber Keith, Paula Klosterman-Pritchard, Ellen Paget, Vicki Rohrer, Autumn Smith Taylor, Nikki Tousley, and the staff at the Bombeck Family Learning Center for loving my family so well.

Thanks to my incredible family: Amanda Carpenter, Steve Daniels, Mary Jo Henning, Ray Henning, Sarah Henning, Shirley Metternick, and Jack Metternick. Without your love and support this work would be so much harder. I am grateful for every late-night phone call and your boundless grandparent and auntie energy that has enriched so many writing days.

Candida Moss, without you I would never have dreamed up this book, nor would I have completed it. You have thought with me since the beginning, shared countless references, graciously shared your own work, and read, reread, edited, and commented on numerous versions of the manuscript—some in the midst of a pandemic. Your daily presence in my life is an indescribable gift that sustains and energizes me. Thank you for your role in my life.

Max and Aria, you are my daily joy, and it is my great honor to be your Mom. Thank you for the laughter, fun, and love that you bring to my life and my work.

This book is dedicated to Doug, the love of my life, who has moved heaven and earth to make my dreams come true, and who has sacrificed the most to make this book possible. Thank you, my darling, for bringing so much light to my life that I am able to make daily forays into hell.

Abbreviations

Titles and abbreviations for ancient and modern works follow the conventions of the *SBL Handbook of Style*, 2d ed. (Atlanta: SBL, 2014).

Primary Sources

Acts Andr.	Acts of Andrew
Acts Andr. Mth.	Acts of Andrew and Matthias
Acts Thom.	Acts of Thomas
Aelian, *Char. An.*	*Characteristics of Animals*
Aelius Aristides, *Sac. Tales*	*Sacred Tales*
Aelius Theon, *Exerc.*	*Preliminary Exercises*
Aëtius, *Philos.*	*Opinions of the Philosophers*
Ambrose, *Vir.*	*On Virgins*
Antyllus, *Health Dec.*	*On Healthful Declamation*
Apoc. Gorg.	Apocalypse of Gorgorios
Apoc. Paul	Apocalypse of Paul
Apoc. Pet.	Apocalypse of Peter
Apoc. Sedr.	Apocalypse of Sedrach
Apoc. Zeph.	Apocalypse of Zephaniah
Aristophanes, *Clouds*	*Clouds*
Frogs	*Frogs*
Aristotle, *Gen. An.*	*Generation of Animals*
Hist. An.	*History of Animals*
Mem. Rem.	*Memory and Remembrance*
Met.	*Metaphysics*
Part. An.	*Parts of Animals*

Pol.	*Politics*
Probl.	*Problems*
Rhet.	*Rhetoric*
Soul	*On the Soul*
Arnobius of Sicca, *Ag. Pag.*	*Against the Pagans*
Arrian, *Diss. Epict.*	*Dissertations of Epictetus*
Artemidorus, *Dreams*	*On the Interpretation of Dreams*
Ascen. Isa.	Ascension of Isaiah
Athanasius, *Hist. Ar.*	*History of the Arians*
Let. Vir.	*Letter to Virgins*
Life Ant.	*Life of Anthony*
Athenagoras, *Plea*	*A Plea for Christians*
Augustine, *Conf.*	*Confessions*
Enarrat. Ps.	*Enarrations on the Psalms*
Let.	*Letters*
Tract. Gos. Jo.	*Tractates on the Gospel of John*
Aulus Gellius, *Attic*	*Attic Nights*
1–3 Bar.	1–3 Baruch
Barn.	Epistle of Barnabas
Basil of Ancyra, *Virg.*	*On Virginity*
Basil of Caesarea, *Let.*	*Letters*
Cedrenus, *Comp. Hist.*	*Compendium of History*
Celcus, *Med.*	*De Medicina*
Chron. Jer.	Chronicles of Yeraḥme'el
Cicero, *Phil. Or.*	*Philippic Orations*
Tusc. Disp.	*Tusculan Disputations*
Clement of Alexandria, *Educ.*	*Christ the Educator*
Ex. Proph.	*Extracts from the Prophets*
Misc.	*Miscellanies*
Cop. Apoc. Eli.	Coptic Apocalypse of Elijah
Cyprian, *Laps.*	*The Lapsed*
Did.	Didache
Dio Cassius, *Rom. Hist.*	*Roman History*

Dio Chrysostom, *Hunt.*	*Hunter (Oration 7)*
Dionysius Halicarnassensis, *Imit.*	*On Imitation*
1–3 En.	1–3 Enoch
Ephrem the Syrian, *Comm. Diat.*	*Commentary on the Diatessaron*
Hymn Chu.	*Hymns on the Church*
Hymn Nat.	*Hymns of the Nativity*
Hymn Par.	*Hymn of Paradise*
Epictetus, *Disc.*	*Discourses*
Ench.	*Enchiridion*
Ep. Tit.	Epistle of Titus
Eth. Apoc. Bar.	Ethiopian Apocalypse of Baruch
Eth. Apoc. Mary	Ethiopian Apocalypse of Mary
Eth. Apoc. Vir.	Ethiopian Apocalypse of the Virgin
Euripides, *El.*	*Electra*
Eusebius of Caesarea, *Eccl. Hist.*	*Ecclesiastical History*
Life Const.	*Life of Constantine*
Martyrs	*The Martyrs of Palestine*
Eusebius of Emesa, *Hom.*	*Homily*
Galen, *Aff. Part.*	*On Affected Parts*
Ant. Caus.	*On Antecedent Causes*
Art	*Art of Medicine*
Blood. Er.	*On Bloodletting, against Erasistratus*
Cap. Soul	*The Capacities of the Soul Depend on the Mixtures of the Body*
Comp. Drug Pl.	*On the Composition of Drugs according to Places*
Diff. Resp.	*On Difficulty in Breathing*
Doct. Hipp. Plat.	*On the Doctrines of Hippocrates and Plato*
Func. Part.	*On the Function of the Parts of the Body*
Health. Cond.	*Healthful Conduct*
Hipp. Aph.	*On Hippocrates's "Aphorisms"*

Hipp. Epid.	*On Hippocrates's "Epidemics"*
Hist. Phil.	*History of Philosophy*
Hyg.	*Hygiene*
Meth. Med.	*Method of Medicine*
Nat. Cap.	*On the Natural Capacities*
Prop. Food	*On the Properties of Foodstuffs*
Semen	*On Semen*
Ther.	*On Theriac to Pamphilianus*
Ther. Glau.	*Therapeutics to Glaucon*
Gk. Apoc. Ez.	Greek Apocalypse of Ezra
Gk. Apoc. Mary	Greek Apocalypse of Mary
Gk. Apoc. Pet.	Greek Apocalypse of Peter
Gos. Pet.	Gospel of Peter
Gos. Ps. Matt.	Gospel of Pseudo-Matthew
Gregory of Nazianzus, *Or.*	*Orations*
Gregory of Nyssa, *Bir. Chr.*	*Birth of Christ*
Grt. Cat.	*Great Catechism*
Life Macr.	*Life of Macrina*
Test. Jews	*Testimony against the Jews*
Heliodorus, *Aeth.*	*Aethiopica*
Herm Vis.	Shepherd of Hermas, Visions
Herodotus, *Hist.*	*History*
Hippocratic Corpus, *Aff.*	*Affections*
Airs	*Airs, Waters, Places*
Anc. Med.	*Ancient Medicine*
Aph.	*Aphorisms*
Art	*Art of Medicine*
Barr.	*Barrenness*
Coan Pre.	*Coan Prenotions*
Crises	*Crises*
Dis.	*On Diseases*
Dis. Yg. Girl.	*Diseases of Young Girls*
Epid.	*Epidemics*

Fem. Dis.	*Female Diseases*
Fist.	*Fistulas*
Genit.	*Genitals*
Glands	*On Glands*
Nat. Boy	*Nature of Boys*
Nat. Child	*Nature of the Child*
Nat. Wom.	*Nature of the Woman*
Prog.	*Prognostics*
Pror.	*Prorrhetic*
Reg.	*Regimen*
Superf.	*Superfetation*
Homer, *Il.*	*Iliad*
Od.	*Odyssey*
Horace, *Sat.*	*Satires*
Ignatius, Ign. *Magn.*	*To the Magnesians*
Ign. *Phld.*	*To the Philadelphians*
Irenaeus, *Ag. Her.*	*Against Heresies*
Isa. Frag.	Isaiah Fragment
Jerome, *Ag. Hel.*	*Against Helvidius*
Let.	*Letters*
John Chrysostom, *Bern. Pros.*	*On Saints Bernice and Prosdoce*
Hom. Act.	*Homilies on the Acts of the Apostles*
Hom. Ep. Rom.	*Homilies on the Epistle to the Romans*
Hom. John	*Homilies on John*
Hom. Matt.	*Homilies on Matthew*
Hom. Pelag.	*Homily on Pelagia, Virgin and Martyr*
Stag.	*To Stagirium*
Vain.	*On Vainglory*
John Malalas, *Chron.*	*Chronography*
Josephus, *Ant.*	*Jewish Antiquities*
Justinian, *Nov.*	*Novels*
Justin Martyr, *1 Apol.*	*First Apology*
Dial.	*Dialogue with Trypho*

Juvenal, *Sat.*	*Satires*
Lactantius, *Death Pers.*	*Death of the Persecuting Emperors*
Lat. Vis. Ez.	Latin Vision of Ezra
Libanius, *Or.*	*Oration*
Lucian, *Civ. War*	*Civil War*
Dial. Dead	*Dialogues of the Dead*
Dial. Gods	*Dialogues of the Gods*
Men.	*Menippus*
Port.	*Essays in Portraiture*
Tyr.	*The Downward Journey or The Tyrant*
Marcus Aurelius, *Med.*	*Meditations*
Mart. Perp. Fel.	*Martyrdom of Perpetua and Felicitas*
Martial, *Epig.*	*Epigrams*
Mary's Rep.	Book of Mary's Repose
Methodius of Olympus, *Res.*	*The Resurrection*
Sym.	*Symposium*
Odes Sol.	Odes of Solomon
Oppian, *Cyn.*	*Cynegtica, or The Chase*
Oribasius, *Coll. Med.*	*Medical Collections*
Origen, *Cels.*	*Against Celsus*
Comm. Jo.	*Commentary on John*
Comm. Rom.	*Commentary on Romans*
Ex. Mart.	*An Exhortation to Martyrdom*
Princ.	*On First Principles*
Pausanias, *Descr.*	*Description of Greece*
Perictione, *Harm. Wom.*	*On the Harmony of a Woman*
Philo, *Contempl. Life*	*On the Contemplative Life*
Spec. Laws	*On the Special Laws*
Phintys, *Temp. Wom.*	*On the Temperance of a Woman*
Plato, *Let.*	*Letters*
Rep.	*Republic*
Tim.	*Timaeus*
Plautus, *Capt.*	*The Captives*
Churl	*The Churl*

Pliny the Elder, *Nat. Hist.*	*Natural History*
Pliny the Younger, *Pan.*	*Panegyric*
Plutarch, *Cons. Wife*	*Consolation to His Wife*
Educ. Ch.	*On the Education of Children*
Mor.	*Moralia*
Mor. Co. Pr.	*Moralia: Advice to Bride and Groom*
Mor. Div. Veng.	*Moralia: On the Delays of the Divine Vengeance*
Quaest. conv.	*Convivial Questions Book IX*
Talk.	*Concerning Talkativeness*
Pomponius Bononiensis, Pros.	*The Prostitute*
Porphyrio, *Sat.*	*Satires*
Procopius of Caesarea, *Build.*	*On Buildings*
Sec. Hist.	*Secret History*
Prot. Jas.	Protevangelium of James
Pseudo-Athanasius, *Virg.*	*On Virginity*
Pseudo-Plutarch, *Educ. Ch.*	*Education of Children*
Ques. Bar.	Questions of Bartholomew
Ques. Ezra	Questions of Ezra
Quintilian, *Inst.*	*Institutes of Oration*
Seneca the Elder, *Cont.*	*Controversies*
Seneca the Younger, *Ben.*	*On Benefits*
Helv.	*To Helviam*
Wise Man	*On the Firmness of the Wise Man*
Severian of Gabala, *Hom. 6 Creat.*	*Homily 6 on Creation of the World*
Hom. Leg.	*Homily on the Legislator*
Shenoute of Atripe, *Liv. Monks*	*Lives of Monks*
6 Bks. Apoc.	Six Books Apocryphon
Soranus, *Gyn.*	*Gynaecology*
Sozomen, *Eccl. Hist.*	*Ecclesiastical History*
Suetonius, *Calig.*	*Gaius Caligula*

Tacitus, *Ann.*	*Annals*
Germ.	*Germania*
Tatian, *Gr.*	*Oration to the Greeks*
Tertullian, *Apol.*	*Apology*
App. Wom.	*The Apparel of Women*
Nat.	*To the Nations*
Pall.	*The Pallium*
Res.	*The Resurrection of the Dead*
Scap.	*To Scapula*
Shows	*The Shows*
Soul	*The Soul*
Val.	*Against the Valententians*
Veil Vir.	*The Veiling of Virgins*
Theophanes, *Chron.*	*Chronography*
Theophilus, *Autol.*	*To Autolycus*
Timotheus, *Frag.*	*Fragments*
Virgil, *Aen.*	*Aeneid*
Xenophon, *Hell.*	*Hellenica*

Secondary Sources

AP	Apophthegmata Patrum
BBR	*Bulletin for Biblical Research*
BETL	Bibliotheca Ephemeridum Theologicarum Lovaniensium
BJRL	*Bulletin of the John Rylands University Library of Manchester*
CBQ	*Catholic Biblical Quarterly*
CCSA	Corpus Christianorum: Series Apocryphorum
CCSL	Corpus Christianorum: Series Latina. Turnhout: Brepols, 1953–.
CH	*Church History*
CJ	P. Krueger, ed. *Codex Justinianus*. Corpus Iuris Civilis (CIC), vol. 2. Berlin: Weidmann, 1877, reprinted 1954.

CMG	Corpus Medicorum Graecorum. Leipzig: Teubner, 1928–.
CSCO	Corpus Scriptorum Christianorum Orientalium
CSEL	Corpus Scriptorum Ecclesiasticorum Latinorum
CTh	T. Mommsen and P. Meyer, eds. *Theodosiani Libri XVI cum Constitutionibus Sirmondianis et Leges Novellae ad Theodosianum Pertinentes*, vols. I.1, I.2, and II. Berlin: Weidmann, 1905, reprinted 1954.
FC	Fathers of the Church
FCNTECW	Feminist Companion to the New Testament and Early Christian Writings
HTR	*Harvard Theological Review*
IC	*Inscriptiones Creticae*
IG	*Inscriptiones Graecae*. Editio minor. Berlin, 1924–.
JAAR	*Journal of the American Academy of Religion*
JBL	*Journal of Biblical Literature*
JDR	*Journal of Disability and Religion*
JECS	*Journal of Early Christian Studies*
JLA	*Journal of Late Antiquity*
JRS	*Journal of Roman Studies*
JSJS	Supplements to the *Journal for the Study of Judaism*
JSNT	*Journal for the Study of the New Testament*
JTS	*Journal of Theological Studies*
Kühn	Karl Gottlob Kühn. *Claudii Galeni Opera Omnia.* 20 vols. Leipzig: Cnobloch, 1821–1833.
LHBOTS	Library of the Hebrew Bible/Old Testament Studies
NHC	Nag Hammadi Codices
NovT	*Novum Testamentum*
NTOA	Novum Testamentum et Orbis Antiquus
NTS	*New Testament Studies*
OTP	*Old Testament Pseudepigrapha*
PG	Patrologia Cursus Completus: Series Graeca. Ed. J.-P. Migne. 162 vols. Paris, 1857–86.
PL	Patrologia Cursus Completus: Series Ecclesiae Latinae. Ed. J.-P. Migne. 217 vols. Paris, 1844–64.

PO	Patrologia Orientalis
RAC	T. Kluser et al., eds. *Reallexikon für Antike und Christentum.* Stuttgart, 1950–.
RBén	*Revue bénédictine*
REJ	*Revue des études juives*
SBLDS	*Society of Biblical Literature Dissertation Series*
SC	Sources Chrétiennes
SL	*Studia Liturgica*
SLA	*Studies in Late Antiquity*
SP	*Sacra Pagina*
VCSup	Supplements to Vigiliae Christianae
WUNT	Wissenschaftliche Untersuchungen zur Geschichte der altchristlichen Literatur. Tübingen: Mohr Siebeck.

Introduction: Eternal Suffering between Reality and Imagination

Today, only 20 percent of the worldwide population, and 56 percent of the U.S. population, believes in the existence of hell. In the popular imagination, however, hell is hotter than ever.[1] Talk of hell is ubiquitous. In 2018, a media fire was ignited when Pope Francis reportedly said that hell did not exist. Afterward, the Vatican clarified that the pope had been misquoted, and that he had affirmed hell as a final destination for the wicked.[2] In a very different cultural arena, the American sitcom, hell took center stage in the critically acclaimed television show *The Good Place*. In this sitcom, viewers experience hell through the eyes of four sinners who appear to have mistakenly landed in heaven. The sinners' discovery of this "mistake" and their bumbling attempts to right it are the psychological tortures of a modern-day hell. In this vision of hell, the characters and the audience members reflect upon ethics, and on what characterizes a "good person."[3]

Both the media frenzy around the pope and *The Good Place* show that hell is a topic that many of us—from those with religious questions to casual television audience members reflecting on moral philosophy—like to think about. We have a propensity to make hell on earth. I'm interested in studying hell as a beginning, not as an end. I'm interested not only in hell, but how we make hell on earth. These hells become testing grounds, a place to develop new forms of torture, and new forms of bodily suffering. This book examines the ancient cultural assumptions about the body that Christians inherited, emended, and employed as they developed a notion of punitive suffering in hell.

The examples above are hardly exceptional. In 2014, after just three seasons of the popular television show *American Horror Story* had aired, critics and fans began to interpret the show as a modern-day version of Dante's *Inferno*. Each season takes place in a different context. Adherents to the Dante thesis argue that each of these contexts, like Dante's circles of hell, corresponds to the punishment of one of the seven deadly sins.[4] The show uses the stock elements of the horror genre to depict the torment of sinners generally. Darkness, filth, clown masks, suspenseful music, and mechanized implements of torture litter each season's episodes. For many, however, these standard elements do not obscure the connections to Dante's *Inferno*, but rather constitute a deeper commentary on questions of ultimate justice. In the context of a religious landscape in which a large portion of the population does not believe in the existence of hell, it is remarkable that fans of a TV show would be drawn to the comparison with Dante's medieval reflection on sin. Viewers' enthusiasm for this theory suggests that Dante's vision of postmortem justice is still very much alive in our world, even if his theological vision of the existence of a postmortem place of punishment has been partly abandoned. Hell is not the end of a life, but the beginning of thinking about torture and controlling the body.

But the elements of the *Inferno* that persist—the classification of crimes, the judgment of sinners, and gruesome bodily punishment as a spectacle that voyeurs willingly consume—invite us to reflect upon the work that hellscapes do in any given historical context as notions of sin, crime, punishment, and the body shift.

But these elements are not the making of Dante's own imagination. Dante's vision of hell is strongly influenced by the Apocalypse of Paul, which he refers to at the beginning of *Inferno*.[5] The Apocalypse of Paul is one of many early Christian "tours of hell," in which a saint or apostle is taken on a journey through hell by a tour guide who explains all the sins and punishments that the tourist saw along the way. In Dante's vision, he is the tourist, and Virgil is his guide on a journey that preserves many of the major generic features of the Apocalypse of Paul.

Given the sensational nature and popularity of the early Christian tours of hell, it is not surprising that the Apocalypse of Paul left such a strong impression on Dante. The early Christian tours of hell, based upon Jewish apocalypses and Greek and Roman descents to Hades, share important features. Each tour has a tourist who is led on a journey through hell where they witness different kinds of bodily torments. In each case, the tourist asks the guide who this suffering person is. The guide responds by identifying the sin, allowing the reader to see the correlation between particular sins and punishments. To adapt a modern phrase, we see the sin, not the sinner.

Most punishments in the tours of hell are thought to be "fitting" in relationship to the sin or crime committed. Indeed, some punishments are very closely related to the sin, matching the ancient judicial standard of *lex talionis*, or measure-for-measure punishment.[6] These punishments were meant to "fit the crime" in measure and intensity, sometimes involving hanging by the offending body part, immersion in fire up to the offending body part, asphyxiation, or tantalization.[7] Some tours are part of larger apocalypses, such as the Apocalypse of Peter or the Apocalypse of Paul, that also contain visions of heaven or other spaces of punishment and reward. Other tours of hell stand alone, as in the Greek Apocalypse of Ezra or the Latin Vision of Ezra. And still others are excursuses to some other story, as in the Acts of Thomas, or the narratives of Mary's Dormition. Few people today are familiar with these tours of hell, likely because they are contained in texts that are outside the biblical canon.[8] And yet, if the viewers of *American Horror Story* are any indication, the vision of hell preserved in these ancient texts has cast long shadows over our contemporary imagination of the afterlife and our sensibilities surrounding notions of justice. When coupled with the theological significance of eternal judgment, hell's images of the body intensify cultural ideals in which femininity and impairment were linked to weakness and moral failing.

The Tours of Hell: Texts, Contexts, and Contents

Despite their relative obscurity today, the apocalyptic tours of hell had become quite popular by the time Dante sat down to write his *Inferno* in the fourteenth century. The early Christian tours of hell are found in extracanonical texts that were written in very diverse circumstances. Since these texts have not typically been the focus of concerted scholarly attention, I will briefly survey the most influential texts here.[9]

Apocalypse of Peter

The Apocalypse of Peter is the earliest of the early Christian tours of hell. It was written in the second half of the second century CE, possibly in Alexandria, but it may have been used liturgically by Christians for centuries.[10] The Apocalypse of Peter is cited as an early Christian writing in several notable texts, including one that is attributed to Clement of

Alexandria and the Muratorian Fragment.[11] In his early third-century work *Extracts from the Prophets*, Clement cites the Apocalypse of Peter as part of his moral teaching against the practice of exposing "undesirable children," describing the scene in the Apocalypse of Peter of children sitting opposite their "bad parents" with lightning bolts coming forth from the children's eyes and striking their mothers' eyes.[12] The Muratorian Fragment indicates not only that the Apocalypse of Peter was considered useful for teaching, but also that it was read in church by some Christians (but not by others): "We receive only the apocalypses of John and Peter, though some of us are not willing that the latter be read in church."[13] In his church history of the mid-fifth century CE, Sozomen tells us that Palestinian churches read the Apocalypse of Peter every year on Good Friday, while fasting in memory of the Passion, and that there was "praise" among "most monks" for the Apocalypse of Paul.[14]

The later tours of hell that are similar to the Apocalypse of Peter either are dependent upon it (like the Apocalypse of Paul) or share similar source material (like the Acts of Thomas). The text is extant in two Ethiopic manuscripts, as well as three Greek fragments.[15] The Ethiopic manuscript tradition is likely to be the best witness to the earliest text of the Apocalypse of Peter, even though the original was likely written in Greek and is no longer extant.

At the opening of the Ethiopic text of the Apocalypse of Peter, the disciples approach Jesus on the Mount of Olives to ask about the return of Christ and the Day of Judgment. In response, Jesus describes what will happen at his return, with particular attention to the separation of the righteous and sinners at the last day. He concludes with the dramatic fiery scene of Judgment Day, when "the whole creation is dissolved," and "an unquenchable fire will drive them and bring them to judgment in a stream of unquenchable fire." Each individual is judged in this fiery river, and those who are found to be "evil creatures" are punished eternally. The remainder of the text contains a scene-by-scene description of each group of sinners, punctuated by vivid descriptions of distinct punishments and demonstrative explanations of their sins.[16] Men who committed fornication are hung up by their thighs (7); slanderers are made to chew their tongues (9). Other groups of sinners undergo general torture. Murderers are consigned to "a place full of venomous beasts, and they are tormented without rest, as they feel their pains and their worms are as numerous as a dark cloud" (7); the damned beg for mercy from Peter (13). At the same time, Christ proclaims that the elect and righteous will be given the baptism and salvation that they seek in the Acherusian Field (14). This interchange becomes a literary trope within the early Christian apocalypses where the damned beg for mercy, and receive some form of respite from their torment. At the end of the Apocalypse of Peter, Christ commissions Peter to go and share what he has seen (14), he undertakes a brief journey to heaven (15–17), and the disciples return to the Mount of Olives (17).

Book of Mary's Repose

The Book of Mary's Repose (the *Liber Requiei Mariae*) contains a tour (chaps. 94–101) that may have been written shortly after the Apocalypse of Peter, in the late second or third century CE. This Dormition narrative traces the story of Mary's miraculous departure from the world. At their request, Mary and the apostles are shown Gehenna, and ask about its inhabitants, following the pattern of questions and demonstrative explanations. This tour focuses on the ecclesial sins of a lector, a deacon, and a priest, describing both their sins and their measure-for-measure punishments in detail. The lector, for instance, "spoke glorious words but he did not do them"; his punishment is to have his mouth become a flaming razor for eternity (95). The parallels between the Book of Mary's Repose and the Apocalypse of Paul have led some scholars to suggest that this Marian tour of hell was source material for the Apocalypse of Paul.[17] While some scholars have argued that the ecclesial sins and punishments of the Apocalypse of Paul originated in a post-Theodosian context, their prominence in a second- or third-century text requires that we emend that thesis, recognizing that punishment for sins of hypocrisy may have been an early stratum of the tours of hell genre.[18]

Acts of Thomas

Another tour of hell that does not occur within an apocalypse is found in the Acts of Thomas. The Acts of Thomas, composed in the first half of the third century CE, contains a tour of hell in chapters 51–58.[19] This tour is framed by the story of a young man who comes to Thomas in a panic over the sin of murder. The young man had fallen in love with a young woman who was working as a prostitute, but murdered her when she refused to "live chastely" with him. Upon hearing his confession, Thomas immediately goes to the young woman, and raises her from the dead. She then recounts for the audience her tour of hell, which follows a similar format and contains some of the same punishments as the Apocalypse of Peter.

Six Books Apocryphon

Like the Book of Mary's Repose, the Six Books Apocryphon contains a very brief tour of hell at the end of a Marian Dormition narrative. This tour, however, focuses not on specific groups of the damned, but on a general group of sinners, "who have neglected my commands." This text was used liturgically as early as the mid-fourth century CE.[20] As in the Book of Mary's Repose, the focus in the Six Books Apocryphon is on Mary's intercession. Mary begs the Messiah to "have mercy on the wicked when You judge them at the day of judgment; for I have heard their voice and am grieved." Jesus does not offer the damned mercy or a day of respite as in other tours of hell, but instead whisks his mother away to paradise. Mary tells John to "guard these things" that she has seen. At the conclusion of the text, Jesus promises Mary that "those who call on your name will be delivered from destruction."[21] This exchange positions the apocalyptic tour of hell, and the larger Dormition narrative as a salvific teaching. Preservation of the text offered future generations of Christian readers the opportunity for efficacious Marian intercession.

Apocalypse of Zephaniah

The Apocalypse of Zephaniah is extant as fragments of a late antique text, which is difficult to date precisely.[22] Most of the text is devoted not to hell, but to a journey through multiple otherworldly places, including the city of life, the dwelling place of the angels, and the judgment scene at which the deeds of each person are read forth from their personalized manuscript. The fragmentary text ends in the netherworld, where the pious are interceding on behalf of a few groups of sinners. The Apocalypse of Zephaniah's short journey to the netherworld also includes several of the key generic features of the tour of hell, including demonstrative explanations, and vivid depictions of fiery punishments.

Apocalypse of Paul

The Apocalypse of Paul, as already mentioned above, was written around 400 CE and is arguably the most influential of the tours of hell, forming the basis of many of the medieval tours of hell, and inspiring Dante's *Inferno*. This Apocalypse was based on the Apocalypse of Peter but surpassed it in popularity. The original text, written in Greek, is no longer extant, but the Apocalypse is extant in Latin, Syriac, Coptic, Arabic, Armenian, Georgian, Church Slavonic, and Ethiopic.[23] The most reliable witness to the original text is one of the Latin manuscripts (L[1]).

The Apocalypse of Paul purports to be a text that was hidden under the apostle Paul's house, revealing what he had seen when he journeyed to the third heaven (2 Cor 12:2–4). This apocalypse begins with an extended description of the souls leaving their bodies at death, and contains longer journeys to heaven and hell than any previous tour of hell. At its conclusion, Paul begs for mercy for the damned, Christ grants the damned a day of respite on Sunday, and Paul returns to heaven. Similarly, in the Book of Mary's Repose the damned are granted nine hours of rest on Sunday, and Mary and the apostles journey to paradise. The hell that Paul witnesses contains measure-for-measure punishments and some hanging punishments, as in the Apocalypse of Peter, but there are more sins punished here, more fiery rivers, and worms, beasts, and angels of torment. The ecclesial sins that were the focus of the Book of Mary's Repose are also featured in the Apocalypse of Paul, including a presbyter who did not execute his ministry properly, a bishop who had no compassion on widows and orphans, a deacon who ate up the offerings and committed fornication, and a lector who did not keep the commandments of God.[24]

Fragmentary Texts

There are two fragmentary texts that are relevant to this discussion. Although the Isaiah Fragment is part of a Jewish text (the Chronicle of Jerahmeel), and likely quite late, the punishments it mentions are like those in the Apocalypse of Peter, and the sins it refers to are similar to those found in the Apocalypse of Peter and the Acts of Thomas.[25] One fragment survives in a fifth-century Latin Christian work called the Epistle of Titus, and contains the punishment of defiled virgins, a distinctively Christian sin among the tours of hell.[26] The Epistle of Titus, the larger work in which the fragment is found, is primarily concerned with chastity and ascetic practice. Martha Himmelfarb has argued that although these texts are found in medieval manuscripts that bear the marks of Christian editing, they are fragments of an earlier Jewish apocalypse that is no longer extant.[27] Apart from her argument for the genetic relationships between these apocalypses, and the primacy of a Jewish apocalyptic tour of hell, however, the "Jewishness" of these fragments is very much debatable. It is equally likely that they are Jewish adaptations of Christian tours of hell, some of which (like the Epistle of Titus) were reworked by the Christians who preserved them. For the purposes of this book, we treat them as texts that are a part of the early Christian tour of hell tradition, noting, where relevant, those fragments that are preserved in Hebrew or that otherwise bear marks of a Jewish reception of the tradition.

Ezra Apocalypses

The Ezra Apocalypses that contain tours of hell are based upon the Apocalypse of Paul, and are likely early medieval texts, although they are difficult to date.[28] Following the tradition of 4 Ezra, both the Greek Apocalypse of Ezra and the Latin Vision of Ezra are framed by an argument between Ezra and God. In both texts, this argument culminates with Ezra's distinctive request to take the place of the damned.[29] In the Greek Apocalypse of Ezra, God meets this request by granting the damned a day of rest. In the Latin Vision of Ezra, God grants the damned a weekly respite on Sunday (Gk. Apoc. Ez. 5.10; Lat. Vis. Ez. 90–91). Both Ezra tours contain hanging punishments and demonstrative explanations.

Medieval Marian Apocalypses

Two additional groups of texts based on the Apocalypse of Paul are the Greek Apocalypses of Mary and the Ethiopic Apocalypse of Mary. In the Eastern Church the texts in which Mary tours hell were even more popular than the Pauline tours, especially in monastic communities in the Byzantine and Slavic worlds.[30] The Greek Apocalypses of Mary (or "The Apocalypse of the All-Holy Mother of God Concerning the Punishments") were written between the fifth and eleventh centuries, and appear, with variations, in several manuscripts.[31] The tours of hell in these texts focus on distinctively Marian doctrinal concerns. For instance, in one of the Greek Apocalypses of Mary, the second group of sinners to be punished (after those who do not worship the Trinity) are those who deny the incarnation and that Mary is the mother of God.[32] The Ethiopic Apocalypse of Mary is a much longer text. This text is concerned with both heaven and hell, and follows the Apocalypse of Paul very closely, but also includes more sins and punishments than any other Christian tour of hell.[33] The Marian tours of hell surpassed the Apocalypse of Paul in popularity in the Eastern Church, perhaps because of the popularity of Mary in the East, or, as Jane Baun has suggested, because it was seen as a tool for promoting social cohesion.[34]

Hell, Apocalypses, and the Punitive Imagination

Tours of hell were popular at least in part because they offered a picture of hell that was lacking in the New Testament texts. In his letters, Paul refers to the judgment of the "sinners" and the "wicked" in general terms, mirroring the tradition of the "Two Ways" from the Hebrew Bible (Ps 1:1–6; 1 Thess 1:10; 5:3; 1 Cor 15:5; Rom 2:5–11).[35] Luke's Gospel has the story of the Rich Man in Hades who begs water from Lazarus, who is ensconced in heaven (Luke 16:19–31). Matthew's "weeping and gnashing of teeth" is a familiar refrain that signals judgment and eternal punishment (Matt 8:12; 13:42, 50; 22:13). Matthew's vision of eternal punishment culminates in Matthew 25 when the Son of Man separates the "sheep" from the "goats" and decides the eternal fate of the righteous and the wicked based upon people's treatment of the "least of these" (Matt 8:12; 13:42, 50; 22:13; 24:51; 25:30). 1 Peter has cryptic references to Jesus descending into Hades after his death that leave the reader wondering exactly what happened on these descents to the underworld (1 Pet 3:18–22; 4:6). And of course the book of Revelation describes the dreaded lake of fire, the eternal home of those who have been judged by their works and do not have their name written in the book of life (Rev 20:12–15). But these glimpses of hell leave many questions unanswered; they represent only the beginnings of the early Christian imagination of the afterlife. And while Matthew's "weeping and gnashing of teeth" or Revelation's "lake of fire" certainly evoked images of bodily torment, they are a far cry from the detailed depictions of the tortures correlated to specific sins that we find in the early Christian tours of hell.

Unlike the New Testament texts about hell, which relied upon the ancient reader's prior knowledge about apocalyptic otherworlds or Greek and Roman visions of Hades, the early Christian apocalypses offered a much fuller picture of hell. Matthew's Jesus refers to the "outer darkness where there is weeping and gnashing of teeth" as a dwelling place for those who do not follow the guidelines of the Sermon on the Mount, but by the second century the early Christian apocalypses contain fulsome descriptions of this space on the "Day of Judgment." In the Apocalypse of Peter, the Day

of Judgment is marked by much gnashing of teeth as the streams of unquenchable fire separate the righteous from the sinners. The nations stand
by and weep, as those who have sinned face their "deeds" and are punished
"each according to his offence" (Apoc. Pet. 5–6). In the "depths of darkness" the "evil creatures, sinners and hypocrites" will be punished eternally
through specific bodily torments (Apoc. Pet. 6). These descriptions of torment are not only more specific than Matthew's references to "weeping and
gnashing of teeth," but they also elaborate upon the New Testament picture
of hell with specific ancient ideas about bodies and judicial torture.

The apocalyptic punishments are keyed to the sins that they punish,
depicting divine judgment as a system that mirrors ancient penal systems.
The murderers of the Apocalypse of Peter 7, for instance, are "cast into the
fire, in a place full of venomous beasts." This punishment is reminiscent
both of exposure to wild beasts and of burning, which were among the
more humiliating forms of punishment.[36] In this imagination of hell, divine
justice looks like ancient Roman justice. For ancient audiences of the apocalypses, this similarity made it easy to imagine an ancient hellscape—the
tortures of the otherworld were proximate and familiar fears.

For some early Christians, though, like Augustine, the apocalyptic imagery of hell was objectionable because it made the ineffable concrete. Augustine argues that the Apocalypse of Paul is "crammed with all manner of
fables" because it is a forgery written by "vain individuals." This surely must
be the case, Augustine argues, because it puts into human language the
"things which it is not lawful for a man to utter."[37] Augustine's objections
reveal that, while some might think of hell as a low-stakes, virtual space,
for early Christians the stakes were quite high. Depictions of hell were intimately connected to one's ideas about God, to the behavioral standards they
hoped to reinforce, and, as we will see below, to the material world of bodies
themselves. Despite Augustine's disapproval, the gruesome images in the
Apocalypse of Paul brought hell to earth well into the medieval period.

While the ancient notions of justice on which the tours of hell draw are
not altogether different from our own concepts of measured relationships
between crimes and punishments or our notion of punishment as deterrent, we must remember that they are also millennia-old remnants from a
different cultural milieu. As such, these judicial remnants carry with them
a host of assumptions about the body that may differ from our own. The
question for this book is what other ancient ideas about bodies and gender

we bring along with those ancient concepts of justice when we reinterpret them in a new era.

Bodies Both Real and Imagined

The sensational depictions of eternal torment in the tours of hell may lead contemporary readers to conceptualize hell as an imaginary space. While we might think of hell as simply the corollary for heaven, or interpret the "weeping and gnashing of teeth" and similar descriptions as metaphors for human suffering, this is decidedly not the case for the second-century author Tertullian. In his reading of John 6:38–40 in *On the Resurrection of the Dead*, Tertullian argues that "eternal life" and being "raised up on the last day" refer to a total bodily resurrection, so that no part of the flesh will perish.[38]

This argument is not surprising, given Tertullian's general attitude toward the incarnation and his overall interest in defending the salvation of the flesh against his pagan opponents.[39] More startling is the fact that the evidence Tertullian adduces for his idea of bodily resurrection in heaven comes from hell. Drawing on Matthew's Gospel, Tertullian argues that the resurrection of the dead must be the resurrection of the flesh because Jesus talks about fearing the Lord who can "slay both body and soul in hell," as well as the place of "outer darkness where there is weeping and gnashing of teeth" (Tertullian, *Res.* 35; cf. Matt 10:28). He explains that weeping and gnashing of teeth is only possible at the final judgment if the resurrected body has eyes and teeth; the outer darkness, for example, is "a torture particularly attaching to eyes" (*Res.* 35). And Tertullian appeals to the final judgment scene of Matthew 25, where the people whose works are not worthy are bound "hand and foot," as evidence that the resurrected dead have hands and feet. Here, hell itself is used as persuasive proof of the existence of complete bodies in heaven. In Tertullian's reading of Matthew, hell is decidedly not imaginary; it is a real space in which bodies are preserved as they were on earth.

As in Tertullian, the Book of Mary's Repose contains an apocalyptic tour of hell in which bodies remain intact despite the extreme extent of their punishments.[40] In this text, Mary describes darkness as a "worse punishment" even than having a mouth made of flaming razors (Mary's Rep. 95 and 97). Like Tertullian, the Mary of this text reads the "darkness" of hell as a punishment that affects the eyes. And her concern about bodily mechanics is evident when she asks Jesus why the man who is beaten with rocks does not fall down or simply turn to dust. The Savior explains that the man "will be in torment while not dying or being dissolved," affirming that his punishment is both bodily and eternal (Mary's Rep. 97–98).[41] Mary's question and Jesus's response bear a striking resemblance to one of the objections of Celsus, a famous second-century opponent of Christianity. Celsus questions the idea of salvation of the flesh: "What sort of body, after being entirely corrupted, could return to its original nature and that same condition which it had before it was dissolved?"[42] The Book of Mary's Repose counters this objection by arguing that bodies are not corrupted or dissolved, even as they are punished violently. This insistence on bodily integrity in the afterlife continues later in the Book of Mary's Repose, where it states that the fleshly wounds of Jesus are preserved in heaven as a teaching tool (Mary's Rep. 133–34).

Even as Tertullian and Mary's tour of hell preserved an idea of the afterlife as a dwelling place for "real bodies," those fleshly bodies inhabited imagined apocalyptic spaces. As John J. Collins has argued, the literary function of apocalyptic literature is to "shape one's imaginative perception of a situation and so lay the basis for whatever course of action it exhorts."[43] Drawing upon ancient rhetoric and postcolonial theory, Greg Carey has demonstrated that ancient rhetoric and language function in these imaginary spaces to shape the orientation of the audience to the apocalyptic author, on the one hand, and to his political opponents, on the other.[44] The imaginative element of apocalyptic literature should not be mistaken for disengagement with the present world, but instead should be viewed as the exact opposite: the imaginative play of the text is the site at which the text's engagement with its own world is most readily discerned.

Imaginary spaces and otherworldly beings are precisely what gives apocalyptic literature the ability to critique and transform real social spaces and figures in the contemporary world. Tina Pippin demonstrates that the book of Revelation's imaginative project allows it to be reinterpreted in new situations of colonial oppression. Pippin traces the way that it has been read and reread by early Christians enduring oppression under Roman imperial rule, and by feminist, womanist, and postcolonial interpreters, who see it also as a "misogynist male fantasy of the end of time."[45] These readings do not seek to "demythologize apocalyptic literature." Rather, as Pippin states, they permit us to "enter boldly into these mythical and fictional worlds," and to harness the power of apocalyptic imagery for change in the contemporary world.[46] Similarly, Jacqueline M. Hidalgo has examined the book of Revelation in relationship to U.S. Chicanx movement texts. Hidalgo demonstrates that the imaginative elements of apocalyptic literature can serve as "utopian homing devices," offering minoritized communities an opportunity to "remake the world into a better inhabitable place for dislocated peoples."[47] The imaginary spaces of the apocalypse invite what Hidalgo calls "social dreaming": the ability to critique and transform social spaces, for groups that are minoritized.[48]

Although Pippin and Hidalgo focus specifically on the book of Revelation and its history of interpretation, a similar set of principles is at work in the imaginative spaces of the apocalypses that describe hell. István Czachesz has argued that the punishments of the Apocalypse of Peter and the Apocalypse of Paul are drawn from Roman implements of torture; their vision of hell offers an imaginary space integrally connected to real bodies and real spaces, reflecting back upon tangible bodies.[49] Although it is tempting to imagine that Christians wrote these texts as a means of protesting the use of these tortures on persecuted Christians, this is not borne out by the evidence. Often the persons who are punished in these visions of hell were not outsiders but Christian leaders themselves.[50] In these apocalypses, the imaginary space of the afterlife is not used to critique imperial methods of torture, or even the empire itself. Rather, the tours of hell critique immorality within the Christian community by imaginatively deploying the colonizer's mechanisms of judicial control. The tours of hell, then, lie at the intersection of "real" and "imagined" spaces and bodies in antiquity. They reflect a view of the afterlife body as continuous with the earthly body and, simultaneously, as a body that is susceptible to the fluctuations of contemporary ideas about the body. The texts that describe hell are grounded in the spaces of everyday life, and at the same time seek to creatively transform those spaces.

In many ways, the apocalyptic landscape is the last early Christian frontier in which scholars have maintained this dualistic tension between "real" and "imaginary" bodies. In part this likely has to do with the fact that scholars in the early twentieth century perceived apocalyptic literature as banal "popular literature" that did not merit as much attention as philosophical or theological texts like Paul's letters or John's Gospel.[51] As late twentieth-century scholars began to interrogate this assumption, interest in apocalyptic literature was renewed, but those conversations have still been largely separate from conversations about the afterlife, gender, and bodies in other genres of early Christian literature.[52] Even in recent works that specifically treat the topic of the afterlife, such as Peter Brown's *Ransom of the Soul*, apocalyptic literature is sidelined, even though Augustine himself sees the tours of hell as important counterpoints to his own view that need to be quashed through argumentation.[53] This work seeks to fill that lacuna, situating the early Christian apocalypses that describe hell within the broader context of early Christian thinking about the afterlife, gender, and the body.

Gender and Bodily Suffering in Antiquity and Early Christianity

As we have seen, the imaginary bodies of the early Christian apocalypses are connected to real bodies in the present world. For this reason, gender is an important category of analysis. The overall system of justice that is described in these visions of hell is dependent upon ancient ideas about the body. The tours of hell are entirely structured around classifying bodies, following the pattern of ancient juridical models of punishment. This model of eternal punishment uses bodily difference and ancient concepts of gender and disability as prominent ways of signaling that difference and sorting the bodies of the righteous and unrighteous in the afterlife.

As each tourist travels around hell, there are landscape descriptors and geographic markers, such as the river of fire, but the primary "landmarks" are the bodies of the punished persons themselves. For instance, the Apocalypse of Peter describes the punishment of young women who did not retain their virginity before marriage: "maidens clad in darkness for raiment . . . shall be seriously punished and their flesh will be torn in pieces" (Apoc. Pet. 11). This same group of sinners, also wearing black, is found in a pit in the Apocalypse of Paul as four "dreadful angels" place fiery chains around their necks (Apoc. Paul 39). In each of these scenes of eternal torment, the young women's bodies are negatively marked by their dark clothing, and visibly tormented through the tearing of their flesh or by fiery collars. As one encounters these scenes, the "high place" and the "pit" in which they take place recede from the memory so that all that remains are the tortured bodies, which serve as signposts demarcating the locale of particular groups of sinners. Ancient ideas about gender and perhaps also ethnicity are in play. The virgin bodies that are tortured here are all female. Their dark clothing differentiates them from virgin brides, who wore white, or may express mourning and grief.[54] Their bodies are punished in ways that connote not only pain, but also humiliation. In the Apocalypse of Peter the tearing of the flesh recalls the punishment of Tityos for the rape of Leto (*Od.* 11.568); in the Apocalypse of Paul the virgin girls' bodies become enslaved bodies, trapped in fiery shackles. These young female bodies act as monuments of shame.

The punishments themselves rely upon ancient notions of bodily difference in order to negatively mark the bodies of the unrighteous. The bodies of the damned are blind, mute, bloody, lacerated, or spewing forth worms. These bodily states were considered nonnormative or "sick" in antiquity. By the same token, the bodies of the righteous are positively identified by their bodily characteristics. In the Apocalypse of Peter the heavenly bodies of Moses and Elijah have hair "like the rainbow in water," and faces that shine so brightly that Peter cannot look at them (Apoc. Pet. 15). In the Apocalypse of Paul David's face shines like the sun, and twelve innocent men with "goodness of heart" sit on golden bejeweled thrones wearing beautiful robes (Apoc. Paul 29).

Since the bodies of the damned and the righteous are central to the early Christian tours of hell, this work builds upon previous scholarship on the body and early Christianity. This scholarship has demonstrated that bodies were an important site for crafting identity.[55] In particular, scholarship on early Christian slavery, martyrdom, sexuality, and asceticism has shown that gender and bodily suffering play an important role in early Christian history.[56] While this work builds upon Perkins's connection between bodily suffering and identity formation, its focus on punitive suffering also challenges the notion that bodily suffering and subjectivity were integrally linked for early Christians. As Chris De Wet has noted, the case of Christian slave owners unveils the multiple discursive frameworks that were operative simultaneously in antiquity.[57]

Gender emerges within the theoretical conversation about the body, as Toril Moi argues, "as an attempt to give to biology what belongs to biology, no more and no less."[58] Thus, invoking the idea of "gender" gestures to a whole complex of ideas that separates the biological "sex" of a body from the social constructs and performative discourses that make up "gender." But even this distinction between sex and gender quickly dissolves because, as Judith Butler argues, it is hard to locate the borders between what is biological and what is socially constructed.[59]

The history of early Christianity is indebted to the ongoing theoretical conversations within gender studies, disability studies, critical race theory, and queer theory concerning the ways in which ideas about the body are developed and transmitted. I will not rehearse the entirety of these theoretical conversations here, but will instead take up two points that are particularly relevant for the bodies we find in the ancient apocalypses: the questions of historical accessibility and discursive reductionism.

First, because our sources for thinking about gender and the body in early Christianity were written by persons with a relatively high degree of social power, we have difficulty accessing what it might have been like to inhabit a body that was wounded, disabled, female, or of low socioeconomic status.[60] As we attempt to understand what particular depictions of the body might mean for the ancient audience, the categories of sex and gender are of "limited value" because, as Jorunn Økland points out, "the cultural assumptions operative in antiquity about anthropology, medicine, and human bodies were vastly different from our own."[61]

Nevertheless, gender studies, or the emphasis on gender as a way of interpreting a body that emerged after the linguistic turn, enables us to talk about the operative cultural assumptions of the body in antiquity despite the elusive nature of that body.[62] No longer preoccupied with recovering "real women," early Christian historians are free to focus instead upon the way in which women and gender are socially constructed in ancient texts.[63] Following Virginia Burrus, I seek "both to reinhabit the world of the ancient texts and to extricate myself from the enveloping fabric of a male-centered 'late antiquity.'" I will do so by circumnavigating the otherworldly and this-worldly realms of these literary tours of hell. In doing so, I will read the afterlife bodies as rhetorical performances of familiar earthly bodies, and as textual products that are both distant from the ancient reader and proximate to her experience of a "culture in which the actors are almost always male and gender is the performance par excellence."[64]

Second, as described above with respect to the apocalyptic genre, conversations about gender and the body often traverse the fundamental fault line between the idea that gender difference is innate and the conviction that it is discursively defined. Much of the secondary scholarship on this question has explored the extent to which it is possible to speak of bodies as *both* real *and* culturally constructed.[65] This work requires that we respect the tensions that are present when multiple ways of talking about gender occur within the same text, rather than forcing a text to fit within a single discursive framework.[66] This approach is instructive for my own project, in which disparate ways of thinking about gender occur within the same apocalypse.

In this regard, my work with the early Christian apocalypses avoids imposing a single theoretical model of gender in antiquity upon the texts under consideration. It will thereby veer away from the allure of Thomas Laqueur's "one-sex model," which has had enormous explanatory power for students of the New Testament and early Christianity in the last two decades. Laqueur argued that ancient Greek and Roman sexual difference was really a spectrum on which there was only one gender—that is, male—and varying degrees to which a person presented masculinity. In this model of gender, female genitals are seen as malformed or inverted male genitals. As we will see in chapter 3, recent critiques have demonstrated that Laqueur's model does not account for all of the gendered discourses we find in antiquity, or even among early Christians.[67]

Disability and the Body in Antiquity and in Hell

Disability might seem like a strange analytical category to apply to the bodies of the damned in hell. One might protest: "But aren't some of these tortured bodies 'just wounded'?" Embedded in this question is the assumption that wounds might be healed, and are thus "not as bad" as having a body that is forever distinguished from the ideal, "able" body. Disability studies interrogates this distinction by considering disability not as a fixed biological category, but as a social one with culturally defined boundaries that vary from place to place.[68] Not only is it impossible to bracket disability as a modern category when approaching our ancient texts, but believing that we can do so risks bringing our own culture's ableism to those texts. Ableism is the insistence that a particular kind of body is the norm, and that any body that differs from this "able" norm is deviant, disabled, or undesirable. Disability, then, is an extremely helpful category for thinking about the bodies in hell that are marked as "deviant." The alignment of specific sins with forms of impairment collapses the distinction among physical, spiritual, and ethical deviance. As Candida Moss has argued, the way that bodies appear in heaven has important consequences for the way that early Christians viewed bodies: "Early Christian insistence on both bodily continuity and eschatological healing reveals the importance of notions of uniformity and proportion in ancient Christian constructions of the afterlife."[69] As Moss notes, this eschatological healing not only has implications for resurrected bodies, but also determines how earthly bodies are valued.

While some people might think of some of the hellbound bodies as wounded and therefore only temporarily, if at all, disabled, such a conception does not fit with ancient understandings of the body and medical practices in which wounds were often fatal. As we will see in chapter 3, even intestinal worms, which we might see as a minor illness, could be a deadly threat to the normative body in the ancient world; these and other parasites still constitute medical problems for people of lower socioeconomic status, especially in the developing world.[70] Although there is no single word for "disability" in antiquity, the bodily differences that we tend to categorize as disabilities in the contemporary world were most frequently seen as deficiencies that removed a person from active participation in society.[71] But, as Warren Carter has noted, we have to be cautious about how broadly we describe disability in antiquity, ever mindful of our tendency to see bodies through the ableism of our own era.[72]

In addition to addressing the historical meanings of the term "disability," disability studies can illuminate what the tortured bodies in hell might have signified for ancient audiences. According to the "social model" of disability, disability is discursively defined: the way people talk about bodies in a given society determines the significance of those bodies.[73] According to the "cultural model" of disability—a poststructuralist response to the "social model"—disability is both "real" and culturally defined.[74] Relying upon the cultural model, disability studies theorists have cast disability in the contemporary world as a big tent that includes any bodily difference that has an impact on the way a person lives, because many different types of bodily difference still have consequences for how a person interacts in her environs in today's world.[75] Nevertheless, disability studies theorists are careful to differentiate between the advocacy needs of different populations within the broad category of "disability."[76] To put it differently, we have to be careful to walk that fine line between being inclusive and not rushing to efface each other's differences as if they needed to be "fixed."[77]

We take this same care with our sources in the ancient world, and it is for this reason that we look to ancient medical texts and other literature that describes bodily states similar to those we find in hell. The hope is that immersing ourselves in the ancient conceptions of the body before we read the tortured bodies of the damned will help us interpret them according to an ancient hermeneutic of the body rather than our own. In developing this hermeneutic of the body, we implicitly rely upon the cultural model of disability that allows ancient cultural norms to determine how ancient bodies were categorized and understood. In developing this hermeneutic of the body in chapter 3, we will discover that there were ancient standards of bodily normativity, and that they were exacting and often gendered.[78] Although the category of "disability" did not exist in antiquity, ancient sources assume a narrowly defined understanding of the normal body that relegates the bodies that deviate from this norm to a stigmatized and excluded existence.[79] Beyond the social stigma that we can discern in our ancient sources, the interpretive value of these nonnormative bodies becomes increasingly obvious as we turn to the bodies of the damned in hell.[80]

In the tours of hell, I argue, the damned inhabit disabled, female, imprisoned bodies for all of eternity. Using bodily normativity as a way to depict eternal torment relies upon familiar imagery of the body to depict the afterlife.[81] These texts use masculinity and bodily normativity to police behavior, equating early Christian ethical norms with masculinity and bodily "health." The punishments of early Christian hell not only mirror the bodies of the disabled in the "real" world, but also intensify and reinforce the ancient idea that bodily difference was a punishment for sin.[82] The disabled bodies mirror the carceral bodies of people in the Roman empire who were punished for crimes; the spaces of hell are topographically analogous to the ancient mines, underground spaces of punishment that were filled with fumes.[83] The overlap between hell's punishments and the carceral bodies and spaces of the ancient world adds a layer of criminality to the characterization of disabled and female bodies. As I will argue in this book, a theology of bodily and spiritual impairment emerges in the early Christian apocalypses, in which the tortured body is a marker of spiritual ignorance and ethical failure, and salvation is described in terms of bodily perfection. In this way, the early Christian apocalypses heighten the ancient "physiognomic consciousness" that correlated physical appearance to ethical behavior.[84]

I see my exploration of these narratives of punitive suffering as a part of the project to critique discourses of disability that inextricably link disability with suffering and other negative valuations of bodily difference. I am also looking for spaces in which early Christian hell might decouple bodily difference from judgment and torment.[85] As Julia Watts Belser has demonstrated in her study of rabbinic images of disability and destruction, even in discourses that rely almost exclusively on the disabled body as a symbol of disaster, there are moments "in which disabled figures flip the conventional script of loss and vulnerability," so that "these very bodies become potent sites of resistance."[86] As we will see with the tears of the saints in chapter 4 and the figure of Mary in chapter 5, there are bodies in hell that have the potential to be valued as weak, compromised, and disabled, but instead reveal the plasticity of the standards of bodily normativity by performing as models of efficacious bodily suffering. These bodies still perform an ancient notion of bodily difference as bodily suffering, but they stretch the mold that could confine that body to insignificant social roles.

Perhaps the most important way that disability studies illuminates the ancient depictions of hell is through its insistence that we must close the perceived gaps between "imaginary" and "real" bodies, between our social contracts around bodies and their medical "reality." While contemporary thinkers about the body are questioning the imagined gulf between "social models" and "medical models" of the body, this work interrogates the idea that tortured bodies within early Christian hell were merely signifiers of an ancient otherworldly imagination, disconnected both from "real" bodies in antiquity and from our contemporary understandings of bodies and punishment.[87] When we talk about bodies in antiquity and the tours of hell, we are not only talking about men's and women's bodies, and the construction of those bodies, we are also participating in a broader conversation about how bodies and social constructions of the body relate to questions of justice. As a category with an unstable nature, disability demands that we look at bodies as subjects that transcend dichotomies like normal-abnormal, and think about "identity" in ways that are multidirectional, and also intersectional.[88]

The Tours of Hell: A History of Scholarship

Beginning with the work of Albrecht Dieterich, just before the turn of the twentieth century, scholars have examined the literary historical development of the tours of hell by investigating their literary antecedents in other cultures. Underlying this debate throughout the nineteenth and twentieth centuries was a desire to identify the origins of a tradition that scholars by turns found fascinating and repugnant. In the late nineteenth century, Dieterich argued that the Apocalypse of Peter had borrowed from the Greek (namely, Orphic Pythagorean) "descent to Hades" traditions.[89] At the end of the twentieth century, Martha Himmelfarb argued that Jewish apocalyptic literature, not Greek Hades traditions, was the primary influence on the genre.[90] Moderating between Dieterich and Himmelfarb, Richard Bauckham and Jan N. Bremmer have argued that the tours of hell in the early Christian apocalypses are influenced by Greek, Roman, *and* Jewish antecedents, and as such share the features of several different types of underworld journeys.[91]

Martha Himmelfarb also shifted the conversation about the tours of hell by turning attention away from literary dependence and toward the mode of presentation of these vivid scenes of torment.[92] Yet for Himmelfarb, as well as for Bauckham and Bremmer, the emphasis of these early investigations was still upon literary dependence, and the mode of presentation of the torments was of interest mostly insofar as it allowed them to say something about each text's date of composition or chronological relationship to other apocalypses, or the "origins" of the idea of hell. More recently, scholarship on the tours of hell has turned to questions about the influence of these depictions of the underworld upon other early Christian literature, attending to the life of these texts after they were written.[93]

Valuable as these approaches are, they fail to consider the impact of these punishments on ancient people. In this book, I examine the tours of hell as rhetoric that engages broader cultural images and notions of the body beyond apocalyptic literature.[94] I have argued that the early Christian tours of hell employed captivating visual rhetoric that was intended to move the audience emotionally. These apocalyptic scenes of torture were part of early Christian education (*paideia*), meant to move hearers to behave according to a particular ethical rubric.[95] As performances of visual rhetoric, these apocalypses drew upon imagery that was familiar to the audience in order to effectively stimulate the imagination.[96] This book expands that line of inquiry, interrogating how this rhetoric used, changed, or amplified bodily imagery to describe hell.

This present study is not directly interested in questions of literary dependence, but it takes as axiomatic the idea that tours of hell are textual performances. Each of these apocalypses is treated as an iteration of the tour of hell tradition that is deployed in a particular historical and geographic context. The diachronic questions engaged throughout the book are informed by the history of scholarship on the early Christian apocalypses and its conclusions about the relationships among these apocalypses. As we trace diachronic changes in the apocalyptic tradition of the tour of hell, we are looking not only at shifting literary traditions, but at shifting sociocultural ways of reading the body and the afterlife.

Previous scholarship on the tours of hell has acknowledged the connection between violence done to bodies in the text and torture in the world, and has attempted to shift the cultural burden for this content in a search for its "origins." The present book, by contrast, analyzes the content of early Christian depictions of hell in order to explain how the bodies of early Christian hell constructed and reconfigured the bodies of those who heard and read these stories. Candida Moss has demonstrated that early Christians engaged the resurrected body in this way when they thought about heaven, arguing that resurrected bodies use the ancient categories of the body to construct and reconfigure Christian identity and the self.[97]

These tour of hell texts are much more pointed, however, because the bodies of the damned actually resemble the real bodies of women and people with disabilities in their midst. In the tours of hell, the sins and violent punishments are not just earthly torture transposed to an eternal locale. Rather, the various elements of these tours create a punitive framework that isolates bodies in order to enforce and rewire gendered social norms by disciplining, criminalizing, effeminizing, and disabling those bodies. For the readers and hearers of these tours of hell, the effeminate and disabled bodies in hell not only offer carceral warnings to discipline earthly bodies, they also reconstruct and intensify the stakes of bodily normativity, criminalizing the real bodies of women and of people with disabilities.

1 Assigned to Suffering: Gendered Bodily Suffering in the Ancient World

In the early third century, Clement of Alexandria, a Christian pedagogue, wrote a guide on the preferred way of life for Christian men and women. In his detailed discussion of how Christian men should dress, Clement derides men who shave their beards, arguing that this goes against the way that God created men's bodies:

> His beard, then, is the badge of a man and shows him unmistakably to be a man. It is older than Eve and is the symbol of the stronger nature. By God's decree, hairiness is one of man's conspicuous qualities, and, at that, hairiness distributed over his whole body. Whatever smoothness or softness there was in him God took from him when God fashioned the delicate Eve from his side to be the receptacle of his seed, his helpmate both in procreation and in the management of the household. What was left (for he had lost all traces of smoothness) remained a man, and revealed that manhood. And to him has been assigned action, just as to her suffering. For, what is hairy is by nature drier and warmer than what is bare; therefore, the male is hairier and more warm blooded than the female; the uncastrated than the castrated; the perfect than the imperfect. Thus, it is unholy to act unlawfully with the symbol of manhood, hairiness.[1]

In this passage, which draws upon and retells the classic creation narrative of Genesis 2, Clement recasts the creation of men and women in terms of traditional ancient Greek understandings of gender: man is "assigned action" (*to dran autō synkechōrētai*), and woman is assigned "suffering" (*hōs ekeinē to paschein*). The Greek verb used to describe the passive body of the woman is the same word that elsewhere denotes physical suffering (e.g.,

Matt 16:21; Mark 5:26). According to Clement, woman's body was defined from the moment of her creation as a passive, suffering body.[2] Women's bodily suffering is natural, and bodily suffering is womanly.

From here Clement develops a physiognomic taxonomy of the characteristics that make up the God-ordained nature of man and woman. The male is active, hairy all over, drier, warmer, and "superior in nature." The female is receptive, smooth, soft, moist, cold, and a (subordinate) partner and helper in parenting and household management.

While the patriarchy may be familiar to us, Clement's descriptions of men's and women's bodies might come as a surprise to the modern reader. Yet these descriptions cohere with the ideas about gender and bodily difference in the writings of ancient physiognomists and in Galen's medical writings, as we will see in the examples below.[3] The assertion that man is "assigned action" and woman "suffering" obscures the hierarchical binary that undergirds these shared ideas about men's and women's bodies. Here, as elsewhere in early Christian literature, broader cultural narratives about gender and the body are tightly woven into Christian theology. Clement's theology was powerfully influenced by ancient medical thought, and Clement, in turn, became an "influential proponent" of "medical Christology." The Christus medicus imagery he introduced remained a prominent part of later Egyptian Christianity.[4]

At the same time, as Benjamin H. Dunning has demonstrated, these androcentric passages are not as straightforward as they might seem. Clement reproduces ancient ideals of gender differentiation, while simultaneously undermining them by insisting that these differences will be effaced at the eschaton.[5] Christians repackaged and modified broadly held ideas even as they reproduced them.

This chapter begins with this passage from Christ the Educator (Educ.) for two reasons. First, Clement's description of the "superior nature" of the male and the corresponding characteristics of male and female illustrates how early Christians engaged with ideas about gender and the body from the surrounding culture. Second, his descriptions of bodily saturation serve as an important reminder that ancient ideas about gender and bodily suffering differ from our own, and require a historical orientation. In his consideration of human physiognomy, Clement drew upon a wide range of ancient theories about the relationship between the body and gender— theories that can be traced back hundreds of years further through diverse medical, cultic, and philosophical traditions. The work of this chapter is to explore how various ancient sources imagined the gendered body and its relationship to suffering, pain, generativity, and unruliness. If we want to understand what early Christians saw when they pictured bodies suffering in hell, we must first appreciate how they constructed nonnormative bodies.

Bodily Difference and Gender in Ancient Thought

As Clement's retelling of Genesis 2 illustrates, ancient concepts of the body operated with a hierarchical understanding of gender in which the superior body was the male body.[6] As Rebecca Flemming has argued, ancient gender hierarchy differed from our own: "It is not so much that the female is inferior as that the inferior is female."[7] Superior (male) bodies were characterized as strong, hot, dry, and compact, or impervious to penetration, whereas inferior (female) bodies were weak, cold, moist, and porous.

Treatments of gender in early Christianity have been greatly influenced by the theory of gender developed by Thomas Laqueur. In *Making Sex*, Laqueur contends that ancient thinkers operated on a "one sex" model in which gender was not a binary but a continuum.[8] This theory is grounded in Aristotle's assertion that women are incomplete men whose bodies have simply never reached the level of heat, dryness, or solidity that characterizes masculinity: "He [Aristotle] . . . insisted that the distinguishing characteristic of maleness was immaterial, and as a naturalist, chipped away at the organic distinctions between the sexes so that what emerges is an account in which one flesh could be ranked, ordered, and distinguished as particular circumstances required."[9]

For Aristotle, male bodies needed to be hot for the purposes of reproduction. Sperm, which he thought was cooked down from the nutritive elements of blood, could not be produced without the greater heat of the male body. Because female bodies are cold, women are unable to cook the nutrients in blood into anything except menstrual blood and milk: "Further, a boy actually resembles a woman in physique, and a woman is as it were an infertile male; the female, in fact, is female on account of inability of a sort, viz., it lacks the power to concoct semen out of the final state of the nourishment (this is either blood, or its counterpart in bloodless animals) because of the coldness of its nature."[10] For Aristotle, bodies exist in a hierarchy in which the female body is an imperfect or deficient male body, that is, "deviant" and "monstrous," a divergence from the normative male body.[11]

Laqueur then turns to Galen, whose treatises he reads as manuals designed to help the physician protect and preserve masculinity by maintaining heat, dryness, and compactness, so that male bodies do not become cold, moist, or porous (i.e., "feminine").[12] A central text for Laqueur's reading is the section of Galen's treatise *On the Function of the Parts of the Body*, in which Galen describes "heat" as the fundamental difference between perfect males and inferior females: "Now just as mankind is the most perfect of all animals, so within mankind the man is more perfect than the woman, and the reason for this perfection is his excess of heat, for heat is Nature's primary instrument. Hence in those animals that have less of it, her workmanship is necessarily more imperfect, and so it is no wonder that the female is less perfect than the male by as much as she is colder than he."[13]

The one-sex explanatory model of the ancient body has been extremely influential among scholars of early Christianity as a means of explaining early Christian ideas about bodies that achieve salvation or glorification by becoming "more male."[14] Its success may be due to the fact that it is sufficiently different from our contemporary model, and yet simple enough to apply broadly to ancient literature.[15]

Recent scholarship by medical historians and classicists has shown that "claims for the dominance of the 'one-sex' model fail to account for the complexity of the classical world."[16] A deeper reading of the works of Galen or the Hippocratic Corpus reveals that a more complex "two sex" concept of the body was operative in antiquity and late antiquity.[17] The Hippocratic Corpus sees woman, not as an incomplete man, but as a radically different, inferior body. Laqueur's error stems in part from a selective reading of the Hippocratic Corpus that does not include the treatises that demonstrate a two-sex understanding of the body. The Hippocratic Corpus's *Female Diseases* 1.62, for example, reminds the audience that women and men must receive different medical treatments, since "the healing of women differs greatly from that of men." According to this text, women are not simply incomplete men because they do not have exterior organs, but their bodies are fundamentally different, too—they are cold, wet, and spongy.[18] And even for Aristotle and Galen, the fundamental "perfection" or "completeness" of the male body lies not in the physical form of genitalia, but in its heat and dryness.[19]

One major idea that Laqueur's emphasis on the one-sex model obscures is the importance of blood flow for both Hippocratic and Aristotelian concepts of gender.[20] As Lesley Dean-Jones notes, "Menstrual blood is the linchpin of both the Hippocratic and the Aristotelian theories on how women differed from men. Whether a woman was healthy, diseased, pregnant, or nursing, in Classical Greece her body was defined in terms of blood-hydraulics."[21] It is for this reason that Soranus argues in his *Gynaecology* that blood flow is of primary importance for female anatomy, saying that "purging is the first function of the womb" (Soranus, *Gyn.* 3.2). Hippocrates believed that the cooler bodies of women made it impossible for them to evacuate their nutrients efficiently; instead, they accumulated their nutrients as cold, wet, menstrual fluid that needed to be expelled once a month.[22] This focus on blood flow is tied to the understanding that women's bodies are cooler than men's bodies, and is applied to nearly every diagnosis of women. The thermal deficit of women, and their resulting poorer blood flow, was thought to be a root cause of illness. Proper blood flow is so important to the body in Galen's eyes that he argues that the menstrually regular female body is actually less susceptible to disease than the healthy male body.[23] Galen also places a host of symptoms in direct relationship to irregular menstruation and excessive cooling, including halted respiration, nausea, shivering, headaches, and fever.[24]

In both the medical literature and Aristotle's one-sex model, the female body is inferior to the male body. That inferiority is integrally linked to the flow of blood. The female body is seen as naturally cooler than the male, resulting in poorer blood flow and greater susceptibility to imbalance (and thus disease and bodily suffering). The centrality of blood flow influences the entire economy of the body, extending to "every part of the flesh: men are firm and hard, women are wet and spongy. In terms of the texture of their bodies as a whole, men are like woven cloth, women are like fleece."[25] While these outward signifiers seem to posit a simple mechanism for identifying, caring for, and preserving male bodies, the outward signs of gender were understood to reflect a more complicated economy of the body.[26]

As we turn to bodily suffering in the early Christian apocalypses, both of these theories of gender are in view. Speaking broadly, using the one-sex model, men and women could move along the hierarchical spectrum upward toward masculinity, or downward into femininity. At the same time, the two-sex model demands that any change in the equilibrium of the perfect male body did not merely initiate a slide down the hierarchical scale to femininity. Any such change also represented a full-scale incursion on that body's perfection, and a more immediate shift in status from a perfect male body to the precarious existence of the weak, porous, cold, and more often dysfunctional female body.[27]

In some ways this understanding of gender allowed for bodies to change, performing the ideal of the impervious male body to a greater or lesser extent, and at the same time it relied upon the hierarchical dualism in which "men and women were perceived as 'opposites' in a very real manner."[28] As we contemplate the bodies of the damned, this binary model of gender means that for the tormented bodies in hell, bodily imperfection represented a total and permanent bodily shift toward femininity.

In particular, for those bodies whose punishment involves blood flow, leaking fluids, or penetration by fire or other objects, the ancient emphasis on the primacy of blood flow and the distinctive porous fabric of the female body is particularly instructive and pertinent. As we will see throughout this book, the punishments that are exacted on the bodies of the damned make these bodies female. This holds true even in descriptions of men hanging by their genitalia. Ancient physiognomic thinking, by contrast, identified the "deformity" of women not in their genitalia, but in their "lack of heat which meant that they could not make semen."[29] If it is true that ancient men and women are differentiated not primarily by their genitals but by their fundamentally different flesh, then the fleshly bodies of the early Christian apocalypses depict bodies that are fundamentally altered versions of their earthly counterparts. For instance, the eschatological punishments that are carried out by male genital mutilation (hanging by the testicles, for example) simultaneously put the once-male body on display while also undermining the masculinity of that body, a body that could no longer make semen. As we look at the intersection of suffering and gender in the medical literature, we will see that more often than not, the female body is equated with suffering, not because of its role, or the interiority of its genitalia, as Laqueur contended, but because of the nature of the whole female body itself.[30]

Gender in Ancient Medicine: Bodily Difference and Bodily Suffering

Our contemporary imaginings of male bodies draw on a host of images from life experience and the media. For ancient audiences, such imaginings drew upon whatever previous encounters an ancient person might have had.[31] Due to medical advances and a culture that largely seeks to avoid pain, when we think about bodily suffering, we imagine something extreme, and hopefully rare. For ancient audiences, pain and bodily suffering were a prominent part of daily life, as we can see from descriptions of ancient medicine in literature, inscriptions, and medical texts themselves. In this context, the medical authors describe sick bodies as "difficult to keep in order and needing outside supervision."[32] As we will see, this understanding of the sick body overlapped with the understanding of the female body, which was also marked by flux, pain, and an unruliness that required constant discipline and regulation. The unregulated, undisciplined bodies—sickly and womanly bodies—provided the building blocks for the torments of early Christian hell.

The Nature of the Evidence

Our evidence for medical understandings of gender and the body in antiquity comes from a variety of sources. The medical texts that were written by ancient physicians like Hippocrates and his followers, Soranus of Ephesus, and Galen, as well as some of the Egyptian medical papyri, offer us detailed descriptions of bodily suffering, protracted reflections on gender and bodily difference, and prescriptions for ameliorating bodily suffering that articulate in detail the epistemological underpinnings of ancient medical practice.[33] Similarly, the physiognomic descriptions that we find in authors like Polemo or Cicero offer us glimpses into ancient understandings of the overlap between bodily comportment and gender.[34] Aristotle, who was not a doctor but a philosopher, had a large influence on Galen, the second-century CE physician who wrote widely on a variety of medical topics.[35] In addition to philosophical sources, ancient literature like the travel diary of Aelius Aristides provides us with insights into the way in which the medical understandings of the body had permeated the cultural imagination of suffering bodies.

Medical praxis is also mediated to us through the inscriptions that recorded healing practices at the ancient Asklepieia. Asklepieia were ancient healing shrines devoted to the god Asklepios. The Asklepios cult and its sanctuaries thrived from the fourth century BCE to the fifth century CE and included more than one hundred temples throughout the ancient Mediterranean.[36] The evidence from the Asklepieia includes financial records, votive offerings (sometimes in the form of body parts that correspond to the types of healing that occurred there), and inscriptions.

Although the inscriptions are diverse, many of them follow the same general pattern: a description of the patient's complaint; a statement that the patient slept in the abaton, or the dormitory where patients waited for their dream cure; and a description of the results and the votive offering. While the inscriptions from the Asklepieia are sometimes viewed as either folk literature or propaganda intended to prop up the temple's infrastructure, they, like ancient medical texts, also reveal common cultural assumptions about men's and women's bodies.[37]

In addition to offering us rich textual descriptions of suffering bodies in antiquity, medical literature is central for an understanding of gender and bodies in the ancient world.[38] These sources often articulate cultural assumptions about male and female bodies. For instance, in *On the Function of the Parts of the Body*, Galen offers a long explanation of why women do not have beards: they do not share the "august nature" of men.

> The hair of the beard not only protects the jaws but also contributes to their seemliness: for the male seems more august, especially as he grows older, if he has everywhere a good covering of hair. On this account also nature has left the so-called "apples" (cheeks) and nose smooth and bare of hair; for otherwise the whole countenance would have become savage and bestial, by no means suitable for a civilized and social animal ... On the other hand, for women, the rest of whose body is always soft and hairless like a child's, the bareness of the face would not be unseemly, and besides, this animal does not have an august character as the male has and so does not need an august form. For I have already shown many times, if not throughout the work, that nature makes the form of the body appropriate to the characteristics of the soul. And female genus does not need any special covering as protection against the cold, since for the most part women stay at home, yet they do need long hair on their heads for both protection and seemliness, and this they share with men.[39]

In order to explain the absence of female facial hair, Galen describes the anatomy of men and women in terms of commonly recognized attributes of women: they do not lead active outdoor lives like men, they are not as dignified as men, and they are generally softer and smoother all over than men. As we will see below, Galen also follows the convention of describing the male body first, and then describing the female body as a relatively deficient body. He places this particular explanation of female deficiency in the context of the main thesis of his anatomical oeuvre: "nature makes the form of the body appropriate to the characteristics of the soul." Galen's anatomical description rationalizes male and female anatomical differences by appealing to nature. Although both males and females have souls, male souls are more august than female ones.[40]

Other medical authors reveal culturally prevalent ideas about the body simply by offering correctives to conventional wisdom. In *On Antecedent Causes*, for instance, Galen warns other doctors not to infer causality where conventional wisdom about the body has. He points out that simply because people believe that indigestion leads to a fever does not mean that the conditions of poor digestion actually caused a person's body to become feverish.[41] In the process of cautioning doctors to question common cultural correlations and eschew prevalent theories about causality, Galen also enumerates for us some of those common theories about causality. So even though Galen and those who read his works knew that bathing in cold water does not cause paralysis, we learn that the belief that bathing in cold water was dangerous was widespread enough that Galen felt he needed to clarify the point for other physicians.[42]

Ancient medical literature not only reveals to us the existing ideas about the body, but it also played a large part in influencing ancient perceptions of the body and the medical practitioners themselves. Due to the popularity of the Asklepios cult and other medical technologies, medicine had a profound impact on society in a way that cut across local cultures.[43]

Gender, Suffering, and Pain

In the medical literature, gender and bodily suffering are mechanisms by which to differentiate between and treat bodies. In order to treat a male or female body, the practitioner had to understand not only its fundamental concerns, but also its general constitution. For this reason, when ancient physicians scrutinized male and female bodies, the broader cultural assumptions about their relative strength and weakness guided both the diagnosis and the treatment. Celsus begins his medical treatise by cautioning against a "healthy man" using a doctor or a massage therapist because he who is "vigorous and functioning on his own volition" should not need medical treatment.[44] Later in the treatise, Celsus advises that massage be used in different quantities for men and women, as well as according to their age, in order to account for differing strength.[45] Celsus reminds his readers that the vigorous, strong, male body could accommodate more vigorous massage, whereas weaker, female bodies, or the bodies of the elderly, had to be treated more delicately. Even within genders this was the case; for example, gladiators could tolerate different kinds of diet than other men.

As we have already seen, the weakness and inferiority of the female body was grounded in its fundamental constitution. The voices of women, children, and eunuchs, for instance, were thought to be inherently weak because of the narrowness of the passages that lined the flesh.[46] And although—according to the Greeks—female fetuses were slower to develop than male, once outside the womb, women's bodies were more susceptible to aging.[47] As Lesley Dean-Jones summarizes, "In the world, male and female are advancing to a negative outcome—death—so the female achieves it first; an inferior entity deteriorates more quickly."[48] The presumption that women's bodies were inferior and deteriorated more quickly may have been founded on the observable fact that women died at considerably younger ages than men in every period of antiquity.[49] While contemporary actuarial tables indicate that women tend to outlive men, in antiquity early pregnancy, childbirth, and bad nutrition caused premature aging and death of women.[50] The female body's weakness and susceptibility to deterioration posed a particular challenge to medical practitioners.

Some authors also attributed greater pain to the female body. The female body's process of menstruation, childbirth, and after-birth recovery was thought to be productive but also painful and dangerous. Menstruation is described by Pliny the Elder in his *Natural History* as "monstrous" and attributed with souring wine, ruining crops, corroding metal, killing bees, and making dogs mad.[51] According to Galen, menstruation is one of the ways nature compensates for the innately soft, weak bodies of women, attempting to bring them into balance despite their lack of heat and blood flow.[52] He elaborates that a woman who is not "well purged" via menstruation is susceptible to a wide range of illnesses and reproductive difficulties, including paralysis and loss of limb function. Aristotle and Soranus describe the process of menstruation itself as painful and a drain on the strength of the female body (Aristotle, *Gen. An.* 727A.22–25; Soranus, *Gyn.* 1.6.29). In the Hippocratic Corpus, the pain of accumulated excess blood is described as particularly severe for unmarried virgins, who are advised to "cohabitate with a man as soon as they can—for if they become pregnant, they recover" (*Dis. Yg. Girl.* 1 [ll. 466–70]).

Although pregnancy and childbirth were also associated with pain, the medical authors observed that women's bodies became accustomed to the pain, so that it was less severe each time. And in some cases, they suggest, women could also experience pain from not bearing children.[53] In short, from puberty to postmenopause, physical pain was an inevitable experience of the female body. In most cases the treatment inflicted more pain to help the spongy female body to properly purge its excesses. So great was the association between female bodies and pain that the Hippocratic Corpus says that a mother's painful period of bleeding after the birth of a female child will be twelve days longer than if she had given birth to a male child. Galen says that bearing and delivering a female child is more difficult and disturbing than giving birth to a male.[54] Female bodies not only endured more pain, they caused more pain as well.

The suffering and leaky female body was also seen as dangerous. Despite the high number of women who sought treatment at the Asklepieia for reproductive problems, childbirth itself was forbidden within the sanctuaries of Asklepios.[55] Of course, at other sanctuaries in the ancient world the bodily fluids of menstruation and childbirth would exempt a woman from entry out of concern for ritual purity. However, at an Asklepieion many of the suppliants (male and female) seeking healing were oozing fluids of some sort.[56] The concern around giving birth at the Asklepieia likely reflects the desire not to have a death occur in the sanctuary. As Lesley Dean-Jones argues, "the body of a woman was thought to be more dangerous for a particular period of her life cycle—menarche to menopause—not for a particular period of her menstrual cycle."[57] From menarche to menopause the female body represents the dangers of childbirth—dangers that were all too real in the ancient world—along with its productive potentials.

Interestingly, at the Asklepieion in particular, the productive potential of pain was widely recognized, and not exclusively associated with the female body. In the *Sacred Tales*, Aelius Aristides describes painful treatments that were prescribed by the god Asklepios, including running barefoot in cold weather, applying cold mud masks to the body, and swimming in icy, turbulent water.[58] These treatments were not unique to Aristides or the Asklepieion; they can be found in other inscriptions and in the medical authors we have surveyed so far. Since these same practices are prescribed by Hippocrates or Galen, it is clear that swimming in cold water is not simply a painful way for suppliants at the Asklepieion "to manifest their obedience through their endurance and bodily submission to painful commands," as Perkins suggests.[59] The healing potential of taking a cold swim or exposing a weakened body to cold weather was based upon a system of medicine in which a man's body had to be brought back into balance by its natural, masculine heat.[60] The treatments that were recommended to Aristides were particular to his sick male body, and do not represent endurance simply for the sake of devotion. Nevertheless, it remains the case that in the *Sacred Tales*, the Asklepieion inscriptions, and the medical authors, the pain of healing is viewed as a "productive" pain that is applied to bodies that are already suffering.

The idea that productive suffering existed at the intersection of humanity and divinity found a home in a number of other contexts. Pain, or *ponos* in Greek, connoted the glory of war and childbirth in Classical Greece, and was associated with hard work and long-lasting but necessary pain that, left untreated, could bring about desired ends.[61] The Hippocratic Corpus compares women's pain and blood to those of a sacrificial animal.[62] Within the Hippocratic Corpus this association is specific to the bleeding of a woman in her menses and lochia, because the first woman to be presented to a man occurred at the institution of sacrifice.[63] The routine pain of a relatively healthy female body is seen as an efficacious sacrifice to the *polis*, whereas the pain of the male body is propitious only in special circumstances, such as sickness or war. These examples show that multiple discursive frameworks of gendered suffering existed side by side in antiquity. The female body could be healthy, in pain, weak, and beneficial simultaneously, while the male body could be in pain and beneficial only when the natural strength and vitality of that body were disrupted.

Gender and Suffering in the Afterlife

Thinking theologically about bodies at the eschaton only complicated matters further, often causing early Christian authors to use multiple (sometimes incompatible) ideas about the body in the service of the same argument. Even the basic question, "Will there be gender differentiation in the afterlife?" provoked a variety of answers. Some early Christian authors were concerned to show that there would be some kind of fundamental equality between male and female bodies at the eschaton. For these writers Galatians 3:28 promised an eschatological ideal in which there would be "no male nor female." This ideal, however, could be realized only by effacing the feminine and collapsing both genders into the androgyne.[64] While Clement of Alexandria does not argue for an androgynous afterlife, he does imagine a future reality in which sexual desire is effaced. Despite his consistent emphasis on procreation and birth as efficacious female bodily suffering, Clement expected the eschaton to be free from sex acts, and he urged married couples who had already had children to live together in celibacy in anticipation of their resurrection bodies.[65] At the eschaton, Clement argues, resurrection bodies will be free from desire because femininity, which he sees as the root of desire, will be erased.

Many other early Christians, however, argued that male and female bodily difference would be preserved at the eschaton, and for widely different reasons. This view was grounded in a belief in the materiality of the afterlife based on ancient Greek and Roman depictions of Hades.[66] The idea that bodies would be "intact" in the ways they existed on earth was so common that Lucian pokes fun at it in *Dialogues of the Dead*; when Mennipus looks at the skeleton of Helen of Troy in Hades, famous for her beauty in life, but a bare skeleton in death, he remarks on how quickly a body "loses its bloom."[67] For early Christians, the idea of bodily resurrection, and the exact nature of that resurrection, became a litmus test for evaluating who was a "true Christian."[68] And although each author interprets Scripture differently, they preserve the Pauline idea that there is some component of continuity and some element of change between earthly and heavenly bodies.[69]

Candida R. Moss has demonstrated that despite the importance of Jesus's wounds in the resurrection appearances, most later Christian thinkers argued that resurrected bodies would be perfected; disability would be effaced, but other defining characteristics, such as gender, would be retained.[70] Likewise, Augustine argues that there will be two sexes at the eschaton, but that there will not be deformity or infirmity. He transfigures the scars of reattached limbs into more aesthetically pleasing tattoos. Pseudo-Justin argues that resurrected bodies will be "whole" and "perfect," whereas Irenaeus viewed disability as an indicator that salvation is incomplete.[71]

Augustine provides an aesthetic rationale for the retention of body parts that would seem to be unnecessary in the afterlife. Nipples, for example, would be retained because they are essential to the beauty of the male form. Eyes, too, will be preserved in heaven, even though they are functionally not needed in the afterlife.[72] Because of this emphasis on aesthetics and materiality, gender difference is important for preserving identity at the eschaton, but sex and reproduction are not. Instead, heavenly bodies are spared the "shame" of desire, birth, and lactation.[73] Because salvation was equated with bodily perfection, intact ideal gender identity, and the absence of pained female bodies, exhibiting those traits on earth became a cipher for moral perfection and future salvation. As Moss argues, "most forms of impairment are not reproduced at the resurrection; they are discarded as part of the dark, chaotic, disordered corpora of corruption. As materialistic identity began to take hold of Western Christianity's notion of the self, impairment became nonessential. Christianity scoured its resurrected bodies and narrated its history so that the salvation of all flesh is completed with the blotting out of impairment."[74] While these forms of impairment are not reproduced at the resurrection, they are used to mark the bodies of the damned that we find in hell. The correlative for Augustine's aesthetically balanced, two-nippled, bearded, resurrected male body is the emasculated, asymmetrical male body hanging by its testicles or having its eyes gouged out in the apocalyptic visions of hell. In the eschatological picture of hell developed by early Christians, bodily impairment, femininity, aesthetic imbalance, and sexual function/dysfunction are preserved as markers of damnation. Men hang by their penis or testicles, women hang by their breasts; men and women wade through rivers of fire so that their bodies are consumed by flames, their lips fall off, and they chew their tongues.[75]

The damned may no longer be actively having sex, but the sexual (dys)function of their body parts is still a central component of their punishment. This point suggests that bodies *could* have functioned sexually at the eschaton, if only they had not sinned on earth. The impact of eschatological punishment is directly tied to the shame of bodily impairment on earth. Such punishments do not simply "fit the crimes" according to the principles of *lex talionis*, but also use the body as a canvas on which to paint familiar images of physical suffering. Martha Himmelfarb and Callie Callon trace the history of specific cases of *lex talionis,* or "mirror punishments," but their emphasis on the literary traditions surrounding each punishment has the unintended effect of separating the apocalyptic rhetoric of punitive suffering from the day-to-day experiences of bodily suffering.[76] And as we have seen with early Christian depictions of the resurrection, the early Christian understanding of what happened to the body after death was frequently framed in discourses of the body that were grounded in lived experience. In turn, the eschatological body determined for Christians what kinds of bodies on earth would be associated with salvation and damnation, with virtue, and with sin. Deformed, disabled, or effeminate bodies were frequently but not exclusively associated with damnation and sin, creating an eschatology that intensified and reinforced the existing social hierarchy of the body.[77]

Gender and bodily suffering were linked in the minds of Christian authors, who frequently drew upon the cultural ideas about the body that we find in the medical literature, but in an unsystematic way. Our sources reveal that Christian eschatology and the medical views of the body are intertwined, to the point that some authors, including Clement and Augustine, struggled to reconcile their understanding of material bodies with the theological telos of the resurrection as they understood it.[78] We might expect the eschatological framework of bodily suffering in the early Christian apocalypses to be even less systematic than that of Clement, who found it difficult to articulate how male and female bodies could coexist at the resurrection. Such is not the case. Because ancient apocalyptic authors drew from earlier apocalypses, their scenes of eschatological punishment are relatively consistent. Recalling that the earliest Christian tour of hell, the Apocalypse of Peter, may have been written in second-century Alexandria—the same environment in which Clement later composed his *Christ the Educator*—we are able to imagine that the tours of hell drew upon ancient medical understandings of gender and the body in similar ways.

Gender and Judicial Punishment

Much recent scholarship on gender in early Christianity has argued that early Christian literature reflects and engages in the ongoing struggle to attain and preserve the ideal male body. But even amid that struggle, the ancient understanding of being male was not fixed. As Maud Gleason has observed, the masculine ideal was somewhat malleable over time.[79] The context of punitive suffering, whether earthly or otherworldly, lays bare the fragility of the ancient masculine ideal. On the whole the suffering body represented a failure to attain normative masculinity. Yet in a culture that used punitive suffering to reinforce those bodily norms and "make men" out of women and slaves, the suffering body is a complicated site that simultaneously symbolizes power and powerlessness.

Chris L. de Wet argues that John Chrysostom's preaching on slavery reflects this tension: "To Chrysostom, Christian identity was founded in being scourged, not flinging the whip. Public and spectacularly violent punishment reflected the degradation of Roman society—a society founded on the brutality of slavery. The harsh punishment of slaves further destabilized masculinity, hence Chrysostom's strict measures to regulate and redistribute the means of punishment."[80] Like the suffering imposed upon the enslaved

Christian, the suffering of bodies in early Christian hell was part of the culture of surveillance meant to ensure productivity and good behavior in a system pervaded by the power of domination. In the context of slavery, "the Christic panopticon" collapses the divine and the enslaver, and in doing so removes any hope of agency, physical, spiritual, or psychological, "creating a powerful spiritual carcerality with no means of escape."[81]

The pedagogical value of these spectacles of torture contributes to the positive view of punishment in early Christian thought. This positive view of punishment is evident in the "lived metaphor" of "exegetical torture" that Origen of Alexandria uses in his biblical exegesis.[82] J. Albert Harrill connects the metaphorical language of dissecting a text to the real bodies of the household slaves of Origen's readers. When Origen describes the ideal interpretive process, he uses the term *basanos*, the "test" or "touchstone," to describe the way that each word must be interrogated: "one must apply every test [*basanos*] even to the words assumed to be clear."[83] The *basanos* was the slate touchstone used to test the purity of gold in the refinement process, as judged by the color of the mark it would leave on the stone. The term was also used, however, to refer to the courtroom process of cross-examination through juridical torture.[84] By invoking this term, Harrill argues, Origen is drawing upon the practice of removing enslaved persons from the courtroom for the purposes of torture. The practice was rationalized as being in service of revealing a hidden truth. The process of aggressively seeking out the truth through a *basanos* was widespread in antiquity. It is mentioned by medical authors, such as Hippocrates and Galen, as well as by philosophers and rhetoricians, all of whom presumed a necessary relationship between the use of physical force and eliciting the truth from an "inferior body."[85] Origen specifically invokes the *basanos* alongside other mentions of "good torture" of enslaved persons.[86] For these early Christian masters, torture was punitive for the enslaved, and pedagogical for both the enslaved and onlookers. Harrill concludes that Origen's use of the metaphor of applying every "test" or *basanos* to Scripture draws upon these real contexts of public bodily torture. Origen's "sanctification of violence extends to a positive view of punishment generally. The ideal body results only from the proper discipline of its flesh."[87] Origen's view of physical punishment as pedagogical mirrors the use of prison within the late antique punitive justice system as both a reform and a deterrent. Prison was reserved primarily for lower ranking offenders, as an educational public spectacle and warning.[88]

The violent spectacle of hell's punishments created a similar "spiritual carcerality" to the public juridical torture of the enslaved and criminals. As an imaginative spectacle, however, hell offered early Christian authors an opportunity to depict the future suffering body in a way that did not threaten masculinity (as Chrysostom feared the punishment of the enslaved would), but actually preserved the masculine body in the present. For example, Chysostom thought that the fires of Gehenna were the only adequate restraint for adolescent sexual desire. He instructs parents on the proper age at which to teach their sons the different stories of punitive suffering. He warns that parents should not tell their sons about hell before they are fifteen, but by eight or ten, they can hear about the flood, Sodom, and the descent into Egypt: "whatever stories are full of divine punishment" will "fortify his hearing."[89]

Chrysostom's zeal for using damnation as a pedagogical tool specifically for boys and young men reminds us that torture and bodily suffering were malleable ideas that could be applied to a wide range of situations beyond the crucifixion.[90] Stories about punitive suffering and images of damnation could be useful tools for forming the ideal Christian man, precisely because they offered up the tortured body and the enslaved body as cautionary tales. "Divine punishment" could "fortify" the young man because it was tied to the prevalent spectacle of violence in the world around these young Christian men, a spectacle they must endeavor to eschew if they were to cultivate and preserve their masculinity.[91] In the judicial context, as in the ancient medical literature, the bodies that are marked as "other" or "inferior" expose the operative bodily norms of the culture. Like the bodies of the sick, or the weak, the enslaved body and the tortured body confound categories. The overwhelming amount of attention paid to these bodies in antiquity reflects an attempt to properly classify the suffering bodies, like those we find in the apocalyptic visions of hell.

Christian Bodies and Ancient Judicial Torture

The spectacle of violence in the judicial context is central for the present study of punitive bodily suffering. Brent D. Shaw has argued that the fear of being involved in a public display of physical torture was "embedded in the conscience of the ordinary people" in antiquity. For early Christians this fear became manifest in the belief in a "final court." As the church fathers continued to develop scriptural notions of divine judgment, the final court began to resemble the judicial proceedings of the Roman world. The relationship between Christians and God came to be defined in judicial terms: "Fairness and justice, vengeance and retribution became the principal qualities of God the Judge. And the final judgment was seen as a court in which Christ was to act as our intercessor or defense attorney."[92] Shaw offers Tertullian, Ambrose, Jerome, and Augustine as prime examples of church fathers who employed the topos of the judicial nightmare in their own descriptions of divine judgment. He also points to the martyrdom literature as a way of memorializing that spectacle.

Whereas martyrdom literature sanctifies the violence by villainizing the Roman as aggressor, the apocalyptic judgment scenes are justified as "appropriate" punishments for the sinful victims.[93] This topos appears in the early Christian apocalypses as well. In the latter, however, the suffering is punitive rather than redemptive, as in the Christian martyrdom accounts. David Frankfurter's study of eroticized voyeurism across "Roman spectacle culture" includes both martyrdom and apocalyptic eschatology. The latter differs from the former, however, in that "the graphic scenes of the suffering of the unrighteous also provided audiences with a safely set-off context for fantasizing aggression."[94]

Within each context gender and bodily suffering draw the audience's eyes to particularly horrifying or confounding elements of the drama. In the apocalyptic visions of punitive suffering in hell, however, the vivid experience is narrated in the third person by an apostolic seer, and the sins are not particular to an individual's life experiences, but encompass a wide range of possible faults. Whereas the judicial nightmares of individual Christians could set up a framework for imagining God as the final judge and Christ as the intercessor, the early Christian apocalypses allowed the Christian to imagine their own scene of torment with greater specificity. Just as the Roman punishments served as theatrically staged events that provided public entertainment and incited fear, the Christian visions of eternal torment provided haunting spectacles that could be generalized to almost any body.

While Shaw suggests that the spectacle "needed a text," the textual nature of the martyrdom accounts and the early Christian apocalypses does not seem to be their only important or even defining feature.[95] To be sure, the repetition of generic elements and the production and preservation of the early Christian apocalypses made it possible for early Christians to hear the vivid scenes of eschatological judgment and punishment on a regular basis, reinforcing the vision of justice and ethical rubric of a specific apocalypse.[96] Since the majority of ancient audiences heard the text instead of reading it themselves, the familiar or most striking words, phrases, and images would have had the greatest impact on listeners. The popularity and influence of the early Christian apocalypses did not depend on their narrative structure (which varied despite some consistent features), nor was it tied to their existence as "texts" that memorialized the drama of punitive suffering. Rather, the imaginative worlds of these apocalypses were influential due to their connection to the real world and their ability to arouse "imprinted memories" grounded in lived experiences of witnessing judicial torment and bodily suffering.[97]

Some of the bodies in early Christian tours of hell undergo torments that fit the ancient standard of *lex talionis*, according to which the punishment should "fit the crime" in measure and intensity. These "measure for measure punishments," as they are also called, sometimes involve hanging by the offending body part, immersion in fire up to the offending body part, asphyxiation, or tantalization.[98] Not only do some of these punishments follow the ancient legal standard of *lex talionis*, they also recall the real torture that ancient persons experienced as a part of the ancient judicial process.[99]

In *City of God*, Augustine connects the scourge of eternal punishment and the penal justice system, making a direct connection between the logic behind Cicero's "eight kinds of penalty" under the law, and the justice of eternal punishment (*City of God* 21.11). For Augustine, the judicial process that was exacted on bodies in this world was an important link to the punishments of hell. Thus, the concept of hell as a prison with "adamantine bars" was a metaphor that linked the early Christian reflections on judgment and eternal punishment to the familiar juridical and disciplinary spaces of the Roman world. The image of Hades or hell as a prison was very prevalent in the ancient world. For example, Virgil depicts Tartarus's screeching gate that is protected by columns of solid adamantine (*Aen.* 6.550–60), and Plutarch envisions Erinys imprisoning souls who are "past all healing" (Plutarch, *Mor.* 564F–65F). In Christian depictions of hell we find similar language, beginning with the "gates of Hades" in Matthew 16. The appropriation of the idea of hell as a prison continues in the early Christian apocalypses with the adamantine bars of hell in the Apocalypse of Peter 4, and the "prison of the underworld" in the Apocalypse of Paul 18.

The connection between the imaginary spaces of hell in the early Christian apocalypses and punitive spaces of the Roman world is not only a literary trope passed on from text to text. In many ways, the types of bodily punishments one finds in hell mirror the judicial punishments of the Roman world. Those who had judicial nightmares might fear imprisonment, hanging, beheading, being thrown to wild beasts, crucifixion, or burning alive.[100] Of these punishments, all but crucifixion occur in the early Christian visions of hell, while hanging, wild beasts, and burning figure prominently as mechanisms of torture. These brutal and public forms of punishment were expanded in the early empire under the jurisdiction of single-judge courts, but the system for handing down these punishments was developed most extensively in the second century. In this system, the bodily torments of judicial nightmares were reserved for those who did not occupy the elite social status (*honestiores*). Julia Hillner explains:

> In consequence, degrading forms of execution, including crucifixion, burning or condemnation to the beasts were reserved for *humiliores*, which may have included everyone below the social category of town councillors (*curiales*), while the death penalty for *honestiores* was decapitation by the sword. Likewise, among the non-lethal penalties, *honestiores* were not to be sentenced to forced labour or corporal punishment, but were to be exiled (with or without the loss of property) or fined. In essence, *honestiores* were spared any punishment that unduly affected their body.[101]

The forms of bodily torment that we find in the apocalypses are the more degrading forms of punishment that were reserved for Roman nonelites and the enslaved, and they are used in the early Christian depictions of hell as a spectacle designed to spare the audience the shame of these punishments in the future.

The arena and geography for punishment mirror the fear-inspiring carceral contexts of forced labor in the mines. Eusebius of Caesarea claims that during the Great Persecution, Christians were dispatched to the mines at Phaeno (modern-day Khibet Faynan) in southwest Jordan as their punishment.[102] The *damnatio ad metallum* (condemnation to the mines) sentence was among the harshest penalties in Roman law and was ordinarily reserved for members of the lower classes and enslaved persons. That Christian tours of hell use the space and conditions of the mines to imagine hell serves to lower the status of those elites whose punishments bring them there.

Whether or not the punishments were as severe as early Christians imagined, mines were perceived as places where prisoners rarely saw sunlight, frequently suffocated from noxious gases, were vulnerable to being crushed by piles of falling rocks, and were exposed to extreme heat and physical exhaustion.[103] The lower a prisoner would descend, the more oppressive and dangerous his experience would be. The descent into the mines prefigured and anticipated the descent into hell and recast the subterranean realm as a place of punishment. In his Homily on Matthew 12, John Chrysostom tells his hearers that hell is like the mines, only indescribably worse.[104]

The traditional approach to the punishments has been to point to their literary antecedents in Greek and Jewish mythology.[105] That there were literary precedents for the mechanisms of torture in the early Christian apocalypses is not in dispute here.[106] Whether the authors of the apocalypses gleaned their images from literature or reality, the audiences of those tours would likely have connected the text with reality and the culturally available imagery of physical violence. While the imagery that ancient hearers encountered may have been borrowed from mythological texts, those images were often edited in ways that standardized these images for mass consumption.[107] As we will see in the martyrdom literature, early Christians built upon this existing connection between torture and truth, welding Jewish and Greek ideas of physical pain into a test that reveals the true identity of the recipient. For the early Christian apocalypses this idea was foundational, allowing early Christian audiences to gaze upon bodies in torment in order to motivate them to reflect upon the "true" state of their own souls.

Gender and Martyrdom: Female Bodies in Pain as a Propitious Spectacle

In martyrdom texts, Christians readily applied the idea of a test, or *basanos*, to redemptive suffering and thought about the physical torture of martyrdom as a public test of the flesh that revealed the true nature of the soul. As we have seen so far, in judicial contexts this test was a way of determining truth by imposing violent torture on an "inferior body." In the Christian eschatological contexts of heaven and hell, the *basanos* reveals not only the veracity of one's words, but the purity of one's soul, just as a touchstone reveals the purity of a metal.[108] This idea may have parallels or antecedents in ancient judicial literature. The test of public torture, once passed by the martyr, enables the elevation of the pure soul.[109] The test was also viewed as part of a propitious public sacrifice that would lead to heavenly glorification.

In the Roman world, martyrdom and judicial punishment served as a public spectacle featuring the violent performance of imperial power.[110] As in the early Christian depictions of hell, these spectacles used the body as a tableau for representing the punitive consequences of particular action or inaction, intended to deter any body in the empire.[111] The early Christian martyrdom accounts certainly played with this framework and resisted the narrative of the empire through their vindication of the martyrs as bodies that suffered righteously. The martyr, once tested and deemed "pure," becomes what Elizabeth Castelli has called a "counter spectacle," glorified through depictions of the martyrs as Christ crucified.[112] Similarly, Virginia Burrus has argued that the Christian martyr, unlike the Roman enslaved person, is not simply a passive object. Rather, the martyr is also a resistant subject who witnesses to the truth against their torturer. For this reason, "the history of martyrdom also illumines the limits of torture's power and the potential sources of its subversion and critique."[113] Yet, even in acts of textual resistance, those accounts participated in performances of gendered bodily suffering, placing the suffering body on display, and drawing attention to the complex ways in which it participated in the ancient gender economy.[114]

Page duBois argues that the concept of excavating for the unadulterated truth through torture is inextricably linked to gender in the ancient world:

> Each of these sites of meaning in ancient culture—epic, oracles, sacred buildings, the medicalized body—lay out a pattern of obscure, hidden truth that must be interpreted . . . These images of interiority are associated in ancient culture with female space, with the containment and potentiality of the female body. And the female is analogous to the slave. The slave's body and the woman's body are marked off as the property of the master; the subject of history in the ancient city, the Greek male citizen, ruled over his subordinates, animals and barbarian slaves, and women, who were seen as like one another in their subordination. Like slaves' bodies, tattooed with signs of ownership and origin, women's bodies were metaphorically inscribed by their masters. The veiled citizen woman, who conceals her true nature with cosmetics and drapery, remains an other, full of potential truth, uncannily resembling the slave, male and female, who awaits torture, who conceals truth.[115]

For duBois, the enslaved body and the female body are both inferior bodies that conceal the truth that demands to be extracted through the physical test of torture. This link between the female body, torture, and truth is evidenced in juridical contexts, ancient medicine, and (as we will see in the next chapter) ancient myths about Hades. DuBois does not include the Christian martyrs in her historical narrative, a gap that Burrus and others have sought to fill.[116] Scholarship on gender and early Christian martyrdom has shown that a female martyr is not simply "a passive container of the truth" and a tortured object, but also a subject who assigns truth and meaning to her own suffering.[117]

One way that early Christian martyrs resist and reinterpret these scenes of torture is through gender-bending reappropriations of the noble death tradition. In antiquity the concept of "dying well" was associated with manliness, heroism, and bravery.[118] Elizabeth Castelli points out that "as the memory work of Christian martyrology unfolds, the capacity of Christian women to be transformed into masculine heroes becomes almost a cliché."[119] Female martyrs are "made male" by fighting in the arena like athletes and warriors. They are also, however, depicted as beautiful mothers and wives, that is, feminized. This tension between the masculinity and femininity of the female martyrs had to be preserved in order for Christians to demonstrate the superiority of Christian witness over and against their Jewish and pagan counterparts: "even Christian women were manlier than their male persecutors."[120] As early Christian martyrdom accounts reenacted scenes of violence, they also resisted this violence through these victorious testimonies to what Virginia Burrus has called the "persistence of the flesh."[121] In this way, female martyrs become important symbols of speaking truth to power, resisting tyranny in the midst of its grand spectacle of violence.

Each of these scholarly attempts to see the Christian martyrdom accounts as an act of resistance is accompanied by the admission that such resistance is only partial, as it reinscribes ancient notions of bodily torture, truth seeking, and gender. Despite their nuances, these scholarly portraits imply that the prevalence and popularity of the female martyrs reflect ancient Christian ideas about the equality of men and women, or at the very least the emergence of the martyr as a mechanism for reclaiming subjectivity amid bodily suffering.[122] But, as Candida Moss has argued, even the most heroic female martyrs were often valued by and interpreted within the patriarchal gaze: "The valorization of the self-sacrifice and the virtues of these women does not necessarily imply, even in these examples, that women transcended the social structures that constrained them."[123]

In fact, the very spaces that draw attention to the masculinized triumph of the female body are mere artifacts of the broader culture's orientation toward the female body as a suffering object. Perhaps "the voyeuristic appreciation of the female corpse may speak more about objectification than masculinization."[124]

As our survey of ancient medical and juridical concepts shows, the prevalence of female martyrs coheres with the dominant ideas about female bodies in pain. The female martyrs who describe their bodily suffering as a sacrifice for Christ their master call to mind the idea of the female body enduring the pain of childbirth as a sacrifice for the household and polis. And the concept of martyrdom as a test that will reveal the truth and purity of their testimony casts the female martyr as one among many other female and enslaved bodies in need of public and violent testing to reveal some interior or hidden truth.

In the *Passion of Perpetua and Felicitas*, for instance, Perpetua's maternal identity and her youthful bravery in the face of suffering are front and center, and contrast with her father's "pathetic old age" (*Mart. Perp. Fel.* 2–6). As Perpetua nurses her newborn, she clings to the title "Christian," and remains intent on revealing the "truth" in spite of her father's repeated request that she "perform the sacrifice." In doing so, Perpetua performs a different kind of sacrifice than that which her father demands, that of the maternal body which suffers for the larger community, ultimately winning her fight with the Devil and gaining heavenly glorification (*Mart. Perp. Fel.* 3, 6, 10, 20–21). To be sure, Perpetua's body is "made male" in her athletic confrontation in the arena, but not before her status as a mother and Christian are secured as unassailable.

Likewise, the story of Felicitas's martyrdom foregrounds her maternal body as a qualification for martyrdom. Just after her arrest Felicitas gives birth to a girl, following a difficult labor in which she "suffered a good deal" (*Mart. Perp. Fel.* 15). Although the text explains Felicitas's difficult labor as the result of a premature delivery (at eight months), readers would also recall the ancient notion that female babies were more painful to birth. During this painful delivery the prison guards taunt Felicitas by asking how she will endure the suffering that awaits her when she is tossed to the beasts. Felicitas responds that in childbirth "I suffer by myself. But then another will be inside me who will suffer for me, just as I shall be suffering for him [Christ]" (*Mart. Perp. Fel.* 15). In addition to modeling calm in the face of torment, Felicitas's response accomplishes something else. Recalling that the ancient medical texts espoused the idea that women's bodies became accustomed to pain through childbirth, Felicitas's explanation is necessary in order to redirect a naturalistic reading of her fortitude in the arena. Without her explanation that she will be able to endure in the arena because she and Christ will suffer for one another, the suffering female body of Felicitas would simply be another example of maternal endurance forged through her difficult delivery of a premature baby girl. In the eyes of the text and the surrounding culture Felicitas is uniquely qualified for martyrdom because she possesses a female body that is primed to suffer. She withstands the "test" by professing that she will "be suffering for him."

Early Christian martyrdom literature drew upon medical and judicial ideas about gender and bodily suffering, using physical pain to depict martyrdom as propitious sacrifice and female martyrs as "true" righteous Christians. In doing so, they simultaneously mounted a Christian resistance against the claims of their torturers while reenacting the broader cultural narratives about the female body. The female martyrs were popular because they already possessed bodies that needed to suffer in order to effect change for others and reveal hidden truths. In short, the ancient Christian woman makes an excellent martyr not in spite of her gender, but because of it, as she conforms to the cultural expectations of the female body as a suffering body.

Conclusion

Ancient men and women lived in a world composed of social structures and practices that equated the female body with the suffering body. Even in contexts that upheld the importance of bodily suffering, like childbirth, the valorization of the suffering body as "productive" or "efficacious" did not always decouple that body from the hierarchical dualisms that also read the suffering body as inferior. The female body was reproductively strong, but it also bore the possibility of death as a constant reminder of human frailty. The male body, by contrast, was like a tightly woven cloth, impervious to penetration, and yet always susceptible to the threat of suffering through which the male body could become like the fleecy, absorbent, weak female body.

At times multiple discourses around the suffering body are at work in the same text. For example, in his discussion of Simeon, Theodoret links excellence in ascetic practice with characteristics associated with the female body. At the same time, Theodoret also recounts Simeon's expulsion from the community as a direct result of another monk discovering his effeminate wounds.[125] And while Tertullian and Augustine both admit that some bodily suffering is propitious (Mary in childbirth, or the bodies of the martyrs), both authors take pains to explain the role of the inferiority and shame of the suffering body in the divine drama. By engaging the discourse of the weak, effeminate suffering body, early Christian authors did not simply supplant that discourse with a novel narrative of redemptive suffering, but often also reinstantiated and reinforced dominant ideas about gender and bodily suffering.

Early Christian discourses of gender and bodily suffering do not diverge radically from the dominant cultural narratives in antiquity. In some ascetic contexts—for example, the admonitions of the fifth-century monastic founder Shenoute to maintain one's vow of celibacy—the recommended practices might have diverged from the daily behavioral patterns of the broader society, but the explanation of those practices was still grounded in a hermeneutic of the body that privileged the maintenance of the superior male body.[126] Martyrdom texts resist the broader narrative of the Christian body as the inferior body that is "tested," but they also reenact the cultural script of the enslaved body and the female body as receptacles of hidden truth and as sites of torture. The female martyrs may win salvation through their manly feats of heroism. Ancient interest in these suffering female bodies, however, is not a sign of their equality or masculinity, but reflects the cultural preference for seeing women's bodies in torment. In drawing on these discourses of gendered bodily suffering, early Christians were not constructing a single cohesive narrative of gendered bodily suffering, but relying upon the culturally available languages of gender difference.

Judith Perkins credits Christians with creating the "suffering subject" out of these narratives of bodily suffering. She argues that "Christianity did not produce its suffering subject alone, but that this subjectivity was under construction and emanated from a number of different locations in the Greco-Roman cultural worlds."[127] But Perkins's notion of the Christian invention of the "suffering self" downplays the preexisting tension in the ancient world in which some suffering was already seen as propitious or voluntary, and sidelines the reality that subjectivity and self-mastery were often out of reach for the vast majority of suffering bodies. As we have seen, the Christian bodies that suffer do so in culturally understandable ways, performing the gendered discourses of suffering as pain, weakness, strength, and efficacious sacrifice. In the next chapters, we look to depictions of bodily suffering in hell. We will see that early Christians used these various topoi of gendered bodily suffering in ways that dramatized and intensified the discursive practices around gender and bodily suffering.

2 Gendered Bodies, Social Identities, and the Susceptibility to Sin

Since 1991, in Cedar Hill, Texas, thousands of teenagers have gone on an annual tour of hell. But they do not have to entreat Charon the ferryman; they simply find a church bus or minivan to take them. When they arrive in hell, they are greeted not by an apostle or angel, but by a guide (youth minister or teen volunteer) who leads them around hell, explaining the sites that they see and subjecting them to scene after scene of violence, screaming, and crying. At the end of their tour they reach a room with an altar call. Within six seconds they are expected to make a decision that, they are told, will change their eternal fate. Unlike the early Christian tours of hell, which were mostly focused on motivating Christians to behave ethically toward others, this tour of hell is keenly focused on individual sins and personal conversion. These tourists are in a very specific kind of hell, one that utilizes the aesthetics of the Halloween haunted house, the commitments of American individualism, the rhetoric of fear, and the notion of eternal torment in the cultural phenomenon known as the hell house.

As in the early Christian tours of hell, tourists on this journey find sinners who mirror the gendered morality of the culture in which each hell is constructed.[1] The moral narrative that the hell house constructs draws its coherence not only from religious texts and traditions, but also from a misogynistic vision of the world that prompts "messages about morality, chastity, and the peril of sexuality."[2] This gendered hellscape did not emerge in a vacuum. Rather, it is a product of the post–Cold War culture in the United States, in which sex and abstinence became objects in a spiritual war between evangelicals and "an enemy within."[3]

This spiritual warfare is depicted at another hell house in Tyler, Texas, in which a drunken husband punches his wife, a girl is raped after she sends text messages to someone she thought was a boy but who turned out to be an older neighbor, and a teen mother who had done meth has her son ripped from her arms in a courtroom. The tour guide explains that this is what happens to women when God is removed from schools.[4] Physical and sexual abuses of the bodies of women and children are depicted to show the collateral damage of a spiritual war between God and those who protect the separation of church and state. This pattern is not unique, but a stock element of the hell house, one that "normalizes male violence while vilifying and damning female victims."[5]

These hell houses are a byproduct of extreme fundamentalist Christianity and the latent patriarchy of the broader culture. But, as we will see, they are also part of a literary and rhetorical tradition that begins in the early Christian apocalypses, which had a gendered morality of their own. Ancient Christian appeals to fear were grounded in "profound longing for relief from the terrors and vulnerabilities" of daily life.[6] Unlike the contemporary hell house, the early Christian tours of hell were not focused on conversion, nor were they targeted exclusively at teenagers. Despite the differences in imagery, in ideas of sin, and in cultural and historical contexts, the rhetorical impact is quite similar: an appeal to fear is used to achieve a specific goal. In both cases, the gendered morality of the parent culture is intensified and reinforced.

In the early Christian Apocalypse of Peter, Peter sees sinners punished for a variety of sins ranging from adultery to sorcery. The earliest manuscript tradition of the Apocalypse of Peter specifies very clearly which punishments include both men and women. The Apocalypse of Peter also distinguishes between spaces of torment in which only men or only women are punished. Both men and women are punished for failing to care for widows or the poor (Apoc. Pet. 9), whereas young women are singled out for abandoning their chastity before marriage (Apoc. Pet. 11).

A comparison of the apocalypses across different time periods and geographic regions reveals a pattern that is more complex than can be seen from the simple contrast between the punishments of men and women in a single apocalypse. Let us compare the parents who are punished in the Apocalypse of Peter with those who are punished in the Greek Apocalypse of Ezra. In the Apocalypse of Peter 8, men and women who commit infanticide are tortured forever by beasts that emerge from the foul breast milk of the mothers. In the fifth-century Greek Apocalypse of Ezra, Ezra sees a woman suspended with four wild beasts sucking upon her breasts (Gk. Apoc. Ez. 5). The angelic tour guide quickly explains that this woman is being punished because she begrudged her milk to her babies and cast them into rivers.

Although these texts are separated by hundreds of years, both texts link the fate of the sinner after death to the way that she performed the social role of parent during her lifetime.[7] In the second-century Apocalypse of Peter, however, both men and women are held responsible for parenting, whereas in the fifth-century Greek Apocalypse of Ezra it is only mothers who are punished in hell for abortion, infanticide, or infant exposure (practices that were separate in the broader culture but come to be conflated by early Christians). In hell, punishments are meted out to those who failed to perform the gender roles prescribed by the wider society in which ancient Christians lived. Although the punishments remain similar over time, the sins do not. Each early Christian apocalypse rewires family and individual culpability for sin.

The Apocalypse of Peter contains a list of sinners that follows the order and gendered hierarchy of the New Testament household codes (e.g., 1 Pet 2:13–3:7). In doing so, they model Christian morality on broader Roman ideals of household and city organization. Male and female heads of household have named social roles and accompanying responsibilities, even as women are clearly subordinated to men. The sins outlined in the Apocalypse of Peter largely reinscribe or intensify the gendered morality of the broader culture. The late antique and early medieval apocalypses move away from the strict ordering of the household codes; in these texts, men and women are no longer culpable for the same sins. The male body is primarily held responsible for sexual self-control and ecclesiastical participation, and the female body is largely held accountable for maintaining virginity until marriage, and for the parental responsibilities that ensue if male efforts at sexual self-control fail. This reordering of the Christian household follows from the shifting social norms of late antiquity, but also amplifies and hyperextends bubbling fears about the precarity of masculinity and the Christian household.[8] As late antique Christians modified the Roman household, men were assigned the social roles that had been previously allotted to women: chastity, self-control, and self-renunciation.[9] In hell, this shift in roles is apparent in the changes in the ways that male and female sins are identified and punished. The gendered bodies in hell offer a window into the way that different groups of early Christians reinstantiated, amplified, or subverted the gendered social norms of the world around them.

Gendered Bodies and the Susceptibility to Sin: The Body as the Locus for Judgment in Hell

Early Christian apocalypses imagined fleshy bodies in hell. In the early chapters of Paul's tour of hell, the angels show him the souls of the righteous and the wicked leaving their bodies on earth. In these scenes both the righteous and wicked souls are instructed to pay close attention to the body they are leaving because they will need to find their body on the "day of the resurrection" in order to receive rewards or punishments (Apoc. Paul 14–15). In the Apocalypse of Paul 15, the angel addresses the wicked, saying, "O unfortunate soul, look at your flesh, which you have left. For on the day of resurrection you will have to return into your flesh to receive what is fitting to your sins and ungodliness."[10] This early fifth-century tour of hell explains that the flesh and blood bodies of sinners are needed in order to receive punishments that fit their crimes.

Although this is the first tour of hell that explains the reason why bodies are in hell, the importance of bodies for punishment predates the Apocalypse of Paul. This emphasis on the bodies in hell is also present in the Jewish tours of hell and in the earliest Christian apocalypses. In the Apocalypse of Zephaniah 10, the reader learns that bodies in hell are very much like real bodies on earth: "And I saw others with their hair on them. I said, 'Then there is hair and body in this place?' He said, 'Yes, the Lord gives body and hair to them as he desires.'" In the Isaiah and Elijah Fragments, the fragmentary Jewish apocalypses that describe hell, the bodies of sinners are hung up by the body part that is associated with their sin. When Isaiah enters the fourth court, he sees "daughters of iniquity hanging by their breasts." The Holy Spirit identifies these women as "the women who uncovered their hair and rent their veil and sat in the open market place to suckle their children, in order to attract the gaze of men and to make them sin, therefore they are punished thus" (frag. 4).[11] In the Apocalypse of Peter the first group of women that Peter sees are punished for a similar sin; they hang by their neck and their hair, and are then cast into the pit. The angel explains to Peter that these women "plaited their hair, not to create beauty, but to turn to fornication, and that they might ensnare the souls of men to destruction" (Apoc. Pet. 7). In both of these texts, these measure-for-measure hanging punishments emphasize the bodily, and gendered, nature of eternal punishment.[12]

All of the later Christian tours of hell follow the example of the Apocalypse of Peter by including some punishments that identify the gender of the tortured bodies. The Apocalypse of Paul, which focuses on the sins of presbyters, bishops, deacons, and lectors, specifies that these church leaders are male, even though readers might have already assumed as much (Apoc. Paul 34–36). The Apocalypse of Paul also contains many of the same female sinners found in the Apocalypse of Peter. Paul sees girls who "defiled their virginity," women who committed adultery, and mothers who exposed infants, though the last two are punished alongside their male counterparts (Apoc. Paul 38–40). These gender distinctions hold throughout the genre, and offer us an opportunity to observe the role gender played in the definition of sins in different historical contexts. The gendered fleshly punishments of these hellscapes can be connected to the concrete bodily and social realities that circumscribed the sins of late antique and medieval Christians.

Sex, Marriage, and the Ancient Christian Household

After failure to care for the poor, the most frequently mentioned sins in the early Christian tours of hell are those that relate to sex and marriage. But early Christian attitudes toward sex and marriage are never just about sex and marriage. In antiquity sex and marriage were tied to understandings of the body, economics, and the sociopolitical order. Sexual practices were often understood according to ancient views of women's bodies as passive receptacles and of men's bodies as active, generative, and penetrating. When early Christian women choose chastity over marriage in the Apocryphal Acts, other characters object on economic grounds, as marriage was a primary mechanism for securing the financial future of the virgin and her family.[13] These views of the body, sex, and a patrilineal economic structure were rooted in the order of the household, which in turn underpinned the entire sociopolitical order of the ancient world. The household was not a private sphere, set apart from the city, but an integral and public part of the empire's social fabric.[14]

One of the ways early Christian depictions of hell classify the bodies of the damned is according to Greek and Roman understandings of household order. In the ancient world, the order and structure of the city and the empire were founded upon the structure of individual households. The household structure was prescribed according to a neatly ordered set of binaries, in which the second member of the binary was accountable and submissive to the first. In the descriptions of this household structure (called the "household code") husbands are the head of the household, and the obedience of their household members determines their level of success in contributing to the order of the city and empire. In the usual organization of the household three relationships are discussed, each characterized by subordination and obedience: husbands and wives, parents and children, and enslavers and the enslaved.[15] Typically, the organization of the household code was from those who had the most social power to those who had the least.[16]

The earliest Christians, who first gathered to worship in households, held ideas about marriage and sex that were formed by the broader culture's understanding of the natural and household orders.[17] But as Christians began to use marriage and sex as a means of reinforcing order, these categories took on a life of their own. Marriage continued to be used as the dominant metaphor for describing the relationship with God, and in hell bodies were tormented for their inability to perform their earthly marital and sexual roles.[18] In short, Christians not only inherited ancient ideas about sex and marriage, but they expanded an existing system of social order by intensifying its specificity and imbuing it with divine and eternal significance.

The Roman household structure is a recognizable focus in apocalypses such as the Latin Vision of Ezra and the Apocalypse of Peter, where there is a similar order.[19] The Apocalypse of Peter 7–10 describes would-be heads of households and men and women who did not live up to their social role, all of whom are punished for a variety of sins, from adultery to idol worship.[20] This catalog of sins is followed by the punishments for children in the place "where the fear is" (Apoc. Pet. 11). Here, in the midst of flowing fire, children receive punishments for sins such as disobeying and failing to honor their parents. Next in order come the enslaved, who are punished for disobedience to their enslavers (Apoc. Pet. 11). After the enslaved, only two categories of sinners remain: those persons who gave alms but did not strive for righteousness, and sorcerers and sorceresses. Their placement at the end of the list suggests that they were lower in the social hierarchy even than enslaved persons.[21]

In the Apocalypse of Peter, the earliest Christian tour of hell, the damned are classified according to their position in the ancient household, beginning with husbands and wives, and concluding with the enslaved. Later tours provide a window into distinctive arrangements of early Christian social order. This order includes many of the same categories of sinners as in the Apocalypse of Peter, but organizes them differently. The tour of hell in the Acts of Thomas begins with sexual and marital sins, but contains no mention of children or enslaved persons (Acts Thom. 55). The Apocalypse of Paul begins with the punishments for those who are "lukewarm" and cannot be deemed righteous or unrighteous, introducing the text's interest in separating authentic practitioners of Christianity from those who are merely claiming Christian identity in vain (Apoc. Paul 31). While the text does include punishments for husbands/wives and parents/children, they are not grouped with each other, but interspersed with other sins, such as sorcery and breaking of a fast before the appointed hour (Apoc. Paul 38–40). As we will see below, the distinctive arrangement of the sins in each apocalypse can reveal something about how each of those sins is viewed in a different historical context.

Adultery, Sexy Hair, and Makeup

The majority of our texts view adultery as a sin for which both men and women are culpable, though they may receive different punishments. The Epistle of Titus, perhaps a fifth-century text, focuses almost exclusively on the punishment for sexual sins, which includes genital tortures for adulterers and those who commit pederasty (Ep. Tit. ll. 408–10).[22] Although both men and women are punished, the text focuses on the adulterous women who are punished "by tortures in their breasts" because they "lasciviously have yielded their bodies to men." Their male partners are found hanging nearby by their "hands," a common euphemism for male genitals (Ep. Tit. ll. 415–17).[23] Adulterous women are punished first, in keeping with their primary responsibility for the adulterous encounter.

Similarly, the Apocalypse of Peter mentions adulterous women before the "men who lay with them." Women are hung by their hair because they "plaited their hair, not to create beauty, but to turn to fornication, and that they might ensnare the souls of men to destruction" (Apoc. Pet. 7). Then the men who committed adultery with them are hung by their thighs, saying to one another, "We did not know that we would come into everlasting torture" (Apoc. Pet. 7). While the complaints of the ignorant adulterers reflect the common cultural understanding that women (particularly those of high social standing) bear a greater responsibility for adultery than men of similar rank, punishment of these men alongside their female paramours might be seen as a critique of this attitude.[24] As we will see below, the claim that the men "did not know" may refer to the adornment of the women, which could have led to their being mistaken as prostitutes. If so, these encounters would not have been considered adulterous under Roman marital law, which only considered sexual intercourse adulterous if it occurred between a *matrona* and a man who was not her husband.[25] Yet even as these men who have been "ensnared" by women with pretty hair plead their innocence, the torment they endure pronounces judgment upon them as co-adulterers. In this way, the Apocalypse of Peter subverts Roman sexual ethics by describing men who go to prostitutes as adulterers and sinners.

The tour of hell in the Acts of Thomas focuses on the chastity of the prostitute who is taking the tour. It is not surprising, then, that punishment of sexual sins takes center stage. In the Greek version of the text, which is thought to be closest to the original Syriac, a variety of sexual practices, including homosexual sex, adultery, and, for women, failure to wear head coverings, are grouped together (Acts Thom. 55–56). The emphasis on sexual continence, and in particular female chastity in the Greek version of the text, fits well with the narrative that frames the tour, in which a young man kills a sex worker because she will not consent to marrying him. Since the tour is seen from the perspective of the prostitute just prior to her resurrection by Thomas, these punishments make the case that the young woman should stop her sex work in order to avoid eternal torment.

There is no similar attempt, however, to pronounce judgment upon her male client, turned suitor, turned murderer. When the young man confesses to Thomas, the apostle's first response is to lament that this poor young man has been driven by uncontrolled lust (Acts Thom. 52.1–2). Next, he washes the young man's hands (presumably to absolve him) and then proceeds to the brothel to resurrect the young woman. There is surprisingly little direct discussion of what the young man was doing in a brothel, or of the fact that he has committed murder (Acts Thom. 52–53). What is more, in the tour of hell that the young woman narrates, there are no murderers or even male adulterers.[26]

The hell of the Acts of Thomas reinscribes an ancient Roman sexual ethic in which a married man is considered an adulterer only when he has sex with a properly married woman, and reflects the view that uncontrolled lust can take control of the masculine body. Distinctively Christian is the murderous man's attempt to marry the prostitute, presumably as a means of both ending her prostitution and controlling his lust. Here too one may see a reflection of Paul's statements about marriage in the Corinthian correspondence (1 Cor 7). Hell's torments in this text reflect an early third-century Christian struggle to redefine sexuality and marriage: marriage is a way to prevent one from "burning with desire," but the sediment still remains of a Roman moral universe in which male sexual sin is defined more narrowly than female sexual sin. Sexual self-control is still firmly coded as the purview of women, and would remain this way until late antique Christians began to shift this responsibility for sexual sin to men.

In general, however, the gender-specific punishments in the earlier apocalypses reinforced a Roman system of morality in which the burden of adultery fell on the adulteress to a greater extent than on the adulterer. Roman women needed to protect their honor as virgin or matron through chastity, but men were free to engage in sex outside of their own marriage "in moderation" as long as it did not involve another man's wife. Adultery is problematic for a virgin or matron because it brings the shame of the enslaved or prostituted down upon her; it is problematic for a man because adultery constitutes the theft of another man's property.[27] This understanding of adultery is motivated largely by class and economic variables.

In many tours of hell the women who commit adultery are punished not simply for committing a sexual act, but for dressing in a way that entices men to have sex with them. The Apocalypse of Peter 7 describes women "plaiting their hair" to "ensnare" the souls of men, while both the Coptic manuscript of the Apocalypse of Paul 39 and the Latin Vision of Ezra 16–17 contain punishments for wives who wore "deceitful cosmetics" to church "for the sake of adultery."[28]

Plaiting one's hair, along with wearing gold jewelry and fine clothing, is expressly forbidden in the household code of 1 Peter 3:1–6, where the guiding principle is obedience to the husband's authority. In the ancient Roman context, the way that a woman dressed indicated rank and status, as well as morality. The married Roman woman, or *matrona*, was expected to wear a *stola*, a long, sliplike garment that went over her tunic, as an indicator of her married status. The household code of 1 Peter 3 parallels the exhortations of Roman moralists like Seneca, who expressed concerns that married women who adorned themselves with cosmetics or forsook the modesty of the *stola* would confuse moral definitions and attract adulterers.[29] In the late second century, the Christian writer Tertullian claims that married women were going out in public without the *stola* for the purpose of practicing prostitution. Like Seneca, Tertullian was anxious that women who were abandoning the *stola*, and even perhaps mimicking the ornate clothing and makeup of prostitutes, would "pervert" the system of dress in which clothing could easily identify the woman's place in the social order (Tertullian, *Pall.* 4.9; *Shows* 25; *App. Wom.* 2.12.3).[30]

In the Apocalypse of Peter, the punishment for women who "plait their hair" may well reflect these second-century concerns about domestic roles and proper dress. Punishment of this sin becomes a trope that extends well beyond the second century. The punishments for adornment for the sake of adultery in the Apocalypse of Paul and the Latin Vision of Ezra indicate that hell was one place in which early Christian concerns about female comportment and fidelity were enshrined for many centuries. In all three of the tours of hell that punish wives for adorning themselves, the intention is clear: they do not beautify themselves for the sake of beauty, nor for their husbands, but in order to attract extramarital partners. The married woman "who ornamented herself for public display was no better than a prostitute," because she eroded chastity by offering her body for the visual consumption of others.[31] The comparison with prostitution indicates the root problem of female adornment: it reverses the primary sexual roles for men and women in antiquity, according to which men are the active, penetrating sexual partners and women are the passive, receiving sexual partners. By beautifying themselves, women play the role of sexual aggressor, which, in this worldview, properly belongs to the man.[32]

For this reason, marriage required ancient Christian women to dress the part of the passive, female sexual partner. Failure to do so made them and the men around them more susceptible to sin. While the ancient Roman woman who was convicted of adultery might be forced to wear a toga instead of the *stola*, the ancient Christian woman who commits adultery is threatened with bodily torment, such as hanging by her hair.[33] As in the writings of the Roman moralist Seneca and the second-century Christian Tertullian, the tours of hell single out the cosmetic adornment as dishonesty at best, and as "whoring" at worst. The woman who dresses ornately is responsible not only for attracting male desire, but also for dragging men down to hell with her.

Blaming wanton women for adultery is also a trope in one of the fragmentary Jewish apocalypses, as well as the Christian tour of hell in the Acts of Thomas. In the Isaiah Fragments (contained in the Chron. Jer. 16.4),

Isaiah witnesses punishments in one court after another. In the fourth court he sees the "daughters of iniquity" hanging by their breasts, and learns that these women had uncovered their hair, rent their veil, and nursed their children in the open marketplace, all "in order to attract the gaze of men and to make them sin."[34] Likewise, in the Greek version of the Acts of Thomas 56.6, the prostitute sees that "the shameless ones hung by their hair are those who have exercised no modesty and have gone about in the world with their heads uncovered." Women's hair may have been understood in different ways in different early Christian communities. In some ancient contexts, women's hair was viewed as a sexual organ and had to be covered in order to preserve female modesty.[35] A story in Mishnah Sotah 1:1–3:4, an early third-century CE rabbinic legal text, offers a parallel to the Isaiah Fragment. Here the rabbinic authorities provide an interpretation of the biblical ritual for the woman who is accused of adultery (Num 5:11–31). In the Mishnaic account, as in the tours of hell, a woman who has committed adultery receives a measure-for-measure punishment. The Mishnah explains that since she adorned herself for adultery, her breasts are bared, and her hair is uncovered or unbound. Unlike the Isaiah Fragment in which the adulteress's bare breasts and hair are her gateway to sin, here the rabbinic authors depict her naked body as a public humiliation that constitutes a part of her punishment.[36]

Although the Isaiah Fragment is difficult to date, it seems likely that both it and the Acts of Thomas were composed long after Paul's writings about head coverings in 1 Corinthians 11:1–15, but still reflect the view that loose or uncovered hair is at best immodest (Acts Thom. 56), and at worst an invitation to extramarital sex (Isa. Frag.). The Isaiah Fragment extends the bounds even further than the Acts of Thomas, to include public nursing, a point not mentioned in any of the other apocalypses.[37] In the Greek text of the Acts of Thomas, the directives to veil pertain not only during worship, as in 1 Corinthians, but also to "going about in the world."[38] Instead of requiring women to avoid the adornments of cosmetics, or plaited hair, as 1 Tim 2:9 does, these texts argue that the female body is itself an invitation to adultery.

In late antique apocalypses like the Apocalypse of Paul, written nearly a century later than the Acts of Thomas, the focus is no longer exclusively on women. Sexual infidelity is mentioned three times; in each case, men are punished alone (Apoc. Paul 31), or are mentioned first, unlike the earlier tours of hell (Apoc. Paul 38, 39), in which women are mentioned first. And unlike the Apocalypse of Peter 7, in which women were hung up by the hair that they used to "ensnare" men, the Apocalypse of Paul does not hold women exclusively responsible for initiating adultery. Instead, the Apocalypse of Paul 39 refers to both men and women, and prescribes the same punishment: they are suspended by their eyebrows and hair in a river of fire. When Paul asks who they are, the angel identifies these men and women as "those who did not give themselves to their own husbands and wives but to adulterers."[39]

These two punishments, which may refer to men and women respectively, are typically associated with initiating adultery in Roman sources. The Roman moralists believed that sin began with the eyes, which introduce evil to the soul.[40] Similarly, ocular punishments in the tours of hell are typically given for allowing one's eyes to wander toward a sinful activity, as in the Epistle of Titus: "Those who hang by their eyes (or have their eyes burnt) are those who have stumbled through their glances and who have looked with craving on guilty acts" (ll. 411–13).[41] In the context of the Epistle of Titus this punishment could cover a number of sins, and does not specifically pertain to looking lustfully at a married woman. In the Apocalypse of Paul 39, however, hanging by one's eyebrows is a punishment reserved for adulterous men, and hanging by their hair is reserved for women who initiated adultery through their ornate dress (Apoc. Pet. 7; Lat. Vis. Ez. 16–17). In the late antique context, the Apocalypse of Paul reflects a major shift in the way that early Christian sexual morality was gendered. In this picture of hell, the men are held accountable not only for adultery, but also for self-control, a virtue that had previously been the domain of women.[42]

In the tours of hell from the early medieval period, the burden for sexual continence has shifted to render men more culpable. The first sinners that Ezra encounters in the Latin Vision of Ezra are those who "have spent the night with women on the Lord's day." For this sin they are beaten by dragons and dogs while they are burned with fire (Lat. Vis. Ez. 8–9). This punishment is unique to this tour of hell, and suggests that this text was composed after the rise of Constantine, who turned Sunday into the Sabbath day of worship and rest. During the second half of the fourth century CE, the church issued a series of orders to prescribe how Christians should observe this day.[43] Other texts include sins pertaining to the Sabbath day. In the Greek Apocalypse of Mary, for example, people are punished for sleeping like the dead on Sundays (Gk. Apoc. Mary 12). Sleeping with women, however, is the only Sabbath-observance sin in the Latin Vision of Ezra.

In the text of the Latin Vision of Ezra, these sinners appear just after Ezra sees the righteous men who engage in the worthy and responsible act of almsgiving.[44] We may speculate that this later Ezra apocalypse has added the punishment for men who have sex on the Sabbath to emphasize that men bear the responsibility not only for almsgiving but also for maintaining ecclesial order through proper observance of the Sabbath regulations. This apocalypse, which begins with ecclesial sins and sexual sins, blends the earlier model of household order with a later emphasis on ecclesial order, connecting the sexual sins of men, women, and children to church order.

In the Latin Vision of Ezra, women who have sex on Sunday do *not* receive punishment alongside the men, but men and women receive the same punishment for adultery. Ezra sees men and women hanging by their hands (again, likely a euphemism for genitals), head downward, as devils administer fire and beat them with clubs (Lat. Vis. Ez. 12–17). This punishment resembles the punishment that adulterous males received in the Apocalypse of Peter 7 (hung by their thighs, head in the mud), but here, by contrast, women receive the same punishment. Whereas the Apocalypse of Peter imagined adulterous adorned women hanging by their sexy hair, the Latin Vision of Ezra focuses on the adultery, not the adornment, as the offense. Although the punishment for adulterous men and women is the same, the sin itself is defined according to gender roles. Men are punished for fornicating with married women, regardless of whether they themselves are married (Lat. Vis. Ez. 15–16).

The Greek Apocalypse of Mary takes a different approach.[45] It imagines that mixed groups of men and women were punished for fornication, but singles out specific groups of women, such as the widows of presbyters who later remarried and the archdeaconess who defiled her body in fornication (Gk. Apoc. Mary 19 and 20).[46] These women are not punished simply because of remarriage or fornication, but because of the sins they committed while proximate to ecclesial authority. In this apocalypse, then, we see a marked shift from emphasizing household order to emphasizing church order.

Early apocalypses view adultery as a consequence of lust; later apocalypses suggest that adultery amounts to theft. In doing so, the latter link the late antique Roman definition of male adultery as "theft" with Christian ethical concern for the other. In the Apocalypse of Paul 31, Paul sees men up to their navels in fire; they are those who, though they attended church and partook in the Eucharist, then "fornicat[ed]" immediately after.[47] Later on his tour, Paul sees "men and women with very black faces in the pit of fire." These people are identified as fornicators and adulterers who "although they had their own wives committed adultery, and similarly the women who committed adultery in the same way, though they had their own husbands" (Apoc. Paul 38). Likewise, the Apocalyse of Paul describes adulterers as "those who did not give themselves to their own husbands and wives, but to adulterers" (39). These are the earliest references to offended wives and husbands found in the apocalyptic punishments for adultery, and suggest that the Apocalypse of Paul views adultery not only as an abrogation of the household order, or theft, but also as an offense against another person. This is a shift from earlier Roman notions of sexual morality, in which male adulterers were accountable to other men, not to their own wives.

And as we saw above, the Latin Vision of Ezra defines an adulterer as a man who has sex with another man's wife. It is irrelevant whether the adulterous man is married himself; the offense is against the other husband, not against his own wife (Lat. Vis. Ez. 12–17). A wife may receive the same punishment as an adulterous man, but her offense is against her own husband. What looks like gender parity when seen through a modern lens is actually in its ancient context consonant with a slow transition in sexual morality that eventually assigned agency to both men and women.[48]

By disrupting the household order, adulterous men and women posed a threat to the social order of the church. Ecclesial order was bolstered by ecclesial organization, and appealed to Christian concern for the "other" and self-control. Whereas Roman sexual morality occasionally acknowledged the problem in correlating behavior and social status, Christian visions of hell harbored no such concern.[49] The earliest Christian apocalypses enshrine Roman imperial concerns that a woman behave chastely to preserve her honor as virgin or matron; not only her honor, but her eternal fate depends on it. As later texts shift part of the burden for sexual sins to men, they also define self-control and ecclesial authority as male virtues. These distinctively Christian shifts worked to both modify and preserve patriarchal gender norms, not to obliterate them.

Homoeroticism

In a few of the apocalypses, the punishments for homoeroticism are grouped with those for adultery and idolatry.[50] In the Ethiopic text of the Apocalypse of Peter, the "men who defiled themselves with one another in the fashion of women" receive the same punishment as worshipers of idols and those who "cut their flesh as apostles of a man" (Apoc. Pet. 10). In the Acts of Thomas 55, the young prostitute sees the "souls who have exchanged intercourse of men and women."[51] In both the Greek and Syriac versions of this text, homoeroticism is likened to the sins of the prostitute, and is immediately followed by punishments for adultery. Like the earliest version of the Apocalypse of Peter, the Apocalypse of Paul focuses on male homoeroticism, punishing those who have "committed the iniquity of Sodom and Gomorrah, men with men" (Apoc. Paul 39). In this text, male homoeroticism is punished alongside other sexual sins, such as loss of one's virginity and adultery, as well as unrelated sins like harming widows and the poor.

Unlike the punishment for adultery, the punishments for same-gender sexual encounters do not involve hanging by the genitals. This difference suggests that the "sin" was understood to be fundamentally different from other sexual transgressions. In the Apocalypse of Peter, this group of the damned repeatedly throw themselves down from a high place, returning again and again as demons drive them to do so. In the Acts of Thomas male and female homoeroticism is punished in a fiery pit, where the "sinners'" souls are suspended on wheels of fire as they dash against one another.[52] In the Apocalypse of Paul, such souls run with bloodied faces in a river or pit of fire and brimstone. These punishments do not enact the *lex talionis* but reflect broader ideas about sex in the ancient world, according to which homoerotic love inverts male-female sexual norms.

These early Christian texts view homoeroticsm not only as interrupting the household order and the social order (as adultery did), but as interrupting the natural order as well. As Bernadette Brooten has argued, the earliest Christian condemnation of homoeroticism, in Paul's letter to the Romans 1:26–32, utilizes a limited form of natural law theory in order to argue that sex between two men or two women is "unnatural" (*para phusin*).[53] In doing so, Paul is following the cultural convention of his time, in which "natural" sex is defined as any sexual relationship between a man and woman, so that there is a dominant (male) partner and a passive (female) partner. In the case of male homoeroticism, nature was thought to be violated because a man must play a passive, and thus effeminate, role. Women who loved other women were seen as masculine and dominant; the real objection to female homoeroticism is that it allowed women to play the sexual role that "naturally" belonged to men. In both cases, the negative cultural valuation of homoeroticism rests on the patriarchal gender hierarchy that defines "nature" according to male dominance.

This same understanding is operative in the early Christian tours of hell. In the Ethiopic and the Greek manuscripts of the Apocalypse of Peter, the passive male partners of a male-male coupling are identified as sinful because they are behaving "like women," but the active male partner does not wind up in hell. In the Greek manuscript, however, the Apocalypse of Peter condemns both partners of a female-female union because they "behaved with one another as men with a woman." The Acts of Thomas uses the Pauline language of "exchange" to describe same-gender sex as "exchanging the union of intercourse that has been appointed by God."[54] These ideas were not uniquely Christian, but the belief that subverting the natural order in this way deserved eternal punishment is not attested in late antique non-Christian texts.

Homoeroticism was also seen as a disruption of the patriarchal household order. In both the Apocalypse of Peter and the Apocalypse of Paul, the description of the sin is ambiguous. The Ethiopic text of the Apocalypse of Peter 10 identifies the damned as "they who cut their flesh as apostles of a man, and the women who were with them . . . and thus are the men who defiled themselves with one another in the fashion of women."[55] It is unclear how the "women who were with them" have themselves sinned. The Greek Apocalypse of Peter 32, which is thought to reflect a later version of the apocalypse than the Ethiopic text, not only punishes the men who "behaved like women," but also the "women . . . who behaved with one another as men with a woman" (Gk. Apoc. Pet. 32).

The Apocalypse of Paul 39 is also unclear and confusing. Although it asserts that the punishment for homoeroticism is for "men and women covered in dust," it describes only male homoeroticism: "they are those who have committed the iniquity of Sodom and Gomorrah, men with men." The inclusion of women at the outset fits with this text's view that men and women are punished in hell for the same sin, such as adultery. But the text then mixes the formulaic description of "men and women," their punishments, and their sins, with an enigmatic description of the sin that emphasized male homoeroticism, like the one in the Ethiopic Apocalypse of Peter.[56] The emphasis on male homoeroticism in these texts is consistent with the ancient focus on male homoeroticism and also reflects the view that a departure from male dominance will cause the Roman household order to crumble. The men who "behaved like women" are singled out by the Christian apocalypses as the symbol of homoerotic love because they challenge the ideal of the active, dominant husband who served as the head of both Roman and Christian households.[57]

The Acts of Thomas groups male and female homoeroticism together for punishment. The Greek version of the text, however, associates homoeroticism with prostitution. As the angelic tour guide tells the prostitute, the souls of those guilty of homoeroticism are her kin (Acts Thom. 55). This comment reflects the ancient association of female homoeroticism with prostitution in antiquity, perhaps because both confused the active-passive sexual roles for men and women, respectively.[58] It is possible that the Acts of Thomas included female homoeroticism with male homoeroticism because the tour of hell is embedded in a story about a female prostitute. At the same time, this particular tour of hell depicts homoeroticism as shameful, extramarital sex that undermines the legal and social structures of marriage.

If we follow Bernadette Brooten's suggestion that the punishment in the later Syriac text is closer to the Syriac original than the older Greek text, the arrangement of the sins themselves reinforces this idea, as it groups homoeroticism with men and women who commit adultery, young men who have sex with prostitutes, and virgins who have broken their virginity.[59] But even apart from this text-critical hypothesis, the interpreting angel himself makes this connection, inviting the reader to equate male and female homoeroticism with the story of the female tourist, a prostitute who refused to "live chastely" with the Christian man who had fallen in love with her at the brothel. In doing so, the Acts of Thomas interprets male and female homoeroticism as an abrogation of the natural order of male-female sexual unions and as the rejection of the household order of marriage. The punishments for homoeroticism in the early Christian apocalypses demonstrate that early Christians not only echoed the judgments cast on homoeroticism by the broader culture, but also intensified those judgments—equating same-gender sexual relationships with the eternal imbalance of toppling off a cliff and the similar fiery torments that were reserved for those who interrupted the household order through adultery.

Pederasty and Incest

It was acceptable for men to engage in pederasty according to ancient Roman cultural standards, as long as the passive male was a child or enslaved: both were thought to be "naturally" subordinate.[60] Pederasty is not often mentioned in the tours of hell. The tour of hell found in the Elijah Fragment, and preserved in the Christian text Pseudo-Titus, declares that "adulterers and pederasts are tortured in their genitals" (Ep. Tit. 1. 410).[61] There are no references to pederasty, however, in the apocalypses that punish male homoeroticism. Perhaps they included pederasty among the sins of those who "behaved like women." It is also possible that Christians were simply following the Roman cultural norm, according to which pederasty was acceptable under certain conditions. Although we do not have a precise date for Pseudo-Titus, sometime in the fifth century CE is plausible, as this would overlap with the sexual persecution when Christian emperors begin to legislate against male homoeroticism. In one sixth-century law, passed early in Justinian's reign, pederasty is singled out, sentencing those who were caught in pederasty to "have their penises amputated," a torture in the genitals just as in the hell of Pseudo-Titus.[62]

Incest is also considered a sin. In the Greek Apocalypse of Ezra 4.21–24, a single man who committed incest is described as a *mētrokoitēs*, a Greek word meaning "motherfucker," and is hung by his eyelids while angels flog him.[63] The man who commits incest is punished in a chain of sins that deal with male abuses of power or influence, including Herod's slaughter of the innocents, eavesdropping, and moving markers. The Latin Vision of Ezra 19–23 prescribes the same punishment for sons who have sex with their mothers and for male and female children "who have done evil to their father and mother and always wished with an evil desire."[64] This arrangement of sins places sons and daughters who had sex with their parents immediately after the punishments for adultery, reflecting the order of the household codes in which references to children follow those to husbands and wives. This novel focus on incest in the late antique and medieval apocalypses likely emerged as a way to rhetorically distance Christians from the common insults that were hurled at them, which included accusations of incest, among other taboo practices.[65]

These references to incest in hell also amplify the late antique Christian concerns about sexual coercion. For early church authors, the potential for incest is used as an argument against having sex with strangers and prostitutes; one could unwittingly be having sex with a child that one had previously abandoned.[66] Like the legislation around prostitution, which was criticized for coercing would-be prostitutes into other arrangements (like conversion and life in the monastery), hell's punishments for incest reveal the dark side of the growing emphasis on sexual agency (Procopius, *Build.* 1.9; *Sec. Hist.* 17.5–6).

In contrast to other tours, the Greek Apocalypse of Ezra and the Latin Vision of Ezra imagine the punishment of children who have experienced pederasty or incest.[67] This detail does not take into account the power differential between children and the adults who have sex with them.[68] The punishment of children in hell is not simply an extension of an old taboo; it holds children accountable for an encounter they cannot control and thereby demonstrates the troubling limits of ancient Christian notions of sexual agency.

The Latin Vision of Ezra adds a punishment for women's incest with their mothers. Including women in the condemnation of pederasty is also unusual in the ancient world, in which the sexual use of boys was regularly practiced, sometimes tolerated and sometimes condemned. Shenoute of Atripe, the head of a large Egyptian monastic community, also broke the pattern of focusing on male pederasty. Shenoute censures both men and women who initiate sex with children.[69] Just as the Apocalypse of Paul began to punish both men and women for sins like adultery, we see similar movement in the Ezra apocalypses with respect to pederasty. In contrast, in the Greek Apocalypse of Mary, only men are punished for pederasty and incest, as Mary finds the men who "debauch mother and daughter" in the outermost ring of fire, a space in which Mary does not make her customary plea for mercy (Gk. Apoc. Mary 23). In this way, the Greek Apocalypse of Mary seems to share the unique concern with the sexual use of girls that we find in the Ezra apocalypses, but does not hold men and women equally accountable for incest and pederasty in the same way that either the Ezra apocalypses or Shenoute of Atripe did. In the Greek Apocalypse of Mary, then, men are still framed as the penetrative sexual aggressor, and thus as the sexual agent.

Parenthood

The early Christian apocalypses frame parental sins as parents' fundamental failures to fulfill their obligations to the household and the *polis*. At the outset, both men and women were seen as responsible for parenting, but over time the focus shifts to mothers exclusively.[70] In the Apocalypse of Peter 8 both mothers and fathers are punished for infanticide, but women alone are punished for having abortions to conceal adultery. The

Apocalypse of Paul 40 avoids this imbalance; in its vision of hell the adulterous women and men who procured abortions to conceal adultery are punished together.

When it comes to parenting failures, however, mothers are punished but fathers are not. In the Greek Apocalypse of Ezra 5.1–6, a woman is suspended as four wild beasts suck at her breasts because she refused to nurse her infants and cast them into the rivers. In the Latin Vision of Ezra 53–54 women are punished by snakes drinking from their breasts for refusing the breast to "infants and orphans." In the Apocalypse of Peter's punishment women are exclusively responsible for children that were the result of adulterous unions, as in Latin Vision of Ezra 52–53. The Isaiah Fragment also envisions punishment for mothers who breastfeed their children in the marketplace in order to attract adulterers (Chron. Jer. 16.4). The Greek Apocalypse of Mary 7 characterizes infant exposure as cannibalism, along with betraying one's brother before kings and governors. The Greek Apocalypse of Mary 23 includes a punishment for "women who strangle their offspring."

The placement of full parental responsibility on women is rooted in ancient attitudes. The father was the head of an ordered household that would contribute well-formed heirs to the broader *polis*. This does not mean that ancient fathers and mothers did not love their children and nurture them.[71] But the primary expression of nurture within the ancient Roman family was education and discipline intended to form the child into an ideal citizen. This nurture began with the mother's gestation and breastfeeding of the infant. Although infant mortality was high, infants were seen as citizens in training whose prenatal and postnatal nourishment and education formed their souls before they could even talk.[72] Mothers could be valorized or damned for the extent to which they engaged in these forms of nurturing.

Parenthood was also foundational to the socioeconomic success of the culture. Ancient Christian ideas about abortion and infanticide were formed in this context. Abortion was practiced in Roman culture, and was not addressed in Roman law until the late fourth century CE.[73] Despite this legal precedent, ancient Roman fears about underpopulation and the view that birthing children was necessary to produce heirs meant that terminating a pregnancy before birth was still viewed negatively.[74] Ovid, for instance, had multiple adulterous affairs that resulted in conception, but he criticized his mistresses harshly for having abortions (*Loves* 2.13). Producing heirs was the prescribed role of free women. An enslaved woman's body, however, was often expected to avoid pregnancy, and so enslaved women experienced economic pressure to remain chaste or have abortions.[75] As Rebecca Flemming has argued, abortion was only problematic "when it became a woman's means to obstruct a man's acquisition of legitimate heirs and pursue instead her own priorities, most dangerously (and characteristically in the eyes of moralists) adultery and vanity."[76]

Infanticide and exposure, like abortion, were both allowed under Roman law in the first and second centuries CE, but were also widely criticized during this same period.[77] Although it was by no means universally acclaimed as a social good, abandonment was treated more mildly than abortion and infanticide, likely because many exposed infants were adopted and therefore survived. As John Boswell notes, "even philosophical texts expressing opposition to infanticide and abortion often treat abandonment as normal and unobjectionable."[78] Ancient discussions about exposure and infanticide often focused on one's duty to the city or the household. For Plato and Aristotle, civic virtue required that one not have too many children; other thinkers held the opposite.[79] And while there were many circumstances in which a parent would be unable to rear their child, recent scholarship has cautioned against hypotheses that single out particular groups of infants as "less desirable" in the ancient imagination.[80] By late antiquity, Roman laws shifted so that abortion and infanticide were no longer concerns of household regulation, and the broader culture's interests in reproduction became enshrined in law. This shift is also reflected in Orphic depictions of the afterlife.[81] And by the medieval period, infant exposure was no longer practiced, as children who could not be cared for could instead be left at the doorsteps of monasteries and churches.[82]

Early Christian writings shared the negative opinion of abortion and infanticide of the Roman moralists, including the close association between female adultery and abortion. Both the Didache and the Epistle of Barnabas issue gender-neutral commands condemning abortion and infanticide (Did. 2.2; Barn. 19.5). But by the late second century, Athenagoras singles out women (Athenagoras, *Plea* 35), and in the early fourth century (305 CE) the Council of Elvira calls for the excommunication of women who had abortions to conceal adultery.[83] In the early Christian apocalypses the broader patterns of Roman and Christian thinking about the household are assigned eschatological and soteriological significance. Since Christian women can be "saved" through childbirth, it is not surprising that ancient

Christian logic also damns women for eschewing childbirth.[84] The greater surprise is that the earliest of these Christian texts view men and women as equally responsible for offspring. This view, however, faded as abortion and infanticide also moved into the legal realm.

The early Christian apocalypses differ in their approaches to the social role of parent, but each apocalypse treats this role in ways that are consonant with the gendered moral expectations of the broader culture of their own time and place. The overall trend to associate abortion, infanticide, and exposure with women's attempts to conceal adultery is also evident in the work of pagan authors (like Ovid), but it seems to have been intensified by late antique Christians.[85] The gender-specific punishments associate abortion, abandonment, or infanticide with adulterous women in the Apocalypse of Peter 8 and Latin Vision of Ezra 52–53.[86] In the fourth century, John Chrysostom preached against married men who committed adultery with prostitutes, arguing that they not only kept these women as harlots, they encouraged them to have abortions, making the women "murderers."[87] For Chrysostom, and for other late antique Christians, the male partner in a sexual union was responsible for the sexual act (adultery), but not for any pregnancies that might result from that act. Even if the man encouraged abortion, his female partner was responsible for the act itself.[88]

As in the broader culture, Christians saw infant exposure and infanticide as distinct practices, but also sometimes conflated the two.[89] In the apocalypses that include punishments for both abortion and infanticide, the latter is treated as a more serious offense. In the Greek Apocalypse of Mary 7, women who expose infants are punished alongside those who betray the martyrs; both sins are equated with cannibalism. This is perplexing as there is no obvious logical connection between infant exposure, martyrdom, and cannibalism. Candida Moss suggests that these three are linked because "both the bodies of the martyrs and (as is explicitly noted here) the bodies of exposed infants were sometimes consumed by animals."[90] Those animals, in turn, could be consumed by humans. By this reasoning, infant exposure and martyrdom facilitated cannibalism. Cannibalism was a common insult hurled at Christians, one that Christians were quick to return. In the Greek Apocalypse of Mary 7, the insult of cannibalism is used rhetorically along with betrayal of the martyrs to criminalize infant exposure, even though this practice did not always result in death and was not consistently viewed negatively in the broader culture.[91] The Greek Apocalypse of

Mary, then, appears to be flipping the rhetoric of a familiar insult that was applied to Christians, leveraging the fear of eating human flesh in order to intensify the social pressure around motherhood.

In the Greek Apocalypse of Mary 23, "women who strangle their off-spring" are punished alongside the man "who debauches mother and daughter," as well as Jews, sorcerers, those who reject baptism, and those who commit fornication. These sins are all linked in the mind of late ancient and medieval Christian audiences. Infanticide was viewed as a practice that was used by women to conceal adultery, while the fear of incest was used as a rhetorical mechanism to scare Christians out of exposing infants.[92] The anti-Semitism of medieval Christian texts also frequently conflated the Jewish body with forms of dangerous sexuality, such as prostitution.[93]

By the medieval period, however, infanticide and infant exposure were not practiced with the same frequency or in the same manner as they were in the early Christian texts that first linked adultery, infanticide, and incest. In the medieval Greek Apocalypse of Mary, gendered rhetoric about women infanticides is coupled with adultery, incest, sorcery, rejection of baptism, and invective against Jews. As these are the only sins for which Mary remains silent, they may be so serious that no one, not even Mary, can intercede on behalf of the damned.

A similar rhetorical move may be evident in the Latin Vision of Ezra 52–53, where women who commit exposure to conceal adultery or do not offer their breasts to infants and orphans are punished. These women, like those who offer false testimony, are punished in the remote parts of hell, just before Ezra descends "four thousand nine hundred steps" (Lat. Vis. Ez. 58). If exposure is no longer being practiced at this point in history, why single out these women as sinners? And if exposure was less common, why make the stakes higher than previous condemnations, rendering women responsible not only for abandoning their own babies, but also for refusing to nurse other infants and orphans? Here, the outdated practices of exposure (and, in a later manuscript tradition, infanticide) are being used along with the bodily technology of wet nursing as a rhetorical device to assert that women are exclusively responsible for all babies.[94]

The Greek Apocalypse of Ezra 5.1–6 castigates a woman who has "begrudged giving her milk." Similarly, the Latin Vision of Ezra 54 characterizes "not offering their breasts" as a sin of neglect. In the Greek Apocalypse, however, the woman's refusal is linked with placing children in the river. In contrast to the earliest Christian apocalypses, which punish both mothers and fathers for infanticide and abortion, the medieval view of hell focuses on the Christian mother and defines her social role quite expansively. According to the Ezra apocalypses, early Christian mothers were responsible for infants to the exclusion of the fathers. What is more, early Christian women not only were responsible for their own infants, but also were expected to act as wet nurses for orphans. Since wet nursing was provided by a household slave or contracted out, this punishment in effect placed Christian women in the role of household slave. An enslaved woman hearing these words might feel pressure to abandon her own children in order to nurse another woman's infant.[95] Like the women who nursed children in the marketplace to attract adulterers in the Isaiah Fragment (Chron. Jer. 16.4), the Latin Vision of Ezra shows that breastfeeding was not a neutral act for medieval Christians, but instead represented a technology of the body that was explicitly linked to particular social roles, and a concomitant gendered morality.

Children and Young Women

Of all the members of the Christian household, children and enslaved persons receive the least censure in the early Christian apocalypses. This may be because they receive the most discipline on earth. For subordinate members of the household, we might expect that the primary sins to be punished in hell are sins of disobedience. The Apocalypse of Peter 11 foresees that children who disobey their parents will be wounded in hell by flesh-eating birds. Their punishment will be witnessed by children and maidens brought forward by the angel, presumably to reinforce the educational message to the text's audience.[96] In the Apocalypse of Zephaniah 3.4, the three sons of the priest Joatham are judged for disobeying their father's, or perhaps the Lord's, commandments.[97] And the Latin Vision of Ezra briefly mentions children who raise a hand against their parents, along with enslaved persons who denied their enslavers and enslavers who did not pay just wages (Lat. Vis. Ez. 50). These examples show that the cultural norm and biblical imperative that children obey their parents persisted, from the second century through medieval Christianity.

The Greek Apocalypse of Mary envisages that children can be punished for the sins of their parents: men and women are immersed in fire up to their waist because they "inherited the curse of father and mother" (Gk. Apoc. Mary 5). Strangely, although it is rooted in a biblical concept (cf. Exodus 20:5), it does not appear in the tours of hell until the medieval period.[98] This may be due to the fact that intergenerational punishment, and the reception history of Exodus 20:5, were the subject of lively late antique Christian debates about whether the God of the Hebrew Bible and the Christian God were one. The absence of a punishment for ancestral sin in the Apocalypse of Peter (and the other apocalypses that draw upon it) represents proto-orthodox concerns.[99] But if medieval Christians were not particularly interested in the concept of ancestral sin, rabbinic authors were.[100]

The final group of children to be punished in the early Christian depictions of hell—young women who "do not keep their virginity until they were given in marriage" (Apoc. Pet. 11)—are not children from the perspective of the broader culture, but their sin is defined in part by their subordinate status in their household of origin. In the Apocalypse of Paul, which otherwise envisions equal punishment for male and female sexual transgressors, young virgins who "defiled their virginity unknown to their parents" (Apoc. Paul 39) are severely punished. The same is true in the Epistle of Titus and the Latin Vision of Ezra, though they omit the reference to parents (Ep. Tit. ll. 407–8; Lat. Vis. Ez. 43–44). In the Apocalypse of Peter and the Apocalypse of Paul, virginity is understood as an economic responsibility to one's father or parents; losing her virginity affected a young woman's marriageability and incurred cost to her parents. In the Apocalypse of Paul and the Latin Vision of Ezra, girls who "violated their virginity," not their parents, pay the economic price by wearing the fiery yoke of slavery for eternity.

In the medieval period, in which the Latin Vision of Ezra is written, virginity retained its material value, but also could signify a variety of other things for Christians.[101] Early Christians adopted the Roman commodification of the virgin body, but also imbued it with theological significance, so that the medieval virgin body became a coherent symbol of Christian wholeness.[102] In hell the loss of virginity signified a violation of Christian covenant. The loss of virginity outside the narrow confines of the masculine system of exchange was no longer simply about economic loss to one's parents. By the time the Latin Vision of Ezra was written, loss of virginity was considered a sin in its own right, as well as a symbol for unholy fragmentation, passion, disobedience, impurity, and ineligibility for eschatological union with God.[103] In this way the apocalyptic tours of hell enfleshed what Christian asceticism had implicitly stated: the compromised virgin body not only failed to achieve unity with the divine, it was eternally broken and isolated in hell. Christian hell not only intensified the gendered Roman moral systems that commodified female bodies, it also amplified the theological significance of the virgin body; the imagery of bodies that were actually broken in the eschaton raised the punitive stakes and reified the perceived threat to physical and spiritual wholeness posed by female "transgressions."

Enslaved Persons

The last members of the household to be addressed in the household codes are enslaved persons. In the early Christian apocalypses their punishment receives the least attention of any group, mentioned in only two texts. The Apocalypse of Peter describes the punishment of disobedient slaves immediately after the punishment of children and maidens (Apoc. Pet. 11). These disobedient slaves chew their tongues and are tormented with eternal fire. The punishment of chewing one's tongue characterizes disobedience as a verbal sin, and associates it with the other speech sins typically associated with enslaved persons, as well as women. This punishment reinforced not only the kyriarchal structure of slavery, but also the patriarchal disciplinary regime that buttressed it. In the medieval Latin Vision of Ezra 50, Ezra witnesses the slaves who "denied their Lord" being thrown into the same furnace of fire with enslavers who denied their servants just wages. In this way, this text restores some measure of equilibrium at least to this aspect of its justice system.

This medieval reference to the punishment of wicked enslavers is unique among the tours of hell. Although enslaved persons appear infrequently, there is ample evidence of their presence in Christian households. The torment of wicked enslavers in hell does not represent widespread pushback against slavery or the abuse of power. Christians in late antiquity and the early medieval period promoted manumission while also permitting slavery, and practiced temperance in disciplining their slaves while also extolling the virtues of flogging.[104] Enslavers engaged in manumission and moderate discipline not so much for humanitarian reasons as to be recognized for their practice of the ascetic ideals of self-control and independence from luxury.[105] These ideals helped to preserve the structure of the Roman household and its gendered hierarchy by refashioning "feminine" characteristics, such as self-renunciation, into masculine ones.[106] The Latin

Vision of Ezra holds enslaved persons and enslavers to the same gendered ideals of self-control, but frames the social accountability of each by reproducing the gendered hierarchy of the household: the enslaved have "lost control" when they commit speech sins or deny their enslavers, and enslavers have "lost control" when they withhold economic remuneration.

Order in the Expanded Household: Church Officeholders and Kings

The Apocalypse of Peter patterns its gendered moral universe on the ancient concept of household order. Other apocalyptic tours of hell expand this vision to reflect shifting concepts of the church as God's household. As ecclesial structures, ascetic communities, and lay leadership positions became more defined, concerns about the abuse of power began to extend beyond husbands, parents, and enslavers to other persons in positions of relative power. Like the household structures and Roman government, ecclesial structures and lay leadership positions were ordered patriarchally; participation in these roles offered opportunities to affirm one's masculinity.[107] As early as the late second or early third century CE, the tour of hell found in the Book of Mary's Repose focuses exclusively on a priest, a deacon, and a lector who did not dispatch their office properly. Including the Book of Mary's Repose in the conversation around the tours of hell requires that we revise previous scholarly hypotheses, including my own, about the distinctiveness of the Apocalypse of Paul.[108] Punishments for wayward church officeholders are included in the Book of Mary's Repose, one of the earliest tours of hell, and developed further in the Apocalypse of Paul and the other Marian tours of hell, but they do not appear in the Ezra apocalypses. In these late antique and medieval tours of hell, the scope is expanded to include both male and female officeholders. In medieval texts, like the Latin Vision of Ezra, concerns about the abuse of power also extend to kings, princes, judges, and governors who exploit the poor, orphaned, or widowed.

Church Officeholders

In a late fourth-century CE letter, Basil castigated priests who were charging money for ordination: they were "on the road to hell" because they were buying and selling the gift of God and covering it up in the name of piety.[109] Basil begs them, "Do not pollute your hands with such earnings, and so make yourselves unworthy to perform the holy mysteries." As we will see, Basil was not alone in his view that church officials who did not live up to their public acts of piety would face the torments of hell. And it was not only priests who were culpable in this regard. The church officials facing punishment in the Book of Mary's Repose include a priest, a deacon, and a lector. In addition to priests, deacons, and lectors, later tours of hell include wayward presbyters, bishops and patriarchs, an archbishop, monks, nuns, and those who wear holy garments (Mary's Rep. 95–98; Eth. Apoc. Mary 104a, 105a, 106b; Apoc. Paul 34–36, 40; Gk. Apoc. Mary 15, 17–18).

The sins of these church officeholders center on a lack of self-control and the failure to care for the poor and marginalized. The Book of Mary's Repose, for instance, refers to a trusted priest who ate the offerings meant for the poor and afflicted or gave them to the unworthy. This wicked priest has his face beaten repeatedly "because he was an infidel from the place of believing" (Mary's Rep. 98), thereby losing his identity for eternity. Hell's punishment of the undisciplined priest reinforces the Christian redefinition of Roman masculinity, which required that the heads of the ecclesial household exhibit self-control, and characterizes his gluttony as a betrayal of the poor and marginalized who trusted him.

As in this earliest Marian tour of hell, most church officeholders punished in hell are identified as men. For instance, the presbyter and bishop in the Apocalypse of Paul 34–35 are identified as "old men" punished for improper execution of their episcopal office. Their characterization as "old men" participates in the broader effeminizing discourse of aging.[110] Age, which in other contexts was a qualification for church office, is here associated with lack of masculine self-control. The presbyter who offered sacrifice at the altar but also ate and drank and fornicated has his intestines pierced or dragged out of his mouth. The bishop who traded on the recognition of his office but did not have compassion on widows and orphans has his face badly disfigured by stoning.[111] Like Basil's priests, these men are judged to be unfit for the holiness of their office, and are punished according to the part of their body that they "polluted" with their unrighteous actions. Whereas participation in rituals and ecclesial activities could have offered these men an opportunity to transcend the effeminizing effects of old age, their failure to execute these offices properly signifies their loss of self-control, and their weak, leaky, and disfigured bodies—in other words, their feminization.[112]

There are, however, a few hells in which female church officeholders are punished. In the Apocalypse of Paul 40, ascetic women "who wear holy garments" are punished alongside their male counterparts, both for failing to have compassion on widows, orphans, and strangers, and for leading an impure prayer life. These women, like male church officials, are punished because they failed to meet the demands of their social role in the church.

The other female officeholders who suffer in hell, however, are punished for sexual sins. The hells described in the Greek Apocalypse of Mary and the Ethiopic Apocalypse of Mary contain the remarried widows of presbyters, an archdeaconess who committed adultery, and a priest and his wife who both committed adultery (Gk. Apoc. Mary 19–20; Eth. Apoc. Mary 103b).[113] In each of these cases the failure to fulfill her social role as wife is what damns each woman, identified as an ecclesial leader based on her proximity to her husband. Like their male counterparts, these women represent a failure to perform the ascetic value of self-control. Yet despite the evidence we have for women who did perform catechetical and sacramental functions as officeholders in the early church, these female officeholders are not held accountable for those roles in hell.[114] In these medieval pictures of hell, female sexual continence takes precedence over the proper execution of church office.

While each of the tours of hell includes punishments for leaders whose behavior does not match their self-presentation, these punishments are not keyed to specific political roles, such as king or governor, until the medieval tours of hell. Although King Herod is mentioned in the heavenly scene in Apocalypse of Paul 26 (the infants he had slain are bathing in a river of milk), he is not punished in the hell scenes of the same apocalypse. He is, however, punished in the Ezra apocalypses (Gk. Apoc. Ez. 4.9–11; Lat. Vis. Ez. 38).

In the Apocalypse of Paul 34–36, the presbyter, bishop, deacon, and lector are engulfed in a river of fire. Similarly, in the Latin Vision of Ezra kings and princes are thrown into a furnace of fire, but here the poor people look on and shout, "Lord these are the ones who deprived us of our power!" (Lat. Vis. Ez. 48–49).[115] In depriving the poor of their power, these kings and princes have failed to serve the poor and have thereby abandoned a central ordering principle of the household of God. In the Latin Vision of Ezra and other medieval Ezra apocalypses, the household of God extends to princes and kings. These rulers must abide by a notion of holiness that is defined by self-control and restraint, and that holds them accountable for their treatment of the poor and weak.

Sexy Hair, Breasts, and Household Order in Hell: Circumscribing Sin and Circumscribing Gender

The earliest tours of hell present two overlapping and interlocking models of moral order: the order of the household and the holiness of the church officeholder. In both categories, subtle shifts in gender roles throughout antiquity are reflected in the sins that are mentioned. In the Apocalypse of Peter, sins are identified according to a descending structure of household hierarchy, in which the husband/father/enslaver has the most power. In the Book of Mary's Repose, sins are identified according to the holiness of the ecclesial roles of priest, deacon, and lector (in this apocalypse, roles that are all held by men). In both of these models, the notion of sin is bounded by the values of a gendered hierarchy that values specific virtues of masculine morality: temperance and bodily control.

Later apocalypses blend these two models, fusing the order of the household and the demands of holiness. As a result, the tours of hell increasingly defined sin or unholiness as the failure to embody particular gender norms. The punishments for these sins are by no means marginal within the early church, as is sometimes thought. Rather, the punishments of the early Christian apocalypses echo church teachings expounded by other early Christian authors from the same or similar eras and regions.

We have also observed some major shifts in the ways in which different sins are punished (or not punished) over time in the early Christian apocalypses. In the earliest apocalypses, hell's punishments were reserved for those who failed to live up to the expectations of their social role in the household or church. Women were accountable for sins that pertained to sex, particularly adultery or the premature loss of virginity, and to childbearing. Men were responsible for maintaining their sexual dominance, dispatching their ecclesial duties with self-control, and ensuring that they produced heirs.

In later apocalypses (Paul, Ezra, Mary), however, women are no longer disproportionately accountable for sexual and marital sins. At the same time, the men became responsible for office holding and women alone for parental sins (the Latin Vision of Ezra) including abortion, often employed by women as a means of concealing adultery.

The shifts in the tours of hell show that household ethics persist but the social roles of the different groups within that household are renegotiated over time. These changes rewire family and individual culpability in ways that place a greater emphasis on gender differences over time. Women were still supposed to exhibit self-control, but the spheres in which they did so were domesticated and also differentiated from the novel ways that men exhibited this virtue. In effect, the damned not only reflected shifting attitudes toward gender, they also helped to reinforce views of the church and the world in which self-control and leadership were synonymous with masculinity.

3 Becoming Female and Deformed through Suffering in Hell

In the previous chapters we have explored a wide range of ancient literature, spanning many centuries, to reveal the different ways that gender and bodily suffering were intertwined in the ancient world. A focus on punitive suffering reveals multiple early Christian narratives about bodily suffering beyond those of self-mastery and propitious suffering. Even amid conceptual diversity, the texts are linked by the use of gender differentiation to describe and assign value (positive or negative) to bodily suffering.

A similar pattern can be seen in the ancient Christian understanding of the suffering body that does more than assert a binary juxtaposition between male and female, and a negative valuation of the feminine. The apocalypses leverage existing cultural ideas about gender and the body to breathe life into the bodies of the damned for their audiences. Whereas previous readings of these punishments have focused on the principle of *lex talionis*—the relationship between the punishment and the crime—here we will examine how these punishments related to the experiences of real bodies on earth. As we shall see, some apocalyptic visions of hell tormented readers with the horror of bodies that were weak, leaky, and porous, like those of healthy ancient women. Others read the bodies of saints and the damned alike as the propitious suffering of a female body in pain. In this genre, different images of gender and bodily suffering could exist alongside one another.

In his letter to Eustochium on "The Virgin's Profession" (384 CE), Jerome combined several images of the female body to depict the precarious nature of chastity: "Note that it is good virgins who are spoken of, for there are bad ones as well. The Scripture says: 'Whosoever looketh on a woman to lust after her hath committed adultery with her already in his heart.'

Virginity therefore can be lost even by a thought. Those are the evil virgins, virgins in the flesh, but not in the spirit: foolish virgins, who, having no oil in their lamps, are shut out by the Bridegroom" (*Let.* 22.5–6).

Jerome goes on to compare these foolish "bodily virgins" who have not controlled their thoughts to a harlot who spreads her legs for any passing man. Jerome equates impure thoughts with the sexual sins of prostitution, and uses the trope of the sad, lonely whore to shame the mentally undisciplined virgin. He concludes that such a virgin would have been better off to have married rather than to fail at chastity, thereby risking eternal torment: "Better had it been for her to have submitted to marriage with a man and to have walked on the plain, rather than to strain for the heights and fall into the depths of hell" (*Let.* 22.5–6). For Jerome the appearance of chastity that masks sinful thoughts is enough to earn a sexually continent virgin a trip to hell.[1]

The bodily punishments of the Apocalypse of Paul, written at approximately the same time as Jerome's letter, unmask the hidden nature of the secretly sinful persons who worried Jerome. The earthly appearances of the pious are called into question; priest and would-be virgin are revealed to be sinner and whore. Hell threatened early Christian readers with a classification system reminiscent of an ancient zoo, placing different species of sinners into spaces set apart from the rest of the world. The visitor to this eschatological zoo could encounter each species in a way that was not possible on earth.[2]

In the early Christian tours of hell the punishments themselves use familiar images of suffering bodies in order to reveal sin. Bodies in hell are seen as they truly are while on earth. Rather, their bodily torment displays the moral and spiritual condition of their souls. These tortured bodies confirm and accentuate ancient ideas about gender and the body. In this chapter we will look at how the damned bodies performed their sins, using bodily torment as a means of classification. Within hell's feminized space, the bodies of saints and sinners alike took on characteristics that were freighted with cultural cues about their relative value in the ancient economy of the body.

Heterotopias and Strategies of Containment: Organizing the Living and the Dead through Imagery

Previous work on the early Christian apocalypses has attempted to anchor these texts to very specific moments in history by viewing the "sinners" in the text as living persons. I argue, however, that these early Christian depictions of hell are not meant to be direct representations of the "real world" but rather that they *both* reflect *and* construct lived reality.

To be sure, some depictions configure hell as a reflection of worldly spaces.[3] These hellscapes include named individuals, or specific groups of people who would be easily identified. While most Christian apocalypses did not name the hellbound sinners, Tertullian peopled his with his opponents—the Valentinians—and imagined their humiliation. Tertullian's heaven is a reflection of the real-world tension between him and those he identifies as "heterodox."[4]

Other netherworlds are not meant to reflect the activities of this world, but to construct human behavior. Here, hell works as a persuasive rhetorical device aimed at persuading audiences to shift their behaviors in order to avoid eternal torment after death. The Apocalypse of Paul 36 depicts an anonymous lector who did not keep the commandments immersed in a river of fire up to his knees while his tongue and lips are lacerated with a "great blazing razor." This lector is identified primarily by his deeds, which place him in the company of other sinners. This anonymity reduces the complexity of human behavior into a binary classification system: a person either committed this particular offense or they did not.

These images place the dead in categories that refer back to the organizing structures of the present world. In contrast to those scholars who have called into question the utility of Michel Foucault's work for thinking about bodily normativity and disability, I argue that the spatial dimension of his thinking is important for understanding what is happening in early Christian hell.[5] In a 1967 public lecture, Foucault described the concept of the "heterotopia" as an "other space," one that is set apart from the social norm but functions in relationship to the spaces we regularly inhabit.[6] Heterotopias, Foucault argues, "are a simultaneously mythic and real contestation of the space in which we live"; they interpret the spaces in which we live our day-to-day lives. Since Foucault was working primarily with modern history, he might have placed otherworlds into the category of "utopia," due to their imaginary nature. For the ancient audiences of the apocalyptic texts, however, these spaces were real indeed, and closely connected to present realities. For this reason, apocalyptic hells fit Foucault's definition of heterotopia as a space that is both mythic and real, and that calls lived spaces into question.[7]

The library, the cemetery, the garden, and the zoo are all spaces that function as a kind of heterotopia because they bring together incongruous spaces.[8] Foucault noted that heterotopias relate to other spaces along a spectrum. At one end of the spectrum are heterotopias that create a "space of illusion that exposes every real space . . . as still more illusory." The other end of the spectrum is occupied by heterotopias that create another "real space, as perfect, as meticulous, as well arranged as ours is messy, ill constructed and jumbled." Somewhere between illusion and "compensation," heterotopias operate on the continuum between a spatial critique of other spaces and a well-ordered alternative.

In this schema, the early Christian apocalypses occupy a central position between the two poles of the spectrum. On the one hand, they are truly "otherworlds" in which the wicked are labeled, contained, and tormented for all to see. These spaces offered a solution to the problem of theodicy by offering a "well ordered" alternative to the chaos of real spaces in which justice does not always prevail. In the Apocalypse of Peter the text opens with a warning to avoid false Christs because the final judgment is imminent, when each person will be judged "according to his work" (Apoc. Pet. 1). Rather predictably, the labels used in the Apocalypse of Peter assign readers to one of two groups: the righteous who resist false Christs and "do good," and the wicked who identify with a false Christ, do wicked deeds, and are consigned to fiery torment. The righteous are discussed only briefly; the wicked are divided into several subcategories of anonymous sinners and discussed at length. The subcategories of the damned invite the reader to take stock of their own world, neatly classifying bodies according to their ethical deeds.[9] Applying taxonomy to the body explicitly invokes ancient hierarchies of the body in which some bodies (male, wealthy, free, whole) are prized over others (female, poor, enslaved, broken).

In other ways, however, hell's punishments expose real spaces as an illusion. The binary that the Apocalypse of Peter establishes at the outset creates a link between the apocalypse and reality that awakens the reader to the need to adjudicate Christianity on earth by identifying "false Christs" and their followers. Other apocalypses go even further, severing the link between membership in Christ and righteousness, so that it becomes even more difficult to identify a Christian on earth.[10] The ecclesial sins that we find in the Book of Mary's Repose, the Apocalypse of Paul, and the Greek Apocalypse of Mary confound any attempt to take earthly categories seriously. The punishments for deacons who ate up the offerings and committed fornication (Mary's Rep. 95–96; Apoc. Paul 36; Gk. Apoc. Mary 15), bishops who were not compassionate to widows and orphans (Apoc. Paul

31–37), those sleeping in on Sunday (Gk. Apoc. Mary 12), and a host of other misbehaving and misleading Christians require readers to redefine the moniker *Christian* and perhaps even to call into question the stability of their own claim to that label. The bodily performance of Christianity on earth was called into question by the deviant bodies in hell.

In addition to calling into question the authenticity of specific claims to Christian identity, the apocalypses also expose real spaces as an illusion simply by juxtaposing many different worldly categories or social spaces in one space. Hell is a heterotopia akin to the ancient garden or the zoo. In a garden or zoo we are able to encounter and compare the familiar and the unfamiliar. Bringing these elements "near" exposes the artificiality of the space in which we encounter them. The spectacle of gardens and zoos, and their very nature as heterotopias, makes them sites to be viewed, toured, visited, and studied, but not inhabited.

By bringing together disparate elements in one space, the heterotopia itself becomes a spectacle that invites viewers to gaze upon its inhabitants and to learn something about all the other spaces they themselves inhabit. Here I depart from Foucault, who in my view distinguished too sharply between "real" and imaginary" spaces. He also does not consider the possibility that sparking imagination may also be an important primary function of some of these "other spaces," which are objects of the visitor's gaze.

In the apocalypses that describe hell, each group of anonymous sinners is "foreign" and unrecognizable to the tourist until the tour guide offers an explanation. Through these explanations, the tourist is invited to reflect upon and learn from the inhabitants. Like the ancient garden or the contemporary zoo, these depictions of the otherworld paradoxically make the origins of its inhabitants seem more remote. The descriptions of the tortured bodies create critical distance between the nonnormative, effeminate body of the damned that is objectified, and the viewer who temporarily maintains the façade of the subject position. Hell's objectified bodies offer a way for the tourist to avoid future travel to hell because they ameliorate all of the deficiencies in the tourist's understanding of the spaces that he or she now inhabits.[11]

The spectator of hell is not allowed to maintain their subject status for long. By bringing the damned near, hell's heterotopia also offers a strategy of containment, a way to keep "sinners" neatly cordoned off from the rest of the church.[12] As we saw in chapter 2, there is a very high level of differentiation in hell. This allows for specific behaviors and subsets of those behaviors to be isolated for punishment. In the Apocalypse of Peter unchaste women are punished in separate places. In Apocalypse of Peter 7, women who plaited their hair for the purpose of fornication are punished. The Apocalypse of Peter 11 describes the punishment for young women who did not maintain their virginity prior to marriage. In later apocalypses the level of differentiation only increases. Hell, like other punitive spaces, singles out the damned, describing their bodies in excruciating detail, while the power exerted over them is less visible and more functional.[13] Such spectacles exert power not only over the punished body, but over all those who observe the punishment as well. In the early Christian apocalypses the disciplinary gaze demands behavioral conformity by insisting that audiences too are under minute scrutiny, and potentially subject to the very same punishments they are observing. Thus, the subject who is viewing the spectacle is quickly collapsed into the object.

There is one crucially important difference between other heterotopias and hell. Unlike the flowers in the garden, or the animals in the zoo, the bodies of the damned in hell look like the weak, female, sick, or deformed bodies of the real people who might hear or read the text. For those audience members, the transition from subject to object is instantaneous. The spectacle of hell's heterotopia is dependent and exacted upon the bodies of the damned and the bodies of the audience. In this way, hell offers a mechanism not only for behavioral containment, but also for bringing hell to earth by imagining a space in which the "true" nature of a sinful person is revealed by the deformed, womanly body they inhabit for eternity. Hell's taxonomy of souls is manifested on bodies, using the nonnormative body as an organizational tool in a punitive system. As the virtual tourist gawks at the different bodies contained in hell, the deviant body becomes a caged animal that exoticized ancient Christian anxieties about sin and bodily weakness.

The Torments of Hell and the Performance of Bodily Deviance

Hell's containment strategies, then, are not simply symbolic; they are also tethered to the real attempts to physically contain or restrain bodily deviance in the ancient world. The tours of hell are replete with unforgettable images of painful hanging punishments, rivers of fire, devouring beasts, and all-consuming worms. And although there are important literary antecedents for some of these punishments, such as the punishments of the Titans in *Odyssey* 11, for many in the audience the primary reference for the torments of hell would have been the spectacle of earthly punishment. As we saw in chapter 1, the punitive spectacle offered its own mechanisms of classification and control.

By late antiquity the more atrocious penalties, such as crucifixion and *ad bestias* (death in the arena), were phased out in favor of the gallows, a faster, less painful, and therefore less entertaining mode of capital punishment.[14] In the absence of these punishments in the "real world," the hell of late antiquity becomes a space in which the Roman juridical fantasy of torture could live on. Even after these practices had ended, the spectacle of the prison supplanted them, an experience that was connected to the concept of bodily suffering in hell in a wide range of late antique contexts.[15] For early Christian thinkers the courtroom, torture, the prison, incarceration, exile, and hell all offered opportunities for education, spiritual reflection, and penance.[16]

In addition to reflecting Roman judicial concepts about punitive suffering, the punishments of early Christian hell also mirror the bodily suffering of other "real bodies."[17] One prominent example is the punishment of blindness. Christian depictions of hell intensified ancient ideas by fusing the conceptions of blindness as a metaphor and punishment. In doing so, they intensified and codified the view that physical disability was the consequence of sin.[18]

Blindness is a punishment in the Apocalypse of Peter 12, the Apocalypse of Paul 40, and the Apocalypse of Zephaniah 10. In other ancient texts, blindness is used as a metaphor for ignorance.[19] The link between blindness and ignorance was so widely accepted that it is woven into stories about bodily healing (John 9:12). A particularly salient example is recorded in an inscription from the Asklepieion at Epidaurus. In this inscription, a woman named Ambrosia who was blind in one eye ridicules the cures at the sanctuary, and is healed only after she repents by offering a silver pig at the sanctuary as a memorial of her ignorance. Like Ambrosia, the blind bodies in the early Christian apocalypses are not merely a metaphor for misunderstanding.[20] Blindness is a real punishment that is exacted on real bodies. In these apocalyptic visions of hell, the theoretical link between the metaphor and the body is substantiated—real bodies are physically changed in order to reflect individual spiritual cognition and ethical success.

In these visions of hell torments are inscribed upon real bodies, linking tortured souls to the disabled body on earth. In the Apocalypse of Zephaniah 10, Zephaniah sees the souls in torment in the netherworld, starting with those who accepted bribes (hands and feet are bound), those who loaned money and accepted interest (covered with mats of fire), and the imperfect catechumens: "And also I saw some blind ones crying out. And I was amazed when I saw all these works of God. I said 'Who are these?' He said to me 'These are the catechumens who heard the word of God, but they were not perfected in the work which they heard.' And I said to him, 'Then do they not have repentance here?' He said 'Yes.' I said 'How long?' He said to me, 'Until the day when the Lord will judge.'"[21]

Unlike other ancient texts that associate blindness with misunderstanding or ignorance metaphorically or metonymically, Zephaniah's vision of hell invokes actual visual impairment as the consequence of intellectual sin. Here blindness is depicted as a physical punishment like the bondage or bodily encasement in mats of fire that precedes it. The description of this punishment is directly followed by a discussion of the hair on the bodies of the damned. These descriptions emphasize that the sinners in torment have real bodies that are analogous to earthly bodies. In this way, the punitive blindness in the Apocalypse of Zephaniah heightens the rhetorical effect of the ancient blindness trope by offering a literal interpretation: not only are the ignorant "like the blind," but here in the otherworld they actually are blind.

Blindness is also invoked in the Apocalypse of Peter 12 as a consequence of ethical failure, in this case, a failure to live out the virtues of the Sermon on the Mount while falsely announcing one's righteousness in public: "[Here] are blind and dumb men and women whose raiment is white. They are packed closely together and fall on coals of unquenchable fire. These are they who give alms and say, 'we are righteous before God,' while they have not striven for righteousness."[22] This passage calls to mind the ancient literary tropes that link physical perception to ethical action. Punitive blindness makes the link between bodily impairment and ethical failure much stronger.[23]

The Apocalypse of Paul 40 explicitly draws upon these earlier depictions of punitive blindness. Paul states: "And I looked and saw men and women clothed in bright clothing, whose eyes were blind, and they were set in a pit of fire; and I asked: 'Who are these sir?' And he said to me: 'They are the heathen who gave alms and did not know the Lord God: therefore they pay unceasingly their own particular penalty.'"[24] Paul describes their sin of idolatry using the language of intellect: they "do not know the Lord God." In this tour of hell, heathen almsgivers are compared with the sinners who bear some outward marker of Christian faith but have failed to live out that faith consistently, such as the deacon who ate up the offerings in the Apocalypse of Paul 36. Like the Apocalypse of Zephaniah and the Apocalypse of Peter, the Apocalypse of Paul imagines that these bodily torments are exacted on real bodies. The Apocalypse of Paul 15 imagines that the wicked will also experience bodily resurrection, so that they can receive their punishments in their own flesh. In this context, the only distinction between blind persons in hell and the blind persons on earth is that in hell the blind are only culpable for one set of sins.

Furthermore, the dark spaces of hell are depicted as an ocular punishment. In Matthew eternal torment happens in the "outer darkness where there is weeping and gnashing of teeth," a set of images that the early Christian apocalypses expand and amplify.[25] In his work on the resurrection, Tertullian states that the darkness of hell is a "torture particularly attaching to the eyes."[26] In the Book of Mary's Repose 97, a person who "has a great punishment more terrible than the others" is bound and kept in darkness while he is struck in the face with stones. Jesus reveals to Mary that this man was a priest who ate the offerings instead of giving them to the poor. This priest is kept in the dark and beaten in the face as an eternal monument to his infidelity to the poor and a visual demonstration of his untrustworthiness. After being beaten in the face repeatedly until he is beyond recognition, the priest is emasculated. In short, he is subjected to the punishment of a slave so severe that he is rendered unidentifiable for eternity.

In both of these texts, the darkness of hell is associated with ocular punishment; simply being in a dark space leads to perceptual deficiency. This understanding of eternal torment is based upon ancient ideas about the body that linked vision to an inner light that was produced by the brain or the soul. For Plato, and later Galen, this inner light source defines vision as the product of understanding, and blindness and darkness as the result of intellectual or cognitive failure (Plato, *Tim.* 45).[27] According to this logic, the outer darkness of hell makes the tormented bodies there blind, thereby concretizing and intensifying the ancient links between light, cognition, and the soul. Physical blindness is the eternal artifact of spiritual blindness.

In Greek and Latin literature, punitive blindness occurred on earth but does not play a role in Hades.[28] Instead, the metaphor of sight and blindness is used repeatedly to describe the education that the soul receives in

Hades. In Lucian's *Menippus*, the title character asks Teiresias what kind of life he considers the best: "Tell me and don't allow me to go about in life blinder than you are" (Lucian, *Men.* 21).[29] In Greek and Roman depictions of Hades, moral or spiritual blindness was a fate far worse than physical blindness. For early Christians, however, punitive and metaphorical blindness were collapsed into one another both on earth and in the afterlife. As David Brakke has argued, "monastic authors shared a general ancient understanding of erotic desire as a 'pathology of the eyes.'"[30] And in the apocalyptic depictions of hell, early Christians do not simply replicate the logic of metaphors in which blindness stood for ignorance or lack of education. Instead, physical blindness is demoted from the place it holds in pagan depictions of Hades; it is no longer preferred to spiritual blindness, but is its artifact. As the conceptions of blindness as metaphor and punishment are fused in the context of the early Christian apocalypse, the idea that physical blindness is the consequence of sin is intensified and codified.

Blindness is not the only disability that is leveraged as a punishment in the apocalypses. Early Christian hells, like the "real world," housed sinners with lacerated or amputated limbs.[31] The Apocalypse of Paul 39 depicts those who harmed widows and the poor "with lacerated hands and feet [*or* with hands and feet cut off] and naked in a place of ice and snow, and worms consumed them."[32] In keeping with the connection between the disabled body on earth and the disabled body in hell, John Chrysostom reasoned that just as gout sufferers were isolated by their extreme pain, so those tortured in hell would not be able to find solace in the company of other sinners there.[33] By threatening bodily difference as a punishment, the bodies that we find in hell intensify and reinforce the ancient idea that having a nonnormative body was a punishment for sin.

Still other hellbound bodies challenge ancient concepts of bodily normativity in ways that might seem strange to the contemporary reader as mechanisms of torture.[34] Several texts describe unceasing consumption by worms (Acts Thom. 56; Apoc. Pet. 9; Apoc. Paul 39, 42) and chattering teeth (Apoc. Paul 42; AP 210). The Apocalypse of Zephaniah refers to ugly angels who carry off the souls of the ungodly that frighten Zephaniah with their "eyes that were mixed with blood" and "hair that was loose like the hair of women" (Apoc. Zeph. 4.4–5). Such afflicted bodies might seem undesirable to the contemporary reader, but ancient texts consider them to be better off than those who suffer hanging punishments, or immersion in a river of fire.[35] All of these punitive spectacles functioned as the means by which hell's heterotopia could contain sin and unveil its insidious hiddenness in the very midst of the readers. Such spaces accomplished these feats by objectifying bodies and consigning them to an eternity of bodily deviance in a feminized space.

Weeping

The power of this unholy space is so all-consuming that everyone who enters it, even the saints who are touring hell, succumbs to its feminizing forces. One image that contributes to the characterization of hell as a gendered space is weeping. Many of hell's inhabitants, righteous and unrighteous alike, weep.[36] According to Apocalypse of Peter 3, the sight of weeping sinners in hell moves both the Savior and Peter to tears. Throughout this passage the narrator and the Savior interpret these tears as a sign of sadness. In the Apocalypse of Paul 33 and 40, Paul weeps vehemently, and the angelic tour guide censures him, asking Paul, "Are you more compassionate than the Lord God?" and interpreting Paul's tears as a merciful response to the sight of the damned (a similar question is put to Peter by the Savior in Apoc. Pet. 3). Likewise, in the Greek Apocalypse of Ezra 5.11, Ezra recalls the beatitudes, but recasts the function of tears in hell, saying, "Blessed are they who weep for their sins."

The tears of the righteous in these tours of hell are an empathetic response to seeing "the sinners who wept in great distress and sorrow" (Apoc. Pet. 3). These damned souls entreat God, the saints, or the angels directly, begging for mercy. In the Apocalypse of Paul 43, the damned entreat the archangel Michael: on earth "tribulations and a worldly minded life did not allow us to repent." In the Latin Vision of Ezra 27, the damned can only be sensed through their cries because their bodies cannot be seen through the fire and torments. In the context of the ancient court, weeping was a sign not of sadness but of guilt and was often accompanied by gestures of subservience and bodily weakness, such as blushing and sweating.[37] Playing upon the culturally prevalent fears of judicial torture, these tears may have had a rhetorical function: to incite fear of divine judgment and encourage repentance.[38]

These weeping bodies also represent compromised male bodies engaged in a feminine response to overwhelming emotion.[39] When Odysseus weeps at the bard's songs of his exploits, he is compared to a wailing widow as she is carried off into captivity during the siege of a city (*Od.* 8.515–35).[40]

Here an uncharacteristically effeminate Odysseus melts into tears, groans, and from shame tries to conceal his tears. And in martyrdom narratives the weeping of a family member could serve as an effeminate foil for the martyr's own performance of the strong, unmoving, masculine ideal. Stephanie Cobb argues that Perpetua, for example, is masculinized through the effusive displays of her father. By way of contrast to her father's leaky, effeminate body, Perpetua's own emotional distance and silence is a model of masculine self-control.[41]

Ancient medical literature describes tears as an involuntary response to advanced stages of illnesses, particularly fever. In the Hippocratic Corpus, crying, "childish weeping," and "crying out" in emotional fits are described as signs of advanced fevers (*Epid.* 4.46; 7.11). *Epidemics* 4 differentiates between intentional crying (which is "not bad") and an "involuntary flow," which is a sign of "crisis" or advanced stages of disease (4.46). Here, the "involuntary flow" of tears is a sign of loss of bodily control, comparable to "collapse of the eye" or "dry hardness of the body." For Galen, swooning and crying are signs that a person is weighed down by very thick and moist humors; these displays are more common in older and weak people. Whereas nonmedical texts viewed weeping as a sign of feminization, in the medical literature weeping, especially when involuntary, is a sign of a weakened body. In nonmedical texts, however, bodily weakness manifested through tears is sometimes, but not exclusively, associated with female bodies.

The view that weeping is pathological is taken up by the patristic authors. For Chrysostom, who used medical language to talk about grief, tears could be a symptom of an underlying disease, and excessive despair could have a demonic etiology.[42] And even in the case of mourning, Chrysostom encourages moderation, so that mourners might avoid the imbalance of the humors brought about by excess. But for Chrysostom tears could also function as a therapy for sin.[43] In his treatise to Stagirius, Chrysostom explains how the tears of repentance work: "Despondency [causing tears] works in exactly this way. One could say that it is a harsh and corrosive medicine that purges us of evil and does great good to the one taking it, when it is given to an indolent and luxurious soul, burdened with a great weight of sins."[44] Tears of repentance were active (not passive as in the case of sorrow), caustic, and could purge the body of excess.

Grief over sin was part of a broader monastic trope in which tears were welcomed and celebrated.[45] Grief, or *penthos*, in the Syrian monastic tradition was characterized by continual tears and lament not only for one's own sins but "for the fallen state of all humanity."[46] These tears were often eschatological in nature, focused on the imminence of death. These tears did not simply serve to mark the monk's piety, but were an active part of the monk's service, and in some cases the mechanism for accomplishing miracles. The male ascetics in Theodoret's *Religious History* produce fluids like tears, which are "normally an index of femaleness," as a means of working miracles in the world.[47] The ability of effeminate fluids like tears to accomplish the miraculous was encapsulated in the story of the "sinful woman" who used her tears to wash the feet of Jesus. This story was extremely popular in late antiquity as an example of the transformative and cleansing power of tears.[48]

In the tours of hell, then, early Christian hell is depicted as a space in which everybody, from Peter to the damned, weeps. Hell is thus a space in which normative masculine bodies are depicted in stereotypically, but also potentially pious, feminine ways. The weeping of the damned not only indicates a weakened and effeminate body but also mirrors the performance of tears that indicates humiliation and guilt in juridical contexts. The apostles' tears, in contrast, represent not humiliation and guilt, but transformative sadness in the face of human sin and punishment. Like male ascetics from the same period, the bodies of the saints in hell display effeminate traits that are understood to have a propitious quality that can transform those who are burdened by sin.[49]

For both the damned and righteous bodies who enter hell, tears offer a way to demarcate the feminizing and weakening effects of sin, and contain them. These weeping, effeminate, weak bodies externalize sin and thereby contest a world in which sin may go unnoticed. The pull of hell's heterotopia forces this bodily sign on all who enter, but for the readers of the text who hope to identify with the righteous and avoid eternal damnation, the feminizing power of the space offers a mythic and real contestation of the space in which they live. Urging the righteous reader toward voluntary, cathartic tears, hell also polices sin in the present by simultaneously mimicking and distancing the person from the body that is involuntarily effeminate and weak. In apocalyptic tours of hell the viewer who weeps voluntarily models the moderation that the medical authors and Chyrsostom urged, while the damned—eternally on display like animals in a zoo—weep for eternity, out of control and demonized like the pathological body. The spatial reasoning of hell's heterotopia objectifies the grieving and sick bodies in all of the other spaces where one lives, in order to pathologize and contain sin.

Fire

Another way in which the normative masculine body is compromised in hell is through bodily torment. As we saw in chapter 1, the types of bodily punishments one finds in hell reflect the judicial punishments of the Roman world. Being burned alive was one of many punishments that was feared by those who had judicial nightmares (among others).[50] In the Apocalypse of Peter 9, those who bore false testimony against the martyrs have their lips cut off as "fire enters into their mouths and their entrails," and the rich are cast upon a stone pillar of fire to suffer unceasing torment.[51] In the Akhmim Fragment of the Apocalypse of Peter 28, the eyes of blasphemers are pierced with fiery rods. In the Apocalypse of Paul 31–37 a variety of sinners are immersed in the river of fire. The deacon who ate up the offerings and committed fornication is seen wading up to his knees in fire: "And his hands were stretched out and bloody, and worms came out of his mouth and from his nostrils and he was groaning and weeping and crying" (Apoc. Paul 36). In the Latin Vision of Ezra 24–32 the greedy and those who were inhospitable to strangers have fiery, fork-shaped yokes pressed onto them. In each of these passages fire and worms penetrate the suffering bodies of the damned. In some cases another form of bodily deformity accompanies this, and in other cases the bodies of the sinners are literally enveloped or consumed by fire or worms.

Fire is associated with hell in numerous contexts, so its presence in the apocalyptic visions of hell is not surprising. The New Testament draws upon the association of fire with judgment, retribution, and punishment in the Hebrew Bible and Jewish apocalypses.[52] Isaiah 66:24, a highly influential text for Jewish and Christian conceptions of hell, connects unquenchable fire and worms to Gehenna.[53] In 1 Enoch 17:5 a river of fire flows from the east to the west end of the earth, but it is not associated with punishment. And in the New Testament "the concept of a fiery hell has been firmly established" (Mark 9:42–48; Matt 5:22; 18:9; Jas 3:6).[54] Fire also appears in some of the Greek depictions of Hades, but is not nearly as prominent there as muck and mire.[55]

The imagery of hellfire also draws upon other spaces in which fire and bodies intersected in ancient culture. In a punitive context fire recalls the juridical torture used to elicit "truth" from the accused. In this schema of torture the truth is hidden in a body that is deemed inferior, and treated violently as a means to an end.[56] For Christians the imagery of *basanos* is leveraged in a variety of contexts, using real or metaphorical force to derive the truth that is hidden in servile bodies as well as in texts.[57] In particular, fire was a common feature of torture in antiquity and late antiquity, and is closely associated with Christian martyrdom.[58]

In the context of ancient medicine fire was seen as the most powerful, and the most dangerous, means of healing. Some patients were advised to sit near a fire to induce vomiting, or to treat a condition caused by excessive cooling.[59] Because the female body was considered to be excessively cold, this advice may have been directed primarily at women.[60] Galen describes the use of fire to redirect blood flow (creating an "eschar," or scab) in a damaged vein. Galen compares this therapeutic use of fire to the prescription of menstruation for a woman who is vomiting blood.[61] Ancient physicians applied fire directly to the body only as a medical last resort. The Hippocratic Corpus sums up the treatment process in this way: "Those diseases that medicines do not cure are cured by the knife. Those that the knife does not cure are cured by fire. Those that fire does not cure must be considered incurable."[62] Fire, then, like tears, could harm the body, but it also had a purgative potential. In the context of hell, however, fire does not purify but in effect signifies incurability. The bodies of the damned are so cold, or effeminate, that even the constant application of fire cannot restore their natural balance.

Further, some fire images in the early Christian apocalypses have a sado-erotic valence.[63] In the tours of hell bodies are routinely penetrated by fire. In the Apocalypse of Peter 9, those who betrayed the righteous have fire penetrate their eyes; in the Greek text of Apoc. Pet. 28 their eyes are pierced with a fiery rod. Next, those who slew the martyrs through false testimony have fire penetrate their mouth and their entrails. Finally, chapter 9 of the Apocalypse of Peter culminates with a phallic pillar of fire that is "sharper than swords." The men and women who "trusted in their riches" and did not care for widows and orphans are thrown upon this stone pillar of fire, suffering the "unceasing torture" of having their bodies pierced by this fiery phallus. In the Apocalypse of Paul 34 a presbyter who drank and fornicated while he offered sacrifices on the altar has his intestines pierced in a river of fire, and in the Apocalypse of Paul 40 the ascetics who wore holy raiment but did not care for others are struck by angels with fiery horns.

These sado-erotic images are a dramatic departure from the "traditional imagery" often cited as an antecedent to early Christian hell fire. The fiery rivers of 1 Enoch 17:5 and the river Pyriphlegethon of *Odyssey* 10.513 are geographic features; in the early Christian apocalypses rivers of fire are mechanisms of punishment. By applying fire directly to the bodies of the damned, the apocalypses combine gendered and sexually charged images of punitive and purgative torment. This complex of gendered fire imagery creates a space in which sado-erotic violence can test and reveal the true nature of hell's inhabitants. In this punitive spectacle, the violence of fiery torments permanently objectifies the damned body that is on display in hell's heterotopia for all to see. For the audience, the weak, out-of-balance damned body is brought near not only by hell's heterotopia, but by the persistent presence of similar "incurable" bodies in all the other spaces they inhabit, perhaps even their own.

Worms

While having fire penetrate the body might strike a chord in contemporary readers and ancient juridical nightmares alike, worms are not a readily transferable cultural fear. Yet they are as prevalent in the tours of hell as fire. According to the Apocalypse of Peter 7: "the murderers and those who have made common cause with them are cast into the fire, in a place full of venomous beasts, and they are tormented without rest, as they feel their pains, and their worms are as numerous as a dark cloud." In the Bible, as in the ancient world, worms are tools of punishment—beginning with Isaiah 66:24 and its "worm that never dies." Martha Himmelfarb notes that worms are "easily associated with the grave," and could have made their way into the apocalyptic tours of hell apart from the influence of Isaiah.[64] I argue, however, that whereas Greek and Latin depictions of Hades associate the imagery of muck and mire so closely with Hades that worms were a logical corollary, muck and mire are not prominent in early Christian depictions of hell.[65] Instead, worms appear as part of the punishment many times in the early Christian apocalypses. While some of them are immortal or "never rest" like the worms of Isaiah 66, many others are just identified as worms, and they devour the damned or are found spewing forth from the body cavities of the damned.[66] For instance, in the Apocalypse of Peter 9, the worm that never sleeps devours the entrails of those who betray the righteous. The Apocalypse of Paul 36 and 37 feature, respectively, a deacon who ate up the offerings and who has worms coming forth from his mouth and his nose, and those who had charged interest being devoured by worms in a river. And in the Latin Vision of Ezra 34–36, the worms devour unrighteous souls, spewing forth fire.

The prevalence of references to suffering from roundworms and tapeworms in the medical literature indicates that this was a fairly common concern for ancient persons, especially women and children. Although the Roman empire had a culture of public bathing, this practice did not reduce the prevalence of intestinal parasites.[67] In the Hippocratic Corpus the practitioner is regularly cautioned to treat for worms early in treatment or to look for the evacuation of worms early in treatment as a sign of promise (*Prog.* 11; *Crises* 2; *Coan Pre.* 338, 458–59, 589). If worms are still present after the time of crisis, the consequence is death (*Fist.* 445–50). It is no wonder that tapeworms are a dreaded punishment in the Apocalypse of Peter 9.

Worms coming forth from the mouth was thought to be a problem that plagued women specifically.[68] In *Epidemics*, the Hippocratic author describes the case of Thersander's wife, who was nursing, and in a late stage of fever; just before death her tongue became hard and there were worms in her mouth (4.10).[69] Women who were fasting were thought to be most vulnerable to vomiting up roundworms,[70] and women's bodies were thought to create roundworms and tapeworms in utero. The treatise *On Diseases* in the Hippocratic Corpus explains this process: "[M]any (sc. untoward) things happen to the fetus in the uterus . . . when caustic pus is generated out of milk and blood growing putrid together and increasing in amount—inasmuch as they are sweet—a living being is formed out of it. Roundworms, too, form there in the same way" (*Dis.* 4.23).[71] As a place where many "untoward things" happen, the uterus provides the perfect conditions for the creation of worms. Evidence for this claim was found in the large number of children who pass intestinal worms immediately after birth. It was a common practice to dose newborns with medications to facilitate this process. An inscription at the ancient Asklepieion associates worms with the uterus: it describes a "false pregnancy" in which the suppliant is alleviated of her condition after she is cut open and two basins of "creatures" are removed.[72] The presence of worms in the uterus and their deadly potential was also noted as a possible form of contraception; Pliny the Elder describes the practice of extracting worms from the head of a wolf spider and placing them inside the uterus for a year.[73]

In the early Christian apocalypses, then, the worms that penetrate bodies and spew forth from the mouth would have reminded readers of a familiar but deadly threat. The threat of bodily penetration by worms was thought to disproportionately affect female bodies, and these deadly worms also originate in the female body precisely because female bodies provide the ideal conditions for their formation. The close association between worms and "womanly diseases" in early Christian sources is illustrated in a story reported by Athanasius. Athanasius tells of a young woman from Busiris Tripolitana who "had a terrible and very hideous disorder" (*Life Ant.* 58).[74] This young woman had fluids coming out of her eyes, ears, and nose that immediately turned to worms when they left her body; in addition, she was paralyzed, and also squinted. He continues: "Her parents having heard of monks going to Antony, and believing in the Lord who healed the woman with the issue of blood, asked to be allowed, together with their daughter, to journey with them."[75] Presumably curing her worms would also have relieved her menstrual symptoms, and perhaps also her paralysis, which was also thought to be the result of improper blood flow to which women were susceptible due to their cool, leaky bodies.[76] The story concludes with the monks leaving Antony and finding the woman and her parents rejoicing because she was "made whole" through her prayers.

The deacon of the Apocalypse of Paul 36 who ate up the offerings and committed fornication also waded weeping and crying through fire with worms spewing from his mouth and his nose. Through this ordeal his body became feminized, penetrable, porous, and therefore vulnerable to vomiting worms. Like the young woman from Busiris Tripolitana, this deacon would readily be recognized as someone suffering from "woman problems" that are "terrible and hideous." The women who committed adultery in the Greek text of the Acts of Thomas 56 are sentenced to spend eternity in a pit welling up with mire and worms, and threatened by womanly diseases.[77] The same applies to those men and women who trusted in their riches and exacted usury at compound interest in the Apocalypse of Paul 37. In short, those whose unrighteousness on earth involved the abuse of power are depicted as weak, powerless, and female in hell. In contrast to other forms of retributive justice, worm-infested men were eternally emasculated and kept in check as a monument of perpetual bodily consumption.[78] The worm-infested, sick womanly body becomes a means of controlling bodies and spaces, by fusing Christian ethical norms, Greek and Roman bodily norms, and Roman disciplinary tactics. In hell's heterotopia, worms critiqued the illusory nature of all other spaces by revealing an ordered underworld in which the effeminate bodies of sinners broadcast the truth of their guilt.

Chattering Teeth and Hell Freezing Over

One example of how bodies are emasculated in hell requires a bit more explanation than the rest. In the Apocalypse of Paul 42, Paul sees those who deny the resurrection in a place of extreme cold and snow that will never become warm: "And I looked from the north towards the west and I saw there the worm that never rests, and in that place there was gnashing of teeth. Now the worm was a cubit in size and it had two heads. And I saw there men and women in the cold and gnashing of teeth." Here the text combines the eternal punishment tropes of gnashing of teeth and the worm that never dies with a third element: extreme cold.

The gnashing of teeth as a reference to emotional distress is found throughout the Septuagint (Job 16:9; Ps 34:16; 36:12; 111:10; Lam 2:16). In Greek literature, gnashing teeth can refer to anger or the passions.[79] The expression "weeping and gnashing of teeth" in Matthew influenced the early Christian apocalypses in which we find different interpretations of those who weep and gnash their teeth in the places of eternal punishment (Matt 8:12; 13:42, 50; 22:13; 24:51; 25:30; cf. Luke 13:28a; Sibylline Oracles 8.231).[80] For an early Christian thinker like Origen, this feature inspired the question of why resurrected bodies would have teeth at all.[81] In contrast to the Apocalypse of Paul, however, Matthew and other early Christian authors often connected "gnashing of teeth" with Gehenna and fiery punishment rather than with cold.[82]

In judicial settings chattering teeth were a sign of guilt or nervousness. Cicero associates chattering teeth with "fright as paralyzing fear which causes paleness, trembling and chattering teeth" (*Tusc. Disp.* 4.8). Such fright is associated with losing control of one's body across a broad span of time (e.g., Homer, *Il.* 10.375–80; Libanius, *Or.* 23.20). In a punitive context chattering teeth are connected not only to fear and guilt, but also to the excessively cold conditions of prison.[83]

In such cold conditions, chattering teeth were also a sign of hunger and diseases such as pleurisy, which ancient medicine associated with an excessively cold body.[84] As we described in chapter 1, women's bodies were thought to be colder and have poorer blood flow, and therefore to be more susceptible to bodily dysfunction or illness. In the Hippocratic Corpus, however, chattering teeth are a symptom of healthy female states, such as fertility and pregnancy, as well as of unhealthy states, such as abortion, pleurisy, and the uterine closing after a stillbirth.[85]

In the Apocalypse of Paul 42, those who deny the resurrection are exposed to extreme cold, similar to the way in which ancient prisoners could expect to dwell in cold or damp conditions that would bring on illness. For those who denied the resurrection, the extreme cold and snow literally make their bodies function like those of women so that they exhibit female traits, such as the loss of bodily control. Here in the early Christian imagination of hell the loss of control of one's body is not simply a metaphor for sin but becomes a judicial mechanism for policing sin. In doing so, it implicitly reinforces the scaffolding of gendered notions of the body. Simultaneously, hell magnifies the ancient desire for bodily conformity, bringing hell to earth for the sick and impaired body. Fear of the out-of-control body became a means of bodily control.

Breast-Milk Beasts and Other Breast Punishments

In the punishments that focus on breasts the sick female body takes center stage as a carceral object. The Ethiopic text of the Apocalypse of Peter 8 envisages the punishments of two groups of potential parents: the mothers who conceived children outside of marriage and procured abortions, and fathers and mothers who have killed their children. The former group have their eyes pierced by lightning or a "flash of fire" that shoots forth from their children.[86] As we discussed in chapter 2, many women in the ancient world were forced by their sexual partners to terminate pregnancies, but were held solely responsible for this choice, experiencing a double standard as result of their lack of cultural capital.[87] In this punishment the adulterous women are punished in a way that hyperfeminizes their bodies, bodies that were vulnerable to penetration before death, but are now violently attacked by their own children, reducing them to a state of total powerlessness.

The mothers and fathers who are attacked by breast-milk beasts receive a unique punishment: "And the milk of the mothers flows from their breasts and congeals and smells foul, and from it come forth beasts that devour flesh, which turn and torture them forever with their husbands, because they forsook the commandment of God and killed their children.

And the children shall be given to the angel Telemakos. And those who slew them will be tortured forever, for God wills it to be so" (Apoc. Pet. 8). The text explains their sin as murder: "These are they that neglected and cursed and transgressed thy commandment. They killed us and cursed the angel who created us and hung us up."[88] Clement of Alexandria remarked that this punishment "teaches that the punishments will come to pass by reason of the sins" (Ex. Proph. 49).[89] Yet this "measure for measure" logic is not crystal clear, since the text itself does not describe their sin as one that pertains to breastfeeding. What is more, the emphasis on the logic of talion should not allow us to lose sight of the gendered imagery of the body that is in play and how it would impact ancient audiences.

These images may be difficult for modern readers to comprehend because lactation and breastfeeding have a different significance in the contemporary world than they did in the ancient world. There is not a single narrative about the significance of breastfeeding in the ancient world. Some authors like Plutarch certainly praised women for nursing their own children.[90] Particularly as the Roman empire worked toward social cohesion after civil wars, moral significance was attached to the act of breastfeeding beyond simply seeing it as an act of providing nourishment to one's child. John Penniman emphasizes the social, political, and spiritual power of milk in this context for both Roman civilization and early Christians.[91] The theorization of breastfeeding took place in political, philosophical, and medical sources, all of which viewed the body of the Roman mother (matrona) or the wet nurse (nutrix) to be the site for the education (paideia) and nourishment of Rome's children.[92] In this framework breastfeeding was not simply nutritive, it was the elemental core of the empire's vitality.[93] Breast milk is seen as connective, made of the same material as the infant itself; according to Galen, milk was thought to be one of the most powerful influences on the humors, able to assist in keeping the body in balance.[94]

Despite the social power attributed to breast milk, and the protest of some moralists, the use of a wet nurse appears to have been quite common in antiquity, generally and among Christians.[95] Some sources explain why an ancient woman might choose to use a wet nurse rather than breastfeeding her own child. Even Soranus, the author of an ancient gynecological treatise, who insists that a mother's breast milk is the best option for feeding a newborn, "then goes on to make things pretty unequal, giving the mother plenty of good reasons not to breastfeed."[96] A new mother might choose not to nurse because of bodily weakness or because she wanted to have more children right away.[97] Wet-nursing contracts frequently precluded the wet nurses from engaging in sexual relationships, from getting pregnant, or from nursing other children during the length of the contract. Enslaved women could have their own babies taken away so that they could wet nurse.[98] As Bernadette J. Brooten argues, the legal wet-nursing contracts for free and enslaved wet nurses show "the purchase of the use of the woman's breasts, but also of her vagina and uterus, which are to remain unused for the duration of the contract" (up to two years).[99] In all these contexts the focus is on a woman's reproductive and nutritive capacities and how they can maximally support the flourishing of the empire through the production of elite male heirs.

The discourse around breastfeeding depended upon ancient understandings of how breast milk worked. Aristotle argued that breast milk was stored-up menstrual blood that had been transformed into milk through the heat of the woman's heart (Aristotle, *Hist. An.* 583a.26–33; *Gen. An.* 4.8, 777a7–8).[100] Soranus and Galen agreed, and saw it as fortuitous that the breasts are located near the heart.[101] Galen describes the regimen of the nursing body as requiring not only a particular diet but also abstention from sex.[102] For Galen and other Roman authors, sex could either provoke menstruation or result in pregnancy—and either condition would divert good blood from being turned into breast milk.[103] Galen advises, "I direct women who are nursing (i.e., providing milk for) little children to abstain from sexual activity altogether. The menstrual flow is stirred up by sexual intercourse and the milk no longer remains sweet. And some women become pregnant; nothing is more harmful than this for the infant being nourished by their milk. In this case, the best of the blood is used up in the fetus, inasmuch as the origin of life is specifically contained in the blood itself and is provided for by this" (Galen, *Hyg.* 9 [46K]). Impure milk could immediately be detected by sight, smell, and taste (*Hyg.* 9 [47 K]).[104]

The Theodosian Code reveals the extent to which ancient thinkers took these guidelines around lactation seriously.[105] Here the nurse who is convicted of misconduct toward her charge has molten lead poured down her throat. In the Apocalypse of Peter such women are attacked by beasts made of spoiled milk. This punishment implies that the sexual or moral corruption of the nursing woman could spoil the milk that was intended to deliver sustenance and pure *paideia* to vulnerable infants.

Outside of this punitive context, physical pain was also associated with breast milk within the body of the nursing woman. Since the breast milk was viewed as a means for the female body to evacuate excess blood, any difficulty with the flow of milk could negatively affect the body's balance. The Hippocratic Corpus notes that breasts can develop cysts and infections when "their milk turns bad" (*Glands* 17). Infection or loss of a breast ultimately results in the suffocation of the woman because the milk is continuing to leave the uterus as blood. Without a point of evacuation this excess milk attacks the central parts of the body like the heart and lungs.[106] Breast milk can not only bring balance to the body, nourishment to the newborn, and *paideia* to the youngest citizens of the empire, it can also be a deadly force when it is unleashed upon the maternal body.

For the women tormented in hell by breast-milk beasts, the mechanics of motherhood are controverted in a punishment that magnified existing cultural fears about lactation. On the surface, the breast-milk beasts may simply represent afterlife torment in which chaos and inversion of the natural order reign; if so, the powerful image of the breast as a source of sustenance becomes a mechanism of bodily torment for male and female bodies. In this reading, the breast-milk beasts channel the available cultural ideas about the female body as the harbinger of both life and death. And for the fathers, the punishment challenges the only space in which male receptivity was acceptable—the nursing male infant—by turning the bodies of the fathers into unwilling receptacles of beastly congealed breast milk.[107]

According to Clement's claim that the breast-milk beasts fit the sin they punish, the sins of the parents relate to infanticide carried out by depriving their offspring of milk (*Ex. Proph.* 41–49).[108] The suggestion that the punishment is one for infanticide or not nursing one's own children fits with the ancient worry over infant mortality and the high value placed on the mother's milk in the Roman republic. But this hypothesis must be nuanced in several ways, given the ancient understanding of the bodily mechanics of nursing, and the popularity of wet nursing even among early Christians. If this is a punishment for not nursing one's children, then the punishment would either apply specifically to enslaved men and women who are to give up their children, or to elite men and women who selected a wet nurse but lost their infant. The description of the milk as "foul smelling" and "congealed" recalls ideas about sexual activity or moral corruption spoiling the milk of a nurse or mother, and real-life punishments that existed for "corrupt" nurses. In any of those cases the punishment reinforces and intensifies the ancient ideals around breastfeeding as a cultural and moral imperative that demanded sexual continence, a principle in tension with the cultural imperative to produce male heirs.

Throughout this passage the emphasis is on the children. Like the widows and the poor elsewhere in the Apocalypse of Peter, they are the "least of these" who are the presumed responsibility of the Christian reader. The breast-milk beasts leverage the vulnerability of the body of the lactating mother as a violent punishment for those parents who neglected their own vulnerable children. The mothers and fathers in this space are tormented in a way that heightens the double bind that the ancient mother faced with respect to her husband and child. Should she nurse, and offer pure nourishment and *paideia* to her child? Or should she hire a wet nurse so that she can be sexually available to her husband and produce more heirs? When it came to lactation, ancient mothers were bad wives if they nursed, but damned if they didn't.

The punishments in later apocalypses draw in various ways upon the imagery found in the Apocalypse of Peter. In the Greek Apocalypse of Ezra 5:2–3, a woman who "begrudged giving her milk but also cast infants into the rivers" hangs while four beasts suck at her breasts. In the Latin Vision of Ezra 53a–54 women who "killed their children" and "did not give their breasts to other orphans" (as we noted in chapter 2, the fathers are absent here) are hanging in fire while serpents suck at their breasts. In one of the Isaiah fragments, women are hung by their nipples because they "uncovered their hair and rent their veil and sat in the open market place to suckle their children in order to attract the gaze of men and make them sin" (Chron. Jer. 16.4). In the Greek Apocalypse of Mary (5–7) infant exposure and abortion are punished by immersing men and women up to their breasts and necks in a river of fire.[109] Later in the Greek Apocalypse of Mary 20, a deaconess is punished for fornication by hanging while a ten-headed beast gnaws at her breasts. Himmelfarb suggests that the breast punishments in the Marian tours of hell submerge the principle of talion, which can, however, be recovered by looking at the relationship between fornication and abortion.[110] I would add to this argument that ancient audiences would have read the Marian tours not solely in the context of retributive logic, but in the more complex and gendered technologies of the body that linked chastity and breastfeeding. To see breasts as a mechanism of punishment would have aroused a knot of images that were entangled with multivalent body politics due to the association between nursing and sexual abstinence. Fornication, infanticide, and nursing are all ways in which a woman makes her body unavailable for the production and sustenance of more male citizens.

The punishments that are tied to breasts and breast milk utilize the mechanics of the female body to depict sinful women as broken or sick.[111] Assertions of retributive logic gloss over the gendered bodily norms that make the punitive spectacle possible. In the Marian tours of hell there is an additional valence of judgment and shame to these punishments, since they are witnessed and narrated by the mother of Jesus, whose identity and religious significance are bound up in her own gestation and nursing of Jesus. This contrast between the nursing mother of Jesus and the women who experience bodily punishments through their breasts appears to be intentional since there are proportionately more breast punishments in the Marian tours of hell than in other apocalyptic tours. These punishments, like the breast-milk beasts in the Apocalypse of Peter, leverage ancient ideas connecting sexual activity to spoiled breast milk, breast pain, and even death.[112] In the zoo of hell's heterotopia it is temporarily possible for Mary's unattainable normative body—the unspoiled ideal of the chaste nursing mother—to come near to the punished and punishing bodies of the sinful women and the beasts. This space magnifies the objectification of the female body and the social pressures around nursing and motherhood. As Mary views the damned, her body holds the subject position only long enough to emphasize the ways in which the damned have fallen short of the ancient maternal ideals. For the audience, however, all of these neatly classified maternal bodies (Mary's included) are objects in a punitive spectacle that contests the messy reality of ancient Christian motherhood.

Toppling Over

Breast-milk beasts leverage the technology of the female body and the body politics of ancient motherhood in order to frighten onlookers; other punishments exploit the ancient body politics around sex. The Apocalypse of Peter refers to sinners whose punishment entails toppling themselves off a cliff:

> And other men and women thrust themselves down from a high place and return again and run, and demons drive them. These are the worshippers of idols, and they drive them to the end of their wits and they plunge down

from there. And this they do continually and are tormented forever. These are they who cut their flesh as apostles of a man, and the women who were with them . . . and thus are the men who defiled themselves with one another in the fashion of women. (Apoc. Pet. 10)[113]

And another very high place . . . the men and women who make a false step go rolling down to where the fear is. And again, while the (fire) that is prepared floweth, they mount up and fall down again and continue their rolling. They shall be punished thus forever. These are they who have not honoured their father and mother, and of their own accord drew themselves from them. (Apoc. Pet. 11)

These punishments are for a range of sins: idolatry, male and female homoeroticism, and the failure to honor one's father and mother.[114] Their repetitive nature is reminiscent of the legend of Sisyphus, who was punished for the hubris of declaring himself more clever than Zeus by having to push his magical rock up the hill only to find himself at the bottom again. But as Bernadette Brooten has demonstrated, the image of toppling over combined with descriptions of homoeroticism appears in the Apocalypse of Peter as a judgment upon men and women who have "reversed their proper roles during their lifetimes . . . going up and coming down, going up and coming down again, reversing their direction just as they reversed the gendered order of society."[115] This explanation also fits well with the notion of measure-for-measure punishment for the sins of idolatry and dishonoring one's parents, which were thought to abrogate the divine and familial order.

The account of this punishment is an *ekphrasis*, or an image that was meant to persuade by bringing to mind other ancient "toppling" images. The image of toppling or being bent over—connoting passivity, weakness, and femininity—was used as an insult expressing a negative valuation of the passive male partner in a homoerotic encounter.[116] The most famous example of this visual image is the Eurymedon vase, which depicts a Persian archer bent over while being approached from behind by a Greek holding his erect penis.[117] The many possible interpretations of this scene center on the overlap between a sexual image and a military one that expresses the pursuit, conquest, and humiliation of the bent figure.[118] The bent-over posture of the Persian is also meant both to code the figure as womanly, and to mock the Persian practice of *proskynesis*, the social gesture of bowing and kissing.[119] Lloyd Llewellyn-Jones contends that this joke parodies the Iranian gesture of respect so that "the Persian's submissive act of bending over—'bottoms up'—is an expression of his natural servility and unbridled nymphomania."[120] The Eurymedon vase painting casts interesting light on the toppling punishments we find in the apocalyptic visions of hell. If being bent over is a recognizable image of weakness and effeminacy, and one that is already associated with homoeroticism, then the men and women who are repeatedly toppling off a cliff may have evoked this imagery and the associated shame.

From this vantage point, the men and women who have committed idolatry, engaged in homoerotic sex, and dishonored father and mother are sentenced to be forever bent over, bending so far that they fall, over and over again. Although some scholars have argued that Christians collapsed all forms of homoeroticism into one category, the punishment described in the Apocalypse of Peter memorializes the shame of male passivity in particular.[121] The visual valence of being bent over was tightly connected not only to pederasty, weakness, and womanliness, but also to the disruption of gender roles and the hierarchy that buttressed an orderly society. This punishment decries the interruption of the hierarchy that was so important for Greek and Roman social order, memorializing these sins as acts of weakness and effeminacy. Unlike the men who engage in these acts in the "real" world, the bodies toppling over in hell do so involuntarily, because they are "driven by demons" or they "make a false step." This point suggests that the choice to resist hierarchical order in other spaces is a mere illusion. Hell's heterotopia demonizes the interruption of hierarchical order in other spaces, intensifying the existing sexual norms, and using the passive homoerotic body as a tool for policing a wide range of other bodies. In the Theodosian Code, this heterotopia is realized on earth, as the early Christian focus on male passivity in sexual intercourse is legislated to be punished with "the avenging flames" (Theodosian Code 9.7.6).[122]

Tongue Laceration, Tongue Chewing, Lip Losing, and Cannibalism

Many common punishments in the tours of hell, after immersion in fire and worms, pertained to the mouth. Like other punishments, mouth torments were tightly tied to gender hierarchy and masculine ideals of self-control. According to the Ethiopic text of the Apocalypse of Peter, those who committed slander are condemned to tongue chewing; in the later Greek text, these same sinners bite through their lips (Apoc. Pet. 9 [28 in the Greek Akhmim text]). In these same texts, those who provided false testimony against the martyrs have their lips cut off (in the Ethiopic; in the Greek they bite through their tongues), and have fire in their mouths and entrails (Apoc. Pet. 9 [29 Akhmim]). In the Apocalypse of Paul the men and women who "reviled the word of God in church" chew their tongues in a fiery confined place (Apoc. Paul 37). In the Book of Mary's Repose, the mouth of the lector who "spoke glorious words" but did not do glorious things becomes a flaming razor (Mary's Rep. 95). This text also contains a particularly disturbing scene in which a deacon who did not care properly for "the glorious blood" is eaten by young children and many others who, presumably, were deprived of the opportunity to partake of the Eucharist.[123]

Like other measure-for-measure punishments, these oral punishments affect the part of the body that was used to commit the sin. They also draw upon and intensify existing ancient ideas about the mouth's relationship to sin in order to terrify audiences.

In the ancient world one's speech was thought to reveal one's character. In Greek and Roman culture improper speech could be a cause for characterizing a person as weak, womanly, and of low socioeconomic standing.[124] Early Christians adopted the value of verbal self-control as a means of promoting their reputation among outsiders.[125] For this reason, Christian texts about improper speech reflected the broader cultural ideas about how speech worked.

Ancient censure of bad speech operated within a gendered hierarchy in which exemplary speech was a display of elite manliness.[126] Marianne Bjelland Kartzow argues that this dichotomous view of speech labeled those men who spoke improperly as effeminate: "These men appeared as lessmales, although they did not become women."[127] In this way the ancient gender hierarchy around speech did not simply separate men and women; it also served to support other ancient hierarchies like class by separating the "legitimate" speech of elite males from other men (like the enslaved) whose speech was labeled as "illegitimate" and womanly.[128] In early Christian tours of hell, the men and women who committed sins through their speech are not simply depicted as "less male." They chew their tongues, their mouths are penetrated by fire, and their lips are cut off. They inhabit bodies that look like leaky, penetrable women's bodies, but they are also unable to speak, exhibiting the symptoms of those with speech impairments.[129] This depiction demonstrates the intersectional nature of eternal punishment in which specific torments reflected ancient ideas of gender, class, and disability.

Not only what came out of the mouth but also what went into it was considered an important marker of character. Ancient philosophical and medical texts described food and drink as nutritive not only for the body but also for the soul. Philosophers thought that a heavy diet weighed down the intellect, while a diet consisting of dry foods brought balance to mind and soul.[130] As John David Penniman observes, "for Galen, the path to a healthy body and a healthy soul begins in the stomach."[131] Penniman argues that this went so far for some early Christian authors (like Gregory of Nyssa) that the Eucharist was actually seen as a dietetic remedy for bodily illness.[132] The case of the deacon who mishandled the Eucharist collapses the nutritive, healing, and pedagogical elements of the communion wine.[133] He is literally eaten in hell because he did not offer appropriate drink to others (Mary's Rep. 95–96). But those who were denied the Eucharist by his neglect are punished as well, presumably because they did not receive the healing and education that were offered by the eucharistic wine. These "young children and many others" are forced to eat the deacon in hell; improper spiritual and material nourishment in this life leads to even worse dining for all eternity. This punishment dramatically reverses the charges of cannibalism (specifically of children) levied at early Christians by taking an anti-Christian epithet and applying it to miseducated children and the Christian deacon who led them astray.[134]

The mouth and especially the tongue also played an important role in ancient diagnostic practices. A yellow or dark tongue was a symptom of pneumonia (Dis. 3.15).[135] The tongue burning or growing hard could also be a sign of death (Epid. 4.10; 7.74). A swollen tongue or loss of speech were also seen as acute conditions that needed to be treated. The laceration of the tongue to draw blood was a common treatment for swelling of the tongue or speech impairments (Dis. 3.89). Galen discusses the practice of tongue laceration as a treatment for a sore throat and swollen tonsils, and elsewhere prescribes it for swelling of the tongue and inflammation in the head and chest (Ther. Glau. 2.4 [line 93K]; 13 [904K]).

For the ancient audiences of the tours of hell, mouth-related torments recalled not only the speech acts that landed sinners in hell, but also the real-life treatments for those with speech impairments or inflamed or swollen tongues. In short, the punishment in hell for bad speech is either eternal speech impairment, a "treatment" that enables blood to flow from the mouth, or both. In the Book of Mary's Repose, the lector whose mouth was a flaming razor and the deacon who did not care for the eucharistic wine properly lost the ability to speak (Mary's Rep. 95–96). Going beyond the principle of *lex talionis*, the early Christian tours of hell use prevalent images of sickness and disability to intensify the punishment for verbal sins. In the case of the deacon who mishandled the Eucharist, the dietetic sin and the spiritual sin are one and the same: denying proper physical and spiritual nourishment to others. Both the deacon and those who did not "drink well" are punished by being consumed or by being forced to consume improper food. Those who exhibited an effeminate loss of control of their mouth were punished in hell in ways that tightly controlled their bodies for eternity. For those who committed speech sins, bodily deviance and the medicalized response to it become a mechanism of bodily control, a punitive spectacle that not only objectifies bodily difference, but unveils the different body as the sinful body. In these punishments, the disabled body is once again an organizational tool, depicting hell's heterotopia as a well-ordered alternative to the earthly mess in which the gendered bodily hierarchy had been interrupted by improper speech or eating.

Hair and Eyes Mixed with Blood

In addition to the emasculated and disabled bodies of the unrighteous, hell also contains angelic bodies that are depicted using bodily descriptors. The Apocalypse of Zephaniah describes the ugly angels who carried off the souls of the ungodly: "Their eyes were mixed with blood. Their hair was loose like the hair of women, and fiery scourges were in their hands. When I saw them I was afraid."[136] Galen describes the presence of blood in the eyes as the easiest way to diagnose an "excess" in the head.[137] Bloodshot eyes signified a sick or abnormal body; this view may have drawn from theories of vision that associated the health of the eyes with ethical conduct.[138]

The loose hair mentioned in the Apocalypse of Zephaniah is explicitly identified as an undesirable female trait. This common trope is made more horrifying by its association with punishing angels who are expected to project strength and masculinity. As Pseudo-Phocylides observes: "Long hair is not fit for males, but for voluptuous women."[139] This view is reflected in Paul's discussion of head coverings (1 Cor 11:2–16) and the exegetical tradition that follows him; the locusts of Revelation 9:8–9, which have "hair like a woman"; and Perpetua's request for a hairpin because it was unfitting for a martyr to die with disorderly hair (*Mart. Perp. Fel.* 20.4–5).[140] But as Maria Doerfler has noted, there was also a "polyvalence of hair in late ancient discourses," as evidenced in the writings of Clement of Alexandria, who was able to criticize Romans for their ornate hair in the same breath that he praised the "barbarians" who wore long hair without adornment (*Educ.* 3.3 [PG 8.589B]).[141]

Similarly, it is difficult to determine the significance of hair in the medical literature. To be sure, both the Hippocratic Corpus and Galen connect hair growth with the strength and capacity of the brain; the more abundant the hair, the larger the brain (Hippocratic Corpus, *Fleshes* 14; Galen, *Art* 6). But Galen also states that those with excess heat (and who are therefore out of balance) have visible veins in the eyes, and considerable black curly hair that grows quickly when they are young, but falls out when they grow older.[142] So for Galen an excess of curly hair could be either a sign of intelligence or a sign of an out-of-balance, sick body.

The association between hair and the brain also explains the relationship between hair and gender in the ancient imagination. According to the Hippocratic Corpus, hair is hollow and grows from the male and female reproductive fluids that flow to it (Hippocratic Corpus, *Nat. Ch.* 20).[143] Because the brain is the place where semen is produced or stored, hair grows best from the head.[144] Men have more body hair than women because they are hotter, and thus better at moving reproductive fluids throughout their bodies.[145] Long hair, however, draws the semen away from the genital area to the head, and therefore hampers sexual reproduction. A woman's long, hollow hair, in contrast, assists in reproduction by increasing the "suction power of her hollow uterus."[146] Excess hair growth could be a symptom of an unbalanced female reproductive system, as in the case of Phaethousa, who grew a beard because her husband's absence prevented her from conceiving a child (Hippocratic Corpus, *Epid.* 6.8.32).[147] Hair was conceptualized as part of female genitalia and also intersected with notions of class and sexuality. Philo, for example, contrasted the long, thick, effeminate hair of enslaved boys and "recent pets of the pederasts" with the appearance of free men, whose appearance contains "no shadow of anything to suggest the slave" (Philo, *Contempl. Life* 48–52, 70–72).[148]

Ancient narratives and satire provide a few more clues for the meaning behind the unkempt hair of Apocalypse of Zephaniah's punishing angels. In Lucian's *Dialogues of the Gods*, Eros exclaims that he is more afraid of Athena than of Zeus: "She scares me with her flashing eyes, and she's terribly like a man . . . and she's got on her breast that terrible face with the snaky hair—that's what scares me most of all. It gives me the creeps and makes me run the moment I see it" (Lucian, *Dial. Gods* 23 [19].1–2). Here Eros reacts to Athena's loose snaky hair in the same way that Lucian does to Medusa in *The Civil War*, and Aeneas to Strife, whose snaky locks were "entwined with bloody ribbons" (Virgil, *Aen.* 6.275–80; Lucian, *Civ. War* 9.670–80).

Such depictions may underlie the description of the punishing angels in the Apocalypse of Zephaniah as having loose, frightening hair as women do. Their bloody eyes would have indicated an imbalanced or sick body, while their womanly hair was fear-inducing. This example illustrates the extent to which ideas about the body influenced imaginative constructions of the afterlife, where even the angels, who never had earthly bodies, are defined by the ancient standards of bodily normativity and masculinity.[149] Early Christian conversation about the resurrected body functions similarly, so that the material differences between male and female bodies are preserved even if the parts of those bodies are "stripped of their humors, desires, and functions."[150]

The gendered significance of hair is also preserved in the hanging punishments that utilize the sinner's own hair as an instrument of torture. In the Greek text of the Acts of Thomas 56, women who do not wear head coverings are hung up by their hair, as are those women in the Apocalypse of Peter 7 and Apocalypse of Paul 39 who adorned themselves for adultery.[151] Because hair was thought to be an extension of female genitals, this punishment was considered apt for the sin of adultery.[152] Martha Himmelfarb notes that Jewish apocalypses describe breasts as the sinful limb for women's sexual offenses, whereas Christian texts use hair. She posits that this difference reflects two different textual traditions. I would add to this that Christian depictions of hell are drawing upon this Greek idea that the hair is an extension of female genitals.[153] In contrast to the punishments that emasculate sinners in hell, these torments preserve the gender differences between male and female bodies precisely in order to punish male and female sexuality in distinctive ways. In hell's heterotopia hair is used to discipline the bodies of women who used their hair on earth to subvert the gendered hierarchy and control men with their powerful uterine vortex. In hell's alternative space, the female body is preserved so that it can be objectified and controlled, critiquing earthly spaces in which women have subverted the gender hierarchy and the order it offered.

Black Garments and Black Faces

The last group of punishments I will consider are those in which gendered ideas about the body intersect with ancient attitudes about pigmentation. Both the Apocalypse of Peter and the Apocalypse of Paul occasionally describe sinners who wore black garments or had black faces. The Apocalypse of Peter 11 refers to "maidens clad in darkness for raiment [who] shall be seriously punished and their flesh will be torn in pieces. These are they who retained not their virginity till they were given in marriage; they shall be punished with these tortures while they feel them." This punishment is present in the Apocalypse of Paul 38–39, where a similar punishment for the would-be virgins is preceded by that of women who committed adultery who have "black faces":

> And again I saw men and women with very black faces in the pit of fire; and sighing and weeping I asked: Who are these, sir? And he said to me: These are fornicators and adulterers who although they had their own wives committed adultery; and similarly the women committed adultery in the same way, though they had their own husbands. (38)
>
> And there I saw girls wearing black clothing and four dreadful angels who had blazing chains in their hands. And they set them (the chains) on their necks and led them into darkness. And again weeping I asked the angel: Who are these, sir? And he said to me: They are those who although they were appointed as virgins defiled their virginity unknown to their parents. (39)

In antiquity black garments were worn when a person was in mourning. Whereas men stopped wearing black after the funeral, women continued to do so throughout the period of mourning.[154] For women this marked a stark contrast to their normal standard of dress, since women typically wore colors while men dressed in white, black, or grey.[155] Black garments were also associated with prostitutes and adulteresses.[156] In practice, prostitutes and adulteresses wore a wide range of clothing, yet the *togata* functioned as a discursive tool for describing "in one word a woman whose morals were easy."[157] The *togata*, Olson argues, "is not a tangible piece of clothing which is indicated by the adjective, but a moral system."[158] A similar symbolic universe exists for the rabbinic authors who linked a woman's clothing and adornment to sexual sin.[159] These authors describe real-life measure-for-measure punishments, in which a woman is stripped of whatever she wore while committing sexual sin: "If she was covered with white garments, they cover her with black. If there were gold items, necklaces, nose rings, and ringed garment fasteners, they remove them from her in order to physically disgrace her."[160] For some of the rabbis, the black garment not only "fits the crime" of female sexual sin, but also is a way to physically and publicly shame the woman.

The tours of hell in the Apocalypses of Peter and Paul may have drawn from these types of moral systems when they invited their audiences to imagine "loose women" in black garments. Ancient men frequently lamented that different types of women could not be as easily distinguished by their dress. Hell, however, provided a uniform so that women of "ill repute" could be easily spotted.[161] The torments in the Apocalypse of Peter include laceration of the flesh, which recalls the punishment for the rape of Leto and draws together several distinct visual markers of sexual sin. For later readers of the Apocalypse of Paul the black garments may have recalled the sixth-century practice of sending women to monasteries—where black clothing was also worn—to atone for sexual crimes. According to Julia Hillner, an index of this practice is found in a story of two noble ladies swept up in the persecution of Miaphysites under Justin II. These two ladies were dressed in black habits, and put to work in a monastery's kitchens and latrines.[162] Dressing wayward girls in black garments in hell reflected gendered punitive practices on earth.

Black skin, too, was seen as a signifier of sexual sin in the Apocalypse of Paul.[163] Black skin was a descriptor in Roman culture that was frequently applied to Egyptians and Ethiopians as a way of depicting them and their culture as distinct or "other" than Romans and Roman culture.[164] Early Christian texts also employ Ethiopian or black-skinned characters as ciphers for evil, in service of what Eric Barreto calls "the full discursive negotiation" of ethnicity in antiquity.[165] Vincent Wimbush and Gay Byron have demonstrated that early Christian monastic stories about Ethiopian characters utilize these characters as a part of ascetic rhetoric of boundary creation and management. Black-skinned characters are introduced precisely because their marginality emphasizes the dominance of other characters.[166] This trope vilifies Ethiopian and other black bodies. These stories not only "demonize Ethiopians," they also "Ethiopianize demons."[167]

In monastic communities the face color was an indicator of ascetic practice. A glowing or bright face meant that the ascetic had attained to the "transformation into the glorified body of the resurrection."[168] Black faces signified failure in ascetic practice and affliction by the demonic. A fitting parallel to the black faces in the Apocalypse of Paul is the monk guilty of fornication who is espied by Paul the Simple: "I see one who is black, and his whole body is dark; the demons are standing on each side of him, dominating him, drawing him to them and leading him by the nose, and his angel, filled with grief, with head bowed, follows him at a distance."[169] After the monk repents, he loses his black appearance, further solidifying the link between his moral state and his countenance.

This story also highlights the link of sexuality to blackness. Ancient jokes and rhetorical exercises about a Roman woman giving birth to an Ethiopian baby unveil cultural fears about political power and boundaries.[170] These jokes not only attest to Roman fears about adultery and the legitimacy of Roman heirs, but also play on a stereotype of Ethiopians as erotically powerful and desirable.[171] Although early Christian asceticism resisted the dominant culture in many ways, monastic thought replicated and even emphasized this Roman discourse around blackness and sexuality.[172] For example, in the *Life of Antony* a demon appears to Antony as a black boy, and after Antony has resisted the sexual temptations of this demon, the demon says, "I am the spirit of fornication."[173]

The Apocalypse of Paul, however, questions the morality not of the male monk but of male and female adulterers. Like the punch line of the Roman jokes in which a black-skinned baby confirms the colonialist fears of tainted Roman blood, the black faces in the Apocalypse of Paul 38 reveal the true identity of the adulterers, unveiling their sexual secrets for all to see. Here, however, the standard is not simply about the preservation of Roman identity, nor is boundary policing solely the responsibility of women (as we saw in chapter 2). In hell's heterotopia, both men and women are depicted as the racialized other as a mechanism for containing their sexuality. This depiction exoticizes adultery as hypersexual behavior and codifies the identification of black skin with sexual sin. Blackness was not simply a way to make visible unseen demonic forces but also became a punishment for sin.

The Wages of Sin Is Womanly: Leaky, Broken Bodies, and Ancient Christianity

Given the cultural and historical contexts in which these apocalypses were written, it is scarcely surprising to see damnation depicted as a womanly condition. Gender also contributed to the attribution of minority status to male bodies, such as the enslaved and eunuchs.[174] The depictions of afterlife Christian bodies evoked emotions of pain and regret by transforming male forms into bloody, leaky, weak, out-of-control, vulnerable womanly bodies. As we saw in the Apocalypse of Paul, the damned body was not only womanly and slavish, but also black. This discourse layered pejorative racial and ethnic associations onto the low-class female body.

Even more surprising is the extent to which the damned bodies are also depicted as disabled, particularly since a large percentage of the ancient audience, and likely the author of the Apocalypse of Paul as well, would have more than a passing familiarity with inhabiting a body that was in some way considered nonnormative.[175] Whether blind, deaf, mute, wounded, trembling out of control, or squirting congealed breast milk, damned bodies would be a cipher for the real bodies of the audience members who had or knew others who had such impairments. While pagan depictions of hell sometimes valorized the bodies of the disabled, the early Christian apocalypses leveraged the ancient cultural association between sin and sickness in order to further demonize bodily difference.[176] As a heterotopia, hell provided an opportunity for audiences to view and learn from these deviant bodies. Despite its strangeness, the damned body has points of reference in the audience's culture that make each body legible as "other." A reader touring this heterotopia is invited to interrogate their own body by identifying with the bodies or the sins of the damned. In hell, as in life, the deviant body is a site for solidifying claims to bodily normativity while also dramatically drawing attention to its impermanence.[177]

In these hellish heterotopias, early Christians employ rhetorical techniques similar to those used by ancient physicians. Here, the apocalyptic authors drew on commonly held ideas about gender, class, ethnicity, and bodily normativity as rhetorical tools aimed at persuading their audience to understand sin and repentance in particular ways. These bodies, much like the disabled bodies in nineteenth-century freak shows, offer a mechanism for the "symbolic containment" of difference. Through this mechanism, tours of hell turn bodily difference and sin into the distant other, even for a culture where bodily difference was the experience of the majority of the population.[178] These early Christian depictions of the damned trouble the assertion that bodily normativity and the disciplinary regime are largely the products of the Enlightenment and the modern medical gaze.[179]

The use of discourse about the body as persuasive rhetoric also has two practical implications for early Christian thought. First, the damned body reinforces and intensifies the stakes surrounding those ideas about the body. While fire, worms, and the gnashing of teeth all have biblical antecedents, the more detailed apocalyptic depictions of these torments amplify their significance within a late antique hermeneutic of the body. Bodies that are penetrated by a fiery phallus or spew forth worms are envisioned as womanly, sick bodies. In hell, those bodies are also perpetually victimized by the porous and moist conditions of that out-of-balance body. The chattering teeth of the damned tortured in the snowy chambers of hell signify a body beyond control. This is a body that trembles due to insufficient blood flow, like the bodies of women, the sick, or the elderly. These punishments use bodily deviance to inspire earthly moral conformity, and simultaneously offer the righteous an opportunity to externalize both the sinful other and their own potentially deficient bodies.[180]

Candida Moss argues that Mark's rhetoric about the afterlife leverages "the contrast between deformed eternal life and normal-bodied damnation," so that audiences are literally encouraged to self-amputate so that they may enter heaven instead of hell.[181] Here, "aesthetics are set on their head," in order to contain sin, and bodily impairment is the path to righteousness and eternal life.[182] The subversive logic of Mark 9 reminds us that although afterlife heterotopias may rely upon bodily normativity, they do so in diverse ways. Some bodies are impaired on earth in order to contain sin in anticipation of the afterlife, whereas other sinful bodies are disabled in hell in order to contain sin in the afterlife.

In contrast, the punishments pertaining to breasts do not simply leverage cultural fears about inhabiting a female or nonnormative body. In addition, the sinful woman's body whose breasts are dysfunctional or sick instrumentalizes the precarious power of the ancient mother who had competing demands on her body. The breast-milk beasts reflect reproduction and lactation as bodily powers that could quickly become dangerous by weaponizing breast milk against men and women alike. These punishments dramatize the ancient ideal of maternal chastity, and the perceived consequences for Christian families if parents fell short of these ideals.

Second, the concepts of the suffering body that emerge from these attempts to persuade different audiences can be incongruent and inconsistent. Tears are effeminate but propitious. The weeping of the damned signals their guilt and humiliation, and elicits potential guilt from the fellow tourists of hell. The tears of the saints are also propitious as they win the damned some respite from their torture. The unruly hair of the punishing angel draws upon the sexually charged visual imagery of powerful women with frightfully uncontrolled hair. Many torments collapse gender differences in order to depict the bodies of the damned as effeminate and weak. The hair-related punishments for women, however, preserve gender differences so that female bodies can be punished by the "sexual organs"— their hair—that they used to commit their crimes.

The fixation on the suffering body in early Christianity may be broader than previously thought. The suffering body is at the nexus of several different discursive practices that allowed ancient audiences to imagine marginalized bodies, and the horror of their own possible fate.[183] Furthermore, the discourses of *damnatio* do not remain submerged in hell. Ancient texts contain gruesome descriptions of a nurse who has molten lead poured down her throat for mishandling her charge, and of women forced to dress in black and remain confined to monasteries to atone for sexual sins.[184] Such tales show that while the apocalyptic strategies of containment may not have succeeded in containing sin, they were powerfully persuasive when it came to shaping the punitive imagination.

4 From Passive to Active: Gender and Atonement in Mary's Tours of Hell

The Marian tours of hell demonstrate an intriguing turn from bodies that are made female in hell to the female body as a soteriological agent. Like the weeping saints discussed in the previous chapter, the bodies who descend, see the damned, lament their fate, and return to tell the tale are not uniformly depicted as virtuous performers of impervious masculinity. For ancient audiences, Mary as woman and mother was the perfect candidate to descend to the damned as she inhabited a weepy but efficacious suffering body. In the texts that describe her descent to hell Mary is biological mother, adoptive mother, spiritual mother, teacher, and intercessor. Not only is Mary the intercessor for the damned, but her ability to intercede is integrally connected to her gender and, especially, to her unique relationships with Jesus and the disciples. The Marian tours of hell display the coexistence of multiple discursive practices around gender and the body, and show the decisive role of Mary's passive female body in the salvation of other bodies.

I will argue that Mary comes to take on the role of apostolic seer in the third century CE and beyond, and thereby subverts the tradition in which only Jesus and male apostles and saints could descend to the depths to witness torment, preach to the damned, or beg for clemency. In the process, the tradition around her tour of hell takes on a different shape than those of the male apocalyptic seers. In addition to inhabiting the roles of apostle, saint, intercessor, and redeemer of the damned, Mary is first and foremost the suffering Mother. In simultaneously mothering, beseeching, and imitating Christ, Mary subverts *and* reenacts the ancient expectations of the female body. In a context that viewed pregnancy and birth as public sacrifices,

Mary's offer to suffer with the damned may have had more impact than the same offer uttered by a male saint, such as Ezra.

The traditions about Mary's descent to hell may have begun as early as the third century, when stories about Mary's Dormition and Assumption began to circulate. Near the end of the Book of Mary's Repose, Gehenna is opened and the archangel Michael takes Mary and the apostles on a tour of hell, where they view the punishments of a lector, a deacon, and a priest (Mary's Rep. 90–100).[1] The damned then entreat Mary: "Mary we beseech you, Mary, light and the mother of light; Mary, life and mother of the apostles; Mary, golden lamp, you who carries every righteous lamp; Mary our master and the mother of our Master; Mary, our queen, beseech your son to give us a little rest" (Mary's Rep. 99). The damned then cry out to the apostles, and are granted nine hours of rest on the Lord's day by the Savior, "because of the tears of Michael, my holy apostles, and my mother Mary" (Mary's Rep. 100). Such traditions may have been the impetus for the development of the miraculous accounts of her departure from the world.[2]

In order to situate Mary's descent in the broader tradition of descents into hell, I will first review the chronology of Marian traditions. This chapter will then turn to early Christian notions of *imitatio Christi* as applied to the "harrowing of hell" motif, according to which Jesus descended to hell prior to his resurrection. I will argue, contrary to previous studies, that the Marian tours of hell draw upon both the *descensus* and the tours of hell. Depictions of Mary as both redeemer of the damned and apocalyptic seer suggest that the earliest Marian journeys to hell develop the motif of descent to the damned at a critical juncture for this tradition, in which the role of the saint and the redemptive role of Christ were beginning to overlap. This chapter will also examine the ways that Mary's redemptive *imitatio Christi* in the Marian tours of hell departs from other *descensus* and tour of hell literature, and in turn influences later tours of hell. Finally, this chapter looks at the way Mary's performance of the role of apostolic seer is informed by her unique role as the mother of Jesus and spiritual mother to the disciples. Specifically, I argue that Mary's maternal roles became tied to her intercessory roles, and eventually culminated in her dramatic and striking offer to suffer with the damned.

Chronology and Influence of Marian Traditions

Previous scholarship does not discuss Marian tours of hell in conjunction with the *descensus*, despite the fact that some of these traditions were developing and were influential at the same time as other stories about the descent to hell. There is scholarly consensus that the Book of Mary's Repose was the earliest of these texts, written no later than the fourth century (and as early as the late second or third century), and that the apocalyptic conclusion of the Book of Mary's Repose was a source for the Apocalypse of Paul (400).[3] Thus, the Book of Mary's Repose and the Six Books Apocryphon serve as early evidence not only for the tradition of Marian intercession, but also for the tradition of Mary's descent to hell, which influenced the most popular tour of hell in Western Christianity.[4] And beyond their importance for establishing early traditions about Mary, these early Dormition narratives were also used liturgically for hundreds of years.[5]

The more complete apocalyptic tours of hell, like those we find in the Greek Apocalypse of Mary or the Ethiopic Apocalypse of Mary, were written later than the Dormition narratives.[6] The sins punished in the Greek Apocalypse of Mary follow the pattern of the Book of Mary's Repose and the Apocalypse of Paul in that the text focuses on the sins of those who are identified as "insiders" to the Christian community, with particular attention on church leaders who do not fulfill their roles.[7] The Ethiopic Apocalypse of Mary was also based on the Apocalypse of Paul.[8] Of these different Marian tours, the Greek Apocalypse of Mary was by far the best known, especially in the Eastern Church, and it eventually supplanted both of the earlier apocalypses that were contained in the Book of Mary's Repose and the Six Books Apocryphon, as well as the Apocalypse of Paul. Given the influence of Marian tours of hell, and the possibility that one of these traditions developed as early as the second century, it makes sense to integrate Mary's descent to hell into the scholarly discussion of the *descensus*.

The Purpose of the Descent

In each of the Marian tours of hell, Mary descends to Hades, sees the unrighteous dead, mourns their fate, and begs God for mercy. This pattern follows the genre expectations of the other apocalyptic tours of hell, but it also calls to mind the early Christian traditions of the descent of Jesus to Hades after his death and prior to his resurrection.[9] Perhaps the most familiar *descensus* text is the Gospel of Nicodemus (the Acts of Pilate), according to which Jesus spoke with Satan, and then freed the patriarchs from hell, and sent them to paradise.[10]

The *descensus* tradition is often traced to late first-century texts like Matthew 27:52–53, John 10, Ephesians 4:9–10, and 1 Peter 3:18–22 and 4:6.[11] These first-century texts, however, do not set a clear precedent for thinking about the relationship between Christ and the dead. They offer neither a cohesive descent narrative nor a consensus around what Jesus accomplishes by descending: does he do anything salvific and if so, for whom? does he preach? if so, to whom?

Richard Bauckham has shown that the first-century authors do not speak with one voice about the descent or with clear soteriological aims in mind; most are interested in the death of Christ and not his activity in Hades.[12] And yet, he and other scholars have asserted that a concept of a descent to hell with salvific significance was already popular in the second century, and demonstrate this point by weaving the second-century patristic references to the *descensus*, such as those of Ignatius or Clement, into a coherent story of doctrinal development.[13] Even in the second century, however, the *descensus* tradition was both diverse and malleable. Nevertheless, they conveyed the same message as did the apocalyptic tours of hell: Christ's descent is salvific not only for the damned, but also, or perhaps even primarily, for the audiences of these texts, who are encouraged to adjust their behavior in the present world in order to avoid postmortem torment.

Early Christian apocalypses contribute to the *descensus* motif through their substantive descriptions of soteriologically significant journeys to hell.[14] In several texts that are later deemed "apocryphal" (Ascen. Isa. 9:17; Apoc. Pet. 17), the dead leave Hades with Christ at his resurrection and ascend to heaven with him at his ascension.[15] Although these texts imagine hell in different ways, they agree that the visit to hell is a critical event in the process of salvation, and that the righteous dead will ascend. In doing so, they configure heaven as the eternal antipode to hell.[16] The conventions of the tour genre dictate that such texts offer visual descriptions of the descent to hell along with theologically laden dialogue between the seer and his or her guide. For this reason, tours of hell provide more details about the mechanics of salvation than many second-century *descensus* texts.

In the Apocalypse of Peter, for instance, Peter learns that on the day of judgment all of the dead will be given back by hell for a final judgment (Apoc. Pet. 4). Toward the end of his tour he sees the righteous fathers in the garden, and learns that the righteous will also enjoy this fate if they have their names written in the book of life (Apoc. Pet. 17). Peter does not preach to the dead during his tour, because the final judgment has already happened and they cannot be saved. Nevertheless, the vision of the righteous patriarchs in heaven shows that Peter's tour is intended to effect salvation. Likewise, in the Ascension of Isaiah, the descent to Sheol is mentioned as a stop along the way in the Son's descent to earth and return to heaven, in

which he "plunders the angel of death" (Ascen. Isa. 9; 10). This confrontation with the angel of death is not the central atoning moment, but rather
belief "on his cross" and "being in the Holy Spirit" (Ascen. Isa. 3:18; 11.40)
are required for salvation and the gift of heavenly robes and crowns.[17] Isaiah
mediates the reader's vicarious vision of the ascent and descent in order to
inculcate salvific beliefs and practices.

Scholars have often bracketed the tours of hell in their discussions of
Christ's descent. Because the texts do not assign soteriological significance
to the descent itself, or conform to the form-critical definition of the *descensus*, they do not fit well into a narrative of historical development of the
tradition except to be listed as "primitive traditions" that can be contrasted
with their more "developed" counterparts.[18] This retrojection of third- and
fourth-century ideas about the descent to hell onto the history of the second century obscures the diversity of second-century Christianity. Even if
the texts do not exhibit the doctrinal or other features of later descent narratives, they nevertheless reflect upon the descent to hell in soteriologically
constructive ways, often through the "inside" knowledge that is mediated
to the reader of the text.

Earlier scholarship on the Marian apocalypses noted the similarity of
Mary's tours to hell as narrated in the Greek Apocalypse of Mary, the Book
of Mary's Repose, and the Six Books Apocryphon, to stories of Jesus's descent to Hades.[19] To be sure, in the apocalypses it is not Christ's preaching
that saves the dead, but the vision of the saint or apostle that saves the
living; the descent is a tableau of salvific information with practical implications for life in "this world." For Richard Bauckham, this distinction is
stark enough to argue that the connection between the apocalyptic tours of
hell and the descent to hell literature is "forced."[20] While these traditions
do have fundamental differences, as Bauckham's work shows, these distinctions did not preclude ancient readers from thinking about these two different types of descent literature in ways that overlapped or even mirrored
each other. The Marian tours of hell enter into this malleable stream of
descent traditions, and develop the idea of an apostle or saint who descends
to hell in ways that reflect the unique character of Mary.

Soteriological Consequences of the Redeemer's Activity in the Descensus

Many of the features of the early Christian apocalyptic tours of hell
were derived from their Greek and Roman antecedents and drew upon the

well-known tradition of touring Hades in order to provide instructions for how early Christians ought to behave in the present.[21] One feature of the early Christian apocalypses that does not have clear precedent in the Greek and Roman journeys to Hades, however, is the intercession of the seer on behalf of the damned. This motif appears only in the traditions about the descent of the Redeemer to hell and the early Christian apocalyptic tours of hell. Because the intercession of Mary in the Marian tours of hell draws fruitfully from both the *descensus* and tour of hell motifs, it is necessary to look at how the seer's intercession is described in both sets of traditions.

The earliest traditions of the descent of the Redeemer are not consistent with regard to who descends or what happens when they do. The Shepherd of Hermas, Similitude 9.15–16, one of the most influential depictions of the descent, depicts the apostles as preaching to the righteous dead. Their preaching is efficacious because it reveals the "name of the Son of God," thereby enabling the righteous dead to "descend through the water dead and arise alive."[22] Here, the concept of the descent to Hades explains the mechanics of baptism, and only secondarily comments on the soteriological effects of the descent itself. The Shepherd of Hermas stands out among second-century descent traditions in two ways. First, the Redeemer himself does not descend, but the apostles.[23] Second, the salvific efficacy of the apostolic preaching is more like a formality that allows "those who were dead" to "lay aside their death." This is a necessary step for the dead saints to escape Hades, but it does not reflect on the intransigence of the saints or their need for salvation. In both of these regards Similitude 9 has much in common with the Apocalypse of Peter, in which the apostle Peter descends and the righteous dead simply have their names written in the "book of life" in order to enter paradise.

In the other descent traditions, it is typically the Redeemer who descends, although who is saved and how may vary. For Ignatius, the Redeemer descends in order to save the righteous dead (including "even the prophets"). He is less concerned, however, with the salvific accomplishments of the Redeemer per se than with the salvation of the prophets as a story of Jewish and Christian continuity.[24] Writing to an audience that was divided over whether they ought to celebrate the Sabbath or the "Lord's Day," Ignatius points to Christ's descent to save the prophets as an example of "embracing new hope" that should encourage Christians to observe distinctive Christian practices and abandon Jewish ones.

Likewise, in Justin's *Dialogue with Trypho* the idea of the descent of the Redeemer is presented as a matter of fact that demonstrates the continuity between the work of Christ and the eternal covenant between God and Israel.[25] Unlike Ignatius, who cites the descent tradition as a novel Christian idea, Justin views it as a concept that was originally present in the book of Jeremiah.[26] Justin states, "From the sayings of the same Jeremiah these have been cut out: 'The Lord God remembered his dead people of Israel who lay in the mounded earth; and he descended to them to preach to them his own salvation.'" Justin is reading a Christian source that attributes the descent story to the prophet Jeremiah, and interprets this material as an excision undertaken by Justin's Jewish opponents due to its Christological and soteriological significance.[27] Justin does not offer any exegesis, as he presumes his audience would recognize its import.[28] In doing so, like Ignatius, Justin presumes that his audience would be familiar with the descent to hell and the Redeemer's preaching there as basic facts. Unlike the Shepherd of Hermas and Ignatius, Justin argues that this story has soteriological significance for all of the dead of Israel (not just the righteous dead).

The Shepherd of Hermas, Ignatius, and Justin all briefly touch upon the concept of a redemptive descent to hell in order to convey some other theological idea like the importance of baptism. By contrast, Irenaeus offers an expansion and sustained interpretation of the story of the Redeemer's journey to hell (*Ag. Her.* 4.27.2).[29] While Hermas and Ignatius maintained the purity and righteousness of the dead, Irenaeus views the descent narrative as a hermeneutical opportunity to connect Jesus's salvific activity to those "for whom the Son of God had not yet suffered" (*Ag. Her.* 4.27.2).[30] Irenaeus and Ignatius disagree with respect to the soteriological significance of the descent itself. They come to a similar conclusion, however, regarding the practical significance of the patriarchs' response, and they both invoke the characters of the Hebrew Bible as exemplars to demonstrate unity between Christianity and Judaism.[31]

Irenaeus's unique retelling of the story presents a universal soteriological schema in which all people, including the heroes of the Hebrew Bible, are susceptible to sin and capable of right repentance.[32] Like Justin, Irenaeus includes the content of Jesus's preaching, but he chooses sayings specifically oriented toward the remission of sin: Jesus descends "proclaiming the good news of his arrival and the remission of sins received by those who believe in him" (*Ag. Her.* 4.27.2).[33] By filling in the message of Jesus's preaching, Irenaeus paints a picture of Jesus offering forgiveness to the sinners of ancient times as he does for Irenaeus's audience. The theological connection between the redemption in Hades and the redemption on earth allows Irenaeus to argue that Christians should "abstain from evil" because

Christ descended once to rescue the patriarchs, but "will not die again on behalf of those who sin now" (*Ag. Her.* 4.27.2). The dead patriarchs are exemplars for the living, who should follow their example and repent. For Irenaeus, as for the early Christian apocalypses, the events in Hades have practical theological implications for the unrighteous dead and the living.

Clement's third-century *Miscellanies* 6.6 weaves many different traditions together in order to depict a descent to hell that is salvific for both Jews and Gentiles.[34] For Clement this universal salvation is grounded in Jesus's preaching to the spirits in Hades as a demonstration of Jesus's concern "that they not be condemned unjustly" (*Misc.* 6.6.52.2–3).[35] Clement then asked: how could Jesus have preached to both the Jews and Gentiles in Hades? He answers this question by citing the Shepherd of Hermas 3.16.49 and Matthew 27:52: even if Jesus preached only to the Jews, his apostles, who imitated him, preached to the Gentiles in Hades as well.[36] Clement reads both passages as evidence for his argument for universal salvation:

> Then a universal movement and exchange happened through the economy of the savior. One righteous man, accordingly, is no different with respect to righteousness, from another righteous man, whether he is of the law or a Greek . . . It is also clear that some who were outside of the law, by means of the peculiar nature of the soul had lived justly, even though they happened to be in Hades, and in prison when they heard the voice of the Lord (whether the authentic voice or even the voice carried through the apostles), they quickly turned and believed. (*Misc.* 6.6.44.2–3)[37]

By juxtaposing the souls who were in prison (1 Peter or 1 Enoch) with the descent of the apostles to Hades (in Hermas) and the resurrection of the dead (in Matthew), Clement constructs a story about the salvation of Jews and Gentiles alike.[38]

Clement's description of a descent to Hades in which the preaching could occur either through the "Lord" or "the apostles" melds the traditions in which Christ descends with the Shepard of Hermas, in which the apostles descend. Here, then, is evidence that for at least one early third-century author the traditions about Christ's descent were connected to or even interchangeable with traditions about the apostles' descent. Clement implies that the Redeemer actively transmits a distinctive voice readily recognized by those in Hades. The apostles not only preach the message of the Redeemer, but they transmit the very voice of Christ. Through this reading of the descent tradition, the apostles become "little Christs," imitating the redemptive activity of Christ's preaching in Hades.[39]

Despite the focus on the salvation of hell-dwellers in early Christian traditions, this motif is not the defining feature of the descent tradition for second-century authors. For Irenaeus, as for the tour of hell narratives, the descent is efficacious for both the dead and the living. By the third century, when the earliest Marian tours of hell were composed, Clement brought descent traditions together to equate the redemptive work of Christ in hell with the redemptive preaching of his apostles. In the Book of Mary's Repose, Mary is initially part of this emerging strand of thinking in which the traditions about Christ and the apostles descending are interwoven. Mary then becomes one of these distinctive voices able to speak to the damned as an imitator of Christ. Mary's voice is distinctive in its ability to speak not only to the damned, but to Christ as well, shaping the nature of her descent in unique ways.

Soteriological Significance of the Apocalyptic Seer in the Tours of Hell

Mary's descents to hell also draw on the tour of hell genre, in which the descent of the apostles can serve a redemptive function for the damned. The major difference between the descent of the Redeemer traditions and the apocalyptic tours of hell is their timing: the Redeemer descended at some point between his death and resurrection, whereas tours of hell either occur after the final judgment, or presume that the wicked are punished immediately after death.[40] As a result, the focus of salvation in the context of the apocalyptic tours is not so much on the damned, but on the living members of the tour's audience who still have time to repent and change their behavior.

Although the primary purpose of the tours of hell was to educate the living, they also contain some soteriological significance for the fate of the damned as well. The earliest instance of the seer interceding for the unrighteous is likely in 1 Enoch 12–13, in which Enoch tries, unsuccessfully, to redeem the fallen watchers.[41] In the Apocalypse of Peter, Peter cries out, saying, "It were better for them that they had not been created," a lament that occurs frequently in the tours of hell.[42] At the close of the Apocalypse of Peter the damned admit that God's judgment is "righteous and good," and resign themselves to the severity of their punishments. In the meantime the elect and righteous are transferred through baptism from the place of torment: "I will grant my called and elect ones whomsoever they request from me, out of the punishment" (Apoc. Pet. 13–14).[43] A similar scene occurs in the Apocalypse of Zephaniah 2, in which Zephaniah begs, "O God, if you remain with the saints, you certainly have compassion on behalf of the world and the souls which are in this punishment."[44] In the Apocalypse of Zephaniah 11, the patriarchs (Abraham, Isaac, and Jacob) run forward and pray to the Lord daily on behalf of those they see in torment; because the text is incomplete, the results of these prayers are unknown.

In the Marian apocalypses, the Apocalypse of Paul, and the Ezra Apocalypses, the plea for the damned becomes more effective, and the divine response is more specific. In the Book of Mary's Repose, the Savior gives the damned nine hours of rest on Sunday "because of the tears of Michael, my holy apostles, and my mother Mary" (Mary's Rep. 100).[45] In the Apocalypse of Paul, Paul's plea for mercy for the damned joins with the weeping of the angels to grant the damned Sunday as a day of rest from their torments (Apoc. Paul 43–44). Mary and Ezra gain the same weekly respite for the damned in the Ethiopic Apocalypse of Mary and the Latin Vision of Ezra.[46] In the Greek Apocalypse of Mary and the Coptic version of the Apocalypse of Paul the damned are pardoned for a period of fifty days, between Easter and Pentecost, annually.[47]

These periods of rest are only temporary, however; the damned are still in torment most of the week and year. The only text in which the sinners are permanently pardoned is the Armenian version of the Apocalypse of Paul, in which Paul's and Mary's entreaties successfully release hell's inhabitants and destroy hell.[48] This wholesale obliteration of hell could be what Augustine feared when he argued against the "compassionate Christians" in *City of God* 21.[49] Here Augustine takes on Christian opponents. These Christians believed that the damned would implore the saints to pray for them, for God "will grant them to the prayers and intercessions of his saints" (*City of God* 21.18).[50] Augustine's wording suggests that his interlocutors are familiar with this concept of saintly intercession and divine mercy from the Apocalypse of Peter 14.1 or the Book of Mary's Repose 99–101.[51] While these early Christian tours of hell were concerned with educating audiences on how they might avoid hell's torments, Augustine worried that the scenes of intercession would undermine the ability of (stories about) hell's punishments to deter the living from their sins (*City of God* 21.24).[52] In other words, for Augustine hell is only an effective educational tool if there is no way out of the torture.

Intercessory scenes, however, held special significance for the communities that preserved the Marian tours of hell. The tradition of the saint debating with God about the fate of the righteous and wicked has its roots in the apocalypse 4 Ezra.[53] And for many of the tours of hell, this dialogue about the fate of the dead, God's mercy, and divine justice is a major narrative framing technique. The apocalyptic seers advance several typical arguments against damnation, including the lament that "it is better not to be born" than to suffer this way, that everybody sins, that humans are God's creation, and that God is merciful.[54] God's responses to these arguments often include reminders that humans chose to behave in sinful ways, and that the seer is not more loving than God.[55] Typically, the divine rejoinders do not satisfy the seer, and they continue to plead for mercy. This type of dialogue is present in part in the Apocalypse of Peter and, more prominently, in the Apocalypse of Paul, Greek Apocalypse of Ezra, Latin Vision of Ezra, and Greek Apocalypse of Mary.[56]

In the Book of Mary's Repose, the earliest tour in which respite for the damned is granted, the dialogue between Mary, the apostles, and God has a slightly different tone. Here Mary and the apostles express sadness and despair upon viewing the damned, rather than consternation and doubts about divine justice. The only hint of a tension is found in the archangel Michael's dialogue with God, in which God responds to Michael's request for mercy by asking if Michael "loves them [the damned] more than the one who created them" (Mary's Rep. 94).[57] The dialogue comes after the damned have implicitly accused Michael of not interceding enough on their behalf; in his guilt, Michael asks God to "give the people rest from this torment and do not make me look at them and think that I have condemned them" (Mary's Rep. 93). God absolves Michael rather than rebuffing his request for mercy.

Mary and the apostles are not as forthright as Michael is. Rather than intercede, they fall down in shock and weep at the sight of the damned. Their tears ultimately win the damned the "little rest" that they ask Mary and the apostles to seek from Jesus on their behalf (Mary's Rep. 99).[58] To sum up, the earliest Marian tour of hell does not portray an "argument" between Mary and the Savior about justice and mercy, but simply silent, efficacious weeping.[59] God is just and merciful, and Mary and the apostles voice no complaint about divine justice but only express compassion for the damned.

It seems, then, that while the Greek Apocalypse of Mary and the Ethiopic Apocalypse of Mary may have drawn upon the apocalyptic tradition of the seer questioning the divine, the earliest Marian apocalypses did not. In these earlier apocalypses Mary's intercession shares some features of the *descensus* tradition by depicting Mary and the apostles as "little Christs"who descend to do different redemptive work in hell for a new age. Although it is not the righteous dead, but the damned who are seeking mercy, the overall focus of Mary's tour is still upon the audience, parallel to the later second- and early third-century *descensus* traditions. Ultimately, though, Mary's intercession for the damned does not line up neatly with any of the preceding traditions. Perhaps this is because Mary's intercession in these early texts is more closely tied to the practices of the audience than to any literary tradition, providing a liturgical framework for understanding Mary's role as intercessor. Marian tours of hell provide a narrative of descent and intercession that influenced the other apocalyptic tours of hell. As we will see, the unique shape of the Marian descent tradition reflects her composite characterization as the apostle who descends and the Mother of Jesus who is uniquely qualified to intercede for the damned with her Son.

Mary as the Apocalyptic Seer in the Tours of Hell

As the seer, Mary has a number of things in common with the other saints who visit hell. Her questions drive the tour forward by drawing attention to specific sins, and she listens attentively to the responses of the angelic tour guide. She responds to the entreaties of the damned and in some cases wins them respite from their suffering. Like the hell-journeys of the apostles and Christ in some early *descensus* traditions, Mary's trip to hell has soteriological significance not only for the damned, but also for the audience of the text, who might be encouraged to connect the sins and her otherworldly intercession with ethical practices and liturgical practices in this world.

Nevertheless, Mary's tours are distinguished by their narrative framing and the emphasis on her role as the Mother of Jesus. In the Book of Mary's Repose the damned cry out to Mary by a number of different names: "light and the mother of light"; "Mary, life and mother of the apostles"; "Mary, golden lamp, you who carries every righteous lamp"; "Mary our master and the mother of our Master"; and "Mary our queen" (Mary's Rep. 99).[60] These names encapsulate the multifaceted nature of Mary's identity. These multiple roles differentiate her from Peter, Paul, Ezra, and the unnamed apostles in Clement's account of the descent. Mary tours hell simultaneously as mother, apostle, and intercessor. These roles lend her both authority and accessibility.

Mary as Mother

Yet there is one respect in which Mary is both more and less relatable: in her unique position as Jesus's mother. The textual accounts of her journeys to hell include repeated references to Mary as the physical mother of Jesus (nursing him, bearing him in her womb), and to her role as the spiritual mother of all the disciples (teaching, leading, and caring for the followers of Jesus after his death). Over time, however, this composite image of Mary shifts so that her biological motherhood is no longer a focus.

Mary's role as mother in the apocalyptic tours of hell is grounded in broader ancient ideas about motherhood as well as earlier Christian ideas about her distinctive relationship to Jesus. Previous scholarship on ancient Christian mothers has compared Christian mothers to the Roman mother, or *materfamilias*, who exerted influence behind the scenes, hovering over the lives of her children, and even remaining actively involved in their adult lives.[61] On this basis, some scholars argue that early Christian martyrdom literature radically changed this image of the mother by introducing the idea of the self-sacrificing mother. Such arguments focus on elite Roman matrons, a focus that fails, however, to account for the ways in which Greek and Roman women's suffering bodies were viewed as vehicles for crafting the ideal family and city state.[62] As we saw in chapter 3, the idea of the ancient mother as a propitious sacrifice for the family and *polis* was rooted in Greek and Roman myth, and also reflected in the medical literature that described the physical suffering of childbirth as emblematic of the entirety of the female life.[63] Christians did not invent the self-sacrificing mother or the distant matron, but chose from among these diffuse ideas in any given depiction of Mary as mother.

Multiple concepts of Mary's motherhood can be seen operating side by side. Luke presents two different images: Mary's voluntary sacrifice and her commitment to act as the *doulos*, or enslaved person, of the Lord. After Mary, a virgin, is told by the angel Gabriel that the Holy Spirit will "overshadow" her so that she will bear a holy child, she responds: "Here I am the slave [*doulos*] of the Lord; let it be with me according to your word" (Luke 1:26–38). The words "let it be with me" combine Mary's willingness to take on the physical and personal sacrifice of unwed motherhood with her sense of obligation as God's slave.[64] Mary's self-description as a "slave of the Lord" can be read in light of the sexual exploitation often experienced by enslaved women. The enslaved woman's presumed sexual availability did not typically include surrogacy, but it did involve wet nursing, a role that required the enslaved woman to remain chaste in order to preserve the purity of her breast milk.

The narrative of John presents Jesus's mother only twice, at the wedding in chapter 2 and at the crucifixion in chapter 19, and never by name. At the wedding at Cana she is depicted as a very involved mother, approaching her adult son when the wine runs out with the expectation that he will resolve the problem, and then interceding to tell the servants to "do whatever he tells you" (John 2:3–5). Here Jesus's mother is depicted as a Roman matron who is actively involved in the adult lives of her children.[65] In the passion narrative, Jesus's mother witnesses the torture and death of her son. As Jesus sees the beloved disciple and his mother from the cross in John 19:26–27, "he said to his mother, 'Woman here is your son.' Then to his disciple, 'Here is your mother.' And from that hour the disciple took her into his own home." In saying this at his death, Jesus not only provides for his mother after his death, but also sets up an example of the malleable boundaries of the Christian family, merging his spiritual and biological families.[66] In John, Jesus's mother is both the hovering matron at the wedding at Cana, and the self-sacrificing mother who watches the violent death of her son, and is commissioned to care for the beloved disciple in a reconfigured family. While these narratives offer alternatives to the cultural script of biological motherhood, the Gospel of John represents the most radical reorganization of the family in which there is no birth, only the "word made flesh" (John 1:14).[67]

Many of the early Christian depictions of Mary link the physical suffering of the incarnation and God. Ancient views about childbirth might suggest that early Christians would view Mary's motherly body as a suffering body that ushers in the suffering of Jesus by delivering him in human form. But in one of the most popular early Christian reflections on Mary, the Protevangelium of James, Mary does not suffer at all. This second-century text was extraordinarily popular in antiquity, as evidenced by the more than one hundred extant Greek manuscripts.

In the Protevangelium of James, the early life of Mary and her miraculous conception and delivery of Jesus take center stage.[68] Both episodes intermingle natural and supernatural technologies of the body. Mary is told that she will not "conceive and give birth like every other woman" (Prot. Jas. 11.2–3), and she gives birth to Jesus via a great flash of light: "And immediately the cloud contracted from the cave and a great light appeared within the cave so that their eyes could not bear it. A little time afterwards the light began to contract until an infant could be seen. And he came and took the breast of his mother, Mary" (Prot. Jas. 19.2). Mary's labor is bloodless and painless, thereby ameliorating the theological problem of an inferior female body participating in the act of bringing the divine into the world. While the birth of Jesus is supernatural, the newborn Jesus is like other infants in his desire to nurse immediately, and Mary, like other mothers, is able to nourish her infant through breast milk.

Mary's characterization in the Protevangelium of James can be read as a function of her impurity as a woman.[69] Mary must leave the Temple at the onset of puberty, a point that draws attention to the onset of menarche and its problematic role within the holiness system.[70] Anna and Mary are both subject to holiness restrictions. Anna, who gives birth to Mary by conventional means, must be purified prior to nursing; Mary, who gives birth to Jesus via a flash of light, can nurse Jesus right away. By contrasting these two images, the Protevangelium of James shows that a woman's body can be the source of pure nourishment. God can work through women's bodies despite their precarious relationship with a patriarchal purity system.[71]

Of course, this does not eclipse that Mary is often the passive object of other characters' actions, nor does it obscure the fact that the Protevangelium of James is a text with theological interests in Mary's body.[72] The image of Mary nursing baby Jesus via conventional technologies of the body may recall the Lukan image of Mary as the *doulos* of the Lord—an enslaved body that is used to sustain another life. But even this image requires readers to reflect upon the complex relationship between biological *and* spiritual motherhood, and between the humanity and divinity of Jesus who is sired by the divine but born as a human with a biological need for nourishment. The unconventional mechanics of motherhood in this text are tied to ancient views of women's bodies as impure and problematic. At the same time, the conventional mechanics of the female body point the reader to ancient views of women's bodies as the locus of human suffering. Mary's female body is both an obstacle to be overcome and a necessary tool for linking the divine and the bodily suffering of the incarnation.

Similarly complex images of Mary's motherhood emerge in Marian apocalypses. In the apocalypses, Mary's pure body highlights the complexity of her spiritual and physical relationship with the child Jesus, and the struggle of early Christians to reconcile ancient understandings of holiness, family, and motherhood.[73] This struggle requires Mary to emerge as a mother who is able to perform her role through both conventional and un-conventional means. Mary's body served this important role as a bridge for early Christians in liturgy as well, in which celebrations of Mary as divine mother assert the reality of Jesus's humanity even as late as Athanasius.[74]

The texts that describe Mary's descent to hell also focus on her complex role as both biological and spiritual mother. In the Marian tours of hell Mary, like other women, has a suffering body, but she is also unique be-cause her son is unique. In the Book of Mary's Repose, which contains our earliest Marian tour of hell, Mary's role as the mother of Jesus is front and center. In the early chapters, she is simultaneously the spiritual mother who receives special knowledge and also the mother who first realizes the power of her Son as she nurses the newborn Jesus (Mary's Rep. 1–3, 5–11, 24, 40, 51, 66, 71). Mary nurses Jesus and expresses worry about where she and Joseph will find food as they are fleeing from Herod. In a demonstration of his power, the newborn Jesus stops nursing and tells Joseph to climb the date palm to collect fruit for his mother. Jesus then commands the tree to lower and raise its head so that Mary and Joseph can eat (Mary's Rep. 7). Here, as in the Protevangelium of James, there is a blending of the supernatural and the natural. The scene begins and ends with the very real bodily hunger of the holy family, and the natural means through which their hunger is sated (breast milk and dates). In the first scene Mary is providing nourish-ment for her son through conventional technologies of the body, and, in the next, Jesus is providing physical and spiritual nourishment for his parents by lowering and raising the date palm (Mary's Rep. 7–11).[75] This reversal of the parent-child relationship reconfigures the Christian family by suggest-ing that spiritual kinship takes precedence over biological relationship (cf. Mark 3:32–34).[76]

Later in the text, as Mary and the apostles tour hell, Mary's mother-hood remains a major theme. When the archangel Michael asks Jesus to have mercy on the damned, Jesus's response indirectly refers to the maternal body of Mary: "Do you love them more than the one who created them, or will you be more merciful to them than the one who gave them breath? And before you asked on their behalf Michael, I did not spare my blood, but I gave it for their sake. O Michael, was there not one who remained in pain, having abandoned the pleasure of Jerusalem? I was conceived of the womb for their sake, to give them rest, and I wept before my Father" (Mary's Rep. 94). This speech takes Jesus's conception and birth as aspects of his sacrifice for the damned; by taking on human form, Jesus "remained in pain." This indirect reference to Mary depicts her womb as an instrument of Jesus's own torture.[77] This jarring image is right at home in a culture that sees the female body during childbirth as an instrument of propitious sacrifice with the potential to bring both life and death.

Throughout the Book of Mary's Repose, the early Christian reconfiguration of family exists alongside notions of biological family. Mary is called sister, mother, and mother of the twelve, and she reminds the apostle John of the Johannine scene in which Jesus places her in a reconfigured family with the beloved disciple (Mary's Rep. 42–43, 45, 51 [cf. John 19:26–27]). Here Mary explicitly identifies John as the beloved disciple. She scolds him by reminding him that as her family member, it is his responsibility to make provisions for her burial.[78]

After Mary's death, Mary and the apostles tour hell as a reconfigured family, sharing this kinship bond with Jesus, interceding together, and ultimately winning a respite for the damned because of their proximate relationships to Jesus. Jesus says that it is "because of the tears of Michael, my holy apostles, and my mother Mary, because they have come and they have seen you," that the damned win nine hours of rest (Mary's Rep. 100). Jesus refers to "my" apostles and to Mary as his own mother, drawing attention to these relationships as the basis for the pardon. This emphasis on Mary *and* the apostles sharing a close relationship with Jesus is not familial language, but together with the text's overall focus on the familial relationships between Mary and the disciples, Mary's tour of hell reads like a reconfigured family trip. This image moves her characterization as mother well beyond biological motherhood.

In the Six Books Apocryphon and the other Marian tours of hell, the focus on motherhood is closely connected to the theme of Mary's intercession. In these texts Mary is addressed through formal titles for her unique maternal role: "my Lady Mary his mother" (6 Bks. Apoc. book 6), "All Holy Mother of God" (Gk. Apoc. Mary 1), and "God Bearer" (Eth. Apoc. Mary).[79] Whereas in the Book of Mary's Repose, Jesus directs the intercession of Michael, Mary, and the apostles, Mary is an active agent of intercession in all her other tours of hell. In these scenes of intercession, however, Mary's role as mother is no longer the primary basis for her success as intercessor. Instead, the focus shifts to the power of calling Mary by name or seeing Mary, themes that were also present in the Book of Mary's Repose.

In the Six Books Apocryphon, Jesus calls Mary "My Lady Mary," and Mary addresses Jesus as "Messiah" and "Lord Rabbūlī." At the end of the

text, Jesus notes her identity as a mother in his response to her intercession, but he pronounces her blessed not because she is his mother but because of what she has seen: "And our Lord Jesus said to my Lady Mary his
mother: 'Blessed art thou, Mary, because of what thine eyes have seen, and
what thou art about to see; because afflictions shall abound unto men, and
those who call on thy name shall be delivered from destruction.'"[80] Mary's
intercessions are efficacious because of the power of her name. Even in this
relatively early Marian tour of hell, the emphasis is shifting from Mary's
roles as *both* biological *and* spiritual mother to her intercessory power as
saint and spiritual mother.

The Greek Apocalypse of Mary and Ethiopic Apocalypse of Mary
codify this trend by widening the gap between Mary and other mothers. In
the Greek Apocalypse of Mary, Mary exclaims at the sight of the damned
that it "was better not to have been born."[81] This exclamation is a traditional
expression uttered by some male saints who tour hell. It is not until the
Greek Apocalypse of Mary, however, that Jesus's mother herself utters these
words that recall the cultural identification of the womb as the beginning of
human suffering as well as the dangers of childbirth (Gk. Apoc. Mary 11).[82]
Like the Book of Mary's Repose, in the Greek Apocalypse of Mary Jesus
includes being "born of Mary, the holy undefiled Mother of God" in the
suffering he has endured for the sake of sinners (Gk. Apoc. Mary 29). The
end of the Ethiopic Apocalypse of Mary contains an even blunter rejection of biological mothers; pregnant women would defile this sacred book
should they come near it.[83] Even the *Theotokos* cannot offset the horrors of
becoming incarnate.

At the same time as these texts distance themselves from biological
motherhood, they also, paradoxically, lay claim to the power that Mary
possesses precisely because of her role as "all-holy Mother of God." Although the evidence for Marian devotion predates the Council of Ephesus
of 431, the rhetorical and theological force of the title *Theotokos* is inextricably linked to the Christological controversies of the fifth century. Roughly
one hundred years after the Nicene Council of 331 affirmed that Christ
was "of the same substance" (*homoousios*) with God, another early Christian movement, Nestorianism, prompted further debates about the nature
of Christ. Nestorius and his followers still held that Christ was both human and divine, but they emphasized that the human and divine natures of
Christ were separate. As part of this argument about the nature of Christ,
Nestorius also rejected the popular title *Theotokos* for Mary, in favor of the

title *Christotokos* (Christ-bearer), on the grounds that this latter title separated the divine and human natures of Christ at the critical moment of the incarnation. In 430, as this controversy had reached a fever pitch, Proclus of Constantinople gave a now-famous sermon, attended by Nestorius and his main supporters, that defended Marian piety against their perceived attacks. This sermon established the "rhetoric and rationale for the cult of the Virgin Mary," formalizing what was already an annual feast.[84] In 431, at the ecumenical council at Ephesus, after extensive debate and political work, Nestorianism was condemned as a heresy and the title *Theotokos* was authorized for use by the entire church. After the Council of Ephesus, the title is associated not only with the feast and veneration of Mary, but with the theological and political weight it bore in the ecumenical council.

As we have already seen, the Marian apocalypses pair these Christological claims with attentiveness to a wide range of images that encompass biological, adoptive, and spiritual motherhood. Both the Greek Apocalypse of Mary and the Ethiopic Apocalypse of Mary emphasize the special nature of Mary's intercession and the Marian devotional practices that exalt her unique role as Mother of God. The Greek Apocalypse of Mary opens with a request from the "all holy Mother of God" to see the punishment. Mary's special interest in the damned is unique; it is not part of the two earlier Marian tours. In the Greek Apocalypse of Mary 23–25, Mary's interest leads her into a dialogue with the commander in chief that allows her to plead for mercy for the Christian sinners. Throughout this conversation the references to Mary as the "Mother of God" and Jesus as the "Son of God" remind the audience of her unique identity. The title *Theotokos* is theologically weighted language that makes Christologically consequential claims about Mary's status; at the same time it casts Mary's relationship to divine power in maternal terms. The Ethiopic Apocalypse of Mary stresses the mother-son relationship even more firmly. Here Jesus is Mary's tour guide, and she addresses him throughout as "my Son."

Both the Greek Apocalypse of Mary and the Ethiopic Apocalypse of Mary connect the mother's tears to the mercy that her prayers effect for the damned (Gk. Apoc. Mary 29 [Oxford ms]).[85] Mary's intercession is efficacious because Mary is the "Mother of God." Both texts make links to Marian devotional practices. In the paradise of the Ethiopic Apocalypse of Mary the male saints recite a formula blessing when they see Mary, saying, "Blessed art thou Mary and blessed is the fruit of thy womb, and blessed are the eyes that see you."[86] Both the Greek Apocalypse of Mary and the

Ethiopic Apocalypse of Mary promise that those who call upon Mary will not be forsaken (Gk. Apoc. Mary 26).[87] The Ethiopic Apocalypse of Mary lists several Marian activities that will merit mercy "to the twelfth generation": celebrating Mary's commemoration; building a shrine to Mary; writing the history of Mary's words. The text concludes with a prayer to Mary that models the practices it describes.[88]

In each of these apocalyptic tours of hell, Mary as mother is a bridge that connects the bodily suffering of human existence with the divine. Later texts, however, downplay her bodily experience of motherhood and distinguish her maternal role from biological motherhood. This distinction enabled devotees to focus on her access to the divine and intercessory power, while also distancing her from the impurity and suffering associated with the female body. This move was more pronounced in Latin Christianity;[89] because Eastern Christianity did not have a doctrinal focus on original sin, Eastern authors did not have to solve the "problem" of Mary's purity. For them, she simply is pure.[90] Even the Ethiopic Apocalypse of Mary, which is based upon the Apocalypse of Paul, demonstrates this Western Christian preoccupation with the impurity of the female body in the admonition about preventing menstruating and pregnant women from touching the text. By contrast, Eastern Christian texts like the Book of Mary's Repose focus on Mary's spiritual motherhood for Christological reasons: to secure her distinctive role as spiritual mother so that she can perform her unique roles as "Master" and "Mother of our Master." For Eastern Christian traditions, Mary's role as mother is not inherently biological, but spiritual, inviting women and men to follow Mary's example regardless of their bodily relationship to the cultural norms of motherhood.

Mary as Apostle and Spiritual Mother

Richard Bauckham has noted that the apocalyptic seers in early Christian tours of hell are all "exemplary figures in Jewish and Christian piety."[91] Mary certainly fits this characterization, and she has the added distinction of being the first woman to fill the role of apocalyptic seer in hell (to be followed much later by Anastasia in the Byzantine Apocalypse of Anastasia).[92] The other prominent seers—Peter, Paul, and Ezra—are male apostles or saints; in the *descensus* tradition, it is typically either Christ or the male apostles who descend. For audiences familiar with the apocalyptic and *descensus* traditions, Mary's presence as seer may have suggested that she was also an apostle.

This portrait of Mary as a follower of Jesus, and a teacher and leader of other disciples, is not directly based on the New Testament. To be sure, as Beverly Roberts Gaventa argued, Luke may consider Mary to be "first and foremost a disciple of Jesus," because she hears the word of God and does it, fulfilling Jesus's criterion for discipleship in Luke 8:21.[93] Mary's response, "be it done to me according to your word," in Luke 1:38 is the primary basis for this claim. Mary's desire to share this news with Elizabeth and to sing it out to the lowly and hungry can also be read as Mary fulfilling her commission as disciple by sharing the Gospel.[94] Other New Testament portrayals of Mary, however, do not have this motif. In the Gospel of John, Jesus's mother is present for Jesus's first miracle (John 2), and she witnesses the crucifixion alongside the beloved disciple (John 19). A faint hint of her future role comes in John 2:1–11, in which she "intercedes" with Jesus on behalf of the parched wedding party. She does not travel with the apostles, teach others, or perform miracles as she does in other, later texts. In Acts, Mary is present at Pentecost (Acts 1:14).

The New Testament traditions about Mary, however, become foundational for later traditions that see her role in the incarnation as a model of discipleship for Christians.[95] In the early Syriac baptismal liturgy that developed around Luke 1:35, "the incarnation . . . doubled as Mary's baptism."[96] Ephrem's Hymns states that Mary was baptized and made holy through the presence of Jesus in her womb, just as the Jordan River was sanctified through his baptism there.[97] Through the sanctifying presence of Jesus in her womb, Mary is both sister to Christ and to all Christians, and the bride of Christ "along with all chaste souls."[98] These traditions locate salvation in the incarnation by focusing on the birth of Jesus rather than on the cross. Michael Peppard's work on the baptistery at Dura-Europos has shown that the Eastern Christian emphasis on the incarnation as salvific is the key to unlocking the significance of the Marian imagery at this ancient church.[99] In this space during the baptismal liturgy Mary invites the initiates to participate in what Peppard calls "birth mysticism," so that they can, like Mary, become impregnated with Christ.[100] Mary becomes the exemplar for all Christians, as the contact point between the human and God, and her pregnancy with Christ is reenacted as Christians have Christ dwell in their bodies through baptism.

Mary is not only mother, but also sister and bride. As the holy virgin bride Mary is a model for chastity that guides the ascetic practices of Syrian monks.[101] Both Western and Eastern Christians viewed Mary as a model for asceticism, as she shaped the exhortations on virginity and monastic living in the works of Alexander of Alexandria, Athanasius, the Cappadocian fathers, Ambrose, and Jerome.[102] The controversies over Mary's virginity in the later fourth century were tied at least in part to the broader concerns about the growth of Christian asceticism and its place within the church.[103] For instance, Athanasius in his *First Letter to the Virgins*, aimed at winning back female ascetic adherents to Arianism, exhorts virgins to pay close attention to Mary's behavior and character traits so that they can live out her ascetic example.[104] Similarly, the arguments made by Ambrose and Jerome about the superiority of asceticism over Christian marriage point to Mary as the model for female ascetics.[105]

Marian devotion was not limited to female asceticism, but had a place in the Roman household as well.[106] An anonymous letter from fourth-century Spain exalts Mary's suffering during childbirth (an uncommon idea by this point) as an ideal to be imitated by married women, who should occasionally abstain from sex and spend time at a monastery.[107] By the fourth century, then, Mary was an exemplar for monastics, for female virgins, for ascetic practices within a marriage, and, indeed, for all Christians.[108]

In the apocalyptic tours of hell, Mary often accompanies, leads, and teaches the other apostles; she is also set apart from the twelve as the "Mother of the Light" and the "all-holy Mother of God." Mary is depicted in the Book of Mary's Repose as a particularly wise disciple who teaches the male disciples from her "profound knowledge of the cosmic mysteries," and leads them in worship.[109] She is the recipient of secret knowledge revealed by a "Great Angel"—in fact, her son Jesus—on the Mount of Olives, and she mediates that esoteric knowledge to the apostles (Mary's Rep. 1–3, 13–15).

Near the end of the Book of Mary's Repose, Mary's death is the occasion for the tour of hell. Here, in contrast to later Marian tours of hell, it is the apostles and not Mary who initiate the tour. Initially Mary and the apostles respond similarly upon viewing the damned—by collapsing with distress (Mary's Rep. 90). As the tour progresses, however, the apostles recede into the background as Mary takes center stage (Mary's Rep. 95–98). The damned who beg for mercy address Mary first, through a series of titles such as "life and mother of the apostles" and "golden lamp." Only then do they address Peter, Andrew, and John, who "have become apostles" and "have been appointed as priests over the cities."

In the Book of Mary's Repose, Mary sometimes works alongside the apostles, but she is also in a unique relationship with them. This special relationship is also a major feature of the Six Books Apocryphon, in which Mary's imminent death becomes the occasion for all of the apostles (even those who are dead!) to reunite and greet her.[110] Here Mary is a teacher and example for the apostles and an ascetic model for a retinue of virgins who have left behind their families and everything they have to follow her.[111] In the scenes leading up to her death, Mary prays in the orans pose, and the apostles immediately follow her example.[112] Her prayer proclaims that the one who was born to her is ruler of heaven and earth. At her death, however, as on her tour of hell, she relates to Jesus as "my Lord Teacher." This title places her in the role of a disciple and apostle able to call other disciples and lead worship.[113]

Yet in both the Six Books Apocryphon and the Ethiopic Apocalypse, Mary's primary role is not as disciple but as intercessor for the living and the dead. The central driving plot line of the Six Books Apocryphon focuses on the throngs who come to Mary during her last days to seek healing. She is promised here and after her death that all who call on her name and commemorate her will be saved.[114] In the Ethiopic Apocalypse of Mary, Mary is an ascetic model for her followers, who proclaim, "You have wearied yourself by every kind of denial, Mary."[115] Although she learns from Jesus on her tour, their interactions are not those of disciple and teacher, but of mother and son. Her intercession for the damned is a function of this special relationship.

In the Greek Apocalypse of Mary, Mary is not primarily a model of asceticism or the teacher of esoteric knowledge, but the all-holy Mother of God. This depiction reinforces theological orthodoxy. After being told that all who call upon her name will be saved, Mary asks about Moses, Paul, the power of the cross, and Michael. Moses, Paul, Michael, and also John then respond in turn. Each one asks that the Lord have mercy on the damned to whom they have each preached. In response to the lament of the saints and apostles that is led by Mary, God promises the damned that they will be judged "according to the law which Moses gave, and according to the Gospel which John gave, and according to the epistles which Paul carried" (Gk. Apoc. Mary 27). Here Mary is depicted not only as a teacher, but as one who leads Moses, John, and Paul, whose teachings form the criteria for eternal judgment. In short, Mary is the merciful teacher who leads the other teachers to join in her intercessory prayers.

In this apocalypse, which was very popular in the East, Mary's teaching and intercessory roles resemble those of the Byzantine deaconesses; she also becomes the powerful intercessor and protectress of Constantinople who intercedes for both women and men.[116] Unlike the apostles, Mary stands alone as the all-holy Mother of God. Although she is beyond comparison with other saints, she is led on an apocalyptic tour of hell, during which she, like the male saints, asks questions and begs for mercy on behalf of the damned. It is difficult, then, to tease her discipleship and teaching out from her roles as mother and intercessor. Her teaching and devotion to Jesus are always cast in light of the incarnation and her special role as *Theotokos*. Mary is the disciple and teacher par excellence because of her unique access to both the divine and human suffering.

Mary as Intercessor, Redeemer, or Co-sufferer

In some ways, Mary's intercession in the apocalyptic tours follows the pattern of intercessory dialogue associated with male apostles and saints. She is unique, however, in her ability to intercede with her son on behalf of sinners. The earliest patristic evidence for Mary's intercession is in an oration of Gregory of Nazianzus from 379. Gregory tells a strange story to commemorate the feast of Cyprian of Antioch.[117] According to the story, Cyprian, who was a magician prior to becoming a Christian, attempted to rape Justina, a beautiful Christian virgin. Justina cried out to Christ and prayed to Mary for help, and took "refuge in a regimen of fasting and sleeping on the ground."[118] Her prayers are successful, and in recognition Cyprian becomes a Christian. Because Gregory included this story of Marian intercession into his oration for Cyprian without comment, it seems likely that by the end of the fourth century prayers to Mary were common practice in Gregory's Cappadocian community. This point is corroborated by the witnesses of Gregory of Nyssa and Sozomen, who describe other types of Marian devotion, particularly tied to apparitions of Mary.[119]

In addition to the Cappadocian evidence for early Marian devotion prior to the Council of Ephesus, Severian of Gabala, a contemporary of John Chrysostom, refers to Marian intercession in his early fifth-century homilies. Severian links Mary's intercessory abilities to the belief in her Assumption: "Of course she hears our prayers, the mother of salvation and the source of light, because she is in the glorious place and the land of the living."[120] Mary is able to intercede for others precisely because she dwells in paradise. This connection may explain the prevalence of the intercessory themes in the Dormition narratives and the Marian tours of hell that are embedded in them.[121]

In another sermon Severian uses the language of spiritual warfare to depict Mary: "The enemy, armed to the teeth, thought that the woman was worthy of derision, but he found her to be a valiant general. He did not think that he would be placed in the tomb, but he found the grave. He thought that she was dead, but was put to death by her."[122] The language here mirrors the "fishhook" metaphor employed in descriptions of Jesus's death as cosmic victory over Satan. Severian presumed that his Antiochine audience understood that Mary's intercession was effective because of her multiple roles. She is the "mother of salvation" ensconced in heaven, and the warrior who is able to kill Satan because he underestimates the battle tactics of a woman. Mary not only intervenes for sinners but also succeeds in vanquishing Satan. This idea is recapitulated in the Eastern Christian traditions about the descent to hell in which hell is overcome entirely.

By the medieval period, Mary's unique role as Jesus's mother means that Jesus cannot refuse her.[123] The effectiveness of Mary's intercession reflects broader cultural ideas about filial piety in which a son is expected to show devotion and deference to his mother.[124] In the Marian tours of hell, Mary's intercession for the damned is very closely tied to her unique position as both mother and disciple, diverging from the ways that male apostles and saints intercede in the other tours of hell. As we have noted before, the intercession of the apostolic seer in the other early Christian apocalypses is initiated by the apostle, who engages in a dialogue with God about why the damned deserve mercy. But in the earliest Marian tour of hell, the Book of Mary's Repose, the intercession of Mary and the apostles is initiated not by Mary or the apostles, but by Jesus, who establishes the opportunity for Mary and the apostles to intercede for the damned: "And when Jesus had said this, he gave them a way by which they could arise from the torment. And the Saviour looked at Michael, and he separated himself from them, and he left Mary and the apostles, so that they would understand them. Then those who were in the torments cried out and said, 'Mary, we beseech you, Mary, light and the mother of light; Mary, life and mother of the apostles; Mary, golden lamp, you who carries every righteous lamp; Mary, our master and the mother of our Master; Mary our queen, beseech your son to give us a little rest.' And others spoke thus: 'Peter, Andrew, and John, who have become apostles'" (Mary's Rep. 99).[125] In this tour of hell, Jesus authorizes the intercession for the damned, giving them "a way by which they could arise from the torment" by leaving them alone with Mary and the apostles. And although the damned beseech Mary as they do the apostolic seer in other tours of hell, their entreaties to her are much more elaborate and specific than their demands of the apostles, whom they simply call by name.

Mary's intercession for the damned is particularly efficacious because of her relationship to Jesus and the titles that refer to that relationship. In the Book of Mary's Repose Jesus tells the damned: "Because of the tears of Michael, my holy apostles, and my mother Mary, because they have come and they have seen you, I have given you nine hours of rest on the Lord's day" (Mary's Rep. 101).[126] Here, Mary and the apostles win a more specific respite for the damned than the Apocalypse of Peter's general statement that the elect and righteous will be saved (entering not heaven but the Elysian fields; Apoc. Pet. 13–14).[127] And in both the Book of Mary's Repose and the Greek Apocalypse of Mary, Jesus himself specifies that it is because of his mother's tears that the damned are awarded a period of rest, emphasizing the effectiveness of a mother's lament upon her son (Mary's Rep. 90, 100; Gk. Apoc. Mary 29 [Oxford ms], 34 [Vatican ms]). All the Marian tours of hell emphasize this connection between Mary's intercession and her unique relationship. This emphasis distinguishes them from the other tours of hell. Whereas the seers in other apocalyptic tours of hell are guided by mediating angels, Mary's tour guide is Jesus, highlighting the special access she has to her son.[128]

In the Six Books Apocryphon, Mary's post-Assumption intercession for the damned is made possible by her role not only as mother of Jesus, but also as an imitator of Jesus in life and in death. In the events leading up to Mary's Assumption, the story follows the structure of the Passion narrative to depict Mary as imitating Christ. She heals the numberless crowds who come to her, "creating a great uproar" that angers priests who go to the praetorium and complain about Mary, and then go to her house with fire and wood.[129] And in a story that is reminiscent of the healing of the centurion's servant (Matt 8:5–13), the hegemon comes to Mary, worships her, and asks her to heal his son, which she does.[130] In the Six Books Apocryphon, Mary's intercession is not only a function of her close relationship to Jesus and her Assumption into heaven, but is also connected to her imitation of Christ, paralleling the intercessory activity of the *descensus* tradition.

In the Greek Apocalypse of Mary, Mary not only begs for mercy for the damned, but also asks to suffer *with* the damned herself. When she encounters a man hung up by his tongue, for instance, Mary says the *Kyrie Eleïson* in his stead, as he is not able to cry out for mercy for himself (Gk. Apoc. Mary 15).

Also in the Greek Apocalypse of Mary, intercession couched in a female body looks very different from the intercession of Paul or Ezra:[131]

> And I, Paul, sighed and said: "Lord God, have mercy on what you have made, have mercy on the children of men, have mercy on your own image." (Apoc. Paul 43)
>
> And Ezra said, "Have pity upon the works of your hands, merciful and greatly pitying one. Condemn me rather than the souls of the sinners, for it is better to punish one soul and not to bring the whole world to destruction." (Gk. Apoc. Ez. 1.11)
>
> And she stretched forth her hands to the undefiled throne of the Father and said: "Have mercy, O Master, on the Christian sinners, for I saw them being punished and I cannot bear their lamentation. May I go forth, and may I myself be punished with the Christian sinners!" (Gk. Apoc. Mary 26 [Oxford manuscript])
>
> And she stretched forth her immaculate hands to the immaculate throne of the Father and said with a great voice, "Holy Trinity, Father, Son, and Holy Spirit, God, the invisible Lord who loves humankind, compassionate master, have mercy on the sinners, for I have seen, Lord, their great afflictions and punishments, and I cannot bear their pain. Command your servant, Master, that I will also be punished with the Christians." (Gk. Apoc. Mary 26 [29] [Vatican manuscript])

Paul and Ezra's requests for mercy follow the apocalyptic literary trope of philosophical and theological debate between the seer and God. Their testimony is delivered in a divine courtroom, a setting that draws upon and also magnifies the judicial fears of the earthly courtroom.[132] Paul reminds God that the damned are made in his own image, whereas Ezra's request recalls the Johannine framing of Jesus's atoning sacrifice.[133] Mary intercedes, not by offering an extended philosophical argument or a theological proposition of substitutionary atonement, but through her willingness to suffer alongside the damned. It is this empathetic suffering that she asks God to alleviate.

Unlike the philosophical and theological pleas of her male counterparts, the bodily compassion exhibited by the suffering mother of Jesus is not limited to the otherworld, but is directly connected to early Marian practices. In the Six Books Apocryphon, the Greek Apocalypse of Mary, and the Ethiopic Apocalypse of Mary, Mary's intercession in hell is linked to the living practice of calling upon the name of Mary or commemorating her.[134] In the Six Books Apocryphon Peter commands the apostles to teach that there should be a commemoration of Mary three times a year so that "everyone who commemorates her be remembered in heaven."[135] An even more specific set of practices is laid out at the end of the Ethiopic Apocalypse of Mary, where Mary herself commands John to instruct the people to celebrate her commemoration on four specific days, and monthly if possible.[136] When Mary asks the archangel Michael for mercy for the sinners in the Greek Apocalypse of Mary, the Lord intervenes, responding, "Hearken all holy Mother of God, if anyone names and calls upon thy name, I will not forsake him, either in heaven or on earth."[137] Here Mary's name, like her son's, offers earthly followers access to the otherworld.

Mary's intercessory work in these tours of hell may seem unremarkable insofar as it conforms to the conventions of the apocalyptic genre; in apocalyptic tours it is common for a saint to request mercy and for the damned to be granted a short respite. Mary's unique identity as both mother and disciple, however, differentiates her from the other apostles who tour hell's landscape.[138] The weight that Mary's appeal carries reflects the broader cultural norms of filial piety in which a good son exhibits devotion to his mother and obedience to her requests. Mary can appeal directly to her son, not as an apostle arguing with a divine Judge, but as his mother.

Conclusion

As intercessor for the damned, Mary's role draws on and reflects ancient ideas about the tortured female body. By depicting Mary simultaneously as mother, teacher, and intercessor, ancient Christian tours of hell subvert and reenact ancient expectations of the female body. The intercessory work that she accomplishes in hell rescues all who call upon her name. In this way, the Marian tours of hell retain the features of the apocalyptic tour, but they function like the *descensus* narratives. This fusion helps to explain the popularity of these Marian texts in the Christian East, in which the *descensus* tradition was thought to abrogate the concept of eternal punishment entirely.[139]

As we have seen, the Marian tours of hell portray the all-holy Mother of God as a seer who accomplishes the work of the descending Redeemer and apostles by securing mercy for the damned and teaching the living about how they ought to live. Mary is the first female apocalyptic seer and the first woman to descend to hell to rescue the damned, subverting the genre expectations and ancient gender expectations at the same time. Her questions, her teaching, her leadership of the other apostles, and the example she sets for asceticism depict her as an *alter Christus* in hell.

At the same time as the Marian tours subvert the ancient expectations of divine justice and male exemplars, their Mary reenacts the ancient
gender norms of a maternal female body who influences her children and
suffers propitiously for them and for the *polis*. As we have seen, Mary's intercession for the damned in the tours of hell is intimately bound up with
her unique position as the mother of Jesus. Mary's entreaties are not in the
form of a theological argument with the divine, in the tradition of the Ezra
apocalypses. Rather, they are the cries of a mother to her son, and they are
efficacious for the damned who call upon her name as the all-holy Mother
of God. When she offers to suffer along with the damned, she embodies
the ancient topos of the maternal body in pain (Gk. Apoc. Mary 25–26).
This focus intensifies and expands the concept of the mother's body in pain
as a propitious bodily sacrifice. Mary acts on behalf of her numerous spiritual children in the reconfigured Christian family.

Conclusion: Making Hell on Earth

By the fifth century, the Theodosian Code brought the hellscapes of the early Christian apocalypses to earth. In this Christian compilation of Roman law, a nurse who mishandles her charge has molten lead poured down her throat, and the passive partner in a homoerotic coupling suffers burning by "avenging flames," amputation of his hands and feet, and glossectomy (surgical removal of the tongue).[1] In these punishments, as in the early Christian apocalypses, the effeminate and disabled body is on display as the sign of moral, social, and spiritual failing. Through Christian laws, hell's womb birthed her inhabitants and their promise of bodily compromise is returned to earth.

The damned body was not simply a mirror for ancient ideas about the body or retributive logic. Rather, the body in early Christian visions of hell *both* reflects *and* constructs lived reality. The permeable barrier between this life and the afterlife allows these images—of tormented and deviant bodies—to act as both mirror and blueprint; hell's punishments for evil also construct evil. The body that threatens in hell becomes the threatening body on earth.

This give and take between the damned body and the punished body on earth belongs to early Christian discourses of bodily suffering that have until now been in the background of scholarly investigations into the roots of subjectivity in early Christian thought. For early Christians, however, the suffering object was an integral part of their cultural milieu and their moral universe. Female bodies were "assigned to suffering," and thereby generated gendered discourses that included suffering as weakness, pain, strength, and propitious sacrifice. As we saw in chapter 1, early Christians drew on this gendered language of bodily suffering to describe the extraordinary bodies in hell. Hell's punitive landscape in turn reified those bodily norms and associated the female, deformed, dysfunctional body with sin and punishment.

This is one of the chief ways "the dead create and recreate social hierarchy."[2] In early Christian hell, the dead inhabit a heterotopia in which their mutilated and dysfunctional flesh is on display in order to evoke fear and disgust in the audience. This heterotopia in turn exoticized the deviant body, leveraging ancient anxieties about bodily weakness to contain sin. As we saw in chapter 3, through the torment of the damned in hell, the effeminate dysfunctional body becomes the artifact of sin. In this way, the womanly, weak bodies that are punished in hell become a way not just to put off sin, but also to distance themselves from the ways in which their own bodies already were or inevitability would become deformed or dysfunctional in some way. In ancient societies in which only a minority of the population could attain the normative body, the violent spectacle of hell reinforced a social hierarchy by demarcating the banal as the grotesque.

This marks a fundamental difference between the impaired body in antiquity and the way that disability studies theory has thought about the disabled body in modernity. Whereas the disabled body often operates at the "margins" of the story in modernity, in a spectacle that works as a kind of sideshow, in the ancient punitive context of hell the spectacle of bodily deviance is the whole show.[3] Because of the punitive focus of this literature, and the prevalence of nonnormative bodies in the cultural milieu, female bodies and deformed bodies are not ancillary to the tours of hell, but at their center. Nevertheless this concerted attention to the nonnormative body does not garner subject status for these bodies. Instead, the nonnormative body is a tool in a punitive schema so comprehensive that it objectifies not only the female and disabled bodies of the damned, but the bodies of the viewers themselves. So while much of disability studies has focused on the Enlightenment or the modern medical gaze as the points of origin for the disciplinary regime and bodily normativity, our study of early Christian hell indicates that these ideas had much deeper roots.

For the audiences of these visions of hell, the effeminate, weak, leaky bodies of the damned represent the persistent threat to the social ideals of self-control. In chapter 2 we saw that moral and social order were depicted through two intersecting models that both emphasized bodily self-control: household hierarchy and the church officeholder's holiness. In the later apocalypses, these two models are fused, and define sin increasingly as a failure to embody particular gender and social norms. This development is most noticeable in the way that women, and women alone, are culpable for sins pertaining to parenthood.

Hell used the deviant bodies of the damned to reveal their true nature. The blind, speechless, or out-of-control bodies of those who have committed a wide range of sins intensify and codify the view that a nonnormative body was a punishment for sin. Their bodies do not simply reflect past sin; rather, the deviant body is itself the artifact of sin. Through the discourses of damnation, the immanent realities of bodily deviance are made more frightening, intensifying the desire to externalize and exoticize the disabled body as "other."

At the same time, the depictions of the damned draw on multivalent cultural discourses about the body. In chapter 3, we saw that the effeminate tears of the damned could exist beside the purgative and propitious tears of the saints. In chapter 4 we explored the ways that Mary's bold plea to suffer with the damned simultaneously draws upon the notions of the propitious suffering of the maternal body and the traditions of male apostles or saints descending to do soteriological work in hell. Even as Mary as *alter Christus* shifts the discourse of the female body in hell from passive to active, from suffering to salvation, her bodily presence in hell is used to reinforce the cultural fetishizing of the maternal body in pain. "Assigned to suffering" even follows the *Theotokos* to hell.

Paradoxically, the early Christian apocalypses set out to exhort readers to care for the strangers in their midst by demonizing and othering a wide range of bodies. In the apocalyptic visions of hell, and the discursive framework of punitive suffering that they bolstered throughout the church, the "suffering self" could quickly shift back from subject to object. The extraordinary body in hell is labeled, policed, contained, and punished. In turn, the effeminate, deviant body on earth is simultaneously othered and instrumentalized. As both punitive object and tool, female bodies and impaired bodies reenacted and intensified the boundaries and stakes of bodily normativity. Hell's filthy, treacherous womb reveals *and* constructs not only the hidden moral truths of her inhabitants, but the social realities of the worlds that her spectators inhabited.

Epilogue: Ancient Christian Hell's Afterlives

Discourses of Damnation

In ancient Christian depictions of hell the body became a way to write out a system of justice. We like to imagine that this gendered, violent scheme of justice is far removed from our world by time, space, Enlightenment reason, liberalism, and advances in human rights. But hell is not a distant heterotopia. The sediment of hell's logic is much nearer, present in the ways that we conceive social responsibilities, justice, and bodies.

Indeed, we fool ourselves if we imagine that the medieval hell of the Latin Vision of Ezra, in which women, and women alone, are accountable for parenting, is some far-off, "primitive" vision of a social world utterly unlike our own. In our own day, female bodies are condemned for having abortions, while male bodies are not, and women are criticized for dressing "provocatively," while male sexual violence is normalized.[1]

We might shudder at the violence of the breast-milk beasts that hunt the women who abandoned or refused to nurse their children. In the United States, we have structured our own society so that new mothers must often return to work just weeks after they have given birth. At the same time, mothers also face social and medical pressure to nurse their children, which is at turns lovely and physically taxing even when breast-feeding is going well for both mother and child. The pressure to breastfeed has become so great that some women feel they should do so even in situations where it is painful for the mother, or physically dangerous for the baby.[2] Hidden in this same landscape are the women who experience miscarriage, stillbirth, or fertility challenges, or who choose not to be mothers and are silenced or cut off from their social networks and faith communities as a result.[3]

We don't need to imagine the breast-milk beasts anymore because they frolic in our midst, tormenting women's bodies. In South Carolina, Regina McKnight was sentenced to twelve years in prison because her baby was stillborn and she tested positive for cocaine use during pregnancy. Even though no evidence links cocaine use and stillbirths, and the Supreme Court ruled that South Carolina had violated Fourth Amendment protections against unwarranted searches, the state still convicted Regina McKnight of murder.[4] The breast-milk beasts are not the distant threat of a faraway place. In at least some U.S. contexts, the pregnant, nursing body is both idealized and penalized. In the following discussion, I do not want to reinscribe the colonial project by arbitrarily adducing examples of this logic from other parts of the world, much less other religions. As a white, temporarily able-bodied woman who resides in the United States, I will focus on examples from the United States, acknowledging that the discourses of gender and disability vary across contexts.

The Punitive Body and Bodily Normativity

Early Christian hells invite us to scrutinize the ways that we think about the carceral body and justice today. We might reject the idea that a woman is assigned to suffering, destined to be passive. But one does not have to look far to find examples of a cultural fixation with female bodies suffering.

The Netflix original series *Orange Is the New Black* offers audiences a tour of a modern-day women's prison, seen through the eyes of an affluent white inmate, Piper Kerman. Based upon the memoir detailing the real-life incarceration of Kerman, who was convicted of money laundering, this show not only details the day-to-day realities of a women's prison, but tells the individual stories of the women who were punished alongside Kerman. In this way *Orange Is the New Black* functions as a kind of modern-day "tour of hell" that offers viewers the opportunity to watch the punitive spectacle from the comfort of their own homes. The show highlights the violence and injustices of mass incarceration in the United States, including racial violence and the ills of for-profit prisons. In a culture that supports a multi-billion-dollar prison industrial complex, in which 93 percent of the inmates are male, why is watching incarcerated women so enthralling?

Orange Is the New Black offers a parafeminist critique of the incarceration of women and minorities by focusing on women's imprisonment at a time when women's incarceration rates were on the rise and the ills of the for-profit prisons were in the forefront of American political discourse.[5] But audiences are also gripped by, and enjoy, the punitive trials of Kerman and her fellow inmates because seeing female bodies in pain is comfortable and even normal, or eroticized. While American action films telegraph the Western masculine ideals of bodily impermeability to the rest of the world, *Orange Is the New Black* offers their inverse—female and minority bodies punished for a wide range of crimes—and holds up the wounded, suffering, incarcerated female body as the tragic hero. Even as the show aspires to undermine the idea of the passive, effeminate minority body in the punitive spectacle, it ultimately does so by first enfleshing it for the viewer. In fact, Netflix markets *OITNB* to both viewers who are critical of mass incarceration and those who simply enjoy the spectacle of violence.[6] In a show operating on a framework of neoliberal multiculturalism, black women's bodies are frequently the target of this violence, often without critical narrative framing.[7]

The gendered way in which moral culpability is tied to social roles in the tours of hell has a long afterlife. Historically, women and minorities are perceived as criminal for stepping outside of the bounds of their prescribed social roles, and are thought as more deserving of punishment than their white male counterparts. In colonial America, for example, a woman could be severely punished for berating her husband or being too vocal in a public setting; the punishment could involve wearing metal headgear that would cause sharp spikes to dig into her any time she moved her tongue.[8] Measure-for-measure punishments, it would seem, persisted long after the Theodosian Code.

And as in the early Christian tours of hell, the female carceral body in the United States was specifically culpable for failing to embody the current gender norms. Women were thought to deserve harsher punishments because they had "fallen further" than their male counterparts, holding out a particular kind of woman as the ideal, and objectifying and criminalizing those whose bodies did not measure up to those standards of femininity. Prison sentences were lighter for women who were already doing domestic labor in a family setting, and harsher for women who transgressed gender roles. Much of the prison reform in the late nineteenth century and most of the twentieth century sought to domesticate these women, training them in things like housekeeping that were thought to restore them to "normal womanhood."[9]

At the same time as prison reformers were using gender norms to punish bodies that stepped out of the social norms of nineteenth-century womanhood, forced labor prisons arose in which black citizens were sent to notoriously brutal prisons, where on flimsy pretexts they were consigned to do hard labor in fields, which resulted in thousands of deaths.[10] Modeled after the slave plantation, these prisons emerged after the Civil War as a way to keep slavery alive long after its abolition, ensuring that black bodies behaved according to the social norms of slavery. These prisons brought the logic of hell to earth, exacting torture on bodies in order to preserve social hierarchy. Even after the closure of forced labor prisons, racial minorities and the poor continue to be imprisoned at higher rates than their white, male, economically secure counterparts.[11]

In the last century, prisons in the United States have functioned like the ancient Christian depictions of hell in that they work to reify ideas about the normative body that are tied to the perceived social roles of people who happened to be female, black, or poor. Female, black, or poor bodies that transgressed their social role were consigned to punishments that were designed to force them into those roles, or ensure that they died trying.

Policing the Normative Body in a Medicalized Society

Unlike some early prison reformers who thought that women had "further to fall," these practices of punishment were also later grounded in the idea that women and minorities were less evolutionarily advanced than white men, and thus had not degenerated as far. According to this line of thinking, criminals among women and racial minorities would be harder to notice, and so were characterized as "monstrous." Their monstrous bodies had all the characteristics of white male criminals, but also the worst characteristics of the female body: "cunning, spite, and deceitfulness," and a lack of "maternal instinct" and "ladylike qualities."[12] This fixation on the monstrous, out-of-control bodies of women as the cause and symbol of crime sounds like something from our early Christian tours of hell. So too, in those ancient hellscapes, the leaky, weak, out-of-control female body made women more susceptible to sin, and was also the emblem of eternal punishment, as bodies were made effeminate in hell.

The idea that women inhabit uncontrolled and monstrous bodies has not left our consciousness, even amid modern medical thinking and practice. Women with endometriosis, called the "most misdiagnosed disease in history," were for centuries presumed to have a psychological condition known as hysteria, and subjected to murder and institutionalization.[13] The medical definition of the disease itself operates on a kind of binary logic, focusing on female reproductive tissue that has spread outside normative boundaries. Women with this condition are described in biomedical studies and also describe themselves as having leaky, weak, and monstrous bodies. These medical and personal descriptors revivify cultural norms in which women are constructed as "inherently monstrous" failed men.[14]

These medical attitudes toward the monstrosity of the female body, like those we saw amplified in the bodies of the damned, can also be seen today amid a variety of health behaviors that equate nonnormative bodies with the female body as the locus of pain and suffering. Working-age men receive greater attention during hospital stays, are more likely than women to be informed of their terminal diagnosis, and are more likely to have their pain taken seriously by medical professionals.[15] When women's bodies are viewed as "normally" in pain and fatigued, women are frequently misdiagnosed, and are treated less aggressively for pain and for illnesses for which pain and fatigue are the presenting symptoms.[16] In many cases the misdiagnosis of women and racial minorities has fatal consequences.[17] In medical charting, healthcare professionals sometimes use the shorthand "LOL," which stands for "little old lady," to mark a patient as one who complains excessively and whose reports of pain should not be taken as seriously as others.[18] Like the ancient Christian visions of hell, the gendered way that the contemporary hospital describes pain not only reflects the conceptions of the broader culture, but helps to construct a gendered morality of bodily suffering.

But healthcare providers are not the only ones who have internalized and reproduced the cultural norm that sick and disabled bodies are effeminate. In the case of male dementia patients, their diagnosis and condition may be described as emasculating.[19] And men with disabilities are often depicted as effeminate even when their disabilities have no connection to bodily attributes that are typically associated with masculinity.[20] As Steve Hoffman reflects on gender and disability, in the 2020 Netflix documentary *Crip Camp*, "If you're a handicapped person, and you happen to have a passive nature about you, you're really screwed." Steve shares this in an interview as a young adult at camp Jened, while a video of him as an adult in a drag show in Berkeley plays on the screen. Steve's experience is held up by the documentary as emblematic of the way that disability, like femininity, assigns bodies to a passive role in our culture.

It is surprising that suffering, physical sickness, and disability are still considered feminine traits, given that women now live longer than men. This overlap between the disabled body and the female body has its roots in the ancient notions of the female body as "assigned to suffering," and flourishes in a society that still extols a very narrow picture of bodily normativity: the young, white, athletic male body. Whereas the punitive discourses of early Christian hell affirmed the elite male impervious body as the narrow, unattainable norm, so too the contemporary medical gaze sees the disabled body as the self-affirming image of the normative white male body. At the same time the disabled body is also a reminder, in early Christian hell and in the contemporary world, that the disorder of the disabled body is a persistent threat to the social ideals of self-control and health.[21]

In 2020, as the world faces a global pandemic, the disabled body has once again taken center stage as the self-affirming image of the normative body. As U.S. leaders try to reassure citizens of their safety, they bandy about ableist language, claiming that the virus will *only* be deadly for the elderly and those with preexisting conditions, or suggesting that the deaths of persons with disabilities are preferable to economic collapse.[22] Such statements attempt to "hide disability in plain sight," ignoring that the elderly and those with preexisting conditions make up nearly half of the national population.[23] This strategy of containment, however, is much more insidious than simply ignoring disability: it externalizes fears of sickness and death onto the disabled body, and then lifts up the disabled body as an acceptable sacrifice, sentenced to death so that others might shop with impunity. Just as ancient hells externalized fears about hidden sins onto the deviant, tortured bodies in hell, today we attempt to contain fears of the sick body by projecting them onto disabled bodies, and marking others as "safe."

But this time those who are attentive can see the narrative of bodily imperviousness laid bare as a myth. In order to flatten the curve, and slow the spread of COVID-19, many states have imposed social-distancing measures that place limits on the body, even for those who consider themselves to be "able-bodied." Persons with all manner of bodies find themselves to be vulnerable to something that they can't see, and public health measures heighten our collective sense of bodily vulnerability—something that persons with disabilities have always known. In some communities that reject social distancing and cling to the idea of bodily invulnerability, the ideals of masculinity and ableism are revealed to be not just "toxic," but deadly.[24] In a global pandemic, the myth of bodily normativity not only imperils those who were already marginalized, it endangers us all.[25]

In the early Christian apocalypses we see the germination of discourses that use the disabled body to mark self-control as a social good, reshaping ancient notions of masculinity. These discourses of damnation placed broken, bloody, stretched, and deformed bodies on display, as monstrous emblems of the sin-sick soul.[26] Through these discourses of damnation the effeminate, disabled body becomes an artifact of sin. Both the ancient Christian tours of hell and contemporary medical surveillance read the disabled body as degeneration from a norm, and then use the disabled body to reinforce and police that norm so that the disabled body becomes the cultural icon of the pathological body or the degenerate soul.

As our journey through hell has shown, the normative body and the way in which the normative body wields power shifts in each new historical context. Recently trans and queer activists have begun to critique campaigns around "body positivity" that were initially developed by feminists to counter narrow cultural norms around body type. These campaigns have become a rallying cry for transexclusionary radical feminism (TERF), which uses body positivity as a weapon against trans bodies. What we can learn from the recent reverberations of TERF and from the early Christian tours of hell is that any society's bodily norms can be weaponized against the bodies that inhabit that society. I propose we think carefully about how to avoid bringing that hell to earth.

Notes

Introduction

1. In the Ipsos/Reuters 2011 poll "Ipsos Global Advisory: Supreme Being(s), the Afterlife and Evolution," about 19 percent of persons from a survey sample of twenty-three countries reported they believed in both heaven and hell. In this same survey 51 percent said they believed in some type of afterlife (https://www.ipsos.com/en-us/news-polls/ipsos-global-dvisory-supreme-beings-afterlife-and-evolution). The Pew Research Center's "Religion and Public Life Project Poll Database," April 8, 2013, reports that in 2013 only 56 percent of people in the United States believed in hell, while 74 percent believed in heaven (http://www.pewforum.org/question-search/?keyword=Hell&x=0&y=0).

2. Jason Horowitz, "Does Hell Exist? And Did the Pope Give an Answer?" *New York Times*, March 30, 2018 (https://www.nytimes.com/2018/03/30/world/europe/pope-francis-hell-scalfari.html). Catholic news outlets reflected on his earlier statements that had distanced hell from the imagery of fire and brimstone. In doing so, they tempered the quality of the pope's idea of hell, even if it could not be categorically dismissed. Thomas Reese, "Pope Francis and Hell," *National Catholic Reporter*, April 3, 2018 (https://www.ncronline.org/news/opinion/signs-times/pope-francis-and-hell).

3. Brandon Katz, "The Good Place Is Way More Popular Than You Think," *Observer*, December 20, 2018 (https://observer.com/2018/12/the-good-place-season-3-netflix-return-date-ratings/); Sam Anderson, "The Ultimate Sitcom," *New York Times Magazine*, October 4, 2018 (https://www.nytimes.com/interactive/2018/10/04/magazine/good-place-michael-schur-philosophy.html).

4. This thesis was first published on the TV fansite Red Herry by Jacqueline Bircher, "Abandon All Hope Ye Who Enter Here," Red Herry, January 7, 2014 (http://www.redherry.com/2014/01/abandon-all-hope-ye-who-enter-here.html), but the theory became widely popular, and received affirmation and support from one of the show's co-creators,

159

Ryan Murphy. Sean Fitz-Gerald, "Ryan Murphy May Have Just Confirmed a Major 'American Horror Story' Fan Theory," Thrillist, August 1, 2017 (https://www.thrillist.com/entertainment/nation/american-horror-story-ryan-murphy-dantes-inferno-theory).

5. Dante, *Inferno* 2.32. For a discussion of the specific ways in which the Apocalypse of Paul is interpreted in medieval fantastic literature, see Tamás Adamik, "The Apocalypse of Paul and Fantastic Literature," in *The Visio Pauli and the Gnostic Apocalypse of Paul*, ed. Jan N. Bremmer and István Czachesz (Leuven: Peeters, 2007), 144–57; Anthony Hilhorst, "*The Apocalypse of Paul*: Previous History and Afterlife," in Bremmer and Czachesz, *Visio Pauli and the Gnostic Apocalypse of Paul*, 19; Theodore Silverstein, *Visio Sancti Pauli: The History of the Apocalypse in Latin, Together with Nine Texts* (London: Christophers, 1935), 93n11. More recently, Gerhard Regn, "Die Apokalypse im Irdischen Paradies. Offenbarung, Allegorie und Dichtung in Dantes Commedia," in *Autorschaft und Autorisierungsstrategien in apokalyptischen Texten*, ed. Jörg Frey, Michael R. Jost, and Franz Tóth (Tübingen: Mohr Siebeck, 2019), 391–412, has argued that Dante was not directly influenced by the Apocalypse of Paul. While I am not convinced, one need not agree that Dante read the fifth-century Apocalypse of Paul in order to see the influence of the Apocalypse and the "tour of hell" genre on Dante's work. By the time of Dante's writing of the *Inferno*, the Apocalypse of Paul had already entered the cultural imagination through images, rituals, and punitive discourse.

6. Patrick Gray, "Abortion, Infanticide, and the Social Rhetoric of the Apocalypse of Peter," *JECS* 9 (2001): 313–37; István Czachesz, "Torture in Hell and Reality: The *Visio Pauli*," in Bremmer and Czachesz, *Visio Pauli and the Gnostic Apocalypse of Paul*, 130–143. On judicial punishment as retribution for a crime in the Roman world, see Julia Hillner, *Prison, Punishment and Penance in Late Antiquity* (Cambridge: Cambridge University Press, 2015), 26, 36, 49, 50, 54, 62, 71, 96.

7. See Martha Himmelfarb, *Tours of Hell: An Apocalyptic Form in Jewish and Christian Literature* (Philadelphia: University of Pennsylvania Press, 1983), 68–105, for a summary of the various kinds of measure-for-measure punishments that occur in the apocalyptic tours of hell. Also Callie Callon, "Sorcery, Wheels, and Mirror Punishment in the *Apocalypse of Peter*," *JECS* 18, no. 1 (2010): 29–49.

8. Tobias Nicklas, "Semiotik-Intertextualität-Apokryphität: Eine Annäherung an den Begriff 'christlicher Apokryphen,'" *Apocrypha* 17 (2006): 55–78; Nicklas, "Christliche Apokryphen als Spiegel der Vielfalt frühchristlichen Lebens: Schlaglichter, Beispiele und methodische Probleme," *Annali di storia dell'esegesi* 23 (2006): 27–44; Nicklas, "'Écrits apocryphes chrétiens.' Ein Sammelband als Spiegel eines weitreichenden Paradigmenwechsels in der Apokryphenforschung," *Vigiliae Christianae* 61 (2007): 70–95; Christoph Markschies, "Models of the Relation between 'Apocrypha' and 'Orthodoxy': From Antiquity to Mod-

ern Scholarship," in *The Other Side: Apocryphal Perspectives on Ancient Christian "Orthodoxies,"* ed. Candida R. Moss, Tobias Nicklas, Christopher Tuckett, and Joseph Verheyden (Göttingen: Vandenhoeck and Ruprecht, 2017), 13–22.

9. This list of texts is by no means exhaustive, but covers the texts that have the greatest influence over the tour of hell tradition, and thus receive more attention throughout the book.

10. Many of the texts that are discussed in this book are not easily dated. I will give approximate dates and direct the reader to the relevant scholarship, but the diachronic arguments adduced here are not dependent upon a precise dating of each text. Richard Bauckham has argued that the Apocalypse of Peter should be dated to 132–35 CE, identifying the liar or antichrist in 2.10 with Bar Kokhba. See Richard Bauckham, *The Fate of the Dead: Studies on the Jewish and Christian Apocalypses,* Supplements to Novum Testamentum 93 (Leiden: Brill, 1998), 160–258. Others have argued that if the liar is not Bar Kokhba, as Bauckham has hypothesized, but rather a cipher for general antagonism toward early Christians, then the Apocalypse of Peter might be more at home somewhere near the early second half of the second century CE. Eibert Tigchelaar, "Is the Liar Bar Kokhba? Considering the Date and Provenance of the Greek (Ethiopic) Apocalypse of Peter," in *The Apocalypse of Peter,* ed. Jan N. Bremmer and István Czachesz (Leuven: Peeters, 2003), 63–77; Meghan Henning, *Educating Early Christians through the Rhetoric of Hell: "Weeping and Gnashing of Teeth" as Paideia in Matthew and the Early Church,* Wissenschaftliche Untersuchungen zum Neuen Testament II. 382 (Tübingen: Mohr Siebeck, 2014), 176; Tobias Nicklas, "Jewish, Christian, Greek? The Apocalypse of Peter as a Witness of Early Second Century Christianity in Alexandria," in *Beyond Conflicts: Cultural and Religious Cohabitations in Alexandria and in Egypt between the 1st and the 6th Century CE,* ed. L. Arcari (Tübingen: Mohr Siebeck, 2017), 5–21; Jan N. Bremmer, "The *Apocalypse of Peter* as the First Christian Martyr Text: Its Date, Provenance and Relationship with 2 Peter," in *2 Peter and the Apocalypse of Peter: Towards a New Perspective: Radboud Prestige Lectures by Jörg Frey,* ed. M. den Dulk, J. Frey, and J. van der Watt (Leiden: Brill, 2019), 75–98; Tobias Nicklas, "Petrus-Diskurse in Alexandria: Eine Fortführung der Gedanken von Jörg Frey," in den Dulk et al., *2 Peter and the Apocalypse of Peter,* 99–127.

11. The Apocalypse of Peter is cited in the list that Eusebius reconstructed and attributed to Clement of Alexandria (*Eccl. Hist.* 6.14.1–7), in the Muratorian fragment, and in the list found in the Claromantanus (D) manuscript. The date of the Muratorian Fragment has been contested by scholars. Some have argued for an early date, in the mid-second century, viewing the fragment as an early precursor to the concept of a canon. For representatives of this view, see Everett Ferguson, "Canon Muratori: Date and Provenance," *Studia Patristica* 17, no. 2 (1982); Joseph Verheyden, "The Canon Muratori: A Matter of Dispute," in *The Biblical Canons,* ed. J. M. Auwers and H. J. de Jonge (Leuven: Peeters,

2003), 487–556. Others have worked to overturn the second-century dating of the fragment, arguing that the document could not have originated before the fourth century, and properly fits within the earliest discussions about the canon that were happening in that era. For examples, see Albert C. Sundberg, "Canon Muratori: A Fourth-Century List," *HTR* 66 (1973): 1–41; Geoffrey M. Hahneman, *The Muratorian Fragment and the Development of the* Canon (Oxford: Oxford University Press, 1992); Clare K. Rothschild, "The Muratorian Fragment as Roman Fake," *NovT* 60, no. 1 (2018): 55–82. While the latter arguments are more persuasive in their circumspect dating of a fragmentary list, the scholarly debate itself warrants caution around using the Muratorian Fragment as evidence in diachronic arguments.

12. Clement of Alexandria, *Extracts from the Prophets*, 41, 48, 49. Wolfgang Grünstäudl, *Petrus Alexandrinus: Studien zum historischen und theologischen Ort des Zweiten Petrusbriefes* (Tübingen: Mohr Siebeck, 2013), argues that these quotes come from an older commentary on the Psalms.

13. Muratorian fragment 71–72, in "The Muratorian Canon," in Bart Ehrman, *Lost Scriptures: Books That Did Not Make It into the New Testament* (Oxford: Oxford University Press, 2003), 331–33. As Attila Jakab, "The Reception of the Apocalypse of Peter in Ancient Christianity," in Bremmer and Czachesz, *The Apocalypse of Peter*, 175, notes regarding the Christians who did not want to read the Apocalypse of Peter in church, "We do not know if they rejected the text because of its content, its authenticity, or for some other reason."

14. Sozomen, *Eccl. Hist.* 7.19.9, 7.9.10.

15. The first of the two Ethiopic manuscripts is published in Sylvain Grébaut, "Littérature éthiopienne pseudo-clémentine," *Revue de l'Orient chrétien* 15 (1910): 198–214, 307–23 (text), 425–39 (translation); the second Ethiopic manuscript was first photographed by Ernst Hammerschmidt, *Äthiopische Handschriften vom Ṭānāsee 1: Reisebericht und Beschreibung der Handschriften in dem Kloster des Heiligen Gabriel auf der Insel Kebrān*, Verzeichnis der Orientalischen Handschriften in Deutschland 20.1 (Wiesbaden: Franz Steiner, 1973), 163–67. A critical edition of the Ethiopic text is available in Dennis D. Buchholz, *Your Eyes Will Be Opened: A Study in the Greek (Ethiopic) Text of the Apocalypse of Peter*, SBLDS 97 (Atlanta: Scholars Press, 1988); and P. Marrassini, "L'Apocalisse di Pietro," in *Etiopia e oltre. Studi in onore di Lanfranco Ricci*, ed. Y. Beyene et al. (Naples: Instituto universitario orientale, Dipartimento de studi e ricerche su Africa e paesi arabi, 1994), 171–232. The Greek texts and a translation are available in Thomas J. Kraus and Tobias Nicklas, *Das Petrusevangelium und die Petrusapokalypse. Die griechischen Fragmente mit deutscher und englischer Übersetzung* (Berlin: de Gruyter, 2004). A "composite translation" of the Ethiopic and the Greek has emerged close to the publication of this volume, and is available in Eric J. Beck, *Justice and Mercy in the Apocalypse of Peter: A New Translation and Analysis of the Purpose of the Text*, Wissenschaftliche Untersuchungen zum

Neuen Testament II. 427 (Tübingen: Mohr Siebeck, 2019), 66–73. Unless otherwise noted, English translations and chapter numbers refer to the Ethiopic text. English translations are adapted from C. Detlef G. Müller, "Apocalypse of Peter," in *New Testament Apocrypha*, ed. Wilhelm Schneemelcher and Edgar Hennecke, trans. R. Wilson (Louisville, KY: Westminster John Knox, 1991), 2:625–38.

16. Himmelfarb, *Tours of Hell*, 45–67, treats the topic of "demonstrative explanations in the tours of hell," and attributes this feature of the text to "pesher-style exegesis," rather than Greco-Roman rhetoric as I have in Henning, *Educating Early Christians through the Rhetoric of Hell*, 86–107. Jan N. Bremmer, *Maidens, Magic and Martyrs in Early Christianity* (Tübingen: Mohr Siebeck, 2017), 292, 318–19, 334–35, also notes the presence of demonstrative pronouns in Virgil's *Aeneid*, and suggests that Virgil may have known 1 Enoch.

17. Bauckham, *The Fate of the Dead*, 332–62; Enrico Norelli, *Marie des apocryphes. Enquête sur la mère de Jésus dans le christianisme antique*, Christianismes antiques (Geneva: Labor et Fides, 2009), 132–36, at 115, 134; Stephen J. Shoemaker, *Mary in Early Christian Faith and Devotion* (New Haven: Yale University Press, 2016), 133–34.

18. See, for instance, Bremmer, *Maidens, Magic and Martyrs in Early Christianity*, 295–312, at 309, who argues that the Apocalypse of Paul is more concerned with social boundaries within the church because of the presence of ecclesial sins, and that this is a function of the later historical context of the Apocalypse of Paul. Whereas previously, I argued that concern for managing community boundaries from within the church was of greater concern in a post-Theodosian context, here I argue that the ecclesial sins in the Book of Mary's Repose suggest that internal boundary policing was of concern in one of the earliest tours of hell. See Meghan Henning, "Lacerated Lips and Lush Landscapes: Constructing This-Worldly Theological Identities in the Otherworld," in Moss et al., *The Other Side*, 99–116, at 116.

19. The Acts of Thomas was composed in the first half of the third century CE, and likely was originally composed in Greek. Unless otherwise noted, translations from the Acts of Thomas are from Harold W. Attridge, *The Acts of Thomas*, ed. Julian V. Hills (Salem, OR: Polebridge, 2010). On date and composition of the Acts of Thomas, see Bremmer, *Maidens, Magic and Martyrs*, 167–70. Although recent research suggests that the text was originally composed in Greek, and the Greek version of the Acts of Thomas is thought to be more representative of the original text, the text was translated into Syriac shortly after it was written and "appropriated by various groups, which have left their imprint on the text" (Bremmer, *Maidens, Magic and Martyrs*, 170). On the priority of the Greek version of the text, see Lautauro Roig Lanzillotta, "A Syriac Original for the *Acts of Thomas*? The Theory of the Syriac Priority Revisited, Evaluated, and Rejected," in *Early Christian and Jewish Narrative: The Role of Religion in Shaping*

Narrative Forms, ed. Ilaria Ramelli and Judith Perkins (Tübingen: Mohr Siebeck, 2015), 105–33. We will discuss the Greek version of the text, noting important differences in the Syriac version where they are noteworthy.

20. Stephen J. Shoemaker, "From Mother of Mysteries to Mother of the Church:
The Institutionalization of the Dormition Apocrypha," *Apocrypha* 22 (2011):
28–39.

21. Six Books Apocryphon, bk. 6. W. Wright, "The Departure of My Lady Mary
from the World," *Journal of Sacred Literature* 6 (1865): 417–48; *Journal of Sacred
Literature* 7 (1865): 110–60 (Syriac text and translation), at 158–60.

22. The text is preserved in two fragmentary manuscripts: a two-page Sahidic manuscript from the fifth century CE, and an eighteen-page Akhmimic manuscript from the fourth century CE. There is also a short quotation (in Greek)
from Clement, *Misc.* 5.11.77, which is not found in either passage. The Coptic
texts and a German translation are available in G. Steindorff, *Die Apokalypse
des Elias, eine unbekannte Apokalypse und Bruchstücke der Sophonias Apokalypse*
(Leipzig: J. C. Hinrichs, 1899), 34–65. The English translations cited are from
O. S. Wintermute, "Apocalypse of Zephaniah," in *The Old Testament Pseudepigrapha*, ed. James H. Charlesworth, 2 vols. (Garden City, NY: Doubleday,
1983), 1:508–15. G. Oegema, *Apokalypsen* (Gütersloh: Gütersloher Verl. Haus,
2001), suggests a date of composition sometime between the second and fourth
centuries. For summary and discussion of the Christian elements of the extant texts, see Bernd J. Diebner, *Zephanjas Apokalypsen* (Gütersloh: Gütersloher
Verl. Haus, 2003), 1141–1246; Bremmer, *Maidens, Magic and Martyrs*, 326–27. See
also the possible "transcultural" relationship between the Apocalypse of Zephaniah and the Egyptian *Book of the Dead* in Michael Sommer, "Roman Tombs
in Alexandria and in the Egyptian Chroa: A Journey through the After-life
of the Apocalypse of Zephaniah," in *Alexandria: Hub of the Hellenistic World*,
ed. Thomas Kraus and Benjamin Schliesser, WUNT (Tübingen: Mohr Siebeck, 2020); Michael Sommer, "Between Jewish and Egyptian Thinking—The
Apocalypse of Sophonias as a Bridge between Two Worlds?" in *Dreams, Visions, Imaginations: Jewish, Christian and Gnostic Views of the World to Come*, ed.
Tobias Nicklas and Jens Schröter (Berlin: De Gruyter, 2021). Sommer argues
convincingly that the extant fragments of the Apocalypse of Zephaniah represent a late antique Christian adaptation of Egyptian ideas about the afterlife
and does not represent second-century Alexandrian Christianity (and is thus
not the same Apoc. Zeph. quoted by Clement).

23. P. Dinzelbacher, "Die Verbreitung der apokryphen 'Visio S. Pauli' im mittel-
alterlichen Europa," *Mittellateinisches Jahrbuch* 27 (1992): 77–90; cf. Hilhorst,
"*The Apocalypse of Paul*: Previous History and Afterlife," 3–4. For a summary of
the arguments supporting the date of 395–416 CE, see Bauckham, *The Fate of
the Dead*, 336; Pierluigi Piovanelli, "The Miraculous Discovery of the Hidden
Manuscript, or the Paratextual Function of the Prologue to the Apocalypse

of Paul," in Bremmer and Czachesz, *Visio Pauli and the Gnostic Apocalypse of Paul*, 23–49; Bremmer, *Maidens, Magic and Martyrs*, 298–302, 313–28. Bremmer argues that the Greek version was written in Egypt around 400 CE, and the Latin translation made at the end of the sixth century. In this dating argument, Augustine's mention of the Apocalypse of Paul in his *Tract. Gos. Jo.* 98.8 (CCSL 36.581) is explained as Augustine having heard the text, but not having read it (as it would not yet have been translated into Latin). Unless otherwise noted, citations of the Apocalypse of Paul are from the best Latin version of the text (L¹); see the critical edition in Theodore Silverstein and Anthony Hilhorst, eds., *Apocalypse of Paul: A New Critical Edition of Three Long Latin Versions* (Geneva: P. Cramer, 1997). English translations are adapted from Hugo Duensing and Aurelio de Santos Otero, "Apocalypse of Paul," in Schneemelcher and Hennecke, *New Testament Apocrypha*, 2:712–47.

24. Apoc. Paul 34–36. Paul's final return to heaven is described in more detail in the Coptic and Syriac manuscripts, which contain a longer ending of Apoc. Paul 51.

25. The Isaiah Fragments are available in Hebrew with a facing English translation in Michael E. Stone and John Strugnell, *The Books of Elijah, Parts 1 and 2* (Missoula, MT: Scholars, 1979), 20–23. Other editions of the Hebrew text of the Isaiah Fragments are available in L. Ginzberg, *Ginze Schechter: Genizah Studies in Memory of Dr. Solomon Schechter*, vol. 1: *Midrash and Haggadah*, Texts and Studies of the Jewish Theological Seminary of America 7 (New York: Jewish Theological Seminary, 1928), 196–98, 204–5; Adolph Jellinek, "A Description of Judgment in the Grave," in *Bet ha-Midrasch* (Jerusalem: Wahrmann, 1967; originally published, 1853–78), 5:50–51. Two different versions of the Elijah Fragment are available in Latin with a facing English translation in Stone and Strugnell, *The Books of Elijah*, 14–19.

26. Himmelfarb, *Tours of Hell*, 34–35. On Pseudo-Titus, see Aurelio de Santos Otero, "The Pseudo-Titus Epistle," in Schneemelcher and Hennecke, *New Testament Apocrypha*, 2:53–74. An edition of the Latin text is available in D. Donatien de Bruyne, "*Epistula Titi, discipuli Pauli, de dispositione sanctimonii*," *RBén* 37 (1925): 47–72. Corrections to the Latin are suggested in Vincenz Bulhart, "Nochmals Textkritisches," *RBén* 62 (1952): 297–99, and noted here where relevant.

27. Himmelfarb, *Tours of Hell*, 131–39; see discussion of this thesis in Bremmer, *Maidens, Magic and Martyrs*, 325.

28. The Greek Apocalypse of Ezra and the Latin Vision of Ezra were likely composed at different dates, but based upon a common Ur-text. While the Ur-text could have been composed as early as the second century CE (just after the Apocalypse of Peter), the Greek Apocalypse of Ezra was written after the Apocalypse of Paul, and the Latin Vision of Ezra can be dated to the mid-sixth century CE. See Jan N. Bremmer's update of Martha Himmelfarb's hypothesis, which had been written prior to the availability of the long version of the Latin Vision: Jan N. Bremmer, "The Long Latin Version of the Vision of Ezra:

Date, Place, and Tour of Hell," in *Figures of Ezra*, ed. Jan N. Bremmer, Veronika Hirschberger, and Tobias Nicklas (Leuven: Peeters, 2018), 162–84. English
translations of the Greek Apocalypse of Ezra and the Latin Vision of Ezra are
cited from M. E. Stone, "Greek Apocalypse of Ezra," in Charlesworth, *Old
Testament Pseudepigrapha*, 1:561–613; and Richard Bauckham, "The Latin Vision
of Ezra," in *Old Testament Pseudepigrapha: More Noncanonical Scriptures*, ed. Alexander Panayotov, James R. Davila, and Richard Bauckham (Grand Rapids,
MI: Eerdmans, 2013), 1:498–528. For the Greek text of the Greek Apocalypse
of Ezra, see O. Wahl, *Apocalypsis Esdrae; Apocalypsis Sedrach; Visio Beati Esdrae*
(Leiden: Brill, 1977). The Latin text of the Vision of Ezra is available in P.-M.
Bogaert, "Une vision longue inédite de la 'Visio Beati Esdrae' dans le légendier
de Teano (Barberini lat. 2318)," *RBén* 94 (1984): 50–70.

29. Meghan Henning, "Substitutes in Hell: Schemes of Atonement in the Ezra
Apocalypses," in *The Ezra Apocalypses*, Studies in Early Christian Apocrypha
(Leuven: Peeters, 2018), 185–204.

30. See Bauckham, *The Fate of the Dead*, 335, for a summary of the prolific and divergent manuscript traditions of the Greek Apocalypse of Mary in Greek, Armenian, Old Slavonic, and Rumanian; as Jane Ralls Baun, *Tales from Another Byzantium: Celestial Journey and Local Community in the Medieval Greek Apocrypha*
(Cambridge: Cambridge University Press, 2007), 375, argues, the popularity of
the Greek Apocalypse of Mary continued into medieval Byzantium as a means
of promoting social cohesion.

31. As Bauckham, *The Fate of the Dead*, 335, notes, at least seven edited manuscripts
of the Greek Apocalypse of Mary have been published, and they vary quite a
bit. Regarding the dating of the Greek Apocalypse of Mary, see Bauckham,
The Fate of the Dead, 335–36; Baun, *Tales from Another Byzantium*, 16–18.
Baun argues for a later date, between the ninth and eleventh centuries, based
upon the development of the cult of Mary as intercessor around this time, but
recent work on Mariology suggests that the cult of Mary originated earlier
than this.

32. Gk. Apoc. Mary 4; English translations of the Greek Apocalypse of Mary are
available in Andrew Rutherford, "The Apocalypse of the Virgin," in *Ante-
Nicene Fathers: The Writings of the Fathers down to A.D. 325*, ed. Alexander Roberts and James Donaldson (Peabody, MA: Hendrickson, 1994; originally published 1896), 9:167–74; and in Baun, *Tales from Another Byzantium*, 391–400.
Those translations are based upon the Oxford manuscript published in M. R.
James, *Apocrypha Anecdota: A Collection of Thirteen Apocryphal Books and Fragments*, Texts and Studies 2.3 (Cambridge: Cambridge University Press, 1893),
115–26. The other manuscript that is an important early witness to this text is
Vatican, Biblioteca Apostolica Vaticana, Ottoboni 1, which is available in the
most recent critical edition of the Apocalypse of the Virgin: Olena Myko-
laivna Syrstova, *Apokryfichna apokaliptyka: filosofs'ka ekzeheza i tekstolohiya z*

vydannyam hretskoho tekstu Apokalipsysa Bohoradytsi za rukupysom XI stolittya Ottobanianus, hr. 1, *Textologia antiquae et mediae aetatis* (Kiev: KM Academia, 2000). A translation of this manuscript is available in Stephen Shoemaker, "The Apocalypse of the Virgin: A New Translation and Introduction," in *New Testament Apocrypha: More Noncanonical Scriptures*, ed. Tony Burke and Brent Landau (Grand Rapids, MI: Eerdmans, 2016), 492–509. See also the e-clavis entry by Tony Burke: https://www.nasscal.com/e-clavis-christian-apocrypha/apocalypse-of-the-virgin/. I will work primarily with the Oxford manuscript and note where the Vatican manuscript diverges in interesting ways.

33. Ethiopic Apocalypse of the Virgin, in M. Chaîne, *Apocrypha B. Maria Virgine*, CSCO: Scriptores Aethiopici: Ser I, 8 (Rome: de Luigi, 1909), 45–80.

34. Bauckham, *The Fate of the Dead*, 335; Baun, *Tales from Another Byzantium*.

35. For a fuller discussion of afterlife imagery in Paul's letters, see Adela Yarbro Collins, "The Otherworld and the New Age in the Letters of Paul," in *Otherworlds and Their Relation to This World: Early Jewish and Ancient Christian Traditions*, ed. Tobias Nicklas et al., JSJS 143 (Boston: Brill, 2010), 189–207.

36. Hillner, *Prison, Punishment and Penance in Late Antiquity*, 51, 91, 137, 201. Lactantius, *Death pers.* 22.2 (SC 39:103), describes the emperor Galerius as a judge who routinely sentenced people to the harshest punishments, such as exposure to the beasts and burning; in 325 CE, however, Constantine replaces condemnation to the beasts with labor in the imperial mines (*CTh* 15.21.1 [325]).

37. Augustine, *Tract. Gos. Jo.* 98.8; cf. 2 Cor 12:4.

38. Tertullian, *Res.* 34. See Candida R. Moss, "'Dying to Live Forever': Identity and Virtue in the Resurrection of the Bodies of the Martyrs," *Irish Theological Quarterly* 84, no. 2 (2019): 155–74. It is certainly possible that Tertullian is an idiosyncratic figure whose opinions represent nothing more than those of an ill-tempered Carthaginian *rhetor*. Certainly, many scholars have viewed him that way. At the same time, the tendency to marginalize Tertullian is reflective of a scholarly trend that tends to deemphasize North African Christianity in general. On this see Candida R. Moss, *Ancient Christian Martyrdom: Diverse Practices, Theologies, and Traditions* (New Haven: Yale University Press, 2012), 123–25.

39. Caroline Walker Bynum, *The Resurrection of the Body in Western Christianity, 200–1336* (New York: Columbia University Press, 1995), 21–58; Virginia Burrus, *Saving Shame: Martyrs, Saints and Other Abject Subjects* (Philadelphia: University of Pennsylvania Press, 2008), 52–57; Carly Daniel-Hughes, *The Salvation of the Flesh in Tertullian of Carthage: Dressing for the Resurrection* (New York: Palgrave Macmillan, 2011), 6–7; Benjamin H. Dunning, *Specters of Paul: Sexual Difference in Early Christian Thought* (Philadelphia: University of Pennsylvania Press, 2011), 124–50; Outi Lehtipuu, *Debates over the Resurrection of the Dead: Constructing Early Christian Identity* (Oxford: Oxford University Press, 2015), 30–31, 109–57; Taylor G. Petrey, *Resurrecting Parts: Early Christians on Desire,*

Reproduction, and Sexual Difference (New York: Routledge, 2015), 86–102; Ellen Muehlberger, *Moment of Reckoning: Imagined Death and Its Consequences in Late Ancient Christianity* (Oxford: Oxford University Press, 2019), 147–82.

40. The Ethiopic textual tradition of the Book of Mary's Repose (*Liber Requiei*) represents a translation of a text (no longer extant) that could date back to the third century CE. On the date and transmission of these traditions, see Stephen J. Shoemaker, *Ancient Traditions of the Virgin Mary's Dormition and Assumption*, Oxford Early Christian Studies (Oxford: Oxford University Press, 2002), 42–46, 253–56, 278–79, 284–86; Hans Förster, *Transitus Mariae: Beiträge zur koptischen Überlieferung mit einer Edition von P. Vindob. K 7589, Cambridge Add 1876 8 und Paris BN Copte 12917 ff. 28 und 29* (Berlin: Walter de Gruyter, 2006), 225–29; Édouard Cothenet, "Traditions bibliques et apocalyptiques dans les récits anciens de la Dormition," in *Marie dans les récits apocryphes chrétiens*, ed. Édouard Cothenet et al. (Paris: Médiaspaul, 2004), 155–75; Enrico Norelli, "La letteratura apocrifa sul transito di Maria e il problema delle sue origini," in *Il dogma dell'assunzione di Maria. Problemi attuali e tentativi di ricomprensione*, ed. Ermanno M. Toniolo (Rome: Edizioni Marianum, 2010), 121–65; Shoemaker, "Mother of Mysteries," 11–47, at 20–21; and Ally Kateusz, "Collyridian Deja Vu: The Trajectory of Redaction of the Markers of Mary's Liturgical Leadership," *Journal of Feminist Studies in Religion* 29, no. 2 (Fall 2013): 75–92. Due to themes in the texts that were later deemed heterodox (such as an early gnostic idea of angel Christology, or Mary's liturgical leadership), the Dormition apocrypha are now thought to predate the Council of Chalcedon. For an alternative view, see Simon C. Mimouni, *Dormition et Assomption de Marie. Histoire des traditions anciennes*, Théologie Historique 98 (Paris: Beauchesne, 1995). English translations of the Book of Mary's Repose are from Shoemaker, *Ancient Traditions*, 290–350; the Ethiopic text is in Victor Arras, ed., *De Transitu Mariae Aethiopice*, 2 vols., CSCO 342–43 (Louvain: Secrétariat du Corpus SCO, 1973).

41. The sinner punished in this passage is a priest who ate up the offerings and gave them to others who were not worthy. As Shoemaker, *Ancient Traditions*, 345, notes in his translation, the Savior explains, "I will tell you how his beauty/ goodness is not dissolved."

42. Origen, *Cels.* 5.14; trans. Henry Chadwick; in John E. L. Outen and Henry Chadwick, *Alexandrian Christianity*, Library of Christian Classics 2 (Philadelphia: Westminster, 1954). For an interesting commentary on Origen's quotations of Celsus's *Alethes Logos*, see Horacio E. Lona, *Die Wahre Lehre des Kelsos. Übersetzt und erklärt*, Kommentar zu frühchristlichen Apologeten 1 (Freiburg: Herder, 2005).

43. John J. Collins, *The Apocalyptic Imagination: An Introduction to Jewish Apocalyptic Literature*, 2d ed. (Grand Rapids, MI: Eerdmans, 1998), 42; cf. Adela Yarbro Collins, "Introduction: Early Christian Apocalypticism," *Semeia* 36 (1986): 7.

44. Greg Carey, *Elusive Apocalypse: Reading Authority in the Revelation to John* (Macon, GA: Mercer University Press, 1999).

45. Tina Pippin, *Death and Desire: The Rhetoric of Gender in the Apocalypse of John* (Louisville: Westminster, 1992), 105; Pippin, *Apocalyptic Bodies: The Biblical End of the World in Text and Image* (New York: Routledge, 1999).

46. Tina Pippin, "The Revelation to John," in *Searching the Scriptures*, vol. 2: *A Feminist Commentary*, ed. Elisabeth Schüssler Fiorenza, Ann Brock, and Shelly Matthews (New York: Crossroad, 1994), 109–30, at 126.

47. Jacqueline M. Hidalgo, *Revelation in Aztlán: Scriptures, Utopias, and the Chicano Movement* (New York: Palgrave Macmillan, 2016), 5–6.

48. Hidalgo, *Revelation in Aztlán*, 5, 14, 238–48; Adela Yarbro Collins, *Crisis and Catharsis: The Power of the Apocalypse* (Philadelphia: Westminster, 1984).

49. István Czachesz, "Torture in Hell and Reality: The *Visio Pauli*," in Bremmer and Czachesz, *Visio Pauli and the Gnostic Apocalypse of Paul*, 130–43; Czachesz, "Why Body Matters in the Afterlife: Mind Reading and Body Imagery in Synoptic Tradition and the Apocalypse of Peter," in *The Human Body in Death and Resurrection*, ed. Tobias Nicklas, Friedrich V. Reiterer, and Joseph Verheyden (Berlin: Walter de Gruyter, 2009), 391–411.

50. Czachesz, "Torture in Hell and Reality," 143.

51. See Collins, *Apocalyptic Imagination*, 1–2, for a discussion of the way that "strong theological prejudice" impeded historical investigation of apocalyptic literature in the nineteenth and early twentieth centuries.

52. Although this theme is underexplored in the literature on apocalypses generally, there are several treatments of gender and the body with respect to Revelation. Pippin, *Apocalyptic Bodies*; Stephen D. Moore, *God's Gym: Divine Male Bodies of the Bible* (New York: Routledge, 1996), 117–29.

53. Peter Brown, *The Ransom of the Soul: Afterlife and Wealth in Early Western Christianity* (Cambridge, MA: Harvard University Press, 2015). Despite Augustine's North African context, the popularity of the tours of hell in late antique Africa, and Augustine's direct engagement with those texts, Brown (57–114) does not include in his discussion the Apocalypse of Peter, or the critical scholarship on the apocalypses, or their ancient readership. Although Brown (113–14, 139–41) does discuss the Apocalypse of Paul, he classifies this as a "post-imperial phenomenon" and does not engage any of the critical scholarship on early Christian apocalypses here. What is more, when Brown (63–65) does discuss Augustine's interlocutors in the debate about the afterlife, he completely ignores the hypothesis proposed by Bauckham in *The Fate of the Dead*, 147–59.

54. Kelly Olson, *Dress and the Roman Woman: Self-Presentation and Society* (New York: Routledge, 2008), 15–22, 41–42. Young upper-class girls wore the toga *praetexta*, a wool toga with a single purple stripe, and brides wore white tunics, which signaled good fortune and purity. Dark-colored clothing in general was worn by women in mourning.

55. Peter Brown, *The Body and Society: Men, Women, and Sexual Renunciation in Early Christianity* (New York: Columbia University Press, 1988); David Brakke, *Demons and the Making of the Monk: Spiritual Combat in Early Christianity* (Cambridge, MA: Harvard University Press, 2006); Burrus, *Saving Shame*.

56. J. Albert Harrill, *Slaves in the New Testament: Literary, Social, and Moral Dimensions* (Minneapolis: Augsburg Fortress, 2006); Stephanie L. Cobb, *Dying to Be Men: Gender and Language in Early Martyr Texts* (New York: Columbia University Press, 2008); Bernadette J. Brooten, ed., *Beyond Slavery: Overcoming Its Religious and Sexual Legacies* (New York: Palgrave Macmillan, 2010); Jennifer Glancy, *Corporeal Knowledge: Early Christian Bodies* (Oxford: Oxford University Press, 2010); Moss, *Ancient Christian Martyrdom*.

57. Chris L. De Wet, *Preaching Bondage: John Chrysostom and the Discourse of Slavery in Early Christianity* (Oakland: University of California Press, 2015), 218. Following Michel Foucault, De Wet argues that the spectacle of bodily punishment deflected shame back onto the slaveholder, leading Chrysostom to argue for moderation as a means of preserving masculinity: "The harsh punishment of slaves further destabilized masculinity, hence Chrysostom's strict measures to regulate and redistribute the means of punishment." As Chrysostom demonstrates, early Christian authors wrote amid multiple discursive frameworks of gender and bodily suffering that were employed in different contexts.

58. Toril Moi, *Sex, Gender, and the Body: The Student Edition of What Is a Woman?* (New York: Oxford University Press, 2005), 14–15.

59. Judith Butler, *Undoing Gender* (New York: Routledge, 2004), 185.

60. As a result, these sources can be seen as part of authoritative traditions that worked to stabilize dominant models of thinking about the body and the self. Max Weber, *Gesammelte Aufsätze zur Religionssoziologie*, 3 vols. (Tübingen: J. C. B. Mohr/Paul Siebeck, [1920] 1978).

61. Jorunn Økland, *Women in Their Place: Paul and the Corinthian Discourse of Gender and Sanctuary Space* (New York: T. and T. Clark, 2004), 12.

62. On the turn from women's studies (social history) to gender studies (hermeneutics) in early Christian history, see Elizabeth Clark, "The Lady Vanishes: Dilemmas of a Feminist Historian after the 'Linguistic Turn,'" *CH* 67 (1998): 1–31; Clark, "Women, Gender, and the Study of Christian History," *CH* 70 (2001): 395–426; Clark, "Engendering the Study of Religion," in *The Future of the Study of Religion: Proceedings of Congress 2000*, ed. Slaviva Jakelic and Lori Pearson (Leiden: Brill, 2004), 217.

63. Clark, "The Lady Vanishes," 31.

64. Virginia Burrus, *"Begotten Not Made": Conceiving Manhood in Late Antiquity* (Stanford, CA: Stanford University Press, 2000), 10–11.

65. Paula M. Cooey, *Religious Imagination and the Body: A Feminist Analysis* (Oxford: Oxford University Press, 1994); Harrill, *Slaves in the New Testament*; Cobb, *Dying to Be Men*; Glancy, *Corporeal Knowledge*. And when we emphasize how

gender is constructed or defined by discourse, there is a move to respect the complexity of those gendered discourses, speaking of masculinities rather than masculinity, and observing the subtle ways masculinity and femininity were morphed and instrumentalized by early Christians. Elizabeth A. Clark, "Foucault, the Fathers, and Sex," *JAAR* 56, no. 4 (1988): 619–41; Stephen D. Moore and Janice C. Anderson, eds., *New Testament Masculinities*, Semeia Studies 45 (Atlanta: Society of Biblical Literature, 2003); Burrus, *"Begotten Not Made,"* 19–22; Chris L. De Wet, *Preaching Bondage*, 172–75.

66. It is constructive to develop "an analytic vocabulary that can verbalize the seams and interstices that inevitably emerge between anatomically distinct bodies (themselves always already culturally constructed) and the manifold cultural ideologies that operate on those bodies." Dunning, *Specters of Paul*, 15–16; cf. Amy Hollywood, *Sensible Ecstasy: Mysticism, Sexual Difference, and the Demands of History* (Chicago: University of Chicago Press, 2002), 284n42. Dunning (74), for instance, reads Clement of Alexandria in this way, preserving the paradox that he finds: "The paradoxical result is a fault line within his theology such that sexual difference is simultaneously created prior to the fall *and* brought about by (or instantiated in) desire."

67. Rebecca Flemming, *Medicine and the Making of Roman Women: Gender, Nature, and Authority from Celsus to Galen* (Oxford: Oxford University Press, 2000); Mathew Kuefler, *The Manly Eunuch: Masculinity, Gender Ambiguity, and Christian Ideology in Late Antiquity* (Chicago: University of Chicago Press, 2001); Helen King, *The One-Sex Body on Trial: The Classical and Early Modern Evidence* (New York: Ashgate, 2013); De Wet, *Preaching Bondage*, 172–74.

68. Lennard Davis, *Enforcing Normalcy: Disability, Deafness, and the Body* (New York: Verso, 1995). In this regard, disability studies is built upon Foucauldian hermeneutics of the body, even as some scholars, like Davis, have pushed past social constructionism. See Lennard J. Davis, *Disability, Dismodernism, and Other Difficult Positions* (New York: New York University Press, 2002); Bill Hughes, "What Can a Foucauldian Analysis Contribute to Disability Studies?" in *Foucault and the Government of Disability*, ed. Shelley Tremain (Ann Arbor: University of Michigan Press, 2008), 78–92; and my arguments in Meghan R. Henning, "In Sickness and Health: Ancient 'Rituals of Truth' in the Greco-Roman World and 1 Peter," in *Disability Studies and Biblical Literature*, ed. Candida R. Moss and Jeremy Schipper (New York: Palgrave Macmillan, 2011), 186–203, at 186–88, nuancing Hughes. Like Lennard Davis, I am a temporarily able-bodied person with research interests in disability studies.

69. Candida R. Moss, "Heavenly Healing: Eschatological Cleansing and the Resurrection of the Dead in the Early Church," *JAAR* 79, no. 4 (2011): 991–1017, at 993.

70. Candida R. Moss, *Divine Bodies: Resurrecting Perfection in the New Testament and Early Christianity* (New Haven: Yale University Press, 2019), 117–18,

describes the impact of socioeconomic class on the contemporary view of heavenly amputation.

71. Nicole Kelly, "Deformity and Disability in Greece and Rome," in *This Abled Body: Rethinking Disability in Biblical Studies*, ed. Hector Avalos, Sarah J. Melcher, and Jeremy Schipper (Atlanta: Society of Biblical Literature, 2007), 31–46. Christian Laes, *Disability in Antiquity* (London: Routledge, 2017), 4, has argued that "infirmity" is a helpful term for thinking about bodily differences in antiquity, stating that "infirmity was a highly fluid differentiating category, often used ad hoc and mostly defined in the context of a person's social role."

72. Warren Carter, "'The Blind, the Lame and Paralyzed' (John 5:3): John's Gospel, Disability Studies, and Postcolonial Perspectives," in Moss and Schipper, *Disability Studies and Biblical Literature*, 129–50, especially 131. Martha Lynn Rose, *The Staff of Oedipus: Transforming Disability in Ancient Greece* (Ann Arbor: University of Michigan Press, 2003), 79, also argues that scholars bring modern ableism to bear on the ancient world when they generalize about ancient attitudes toward blindness, assuming that all Greeks equated blindness with punishment, based upon the "grand sweep of legend and tragedy." See also Lisa Trentin, "Exploring Visual Impairment in Ancient Rome," in *Disabilities in Roman Antiquity: Disparate Bodies A Capite ad Calcem*, ed. Christian Laes, C. F. Goodey, and M. Lynn Rose (Leiden: Brill, 2013), 89–114.

73. Davis, *Enforcing Normalcy*; Rosemarie Garland-Thomson, *Extraordinary Bodies: Figuring Physical Disability in American Culture and Literature* (New York: Columbia University Press, 1997); Robert McRuer, *Crip Theory: Cultural Signs of Queerness and Disability* (New York: New York University Press, 2006); Alison Kafer, *Feminist, Crip, Queer* (Bloomington: Indiana University Press, 2013).

74. Garland-Thomson, *Extraordinary Bodies*, 23: "Both constructionism and essentialism, then, are theoretical strategies—framings of the body—invoked for specific ends, such as psychologically liberating people whose bodies have been defined as defective or facilitating imagined communities from which positive identities emerge. Strategic constructionism . . . Strategic essentialism . . . The identity 'disabled' operates in this mode as a life-enhancing fiction that places the reality of individual bodies and perspectives within specific social and historical contexts."

75. See Garland-Thomson, *Extraordinary Bodies*, 8–12, for a discussion of the narrow limits of the "normate" and the resulting plethora of deviant others who help to define the cultural boundaries of the normate.

76. For one example, see the capitalization of "Deaf" and the cultural valuation of "Deafness," as opposed to the move to use person-first language when referring to other disabilities. H.-D. L. Bauman and J. J. Murray, eds., *Deaf Gain: Raising the Stakes for Human Diversity* (Minneapolis: University of Minnesota Press, 2014).

77. As Garland-Thomson, *Extraordinary Bodies*, 23, cautions, "Thus, the postconstructuralist logic that destabilizes identity can free marginalized people from

the narrative of essential inadequacy, but at the same time it risks denying the particularity of their experiences. The theoretical bind is that deconstructing oppressive categories can neutralize the effects of real differences."

78. As Garland-Thomson, *Extraordinary Bodies*, 9, asserts, "The non-normate status accorded disability feminizes all disabled figures." She traces the overlap of gender and disability to Aristotle (19–28).

79. Julia Watts Belser, *Rabbinic Tales of Destruction: Gender, Sex, and Disability in the Ruins of Jerusalem* (Oxford: Oxford University Press, 2017), xxviii, calls this "an implicit category of disability," in which people with bodies that deviated from physical and sensory norms were "recognized" and constituted "a stigmatized identity."

80. As Candida R. Moss and Jeremy Schipper, "Introduction," in *Disability Studies and Biblical Literature*, 4, point out, in much of the scholarship on disability in the biblical world the focus is not on social discrimination but on the interpretive value of disability for a given culture. Thus, biblical scholars frequently rely upon the cultural model of disability, which "understands disability as product of the ways that cultures use physical and cognitive differences to narrate, organize, and interpret their world." Specifically, Moss and Schipper cite David T. Mitchell, *Cultural Locations of Disability* (Chicago: University of Chicago Press, 2006), 5–11; Jeremy Schipper, *Disability Studies and the Hebrew Bible: Figuring Mephibosheth in the David Story* (New York: T. and T. Clark, 2006), 18–21; Rebecca Raphael, *Biblical Corpora: Representations of Disability in Hebrew Biblical Literature*, LHBOTS 445 (New York: T. and T. Clark, 2008), 8–11.

81. As Garland-Thomson, *Extraordinary Bodies*, 9, has theorized, the disabled have often functioned this way in literature, "as uncomplicated figures or exotic aliens whose bodily configurations operate as spectacles, eliciting responses from other characters or producing rhetorical effects that depend on disability's cultural resonance."

82. This is one concept of disability that exists within biblical literature. As Jeremy Schipper has demonstrated, biblical narratives use disability imagery to communicate a wide range of complex ideas about bodies, beauty, national identity, and political ideology. Schipper, *Disability Studies and the Hebrew Bible*; Schipper, *Disability and Isaiah's Suffering Servant* (New York: Oxford University Press, 2011).

83. On forced labor in the mines, see Eusebius, *Eccl. Hist.* 8.8, 10; *Martyrs* 7.4, 8.1; Athanasius, *Hist. Ar.* 60; Fergus Millar, *Government, Society and Culture in the Roman Empire* (Chapel Hill: University of North Carolina Press, 2004), 137–45; Megan A. Perry, Drew S. Coleman, David L. Dettman, John P. Grattan, and Abdel Halim al-Shiyab, "Condemned to Metallum? The Origin and Role of 4th–6th Century A.D. Phaeno Mining Camp Residents Using Multiple Chemical Techniques," *Journal of Archaeological Science* 38 (2011): 558–69. In addition to the punishments mirroring the carceral spaces of the mines, the narrative exchanges of the apocalypses recall ancient judicial spaces, or courtrooms.

See Meira Z. Kensky, *Trying Man, Trying God: The Divine Courtroom in Early Jewish and Christian Literature*, WUNT 289 (Tübingen: Mohr Siebeck, 2010), 255–92.

84. In Meghan R. Henning, "Metaphorical, Punitive, and Pedagogical Blindness in Hell," *Studia Patristica* 81, no. 7, ed. Jared Secord, Heidi Marx-Wolf, and Christoph Markschies (Fall 2017): 139–52, I argue that in particular the punishments of blindness function this way. See also Edward Wheatley, *Stumbling Blocks before the Blind: Medieval Constructions of a Disability* (Ann Arbor: University of Michigan Press, 2010), who argues similarly that the use of blinding as a punishment essentially criminalized the unilateral experience of blindness. On the physiognomic consciousness in the Greek and Roman worlds and in the New Testament, see Robert Garland, *The Eye of the Beholder: Deformity and Disability in the Graeco-Roman World* (Ithaca, NY: Cornell University Press, 1995), 87–104; Nicholas Vlahogiannis, "Disabling Bodies," in *Changing Bodies, Changing Meanings: Studies on the Human Body in Antiquity*, ed. Dominic Monserrat (New York: Routledge, 1998), 13–36, especially 15–23; Mikeal Parsons, *Body and Character in Luke and Acts: The Subversion of Physiognomy in Early Christianity* (Grand Rapids, MI: Baker Academic, 2006); Chad Hartsock, *Sight and Blindness in Luke-Acts: The Use of Physical Features in Characterization* (Leiden: Brill, 2008), 146–55. On the physiognomic consciousness in the Qumran literature, see Mladen Popović, *Reading the Human Body: Physiognomics and Astrology in the Dead Sea Scrolls and Hellenistic–Early Roman Period Judaism* (Leiden: Brill, 2007).

85. This impetus to disentangle disability from suffering and tragedy is a key principle within disability studies. See Rosemarie Garland-Thomson, "The Case for Conserving Disability," *Journal of Bioethical Inquiry* 9, no. 3 (2012): 339–55.

86. Belser, *Rabbinic Tales of Destruction*, xxx.

87. See Deborah B. Creamer, *Disability and Christian Theology: Embodied Limits and Constructive Possibilities* (New York: Oxford University Press, 2009), whose model of "limits" challenges the notion that the social model and the medical model are mutually exclusive, proposing a third option. See also the special issue of the *Journal of Disability and Religion* devoted to new models for thinking about disability and theology: Jana M. Bennett and Medi Ann Volpe, eds., "Models of Disability from Religious Tradition," *JDR* 22, no. 2 (2018).

88. Lennard J. Davis, "Identity Politics, Disability, and Culture," in *Handbook of Disability Studies*, ed. Gary I. Albrecht, Katherine D. Seelman, and Michael Bury (Thousand Oaks, CA: Sage, 2001), 535–45. Kimberly W. Crenshaw, "Demarginalizing the Intersection of Race and Sex: A Black Feminist Critique of Antidiscrimination Doctrine, Feminist Theory and Antiracist Politics," *University of Chicago Legal Forum* (1989): 139–67, at 140, demonstrated that feminist thought needed to consider the way in which multiple vectors of power act upon a body, coining the term "intersectionality."

89. Albrecht Dieterich, *Nekyia: Beiträge zur Erklärung der neuentdeckten Petrusapokalyse* (1893, 1913; reprint, Stuttgart: B. G. Teubner, 1969), 19–45.

90. Himmelfarb, *Tours of Hell*. Prior to the publication of this work, the tours of hell had received little scholarly attention.

91. Bauckham, *The Fate of the Dead*, 50–52; Bremmer, *Maidens, Magic and Martyrs*, 274–80, 313–28; Jan Bremmer, "Orphic, Roman, Jewish and Christian Tours of Hell: Observations on the Apocalypse of Peter," in *Other Worlds and Their Relation to This World: Early Jewish and Ancient Christian Traditions*, ed. Tobias Nicklas et al. (Leiden: Brill, 2010), 318–21.

92. Himmelfarb, *Tours of Hell*, 45–46.

93. Kirsti Barrett Copeland, "'The Holy Conquest': Competition for the Best Afterlife in the Apocalypse of Paul and Late Antique Egypt," in Nicklas et al., *Other Worlds and Their Relation to This World*, 369–89; Tobias Nicklas, "Resurrection-Judgment-Punishment: Apocalypse of Peter 4," in *Resurrection from the Dead: Biblical Traditions in Dialogue*, ed. Geert Van Oyen and T. Shepherd, Traditions bibliques en dialogue BETL 249 (Leuven: Peeters, 2012), 461–74; Tobias Nicklas, "Gute Werke, rechter Glaube: Paulusrezeption in der Apokalypse des Paulus," in *Ancient Perspectives on Paul*, ed. Tobias Nicklas, Andreas Merkt, and Joseph Verheyden, NTOA 102 (Göttingen: Vandenhoeck and Ruprecht, 2013), 151–70.

94. Henning, *Educating Early Christians through the Rhetoric of Hell*; Henning, "Metaphorical, Punitive, and Pedagogical Blindness in Hell," 139–52; Henning, "Lacerated Lips and Lush Landscapes," 99–116; Henning, "Weeping and Bad Hair: The Bodily Suffering of Early Christian Hell as a Threat to Masculinity," in *Phallacies: Historical Intersections of Disability and Masculinity*, ed. Kathleen M. Brian and James W. Trent Jr. (Oxford: Oxford University Press, 2017), 282–300; Henning, "Substitutes in Hell," 185–204; Henning, "Hell as 'Heterotopia': Edification and Interpretation from Enoch to the Apocalypses of Peter and Paul," in *Between Canonical and Apocryphal Texts: Processes of Reception, Rewriting and Interpretation in Early Judaism and Early Christianity*, ed. Jörg Frey, Claire Clivaz, and Tobias Nicklas, with the collaboration of Jörg Röder (Tübingen: Mohr Siebeck, 2019), 297–318.

95. Henning, *Educating Early Christians through the Rhetoric of Hell*, 224–32.

96. Henning, "Eternal Punishment as *Paideia*: The *Ekphrasis* of Hell in the *Apocalypse of Peter* and the *Apocalypse of Paul*," *Biblical Research* 58 (2013): 29–48.

97. Moss, "Heavenly Healing," 991–1017; Moss, *Divine Bodies*, 155–74.

Chapter 1. Assigned to Suffering

1. Clement of Alexandria, *Educ.* 3.3.19.1–2. Greek text in M. Marcovich, ed., *Clementis Alexandrini Paedagogus*, VCSup 61 (Leiden: Brill, 2002), 159. English translation adapted from Simon P. Wood, *Clement of Alexandria: Christ the*

Educator, FC 23 (Washington, DC: Catholic University of America Press, 1954), 214–15.

2. Later, Clement describes male homoeroticism as "suffering the things of women" (*ta gunaikōn hoi andres peponthasin*), *Educ.* 3.3.21.3. Marcovich, *Clementis Alexandrini*, 161. See Denise Kimber Buell, *Making Christians: Clement of Alexandria and the Rhetoric of Legitimacy* (Princeton, NJ: Princeton University Press, 1999), for a discussion of Clement's use of procreative language as a metaphor for the origins of the universe.

3. Maud W. Gleason, *Making Men: Sophists and Self-Presentation in Ancient Rome* (Princeton, NJ: Princeton University Press, 1995), 58–81; Rebecca Flemming, *Medicine and the Making of Roman Women: Gender, Nature, and Authority from Celsus to Galen* (Oxford: Oxford University Press, 2000), 294–329.

4. Andrew Crislip, *Thorns in the Flesh: Illness and Sanctity in Late Ancient Christianity* (Philadelphia: University of Pennsylvania Press, 2013), 50; Andrew Crislip, "Shenoute of Atripe on Christ the Physician and the Cure of the Souls," *Le Muséon* 122 (2009): 265–95. See also Kyle Harper, *From Shame to Sin: The Christian Transformation of Sexual Morality in Late Antiquity* (Cambridge, MA: Harvard University Press, 2013), 85, who states, "Clement more than any other representative of the early church, presented his views in the language of the culture around him."

5. Benjamin H. Dunning, *Specters of Paul: Sexual Difference in Early Christian Thought* (Philadelphia: University of Pennsylvania Press, 2011), 61–74.

6. Flemming, *Medicine and the Making of Roman Women*, 119.

7. Flemming, *Medicine and the Making of Roman Women*, 119.

8. Thomas W. Laqueur, *Making Sex: Body and Gender from the Greeks to Freud* (Cambridge, MA: Harvard University Press, 1992), 25–62.

9. Laqueur, *Making Sex*, 28.

10. Aristotle, *Gen. An.* 2.728.A17. See also *Gen. An.* 2.721.A30–730.B31, 4.775.A15; *Hist. An.* 588.B4–589.A9; *Met.* 1058.A29; *Part. An.* 681.A12–28. A notable exception to the idea that women are colder than men occurs in Hippocratic Corpus, *Fem. Dis.* 1.1, in which women's blood is presumed to be hotter than men's.

11. Aristotle, *Gen. An.* 4.767.B7. See Rosemarie Garland-Thomson, *Extraordinary Bodies: Figuring Physical Disability in American Culture and Literature* (New York: Columbia University Press, 1997), 19–28.

12. Laqueur, *Making Sex*, 25–30, 52–62. Galen, *Func. Part.* 14.6–7.

13. Galen, *Func. Part.* 14.6 (2.299 in C. G. Kühn, *Galena Opera Omnia*, 20 vols. [Leipzig: Cnoblauch, 1821–23]). Translation in Margaret May Tallmadge, *Galen: On the Usefulness of the Parts of the Body*, 2 vols. (Ithaca, NY: Cornell University Press, 1968), 2:630.

14. Dale B. Martin, *The Corinthian Body* (New Haven: Yale University Press, 1995), 32–33, explains Hippocrates and Galen through the lens of Aristotle and Laqueur. And again, Dale B. Martin, *Sex and the Single Savior* (Louisville: West-

minster John Knox, 2006), 84, introduces the one-sex model, explaining its significance for salvific changes to the body. Martin's work on the body and gender, and the body in early Christianity, was highly influential, maximizing the impact of Laqueur's thinking on the subdiscipline. See, for instance, the work of Stephanie L. Cobb, *Dying to Be Men: Gender and Language in Early Martyr Texts* (New York: Columbia University Press, 2008). Notable exceptions to this trend include Chris L. de Wet, *Preaching Bondage: John Chrysostom and the Discourse of Slavery in Early Christianity* (Oakland: University of California Press, 2015); and Mathew Kuefler, *The Manly Eunuch: Masculinity, Gender Ambiguity, and Christian Ideology in Late Antiquity* (Chicago: University of Chicago Press, 2001), 304n5.

15. In her corrective to Laqueur, Helen King, *The One-Sex Body on Trial: The Classical and Early Modern Evidence* (New York: Ashgate, 2013), 13–15, cites the simplicity and accessibility of Laqueur's argument as part of the reason for its influence across disciplines.

16. King, *The One-Sex Body on Trial*, 25.

17. As Helen King has noted, Laqueur's initial position was more nuanced than that of those who appropriated it, arguing that *both* a two-sex and a one-sex model have always been a part of the conversation about gender and the body. King, *The One-Sex Body on Trial*, 25. See also Flemming, *Medicine and the Making of Roman Women*, 357–58. King (8) recounts the discrepancy between Laqueur and the reception of Laqueur: "I agree with an assertion found in the preface to *Making Sex*, one which is at odds with Laqueur's subsequent work and its reception; in his words, 'the startling conclusions that a two-sex and a one-sex model [have] always been available to those who thought about difference.'"

18. King, *The One-Sex Body on Trial*, 44. Hippocratic Corpus, *Fem. Dis.* 1.1. See also Lesley Ann Dean-Jones, *Women's Bodies in Classical Greek Science* (Oxford: Oxford University Press, 1994), 111.

19. Aristotle, *Gen. An.* 721.A30–730.B31; Galen, *Func. Part.* 14.6–8.

20. King, *The One-Sex Body on Trial*, 46, argues contra Laqueur, *Making Sex*, 35, 37, and 105, "Not being aware of the *Gynaikeia* tradition, Laqueur plays down the pre-modern importance of menstruation in defining what it is to be female, replacing this with his focus on inside/outside organs."

21. Dean-Jones, *Women's Bodies in Classical Greek Science*, 225.

22. Hippocratic Corpus, *Glands* 16.8.572.13; *Fem. Dis.* 1.1.8.12.6–12. See also Aristotle, *Gen. An.* 726B.31–727A.19.

23. Galen, *Aff. Part.* 5.7 and *Blood Er.* 5. Flemming, *Medicine and the Making of Roman Women*, 339.

24. Galen, *Aff. Part.* 6.5. On the centrality of childbearing and menstruation to healthy bodies in Hippocrates and Galen, see Dean-Jones, *Women's Bodies in Classical Greek Science*, 136–46; and Flemming, *Medicine and the Making of Roman Women*, 331–43.

25. King, *The One-Sex Body on Trial*, 48, citing Hippocratic Corpus, *Fem. Dis.* 1.1. See also Meghan Henning, "Paralysis and Sexuality in Medical Literature and the *Acts of Peter*," *JLA* 8, no. 2 (2015): 306–21, for further discussion of the intersection between blood flow and gender in antiquity and late antiquity.

26. Flemming, *Medicine and the Making of Roman Women*, 369–70. See also Teresa M. Shaw, *The Burden of the Flesh: Fasting and Sexuality in Early Christianity* (Minneapolis: Fortress Press, 1998), 64–78, who discusses the ways in which ancient medical texts reflected broader cultural ideas about gender and the body.

27. Martin, *The Corinthian Body*, 32–33, argues, "Much of Galen's hygienic and therapeutic method reads like a training manual designed to maintain the right degree of heat, dryness, and compactness for the masculinization of the young man's body and to keep it from slipping down the precarious slope to femininity." See also Martin, *Sex and the Single Savior*, 84, which describes this "spectral hierarchy" of gender and women's salvation as "movement upward into masculinity."

28. Kuefler, *The Manly Eunuch*, 20.

29. Flemming, *Medicine and the Making of Roman Women*, 119; King, *The One-Sex Body on Trial*, 41, 44–45.

30. Flemming, *Medicine and the Making of Roman Women*, 357–58; and Galen, *Doct. Hipp. Plat.* 9.3.25–26.

31. Aristotle, *Mem. Rem.* 450 AB; *Rhet.* 2.2–11. Aristotle offers an anthropological explanation for how visual imagery works, arguing that an original sensory perception impresses a mental image on the soul, just as an image is stamped into wax. The soul then associates this image with similar images and emotional responses that are already familiar, responding in kind. I am grateful to Troy W. Martin for these references to Aristotle's understanding of the way that mental imagery works. Similarly, Quintilian, *Inst.* 8.3.71, argues that the mind "finds it easiest to accept what it can recognize."

32. Judith Perkins, *The Suffering Self: Pain and Narrative Representation in the Early Christian Era* (New York: Routledge, 1995), 169.

33. Vivian Nutton, *Ancient Medicine*, 2d ed. (New York: Routledge, [2004] 2013), 70–71. As Nutton notes, it is almost impossible to distinguish the small number of authentic writings of Hippocrates from the rest of the corpus.

34. Gleason, *Making Men*, 62–70, 105–8.

35. Vivian Nutton, "From Galen to Alexander: Aspects of Medicine and Medical Practice in Late Antiquity," *Dumbarton Oaks Papers* 38 (1984): 2–5.

36. While Epidaurus "reached its peak" in the fourth and fifth centuries BCE but remained open until 426 CE, Athens was functioning from 420 BCE to the fifth century CE, Kos opened in the fourth century BCE, and Pergamon opened in 350 BCE and underwent a major renovation during the reign of Hadrian (117–38 CE). Hector Avalos, *Illness and Health Care in the Ancient Near East: The Role of the Temple in Greece, Mesopotamia and Israel* (Cambridge, MA: Harvard

University Press, 1995), 37–98; Louise Wells, *The Greek Language of Healing from Homer to New Testament Times* (Berlin: Walter de Gruyter, 1998), 19–83.

37. Sara B. Aleshire, *The Athenian Asklepieion: The People, the Inscriptions, and the Inventories* (Amsterdam: J. C. Gieben, 1989); Lynn R. LiDonnici, *The Epidaurian Miracle Inscriptions: Text, Translation and Commentary*, Texts and Translations: Graeco-Roman Religion Series (Atlanta: Scholars, 1995), 20–39; Wells, *The Greek Language of Healing*, 17–22.

38. Laqueur, *Making Sex*; Dean-Jones, *Women's Bodies in Classical Greek Science*; Flemming, *Medicine and the Making of Roman Women*; King, *The One-Sex Body on Trial*.

39. Galen, *Func. Part.* 11.14. Musonius Rufus, frag. 21, and Arrian, *Diss. Epict.* 1.16.10–14, offer similar, Stoic explanations of the significance of beards.

40. Flemming, *Medicine and the Making of Roman Women*, 321–22, 365–66. "For Galen, the reasoning runs this way in this particular instance because he is interested in explaining why women do not have beards, not why they lack dignity and an active outdoor life. Neither he, nor any other surviving author, is really in the business of explicating or justifying women's roles in society, or any particular aspect of contemporary culture. They do not try to persuade people that the female is a relatively worse human being than the male: rather, they are making that already existing situation medically manifest in a number of ways, ranging from the subtle to the emphatic" (365).

41. Galen, *Ant. Caus.* 15.118. Earlier, in 8.109–11, Galen explains, "It is not our task here to explain what exactly the seeds of fever are; rather it suffices to show that the conditional inference is not sound."

42. Galen, *Ant. Caus.* 8.109–11. Plato, *Tim.* 62b, and Hippocratic Corpus, *Anc. Med.* 22, offer further evidence that numbness, deadness of the limbs, and trembling were associated with being chilled to the point of shivering or freezing. Meghan Henning, "Paralysis and Sexuality in Medical Literature," 306–21.

43. Perkins, *The Suffering Self*, 173–74. For a discussion of the overlap between medical practices at the Asklepieia and Hippocratic practices, see René Josef Rüttimann, "Asklepios and Jesus: The Form, Character and Status of the Asklepios Cult in the Second Century CE and Its Influence on Early Christianity" (PhD diss., Harvard University, 1986), 46–47; Avalos, *Illness and Health Care*, 78; Wells, *The Greek Language of Healing*, 81–83; Laura Bronwen Wickkiser, *Asklepios, Medicine, and the Politics of Healing in Fifth Century Greece: Between Craft and Cult* (Baltimore: Johns Hopkins University Press, 2008), 49. On the extent to which the broader population would have understood ancient medical concepts, see Flemming, *Medicine and the Making of Roman Women*, 50–70; Nutton, *Ancient Medicine*, 284–91.

44. Celsus, *Med.* 1.1. Sarah E. Bond, "'As Trainers for the Healthy': Massage Therapists, Anointers, and Healing in the Late Latin West," *JLA* 8, no. 2 (2015): 386–404, at 398.

45. Celsus, *Med.* 2.14.9. Flemming, *Medicine and the Making of Roman Women,* 177.

46. See the passage *On Healthful Declamation* that is attributed to Antyllus by Oribasius (Antyllus, *Health Dec.,* ap. Oribasius, *Coll. Med.* 6.10.1–25): "These *poroi* are part of an integrated pneumatic system within the body, of which the vocalization process is a part, so their dimensional deficiency has a detrimental effect on the quality and tone of both voice and flesh as the flow of *pneuma* is impeded." See also Pliny the Elder, *Nat. Hist.* 11.112.269, who describes the fundamental weakness of all female bodies (except those of leopards and bears).

47. Pliny the Elder, *Nat. Hist.* 7.5.41, asserts that whereas male fetuses move on the fortieth day, female fetuses do not move until the ninetieth day.

48. Dean-Jones, *Women's Bodies in Classical Greek Science,* 104.

49. The shorter life expectancy for ancient women is supported by osteoarchaeological studies. Mirko D. Grmek, *Diseases in the Ancient Greek World,* trans. Mireille Muellner and Leonard Muellner (Baltimore: Johns Hopkins University Press, 1991), 104; originally *Les maladies à l'aube de la civilisation occidentale* (Paris: Payot, 1983). Saskia Hin, *The Demography of Roman Italy: Population Dynamics in an Ancient Conquest Society, 201 BCE–14 CE* (Cambridge: Cambridge University Press, 2013), 129–34, provides important qualifications for these data, arguing that more research is still needed to understand why this was the case.

50. Dean-Jones, *Women's Bodies in Classical Greek Science,* 105.

51. Pliny the Elder, *Nat. Hist.* 7.13.63–67; 14.66; 28.23.77–78.

52. Galen, *Blood. Er.* 5 (11.164–66 in Kühn, *Galena Opera Omnia*); translation is from Flemming, *Medicine and the Making of Roman Women,* 311–12. See also Galen, *Func. Part.* 14.7; Galen, *Ther. Glau.* 1.15 (11.47–50 in Kühn, *Galena Opera Omnia*); and the discussion of blood flow, sexual disfunction, and paralysis in Henning, "Paralysis and Sexuality in Medical Literature," 316–17. This emphasis on blood flow and gynecological health is one of the few overlaps between Greek medicine and the Egyptian papyri. For example, *Kahun* 26 describes dilated blood vessels in the breasts as a necessary sign of fertility or early pregnancy. See *Kahun* 26 in John F. Nunn, *Ancient Egyptian Medicine* (Norman: University of Oklahoma Press, 1996), 192.

53. On the pain of childbirth and recovery dissipating with each birth: Hippocratic Corpus, *Nat. Child* 7. For discussion of women who experienced pain as a result of not bearing children, see Hippocratic Corpus, *Epid.* 6.832; Galen, *Hipp. Epid.* 6.8 (*CMG* 5.10.2.2.506.21–38); Galen, *Aff. Part.* 6.5 (8.417 in Kühn, *Galena Opera Omnia*); Galen, *Comp. Drug Pl.* 9.10 (13.319–20 in Kühn, *Galena Opera Omnia*); Galen, *Diff. Resp.* 3.13 (7.959 in Kühn, *Galena Opera Omnia*). Flemming, *Medicine and the Making of Roman Women,* 334; King, *The One-Sex Body on Trial,* 20, 96–97, 108–9.

54. Hippocratic Corpus, *Nat. Child* 7; Galen, *Hipp. Epid.* 2.2 (*CMG* 5.10.1.230.31–231.6); Galen, *Hipp. Aph.* 5.55 (XVIIB 834–35 in Kühn, *Galena Opera Omnia*). Hippocratic Corpus, *Nat. Child* 20.1, argues that male fetuses develop more

quickly than female fetuses because the males are stronger, made from stronger, thicker seed than the females. Pliny also says that female fetuses are "burdensome" during pregnancy and delivered with greater difficulty. Pliny the Elder, *Nat. Hist.* 7.3.37 and 7.5.41.

55. For instance, at the Athenian Asklepieion the inventories record a higher percentage of female dedicants and there are more female anatomical votives (specifically breasts) than male body parts. Aleshire, *The Athenian Asklepieion*, 45–46. On the rule against childbirth at the Asklepieia, see E. D. Phillips, *Aspects of Greek Medicine* (London: Croom Helm, 1973), 199; Susan G. Cole, "*Gunaixi ou Themis*: Gender Difference in the Greek *Leges Sacrae*," *Helios* 19 (1992): 104–22 at 109–10. An example of women being expected to leave the sanctuary to give birth is the inscription detailing the story of Ithmonika of Pellene, in which she has to leave the sanctuary to give birth, even though that is her "cure" for a "three year pregnancy" (*IG* IV², 1, no. 121:2).

56. See, for instance, *IC*, 1.17, no. 17, in which a man comes to the Asklepieion coughing up bloody pieces of flesh. And in *IG* IV², 1, no. 122:21, a woman is cured of dropsy by having her head cut off and a large quantity of fluid drained, then having her head and neck reattached. Dean-Jones, *Women's Bodies in Classical Greek Science*, 246, tells a story from Euripides, *El.* 654, 1131–33, in which Iphigeneia speaks for Artemis, saying that any man whose hand is stained with blood, childbirth, or burial is unclean and cannot approach the altar.

57. Dean-Jones, *Women's Bodies in Classical Greek Science*, 247.

58. Aelius Aristides, *Sac. Tales* 47.59, 65, 74; 48.18, 50, 51; 51.49; Marcus Aurelius, *Med.* 5.8. Perkins, *The Suffering Self*, 179.

59. Perkins, *The Suffering Self*, 179.

60. See, for instance, *IG* IV², 1, no. 122:37, in which a paralyzed man is instructed by Asklepios to bathe in an exceedingly cold lake, and is told that he will not be healed if he is "too cowardly" to do so. According to Vitruvius, 8.3.4, for those who were paralyzed or lacking proper blood flow, bathing in natural hot springs might be recommended. See also Flemming, *Medicine and the Making of Roman Women*, 65–76, who also critiques Perkins, arguing that the relative power of the physician and the patient's dependence on their prescriptions somewhat undermines the narrative of suffering as "self-mastery" that Perkins is trying to construct.

61. Nicole Loraux, "*Ponos*. Sur quelques difficultés de la peine comme nom du travail," *Annali dell'Instituto Orientale di Napoli* 4 (1982): 171–92; Helen King, *Hippocrates' Woman: Reading the Female Body in Ancient Greece* (London: Routledge, 1998), 123–26.

62. Hippocratic Corpus, *Fem. Dis.* 1.6 (8.30.16–17), 1.72 (8.152.7); and *Nat. Ch.* 18 (7.502.6–7). Helen King, "Sacrificial Blood: The Role of the *Amnion* in Ancient Gynecology," *Helios* 13 (1987): 117–26; Dean-Jones, *Women's Bodies in Classical Greek Science*, 101.

63. Lesley Dean-Jones observes that "a woman's menarchal blood was an auspicious sign indicating that she was ready to assume her allotted role in the service of the *oikos* and therefore of the *polis*," and likewise, the blood of a woman after childbirth was like "that of a propitious sacrifice" because it represented the "culmination of this role." Dean-Jones, *Women's Bodies in Classical Greek Science*, 215.

64. Basil of Ancyra, *Virg.* 51 (*PG* 30:772B–C); Pseudo-Athanasius, *Virg.* 10: "For in the kingdom of heaven 'there is neither male nor female,' but all well-pleasing women take on the rank of men." Shaw, *The Burden of the Flesh*, 235, 253; see also Gregor Emmenegger, *Wie die Jungfrau zum Kind kam. Zum Einfluss antiker medizinischer und naturphilosophischer Theorien auf die Entwicklung des christlichen Dogmas* (Fribourg: Academic Press, 2014).

65. Clement of Alexandria, *Misc.* 3.7.58; Dunning, *Specters of Paul*, 65, 74; Taylor Petrey, *Resurrecting Parts: Early Christians on Desire, Reproduction, and Sexual Difference* (London: Routledge, 2015).

66. Candida R. Moss, "Heavenly Healing: Eschatological Cleansing and the Resurrection of the Dead in the Early Church," *JAAR* 79 (2011): 991–1017.

67. Lucian, *Dial. Dead.* 1.3, 5.1; while there was not a single view of the afterlife in the ancient world, the idea that the soul continued as a shade of some form was prevalent, and the literature that was used for classical education (Homer's *Odyssey* and Virgil's *Aeneid*) reinforced the idea of a bodily postmortem existence. On the prevalence of these texts in ancient paideia, see Quintilian, *Inst.* 1.8.4–12; Augustine, *Conf.* 1.13–14; Raffaella Cribiore, *Gymnastics of the Mind: Greek Education in Hellenistic and Roman Egypt* (Princeton, NJ: Princeton University Press, 2001) 197; Meghan Henning, *Educating Early Christians through the Rhetoric of Hell: "Weeping and Gnashing of Teeth" as Paideia in Matthew and the Early Church*, Wissenschaftliche Untersuchungen zum Neuen Testament II. 382 (Tübingen: Mohr Siebeck, 2014), 65.

68. Outi Lehtipuu, *Debates over the Resurrection of the Dead: Constructing Early Christian Identity* (Oxford: Oxford University Press, 2015), 67–108.

69. Lehtipuu, *Debates over the Resurrection*, 109–58.

70. Moss, "Heavenly Healing," 1–27.

71. Pseudo-Justin Martyr, *On the Resurrection* 3–4; Irenaeus, *Ag. Her.* 5.12.6; cited in Moss, "Heavenly Healing," 15–17.

72. Augustine, *City of God* 22.17.1145; 22.20.1152; Moss, "Heavenly Healing," 18–19.

73. For discussion of the way that Tertullian directly addresses the broader cultural association between childbirth and shame, see Virginia Burrus, *Saving Shame: Martyrs, Saints, and Other Abject Subjects* (Philadelphia: University of Pennsylvania Press, 2008), 52–57; Taylor Petrey, *Resurrecting Parts: Early Christians on Desire, Reproduction, and Sexual Difference* (New York: Routledge, 2016), 98.

74. Moss, "Heavenly Healing," 21–22.

75. Acts Thom. 55–57; Apoc. Pet. 7 and 9; Apoc. Paul 34–39.

76. Martha Himmelfarb, *Tours of Hell: An Apocalyptic Form in Jewish and Christian Literature* (Philadelphia: University of Pennsylvania Press, 1983); Callie Callon, "Sorcery, Wheels, and Mirror Punishment in the *Apocalypse of Peter*," *JECS* 18, no. 1 (2010): 29–49.

77. Meghan Henning, "Metaphorical, Punitive, and Pedagogical Blindness in Hell," *Studia Patristica* 80, no. 3 (2017); Meghan Henning, "Weeping and Bad Hair: The Bodily Suffering of Early Christian Hell as a Threat to Masculinity," in *Phallacies: Historical Intersections of Disability and Masculinity*, ed. Kathleen M. Brian and James W. Trent Jr. (New York: Oxford University Press, 2017), 282–300.

78. As Moss, "Heavenly Healing," 20, demonstrates, Augustine had to create two separate categories of beauty (beauty of virtue vs. beauty of body) in order to reconcile the idea that the martyrs kept their wounds in heaven with his bodily aesthetic of perfection (Augustine, *City of God* 22.19.1149). Contra Beth Felker Jones, *Marks of His Wounds: Gender Politics and Bodily Resurrection* (Oxford: Oxford University Press), 29, who argues that Augustine redefines blemishes as beautiful.

79. See Maud W. Gleason, *Making Men: Sophists and Self-Presentation in Ancient Rome* (Princeton, NJ: Princeton University Press, 1995), 160–62. De Wet, *Preaching Bondage*, 174–83, describes the way that the different ideals of Roman masculinity, or "masculinities," shaped slaveholding discourse.

80. De Wet, *Preaching Bondage*, 218.

81. De Wet, *Preaching Bondage*, 199.

82. J. Albert Harrill, "'Exegetical Torture' in Early Christian Biblical Interpretation: The Case of Origen of Alexandria," *Biblical Interpretation* 25 (2017): 39–57. I am extremely grateful to J. Albert Harrill for sharing a prepublication version of this article, which has had a tremendous impact on my thinking about ancient judicial punishment and the early Christian imagination.

83. Origen, *Comm. Jo.* 20.323, quoted in Harrill, "Exegetical Torture," 40; for a translation, see Ronald E. Heine, *Origen: Commentary on the Gospel according to John*, FC 80 and 89, 2 vols. (Washington, DC: Catholic University of America Press, 1989).

84. On the juridical practice of the *basanos* and the brutality of the torture used, see Keith Bradley, *Slavery and Society at Rome* (Cambridge: Cambridge University Press, 1994), 165–70; David Mirhady, "The Athenian Rationale for Torture," in *Law and Social Status in Classical Athens*, ed. Virginia Hunter and Jonathan Edmonson (Oxford: Oxford University Press, 2000), 53–74; Jane F. Gardner, "Slavery and Roman Law," in *The Cambridge World History of Slavery*, vol. 1: *The Ancient Mediterranean World*, ed. Keith Bradley and Paul Cartledge (Cambridge: Cambridge University Press, 2011), 431.

85. Plato, *Let.* 2.313c–d; Hippocratic Corpus, *Airs* 3; Philo, *Spec. Laws* 4.156–57; Plutarch, *Mor.* 574, 645b–c; Plutarch, *Quaest. conv.* 3; *De fato* 11; Galen, *Nat. Cap.*

3.10.178–80; *Semen* 1.16.25; cited in Harrill, "Exegetical Torture," 49–54. See also Page duBois, *Torture and Truth* (New York: Routledge, 1991), 35–36.

86. Origen, *Comm. Rom.* 7.14.4; Origen, *Princ.* 3.1.11; cited in Harrill, "Exegetical Torture," 56.

87. Harrill, "Exegetical Torture," 56.

88. Julia Hillner, *Prison, Punishment and Penance in Late Antiquity* (Cambridge: Cambridge University Press, 2015), 58–63, 131–50.

89. John Chrysostom, *Vain.* 76 and 52, gives specific guidance about how parents should use hell to teach their children, stating that parents should wait until their sons are fifteen to tell them about hell.

90. Harrill, "Exegetical Torture," 55–56, also observes this with respect to the range of Origen's uses of torture.

91. According to John Chrysostom, *Hom. Matt.* 30.6, these punishments had to be used with more care when instructing women, who should only receive instruction on hell's punishments for outward adornment after they have been eased into the subject matter.

92. Brent D. Shaw, "Judicial Nightmares and Christian Memory," *JECS* 11, no. 4 (2003): 533–63, at 556.

93. Shaw, "Judicial Nightmares and Christian Memory," 239.

94. David Frankfurter, "Martyrology and the Prurient Gaze," *JECS* 17, no. 2 (2009): 215–45, at 238–39.

95. Shaw, "Judicial Nightmares and Christian Memory," 551, says that the judicial spectacle was replayed through the end of antiquity, "but it needed a literary text." He argues that the martyrdom literature provides the narrative that memorializes this spectacle, however transitory the genre. Shaw nuances this claim in several places, admitting that the literary product itself is representative of the highest, literate stratum of a given culture.

96. Himmelfarb, *Tours of Hell*, 41–51; the Apocalypse of Peter, for instance, was included in several Scripture lists, and was read in some churches. The Apocalypse of Peter is cited in the list that Eusebius (*Eccl. Hist.* 6.14.1–7) reconstructed and attributed to Clement of Alexandria, in the Muratorian fragment, and in the list found in the Claromantanus (D) manuscript. Sozomen, *Eccl. Hist.* 7.19.9 (mid-fifth century CE), details the practice of some Palestinian churches that still read the Apocalypse of Peter every year on Good Friday. Those Christians read the text while fasting in memory of the Passion.

97. Henning, *Educating Early Christians*, 60–64, 207–10.

98. See Himmelfarb, *Tours of Hell*, 68–105, for a summary of the various kinds of measure-for-measure punishments that occur in the apocalyptic tours of hell, including charts that summarize the correlation between specific sins and punishments.

99. Himmelfarb, *Tours of Hell*, 75–78; Patrick Gray, "Abortion, Infanticide, and the Social Rhetoric of the Apocalypse of Peter," *JECS* 9 (2001): 313–37; István

Czachesz, "Torture in Hell and Reality: The *Visio Pauli*," in *The Visio Pauli and the Gnostic Apocalypse of Paul*, ed. Jan N. Bremmer and István Czachesz (Leuven: Peeters, 2007), 130–43. *Lex talionis* is not the primary form of punishment in Roman law codes, but it remained in the cultural memory and does appear in the *Laws of the Twelve Tables* 7.9, where a person who has their limb broken by another person is allowed to retaliate in kind if the offender does not make a settlement.

100. Shaw, "Judicial Nightmares and Christian Memory," 537; cf. Artemidorus, *Dreams* 1.40; 2.49–54.

101. Hillner, *Prison, Punishment, and Penance*, 51.

102. Eusebius, *Eccl. Hist.* 8.8, 10; *Martyrs* 7.4; 8.1; Athanasius, *Hist. Ar.* 60.

103. For an archaeological study of graves associated with the Phaeno mines, which notes that few human remains there show evidence of ill health, see Megan A. Perry, Drew S. Coleman, David L. Dettman, John P. Grattan, and Abdel Halim al-Shiyab, "Condemned to Metallum? The Origin and Role of 4th–6th Century A.D. Phaeno Mining Camp Residents Using Multiple Chemical Techniques," *Journal of Archaeological Science* 38 (2011): 558–69.

104. John Chrysostom, *Hom. Matt.* 43.5: "But as those who work in the mines [Gk. *metalla*] are delivered over to certain cruel men, and see none of the people they live with [Gk. *tōn oikeiōn*], but only their overseers; so will it be then also: or rather not so, but even far more cruel [Gk. *xalepōteron*]. For here it is possible to go unto the king, and entreat, and free the condemned person: but there, no longer; since it is not permitted, but they continue in the scorching torment, and in such great bodily pain [Gk. *odunēn*], as it is not possible for words to tell." PG 57:462.56–59; translation mine. In a law addressing prostitution passed by Theodosius II, the horror of the mines is used to condemn those who sexually traffic women, arguing that the punishment of pimps in the mines is fitting because it is better than what torture they have imposed upon women who are forced to have sex (*CTh* 15.8.2).

105. Albrecht Dieterich, *Nekyia: Beiträge zur Erklärung der neuentdeckten Petrusapokalyse* (1893; 1913²; repr., Stuttgart: B. G. Teubner, 1969), 196–201; Himmelfarb, *Tours of Hell*, 107–10.

106. However, as István Czachesz notes, it is hard to say that the overlap between real-life torture and the tours of hell is mere "coincidence"; he questions "whether such punishments came to the Apocalypses from mythological texts or from historical experience" (Czachesz, "Torture in Hell and Reality," 142).

107. Ernst Emanuel Mayer, *The Ancient Middle Classes: Urban Life and Aesthetics in the Roman Empire, 100 BCE–250 CE* (Cambridge, MA: Harvard University Press, 2012), 166–213.

108. Pliny the Elder, *Nat. Hist.* 33.126, describes the way in which the *basanos*, or touchstone, was used, comparing the metal that is being tested against a sample that is known to be a true or pure representation of that metal. Translated

in John W. Humphrey, John P. Olsen, and Andrew N. Sherwood, eds., *Greek and Roman Technology: A Sourcebook: Annotated Translations of Greek and Latin Texts and Documents* (New York: Routledge, 1998), 166.

109. Virginia Burrus, "Torture, Truth, and the Witnessing Body: Reading Christian Martyrdom with Page duBois," *Biblical Interpretation* 25 (2017): 5–18, at 13; J. Albert Harrill, "Exegetical Torture," 55; Candida R. Moss, *Divine Bodies: Resurrecting Perfection in the New Testament and Early Christianity* (New Haven: Yale University Press, 2019), 105.

110. Elizabeth Castelli, *Martyrdom and Memory: Early Christian Culture Making* (New York: Columbia University Press, 2007), 33–68, 104–33; Frankfurter, "Martyrology and the Prurient Gaze," 238–40.

111. Shaw, "Judicial Nightmares and Christian Memory," 535.

112. Castelli, *Martyrdom and Memory*, 126.

113. Burrus, "Torture, Truth, and the Witnessing Body," 15, 17.

114. As Frankfurter, "Martyrology and the Prurient Gaze," 228, has argued, the sado-erotic themes of the martyrdom accounts are "far more complex imaginative experiences than simply tableaux for male misogyny." See also Elizabeth Castelli, "Visions and Voyeurism: Holy Women and the Politics of Sight in Early Christianity," *Protocol of the Colloquy of the Center for Hermeneutical Studies* n.s. 2 (1995): 1–20; J. Albert Harrill, *Slaves in the New Testament: Literary, Social, and Moral Dimensions* (Minneapolis: Augsburg Fortress, 2006), 157–63; Candida R. Moss, "Blood Ties: Martyrdom, Motherhood, and Family in the *Passion of Perpetua and Felicitas*," in *Women and Gender in Ancient Religions: Interdisciplinary Approaches*, ed. Stephen P. Ahearne-Kroll, James A. Kelhoffer, and Paul A. Holloway, WUNT 1.263 (Tübingen: Mohr Siebeck, 2010), 198–204.

115. DuBois, *Torture and Truth*, 90.

116. Burrus, "Torture, Truth, and the Witnessing Body," 6, 14. See also Kate Cooper, "The Voice of the Victim: Gender, Representation and Early Christian Martyrdom," *BJRL* 80, no. 3 (1998): 147–57.

117. Burrus, "Torture, Truth, and the Witnessing Body," 5; Perkins, *The Suffering Self*, 15–40; Cooper, "The Voice of the Victim," 148–54; Virginia Burrus, "Torture and Travail: Producing the Christian Martyr," in *A Feminist Companion to Patristic Literature*, ed. Amy-Jill Levine with Maria Mayo Robbins, FCNTECW 12 (London: T. and T. Clark, 2008), 56–71; Burrus, *Saving Shame*, 23–32; Stepanie Cobb, *Divine Deliverance: Pain and Painlessness in Early Christian Martyr Texts* (Berkeley: University of California Press, 2017), 146–47.

118. Moss, *Ancient Christian Martyrdom*, 28–29.

119. Castelli, *Martyrdom and Memory*, 126.

120. Cobb, *Dying to Be Men*, 126.

121. Burrus, "Torture, Truth, and the Witnessing Body," 17.

122. Buell, "Ambiguous Legacy," 50–51; cf. Annewies van den Hoek, "Clement of Alexandria on Martyrdom," *Studia Patristica* 26 (1993): 324–41. Van den Hoek

argues that Clement has mixed views on women, but his treatment of martyrdom "evokes women as heroines and brings out their equality with men" (338–39).

123. Moss, *Ancient Christian Martyrdom*, 32.

124. Moss, *Ancient Christian Martyrdom*, 32.

125. Ellen Muehlberger, "Simeon and Other Women in Theodoret's Religious History: Gender and the Representation of Late Ancient Christian Asceticism," *JECS* 23, no. 4 (2015): 583–606, at 604–6.

126. On this see David Brakke, *Demons and the Making of the Monk: Spiritual Combat in Early Christianity* (Cambridge, MA: Harvard University Press, 2006); Muehlberger, "Simeon and Other Women," 583–606.

127. Perkins, *The Suffering Self*, 214.

Chapter 2. Gendered Bodies, Social Identities, and the Susceptibility to Sin

1. Scholars, like Ethan Blue, who have analyzed the contemporary hell house note that the sins that are punished in these haunted spectacles are not randomly chosen, but are "symbolic expressions of real existential indeterminacies," channeling "the fears of a chaotic world into a coherent historical and moral narrative." Ethan Blue, "National Trauma, Church Drama: The Cultural Politics of Christian Fear," Bad Subjects Online, February 2005, http://bad .eserver .org/ issues/ 2005/ 72/ blue .html; quoted in Brian Jackson, "Jonathan Edwards Goes to Hell (House): Fear Appeals in American Evangelism," *Rhetoric Review* 26, no. 1 (2007): 42–59, at 52–53. I am extremely grateful to Joseph Valenzano III, for drawing my attention to this scholarship, and for robust conversations about the rhetoric of hell in and out of our shared classroom.

2. Kelly J. Baker, "Hell House," *Sacred Matters*, October 29, 2015, https://sacred mattersmagazine.com/hell-house/.

3. Jeff Sharlet, "Hell House," *Lapham's Quarterly* 11, no. 1 (2009), https://www .laphamsquarterly.org/eros/hell-house.

4. Sharlet, "Hell House"; Jason Bivins, *The Religion of Fear: The Politics of Horror in Conservative Evangelicalism* (Oxford: Oxford University Press, 2008).

5. Baker, "Hell House."

6. Kelly J. Baker and John David Penniman, "Hell Houses and the Terror of the Gospel: A Conversation," *Sacred Matters*, December 1, 2016, https:// sacredmattersmagazine .com/ hell -houses -and -the -terror -of -the -gospel -a -conversation/.

7. While there are many bodies in the apocalyptic visions of hell that are punished irrespective of gender, those punishments are still tightly tied to the performance of one's social role.

8. On the idea that Roman masculinity was in crisis during this period, see Matthew Kuefler, *The Manly Eunuch: Masculinity, Gender Ambiguity, and Christian*

Ideology in Late Antiquity (Chicago: University of Chicago Press, 2001), 37–69. On the reorganization of the Christian household, see Kate Cooper, *The Fall of the Roman Household* (New York: Cambridge University Press, 2007); Kristina Sessa, *The Formation of Papal Authority in Late Antique Italy: Roman Bishops and the Domestic Sphere* (New York: Cambridge University Press, 2011), 127–73; Chris L. de Wet, *Preaching Bondage: John Chrysostom and the Discourse of Slavery in Early Christianity* (Oakland: University of California Press, 2015), 84–86, 124–25.

9. Virginia Burrus, *Begotten Not Made: Conceiving Manhood in Late Antiquity* (Stanford, CA: Stanford University Press, 2000), 19–22.

10. The righteous are told in Apoc. Paul 14, "Soul take knowledge of your body which you have left, for in the day of resurrection you must return to that same body to receive what is promised to all the righteous."

11. Chron. Jer. 16.4. For the Hebrew text and translation see Michael E. Stone and John Strugnell, *The Books of Elijah, Parts 1 and 2* (Missoula, MT: Scholars Press, 1979), 20.

12. See Maud W. Gleason, *Making Men: Sophists and Self-Presentation in Ancient Rome* (Princeton, NJ: Princeton University Press, 1995), 160–62, on how the Roman masculine ideal was somewhat malleable, especially over time. De Wet, *Preaching Bondage*, 174–83, describes the way that the different ideals of Roman masculinity, or "masculinities," shaped Christian slaveholding discourse.

13. Virginia Burrus, *Chastity as Autonomy: Women in the Stories of the Apocryphal Acts* (Lewiston, NY: E. Mellen, 1987); Kate Cooper, *The Virgin and the Bride: Idealized Womanhood in Late Antiquity* (Cambridge, MA: Harvard University Press, 1996). Later scholarship has continued the dialogue around the extent to which the women in these texts represent real or idealized women, but no matter where one comes down on that question, the matrix of possible ways of performing and representing ancient womanhood still involves some interplay between household order, economics, marriage, and sex. For representative examples of this broader scholarly conversation, see Shelly Matthews, "Thinking of Thecla: Issues in Feminist Historiography," *Journal of Feminist Studies in Religion* 17, no. 2 (2001): 39–55; Outi Lehtipuu, "The Example of Thecla and the Example(s) of Paul: Disputing Women's Role in Early Christianity," in *Women and Gender in Ancient Religions: Interdisciplinary Approaches*, ed. Stephen P. Ahearne-Kroll, Paul A. Holloway, and James A. Kellhoffer, WUNT 263 (Tübingen: Mohr Siebeck, 2010), 350–78; Ross Shepard Kraemer, *Unreliable Witnesses: Religion, Gender, and History in the Greco-Roman Mediterranean* (Oxford: Oxford University Press, 2011), 117–52.

14. On the intertwining of the domestic and civic, see Susan Hylen, *A Modest Apostle: Thecla and the History of Women in the Early Church* (Oxford: Oxford University Press, 2015), 18–22, 24–31.

15. Within Roman culture the particular nature of this accountability or obedience had become a matter of discussion, with wives in particular gaining more power

and agency, but still needing to act to choose from among choices within their social conditioning regarding what it means to be a good Roman woman (deference, respect, industry, loyalty to the gods, etc.). Carolyn Osiek and David L. Balch, *Families in the New Testament World: Households and Churches* (Louisville, KY: Westminster John Knox, 1997), 60–64; Hylen, *A Modest Apostle*, 18–42.

16. 1 Pet 2:11–3:7, however, is not organized this way, beginning instead with slaves. This is one of several ways 1 Peter's household code offers a unique Christian response to the broader diaspora understanding of "household." For an incisive and thorough discussion of Christian revision and appropriation of this material in 1 Peter, see Shively T. J. Smith, *Strangers to Family: Diaspora and 1 Peter's Invention of God's Household* (Waco, TX: Baylor University Press, 2016), 61–83.

17. Osiek and Balch, *Families in the New Testament World*, 103–55. David Hunter, *Marriage, Celibacy, and Heresy in Ancient Christianity: The Jovinianist Controversy* (Oxford: Oxford University Press, 2007), 90–97, offers a clear and concise explanation for how the New Testament household codes laid the foundation for "clerical hierarchy and conformity to the established values of Greco-Roman society" (96). Hunter goes on to show that the household codes gave way to second-century conflicts between marriage and sexual renunciation, and then to the discursive practice of heresy. It is this discursive practice to which our apocalypses belong, seeking to circumscribe Christian orthodoxy and orthopraxy.

18. See, for instance, Eph 5, in which marriage is an analogy for the love between Christ and the church. As Candida R. Moss and Joel S. Baden, *Reconceiving Infertility: Biblical Perspectives on Procreation and Childlessness* (Princeton, NJ: Princeton University Press, 2015), 220–28, argue, heavenly bodies offer a surprising reversal of this social hierarchy, because they do not procreate or engage in sex, enshrining the barren body as the eschatological ideal.

19. Jan N. Bremmer, "The Long Latin Version of the Vision of Ezra: Date, Place, and Tour of Hell," in *Figures of Ezra*, ed. Jan N. Bremmer, Veronika Hirschberger, and Tobias Nicklas (Leuven: Peeters, 2018), 162–84, at 169. See a similar ordering principle at work in P. W. van der Horst, *The Sentences of Pseudo-Phocylides* (Leiden, 1978), 110–11.

20. The sins punished here include adultery, murder, abortion, infanticide, slander, false testimony against the martyrs, not caring for widows, lending money for interest, homosexual sex, and idol worship. These sins are also punished in the Greek manuscript of the Apocalypse of Peter (Apoc. Pet. 21–34). See Thomas J. Kraus and Tobias Nicklas, *Das Petrusevangelium und die Petrusapokalypse. Die griechischen Fragmente mit deutscher und englischer Übersetzung* (Berlin: de Gruyter, 2004), 109–17. The Greek text actually ends here, and does not include the rest of the household, whereas the Ethiopic text goes on to describe the sins of children and slaves. See Dennis D. Buchholz, *Your Eyes Will Be Opened: A Study in the Greek (Ethiopic) Text of the Apocalypse of Peter*, SBLDS 97 (Atlanta: Scholars Press, 1988), 216–21.

21. Callie Callon, "Sorcery, Wheels, and Mirror Punishment in the *Apocalypse of Peter,*" *JECS* 18, no. 1 (2010): 29–49.

22. *Per ipsa uero uaria supplicia ostenditur uniuscuiusque actus: naturalium dolor utique adulteri sunt et pederasti.* An edition of the Latin is available in D. Donatien de Bruyne, "*Epistula Titi, discipuli Pauli, de dispositione sanctimonii,*" *RBén* 37 (1925): 47–72. Corrections to the Latin are suggested in Vincenz Bulhart, "Nochmals Textkritisches," *RBén* 62 (1952): 297–99, and noted here where relevant. For a translation, see Aurelio de Santos Otero, "Epistle of Titus," in *New Testament Apocrypha*, ed. Wilhelm Schneemelcher and Edgar Hennecke, trans. R. Wilson (Louisville, KY: Westminster John Knox, 1991), 2:53–74, at 64.

23. *Nam quod foeminae mammillis torqueri iubentur istae sunt quae in ludibrio corpus suum tradiderunt masculis, ideoque et ipsi iuxta erunt in tormentis manibus pendentes p<ropt>er hanc rem.* On "hands," "thighs," or "feet" as a euphemism for "penis," see Richard Bauckham, "Hell in the *Latin Vision of Ezra*," in *Other Worlds and Their Relation to This World*, ed. Tobias Nicklas, Joseph Verheyden, Erik M. M. Eynikel, and Florentino García Martínez (Leiden: Brill, 2010), 323–42, at 328–29.

24. Thomas McGinn, *Prostitution, Sexuality, and the Law in Ancient Rome* (New York: Oxford University Press, 1998), 147–56, argues that the Roman legal definition of adultery largely hinged upon the social status of the woman. If she was a *matrona* or *materfamilias*, then she and her partner were liable under the law. Women who were enslaved, prostitutes, procuresses, peregrines (foreign women not married to a Roman citizen), or convicted adulteresses were exempt from the law.

25. Amy Richlin, "Approaches to the Sources on Adultery at Rome," *Women's Studies* 8 (1981): 225–50, 228. As a result there were a lot of extramarital sexual relationships a married man could engage in that were not considered adulterous.

26. With the exception of the Syriac manuscript tradition, which includes punishments for men who leave their wives and have sex with the wives of their friends, women who have sex outside of their marriage, young men who seek prostitutes, young men who have sex with virgins, and maidens who do not preserve their virginity. For a translation of the Syriac text, see A. F. J. Klijn, *The Acts of Thomas: Introduction, Text, and Commentary*, 2d ed. (Leiden: Brill, 2003), 132–37. See punishments for murder in Ethiopic Apoc. Pet. 7; Gk. Apoc. Pet. 25; Apoc. Paul 18.

27. Kyle Harper, *From Shame to Sin: The Christian Transformation of Sexual Morality in Late Antiquity* (Cambridge, MA: Harvard University Press, 2013), 43.

28. The Coptic text of the Apoc. Paul has not received as much scholarly attention as the Latin, but as Lautaro Roig Lanzillotta, "The Coptic Apocalypse of Paul in Ms Or 7023," in *The Visio Pauli and the Gnostic Apocalypse of Paul*, ed. Jan N. Bremmer and István Czachesz (Leuven: Peeters, 2007), 158–97, has argued, the Coptic is not an expanded or inferior version of the Apoc. Paul, but "often provides better readings that help us to understand sections that in Latin are

clearly corrupt." Here the Coptic adds, "These are those who beautify themselves with unguents of the devil. They go to the church [searching] for adultery and not for their husbands. They made of God their enemy because of these deceitful unguents. Therefore they will receive eternal punishment" (translated in Lanzillotta, 189).

29. Seneca the Elder, *Cont.* 2.7.3–4; Propertius 3.21.3; Ovid, *Loves* 2.2.3–4; 3.2.34; 2.19.19. The *stola* does not appear in artistic renderings after 175 CE, and appears to have been in fashion for a relatively short period (two centuries roughly) compared to the male toga. Birgit Scholz, *Untersuchungen zur Tracht der römischen matrona* (Cologne: Böhlau, 1992). Beyond the *stola*, women's dress and the importance of eschewing fancy hairstyles, jewelry, and so on is a popular topic among Greek and Roman authors. Phintys, *Temp. Wom.* 153.15–18; Perictione, *Harm. Wom.* 143.10–14; Seneca the Younger, *Helv.* 16.4; *Ben.* 1.10.2; 7.9.4–5; Dio Chrysostom, *Hunt.* (*Or. 7*) 117; Juvenal, *Sat.* 3.180–81; 6.457–63; 495–511; Plutarch, *Mor. Con. Pr.* 141 E; *Mor.* 133A; Epictetus, *Ench.* 40; Pliny the Younger, *Pan.* 83.7; Tacitus, *Ann.* 3.54; Lucian, *Port.* 11. Cf. Paul J. Achtemeier, *1 Peter*, Heremeneia (Minneapolis: Fortress, 1996), 212.

30. Kelly Olsen, "Matrona and Whore: Clothing and Definition in Roman Antiquity," in *Prostitutes and Courtesans in the Ancient World*, ed. Christopher A. Faraone and Laura K. McClure (Madison: University of Wisconsin Press, 2006), 186–204, at 198–99. See also Clement of Alexandria, *Educ.* 2.11–13; 3.1–2.

31. Olsen, "Matrona and Whore," 199.

32. Bernadette Brooten, *Love between Women: Early Christian Responses to Female Homoeroticism* (Chicago: University of Chicago Press, 1996), 1–2, 116, 324. See, for instance, Clement of Alexandria, *Educ.* 3.3.19.1, who says that women who marry other women reject their passive role and are characterized as "lawless." Brooten demonstrates that these attitudes toward sexuality are not unique to Christians, but reflect those of the broader culture.

33. Horace, *Sat.* 1.2.63; Martial, *Epig.* 2.39, 10.52; Juvenal, *Sat.* 2.68–70; Porphyrio, *Sat.* 1.2.63. McGinn, *Prostitution, Sexuality, and the Law*, 157–60, notes that the law forbidding prostitutes from wearing the *stola* was no longer enforced by the second century CE, if it ever was. But the public shaming of adulterers as prostitutes was still social convention. Olsen, "Matrona and Whore," 186–204; Kelly Olsen, *Dress and the Roman Woman: Self-Presentation and Society* (New York: Routledge, 2008), 80 and following; Alicia J. Batten, Carly Daniel-Hughes, and Kristi Upson-Saia, "What Shall We Wear," in *Dressing Judeans and Christians in Antiquity*, ed. Kristi Upson-Saia, Carly Daniel-Hughes, and Alicia J. Batten (Burlington, VT: Ashgate, 2014), 1–20, at 17.

34. *Chron. Jer.* 16.4. For the Hebrew text and translation see Stone and Strugnell, *The Books of Elijah*, 20.

35. Troy W. Martin, "Paul's Argument from Nature for the Veil in 1 Corinthians 11:13–15: A Testicle Instead of a Head Covering," *JBL* 123, no. 1 (2004): 75–84.

36. Naftali S. Cohn, "What to Wear: Women's Adornment and Judean Identity in the Third Century Mishnah," in Upson-Saia, Daniel-Hughes, and Batten, *Dressing Judeans and Christians in Antiquity*, 21–36, at 29–30; Ishay Rosen-Zvi, *The Mishnaic Sotah Ritual: Temple, Gender, and Midrash*, trans. Orr Scharf (Leiden: Brill, 2012; originally published in Hebrew as *The Rite That Was Not*, 2008).

37. The absence of this sin in the early Christian apocalypses could be explained by the overwhelming emphasis on the nursing mother in Roman art and literature, and in early Christian thought as well. See John David Penniman, *Raised on Christian Milk: Food and the Formation of the Soul in Early Christianity* (New Haven: Yale University Press, 2017), 37–43. In particular, in the Marian apocalypses, some of which depict Mary breastfeeding the infant Jesus, this punishment would be a particularly odd juxtaposition.

38. The later Syriac manuscript tradition merely contains a general mention of adultery (both men and women) in chapter 56. It seems that the Syriac text has shortened the list of sins so that the sins punished in the prostitute's tour of hell still focus on sexual continence, but specifically on adultery.

39. *Et uidi alios uiros ac mulieres suspensos a superciliis et capillis suis et igneum flumen traebat eos et dixi: Qui sunt hii, domine? Et dixit mihi: Hii sunt comitentes se non propriis uiris ac mulieribus sed mecis. Et ideo indeficientes persoluunt proprias penas.* Although the Coptic manuscript of this passage describes a sin that is specific to wives (see below), the two punishments here seem to indicate that men and women were both punished in the earlier version of the apocalypse, and that the Coptic manuscript reflects an attempt to bring this punishment back into line with earlier versions of this punishment like that of Apoc. Pet. 7.

40. As Martha Lynn Rose, *The Staff of Oedipus: Transforming Disability in Ancient Greece* (Ann Arbor: University of Michigan Press, 2003), 92–93, emphasizes, the notion that blindness overlapped with sexual sins specifically was one physiognomic interpretation of blindness among several. Lisa Trentin, "Exploring Visual Impairment in Ancient Rome," in *Disabilities in Roman Antiquity: Disparate Bodies A Capite ad Calcem*, ed. Christian Laes, C. F. Goodey, and M. Lynn Rose (Leiden: Brill, 2013), 89–114, makes a point similar to Rose's about the understanding of blindness in ancient Rome. See also Nicholas Vlahogiannis, "Disabling Bodies," in *Changing Bodies, Changing Meanings: Studies on the Human Body in Antiquity*, ed. Dominic Monsterrat (New York: Routledge, 1998), 28–32; Chad Hartsock, *Sight and Blindness in Luke-Acts: The Use of Physical Features in Characterization* (Leiden: Brill, 2008), 68–69.

41. *Qui oculis uero cremantur hii sunt qui in adten<den>do scandalizati sunt respicientes in concupiscencia reatu gesta.* This text reflects the correction of Bulhart, "Nochmals Textkritisches," 298, who suggested that the text should read *adten<den>do*, in place of *uidendo* (*videndo*) in de Bruyne's text, arguing that de Bruyne unnecessarily used *videndo*, when the text's use of *attendere* is plausible.

Men are also found hanging by their eyes in the Elijah fragment that is found in Reshith Ḥokhmah in Stone and Strugnell, *The Books of Elijah*, 14–19. Martha Himmelfarb, *Tours of Hell: An Apocalyptic Form in Jewish and Christian Literature* (Philadelphia: University of Pennsylvania Press, 1983), 90–91, summarizes all of the ocular punishments throughout the tours of hell, including a similar punishment for those who look at married women and covet the money of others in Gedulet Moshe 13.

42. Burrus, *Begotten Not Made*, 19–22.

43. Eusebius, *Life Const.* 4.18–20; *CJ* III.12.2, *CTh* II.8.1; Willy Rordorf, *Sabbat und Sonntag in der Alten Kirche* (Zürich: Theologischer Verlag, 1972); Wolfram Kinzing, "'Auszeit': Anmerkungen zu Ursprung und Sinn von Sonn-und Feiertagen aus kirchenhistorischer Sicht," *Theologische Zeitschrift* 62 (2006): 357–75. Cf. Jan N. Bremmer, "Long Latin Version," 179–80. See also Andrew B. McGowan, *Ancient Christian Worship* (Grand Rapids, MI: Baker Academic, 2014), 217–24.

44. In the third and fourth centuries CE almsgiving is linked with repentance, through penitential practices. See David J. Downs, *Alms: Charity, Reward, and Atonement in Early Christianity* (Waco, TX: Baylor University Press, 2016), 284; Gus George Christo, trans., *St. John Chrysostom: On Repentance and Almsgiving*, The Fathers of the Church: A New Translation 96 (Washington, DC: Catholic University of America Press, 1998); Alexis Torrence, *Repentance in Late Antiquity: Eastern Asceticism and the Framing of the Christian Life c. 400–650 CE*, Oxford Theology and Religion Monographs (Oxford: Oxford University Press, 2012).

45. Gk. Apoc. Mary 6 contains a punishment for fornication, in which the sinners are submerged to their chests in fire. This punishment is similar to the punishment for those who receive the Eucharist and then fornicate and do not cease from their sins until they die, standing in fire up to their navel, in the Apoc. Paul 31. Gk. Apoc. Mary 23 does mention in passing "those who fornicate and sin against the sweet and passionless perfume of marriage," along with five other groups of sinners standing in a river of fire, but does not go into detail about whether there are men or women in this group.

46. In the Oxford manuscript of the Gk. Apoc. Mary (Oxford Bodl. Misc. gr. 56), chapters 6 and 20 use the same Greek phrase (*eis porneian*) to describe the sexual sins of an unspecified group (6) and women (20). M. R. James, *Apocrypha Anecdota*, Texts and Studies 2.3 (Cambridge: Cambridge University Press, 1893), 109–26, at 118 and 122. The Vatican manuscript of the Greek Apocalypse of Mary punishes the wives of priests instead of presbyters (21) and a deaconess instead of an archdeaconess (22).

47. These men are punished immediately after men and women who commit speech sins after church (a set of sins that were notoriously identified with women), in what seems like an attempt to make sure both men and women who engage in disingenuous piety are punished.

48. Harper, *From Shame to Sin*, 172–90, traces the way that a concept of "free will" was mapped onto sexual morality by Augustine and others, even forcing Theodosius II and Justinian to make legal changes to prevent the sexual coercion of prostitution, as a means of protecting female sexual agency and preventing forced sin.

49. Harper, *From Shame to Sin*, 50.

50. The punishments for homoeroticism in hell are also part of the reception history of Romans 1:18–32. See Brooten, *Love between Women*, 189–350; Diana Swancutt, "'The Disease of Effemination': The Charge of Effeminacy and the Verdict of God (Romans 1:18–2:16)," in *New Testament Masculinities*, ed. Stephen D. Moore and Janice Capel Anderson (Atlanta: Society of Biblical Literature, 2003), 193–233; Joseph A. Marchal, "The Exceptional Proves Who Rules: Imperial Sexual Exceptionalism in and around Paul's Letters," *JECH* 5 (2015): 87–115. Here I am following Brooten in using the terminology of *homoeroticism* over *homosexuality*, because the latter is sometimes thought to refer only to love between men in the contemporary world. Brooten, *Love between Women*, 8.

51. The Syriac text of the Acts of Thomas 55 has "the souls which change the intercourse that has been appointed by God." This terminology follows closely the argument made in Romans 1:18–32. See Brooten, *Love between Women*, 309–13. In contrast, Himmelfarb, *Tours of Hell*, 96, has interpreted this sin as "committed abortion and infanticide," because of the punishment in the Greek text that includes accusing infants, construing abortion and infanticide as perverting the procreative purpose of intercourse. Since the narrative frame of this tour of hell is advocating for a chaste (and thus childless) marriage, this does not seem to be a satisfactory explanation for the meaning of "exchanging intercourse."

52. See Callon, "Sorcery, Wheels, and Mirror Punishment in the *Apocalypse of Peter*," 35–46, for discussion of the fiery wheel as a mirror punishment for sorcery in the Apocalypse of Peter and other ancient literature. In the Orphic tradition, Ixion revolves on a wheel in the underworld. See David Fiensy, "Lex Talionis in the Apocalypse of Peter," *Harvard Theological Review* 76 (1983): 255–58, at 257; Virgil, *Aen.* 6.616–17. Fire may be associated with these punishments because of the biblical punishment of Sodom, or simply because fire was a popular punishment in apocalyptic literature. Matt 18:8; 25:41; Rev 19:20; 20:10; Enoch 10:6; 18:11; 21:7–11. The Greek manuscript of this text, which is usually thought to be the earlier, more reliable manuscript tradition, also describes these souls dwelling in a pit with infant souls who are described as their children, a punishment that is usually reserved for abortion or infanticide. As Brooten, *Love between Women*, 309–12, has argued, this punishment is enigmatic and does not really fit with the sin of "exchanging intercourse of men and women," and thus the Syriac version of the text (which does not include the accusing infants) more accurately reflects the earliest version of the text at this point. In the Syriac version of the text, as we will see below, homoeroticism is grouped with adultery,

men having sex with prostitutes, and virgins who were not chaste. Brooten argues that this grouping was original to the earlier Syriac text that was used by the Greek translator, and that the accusing infants were listed as part of the punishment for fornicators, not homoeroticism. Or alternatively, if this punishment did originally refer to the sin of homoeroticism, a Syriac scribe might have noticed the mismatch between the punishment and the sin and corrected the original Syriac text.

53. Brooten, *Love between Women*, 267–302.

54. Brooten, *Love between Women*, 311–13.

55. See also Hugo Duensing, "Ein Stücke der urchristlichen Petrusapokalypse enthaltener Traktat der äthiopischen Pseudoklementinischen Literatur," *ZNW* 14 (1913): 65–78, at 71, who noted that the text is corrupt at this point. The Greek text has *hai sunkoimētheisai allēlais hōs an anēr pros gunaika*. See Kraus and Nicklas, *Das Petrusevangelium und die Petrusapokalypse*, 114–17.

56. Brooten, *Love between Women*, 314, also notes that the author of the Apocalypse of Paul may have only mentioned male homoeroticism because this was "the more commonly discussed of the two types."

57. Female sexual dominance was certainly seen as problematic to Christians as well, but it did not involve dominance over a man, and thus was primarily seen as a crime against nature and not as an interference with the heteronormative patriarchal family structure. See, for instance, Brooten, *Love between Women*, 324, regarding the "fundamental asymmetry between Clement's views of woman and man" when it comes to homoeroticism.

58. Brooten, *Love between Women*, 51–54, 121–22, 131–32, 135–36, 138–39; Allison Glazebrook, "The Bad Girls of Athens: The Image and Function of *Hetairai* in Judicial Oratory," in Faraone and McClure, *Prostitutes and Courtesans in the Ancient World*, 125–38; Kate Gilhuly, "The Phallic Lesbian: Philosophy, Comedy, and Social Inversion in Lucian's Dialogues of the Courtesans," in Faraone and McClure, *Prostitutes and Courtesans in the Ancient World*, 274–91.

59. Brooten, *Love between Women*, 309–13. Brooten does not, however, make the connection between this grouping of the sins in the Syriac text and the Greek text's assertion that these sinners are "kin" of the prostitute.

60. Craig A. Williams, *Roman Homosexuality*, 2d ed. (Oxford: Oxford University Press, 2009), 17–29.

61. Schneemelcher and Hennecke, eds., *New Testament Apocrypha*, 2:64.

62. As Harper, *From Shame to Sin*, 156, notes, there are varying historical accounts of the law and its enforcement: John Malalas, *Chron.* 18.167–68; Procopius of Caesarea, *Sec. Hist.* 11.34–36; 16.18–22; Theophanes, *Chron.* (PG 108:col. 408); Cedrenus, *Comp. Hist.* 368 (PG 121:704). Harper goes on to add that even after the passage of this law, pederasty was still "not an unlikely occurrence."

63. As Bremmer, "Long Latin Version," 171, notes, this word occurs in only one other text. Bremmer also argues that the male incest of the Greek Apocalypse of Ezra

seems more authentic than the women's incest with their mothers in the Latin Vision of Ezra.

64. Bauckham, "The Latin Vision of Ezra," v. 20, adds in a note with his translation that one manuscript has "have spent the night with their mother," and notes that "the reference is certainly to incest."

65. Tertullian, *Apol.* 2.5; Eusebius, *Eccl. Hist.* 4.7.11. Incest and cannibalism are linked in ancient invective as a way to exoticize one's opponents, and Christians also used this rhetoric against those they deemed heretics. Candida R. Moss, "Infant Exposure and the Rhetoric of Cannibalism, Incest, and Martyrdom in the Early Church," *JECS* 29, no. 3 (2021), forthcoming, demonstrates how these rhetorical categories intersected in the ancient imagination and worked as vituperative rhetoric for both Christians and their opponents. See also Andrew McGowan, "Eating People: Accusations of Cannibalism against Christians in the Second Century," *JECS* 2 (1994): 413–42; James B. Rives, "Accusations of Human Sacrifice among Pagans and Christians," *JRS* 85 (1995): 65–85; J. Albert Harrill, "Cannibalistic Language in the Fourth Gospel and Greco-Roman Polemics of Factionalism (John 6:52–66)," *JBL* 127, no. 1 (2008): 133–58; Bart Wagemakers, "Incest, Infanticide, and Cannibalism: Anti-Christian Imputations in the Roman Empire," *Greece and Rome* 57 (2010): 337–54.

66. Clement, *Educ.* 3.3 (PG 5:585); Justin Martyr, *1 Apol.* 27 (PG 6:369–72). Under the reign of Theodosius II and Justinian, Christians began to legislate around their concerns about prostitution, with particular concern that prostitutes not be economically or otherwise coerced into a sexual relationship. Under Theodosius II pimps were banned, and Justinian eventually made prostitution illegal (Harper, *From Shame to Sin*, 183–89; *CTh* 15.8.2; Justinian, *Nov.* 14). These laws were part of a gradual shift in early Christian and public perceptions of sexual morality that began to focus on the agency of individuals. The punishments for incest appear at home in this late antique and early medieval moral world of perceived sexual agency.

67. Philo censures both the adult and the child (Philo, *Spec. Laws* 3.37–39). Shenoute of Atripe only condemns the adults who have sex with children (Shenoute, *Liv. Monks* 25–26). Brooten, *Love between Women*, 257, 349–50.

68. In a way these punishments are a continuation of mythological treatments of incest, in which it did not matter much whether one intended to commit incest, only that it happened. See McGowan, "Eating People," 431n51.

69. Shenoute, *Liv. Monks* 25–26. In his monastic context, Shenoute's inclusion of women exhibits a concern about bringing in the outside world.

70. Parental responsibility is also framed as maternal responsibility in Titus 2:4, in which older women are instructed to teach younger women to love their children.

71. Suzanne Dixon, *The Roman Family* (Baltimore: Johns Hopkins University Press, 1992), 107, cautions against looking for cultural consistency in the Ro-

man views of family. For an excellent discussion of the tension between ancient pragmatism toward children and parental adoration of children, see Robert H. von Thaden Jr., "Procreation, Children, and Family," in *The Handbook of New Testament, Gender, and Sexuality*, ed. Benjamin H. Dunning (Oxford: Oxford University Press, 2019), 539–56, at 543–45. John Boswell, *Kindness of Strangers: The Abandonment of Children in Western Europe from Late Antiquity to the Renaissance* (New York: Pantheon, 1988), 92–93, argues that in spite of the widespread practice of abandonment of one's children, "the great majority of Roman sources do, in fact, assume strong parental affection."

72. Penniman, *Raised on Christian Milk*, 9, argues, "The proper education and formation of children was, throughout antiquity, wrapped up in the material provision of food and the ways in which that provision was theorized and regulated." Penniman adduces a number of pre-Christian and Christian sources to support this point, but in particular gleans the titular phrase of his book from a passage in which Tertullian remarks that the emperor's son benefited from the physical, intellectual, and spiritual formation of his Christian wet nurse, "raised on Christian milk." Tertullian, *Scap.* 4.5 (CCSL II.2:1130–31).

73. Non-Christian authors reflect the broader cultural acceptance of these practices. Plautus, *Churl* 179; Polybius 36.17; Ovid, *Loves* 2.14; Juvenal, *Sat.* 2.6; Suetonius, *Calig.* 5; and Seneca the Younger, *Helv.* 16.3–4. Tara Baldrick-Morrone, "'Let's Not Retell This Myth about the History of the Thing': Disrupting John T. Noonan, Jr.'s Grand Narrative of Christian Opposition to Abortion" (PhD diss., Florida State University, 2020), addresses the contemporary rhetorical dimensions of the reception of these sources in secondary scholarship on ancient ideas about abortion. For representative examples of two divergent readings of these materials, see, on the one hand, John T. Noonan Jr., *Contraception: A History of Its Treatment by the Catholic Theologians and Canonists* (Cambridge, MA: Belknap Press of Harvard University Press, 1986 [1965]); Michael J. Gorman, *Abortion and the Early Church: Christian, Jewish, and Pagan Attitudes in the Greco-Roman World* (Eugene, OR: Wipf and Stock Publishers, 1982); and, on the other hand, Beverly Wildung Harrison, *Our Right to Choose: Toward a New Ethic of Abortion* (Boston: Beacon Press, 1983); Daniel A. Dombrowski and Robert Deltete, *A Brief, Liberal, Catholic Defense of Abortion* (Urbana: University of Illinois Press, 2000).

74. On concerns about infant mortality and population, see Tim Parkin, "The Demography of Infancy and Early Childhood in the Ancient World," in *The Oxford Handbook of Childhood and Education in the Classical World*, ed. Judith Evans Grubbs and Tim Parkin (Oxford: Oxford University Press, 2013), 40–61. As Lesley Dean-Jones and Helen King have argued, childbirth and menarche were seen as propitious sacrifices that women made in service of the household and the city-state. See Lesley Ann Dean-Jones, *Women's Bodies in Classical Greek Science* (Oxford: Oxford University Press, 1994), 215; Helen King,

"Sacrificial Blood: The Role of the *Amnion* in Ancient Gynecology," *Helios* 13 (1987): 117–26. See chapter 3 for further discussion on ancient views of childbirth as sacrifice.

75. Anna Rebecca Solevåg, *Birthing Salvation: Gender and Class in Early Christian Childbearing Discourse* (Leiden: Brill, 2013), 53–54. Chastity and not becoming pregnant were explicitly outlined requirements in wet-nursing contracts. See Keith R. Bradley, "Wet-Nursing at Rome: A Study in Social Relations," in *The Family in Ancient Rome: New Perspectives*, ed. Beryl Rawson (Ithaca, NY: Cornell University Press, 1987), 201–29.

76. Rebecca Flemming, *Medicine and the Making of Roman Women: Gender, Nature, and Authority from Celsus to Galen* (Oxford: Oxford University Press, 2000), 169. Helen King, *The One-Sex Body on Trial: The Classical and Early Modern Evidence* (New York: Ashgate, 2013), 162–63, argues that women doctors were not trusted because they would perform abortions.

77. Judith Evans Grubbs, "Infant Exposure and Infanticide," in Grubbs and Parkin, eds., *Oxford Handbook of Childhood and Education in the Classical World*, 99; O. M. Bakke, *When Children Became People: The Birth of Childhood in Early Christianity*, trans. Brian McNeil (Minneapolis: Fortress, 2005), 32–33; and Beryl Rawson, *Children and Childhood in Roman Italy* (Oxford: Oxford University Press, 2003), 362; cited in von Thaden, "Procreation, Children, and Family," 547. Although Jews and Christians were known for their rejection of infanticide and exposure, they appear to have drawn upon the growing discomfort with these practices in the broader culture in order to effect Roman legal changes condemning this treatment of children.

78. Boswell, *Kindness of Strangers*, 89.

79. Plato, *Rep.* 2.12 (372B); 5.8 (459E); 5.9 (460C); Aristotle, *Pol.* 7.14.10 (1335B) contra Musonius Rufus, *Should Every Child That Is Born Be Reared*, in Stobaeus (*Florilegium*, ed. C. Wachsmuth and O. Hense [Berlin, 1884–1923], 4.24.15, p. 605); Hierocles, in Stobaeus, 4.24.14 (Wachsmuth and Hense, 4.603). As Boswell, *Kindness of Strangers*, 86, 89, argues, only Epictetus, *Disc.* 1.23, raises concerns about parental responsibility.

80. Eleanor Scott, "Unpicking a Myth: The Infanticide of Female and Disabled Infants in Antiquity," in *TRAC 2000: Proceedings of the Tenth Annual Theoretical Roman Archeology Conference*, ed. Gwyn Davies, Andrew Gardner, and Kris Lockyear (Oxford: Oxbow Books, 2001), 143–51, offers a compelling critique that previous historiography has read contemporary ideas about gender and disability in antiquity onto the ancient archaeological record, vastly overstating the extent to which female and disabled infants were exposed or killed.

81. There were also punishments for infanticide in Orphic depictions of the afterlife. Virgil, *Aen.* 6.428, begins with Aeneas hearing the sounds of babies' souls. The Bologna papyrus, a third- or fourth-century text of early imperial origin, condemns infanticide and abortion. Robert Turcan, "La catabase orphique du

papyrus de Bologne," *Revue de l'histoire des religions* 150 (1956): 149–55. Jan N. Bremmer, *Initiation into the Mysteries of the Ancient World* (Berlin: De Gruyter, 2014), 185–87, argues that these punishments are added to the Orphic tradition later, as a result of the influence of Judaism and Christianity. However, the broader cultural concerns about infanticide noted by Grubbs, "Infant Exposure and Infanticide," 99, indicate that these punishments and whether or not they were included in the original Orphic sources should be revisited.

82. Boswell, *Kindness of Strangers*, 228–66.

83. A penalty that was reduced to ten years' penance in the Council of Ancyra in 314 CE.

84. Solevåg, *Birthing Salvation*, 98–99, 130; Von Thaden, "Procreation, Children, and Family," 547.

85. See Methodius of Olympus, *Sym.* 2.6.45, in which the infants who were exposed call their parents before the judgment seat, to judge them for their adulterous sexual acts that produced the infants (not for abandonment itself). Boswell, *Kindness of Strangers*, 166, argues that Christian writers initially focused their critiques of abandonment on adultery, but that this gradually abated in the third and fourth centuries, and "was supplemented by moderate misgivings about parents limiting the number of legitimate heirs and sympathetic views of the circumstances of the poor."

86. While the long Latin MS B of the Lat. Vis. Ez. 52–53 punishes women who had their children from adultery and "rejected" them, the shorter H MS (Heiligenkreuz, Stiftsbibliothek, 11, fols. 272^v–273^r) reads "killed them." Bauckham, "The Latin Vision of Ezra," v. 52 n. f, 522. Nuns and widows who have abortions as the result of sex that "destroyed their virginity" are also punished in gender-specific punishments in Eth. Apoc. Mary fol. 105 a. The second half of the punishment follows the Apoc. Paul 40 almost verbatim, awkwardly mixing a gender-specific punishment for nuns and widows with the Apoc. Paul's formulation.

87. Chrysostom, *Hom.* 24 *Ep. Rom.* (PG 60:626).

88. See also Basil, *Let.* 217.52 (PG 32:796), who singles out women who "despise the child they have borne and abandon it in the road when it could have been saved or who hope thus to hide sin, or who are motivated by bestial and inhuman thoughts."

89. Tertullian, *Nat.* 1.15 and *Apol.* 9.7, for example, compares infanticide and exposure, and even surmises in *Nat.* that exposure is worse. As Moss, "Infant Exposure," forthcoming, argues, "while many Christian authors deliberately and strategically conflate abortion, infanticide, and infant exposure, and rhetorically bind these practices to the socially abhorrent practice of human sacrifice, this classification scheme would not have been familiar to most ancient Greeks and Romans."

90. Moss, "Infant Exposure," forthcoming.

91. On reproaching early Christians with cannibalism, see Jan N. Bremmer, "Early Christian Human Sacrifice between Fact and Fiction," in *Sacrifices humains. Discours et réalité*, ed. Agnes Nagy and Francesca Prescendi (Turnhout: Brepols, 2013), 165–76. Moss, "Infant Exposure," forthcoming, reads this passage as a reversal of the rhetoric aimed at Christians. As Moss argues, we find a similar trope of rhetorical reversal in the *Letter of the Churches in Lyons and Vienne to the Church in Smyrna* (Eusebius, *Eccl. Hist.* 5.1.1–5.3.4), in which those who persecute the martyrs are accused of cannibalism.

92. Tertullian warns that the major threat of abandonment was sexual impurity, making unwitting parents liable to future acts of incest. Tertullian, *Apol.* 9.

93. Ruth Evans, "The Jew, the Host, and the Virgin Martyr: Fantasies of the Sentient Body," in *Medieval Virginities*, ed. Anke Bernau, Ruth Evans, and Sarah Salih (Cardiff: University of Wales Press, 2003), 180, argues, "The conflation of penitent prostitutes with penitent former Jews suggests that Jewish female sexuality (like Jewish male sexuality) is viewed as deviant." See also Louise O. Fradenburg, "Criticism, Anti-Semitism, and the Prioress's Tale," *Exemplaria* 1 (1989): 69–115; Kathleen Biddick, "Genders, Bodies, Borders: Technologies of the Visible," in *Studying Medieval Women*, ed. Nancy F. Partner (Cambridge, MA: Mediaeval Academy of America, 1993), 87–116; Jocelyn Wogan-Browne, *Saint's Lives and Women's Literary Culture, c. 1150–1300: Virginity and Its Authorizations* (Oxford: Oxford University Press, 2001), 118.

94. As Brooten has demonstrated, Christians mention wet nurses in passing, and in metaphor, indicating that they were commonplace and that the practice was not worthy of comment. Bernadette J. Brooten, "Early Christian Enslaved Families (First to Fourth Century)," in *Children and Family in Late Antiquity: Life, Death and Interaction*, ed. Christian Laes, Katarina Mustakallio, and Ville Vuolanto (Leuven: Peeters, 2015), 111–34, at 121n32, citing Tertullian, *Soul* 19; Cyprian, *Laps.* 25; Gregory of Nyssa, *Life Macr.* 972M. Augustine says that he was fed by both his mother and wet nurses (*Conf.* 1, 6). And Arnobius of Sicca, *Ag. Pag.* 2.21, uses the image of a wet nurse metaphorically.

95. Slave women could be forced to wet nurse and not nurse their own baby, frequently having their baby taken from them, or abandoning their own infant.

96. Meghan Henning, *Educating Early Christians through the Rhetoric of Hell: "Weeping and Gnashing of Teeth" as Paideia in Matthew and the Early Church*, Wissenschaftliche Untersuchungen zum Neuen Testament II. 382 (Tübingen: Mohr Siebeck, 2014), 212–13.

97. Despite attempts to connect these disgraceful sons and the priest Joatham with a specific priest mentioned by Josephus (*Ant.* 8.12), it is not clear who is in the mind of our author. Wintermute, "Apocalypse of Zephaniah," 511 n. c.

98. Bernard M. Levinson, *Legal Renewal and Religious Renewal in Ancient Israel* (Cambridge: Cambridge University Press, 2008), and Hilary Kapfer, "Collective Accountability among the Sages of Ancient Israel" (PhD diss., Harvard University 2013), have argued that there were multiple perspectives on the concept of

collective accountability even within Wisdom tradition and the biblical text itself.

99. Meghan R. Henning, "Lacerated Lips and Lush Landscapes: Constructing This-Worldly Theological Identities in the Otherworld," in *The Other Side: Apocryphal Perspectives on Ancient Christian "Orthodoxies,"* ed. Candida R. Moss, Tobias Nicklas, Christopher Tuckett, and Joseph Verheyden (Göttingen: Vandenhoeck and Ruprecht, 2017), 99–116; Christoph Markschies, "Models of the Relation between 'Apocrypha' and 'Orthodoxy' from Antiquity to Modern Scholarship," in Moss et al., *The Other Side*, 13–22.

100. As Dov Weiss, "Sins of the Parents in Rabbinic and Early Christian Literature," *Journal of Religion* 97, no. 1 (2017): 1–25, argues, early Christian thinkers like Origen and John Cassian frequently interpreted Exodus 20 through an ethical or allegorical lens that neutralized the concept of ancestral punishment, whereas rabbinic authors limit, reinterpret, or affirm the concept. So in the Greek Apocalypse of Mary we end up with an example of a medieval text with a very strong anti-Judaic orientation that seems to share the biblical reading practices of the rabbis. In this way, the Greek Apocalypse of Mary renews the idea that potentially innocent subordinate members of the Christian household, such as children, could be held responsible for the sins of their parents. All of the medieval versions of the Greek Apocalypse of Mary contain anti-Jewish references to "the Jews," but two versions (Vienna Theol. 333 and Oxford Bod. Rawlinson G.4) omit the reference in Gk. Apoc. Mary 23 to "the Jews" as those who crucified Christ. See Jane Baun, *Tales from Another Byzantium: Celestial Journey and Local Community in the Medieval Greek Apocrypha* (Cambridge: Cambridge University Press, 2007), 54–57.

101. On the material value of virginity in the medieval period, see Kim M. Phillips, "Four Virgins' Tales: Sex and Power in Medieval Law," in Bernau, Evans, and Salih, eds., *Medieval Virginities*, 80–101.

102. Elizabeth A. Castelli, "Virginity and Its Meaning for Women's Sexuality in Early Christianity," in *A Feminist Companion to Patristic Literature*, ed. Amy-Jill Levine with Maria Mayo Robbins (London: T. and T. Clark, 2008), 94–95; and Evans, "The Jew, the Host, and the Virgin Martyr," 179. See also Cooper, *The Virgin and the Bride*, 116–43.

103. Rape was thought to make virgins ineligible for the celestial bridal chamber, which sometimes led to virgins committing suicide in order to avoid rape. Eusebius of Emesa, *Hom.* 6, 25–28; Eusebius of Caesarea, *Eccl. Hist.* 7, 12, 3–4; John Chrysostom, *Hom. Pelag.* (PG 50:579–84); *Bern. Pros.* (PG 50:629–40); Ambrose, *Vir.* 3, 7 (PL 16:229–32); Augustine, *City of God* 1, 26 (PL 41:39–40); cited in Castelli, "Virginity and Its Meaning," 95. On the way in which the Christian virgin is represented in ascetic literature, see Teresa M. Shaw, "The Virgin Charioteer and the Bride of Christ: Gender and the Passion in Late Ancient Ethics and Early Christian Writings on Virginity," in Levine and Robbins, *Feminist Companion to Patristic Literature*, 193–210.

104. DeWet, *Preaching Bondage*, 113.
105. DeWet, *Preaching Bondage*, 124–26, refers to these practices as "tactical slavery," meant to preserve Roman masculinity and household order in the face of the crisis that the growing power of the principate posed to men's civic participation. See also Matthew Kuefler, *The Manly Eunuch*, 37–69.
106. Burrus, *Begotten Not Made*, 19–22.
107. DeWet, *Preaching Bondage*, 124, argues that this held for lay leaders as well as for vowed religious: "Ecclesiastical participation was an attractive alternative for some men, who saw it as a way to reestablish their patriarchy and kyriarchy. Transforming the *paterfamilias* into a lay domestic 'priest' already instilled a sense of masculinity. Pastoralization then also became a form of masculinization."
108. Contra Meghan Henning, "Lacerated Lips and Lush Landscapes: Constructing This-Worldly Theological Identities in the Otherworld," in Moss et al., *The Other Side*, 99–116, at 116; Jan N. Bremmer, *Maidens, Magic and Martyrs in Early Christianity* (Tübingen: Mohr Siebeck, 2017), 304–9. On the relationship between the Marian apocalypses and the Apocalypse of Paul, see my discussion in the introduction. See also Richard Bauckham, "The Four Apocalypses of the Virgin Mary," in *The Fate of the Dead*; Enrico Norelli, *Marie des apocryphes. Enquête sur la mère de Jésus dans le christianisme antique*, Christianismes antiques (Geneva: Labor et Fides, 2009), 132–36, at 115, 134; Stephen J. Shoemaker, *Mary in Early Christian Faith and Devotion* (New Haven: Yale University Press, 2016), 133–34.
109. Basil, *Let.* 53. "Therefore, I beg you, abandon this way to revenue, or rather, this road to Hell." Basil was writing around 370 CE to the Chorepiscopi, a class of priests that was between bishops and ordinary priests and presbyters, appointed to supervise remote parts of large dioceses.
110. Chris L. De Wet, "Grumpy Old Men: Gender, Gerontology, and the Geriatrics of Soul in John Chrysostom," *JECS* 24, no. 4 (2016): 491–521.
111. The Latin of Apoc. Paul 34 describes the punishment as piercing the intestines, whereas the Coptic and Syriac have the old man's entrails being dragged out of his mouth. The Coptic text and translation are available in E. A. W. Budge, *Coptic Texts*, vol. 5, reprint of *Miscellaneous Coptic Texts in the Dialect of Upper Egypt* (New York: AMS, 1977 [1915]). For the Syriac see Cod. Vatican Syriacus 180 in G. Ricciotti, *L'Apocalisse di Paolo Siriaca. I. Introduzione, traduzione e commento*, vol. 1 (Brescia: Morcelliana, 1932), and digitally through the Vatican library: https://digi.vatlib.it/view/MSS_Vat.sir.180.
112. De Wet, "Grumpy Old Men," 494–507, at 520–21; cf. Keufler, *Manly Eunuch*, 206–44.
113. The Vatican manuscript of the Greek Apocalypse of Mary punishes the wives of priests instead of presbyters (21) and a deaconess instead of an archdeaconess (22).

114. Ute E. Eisen, *Women Officeholders in Early Christianity: Epigraphical and Literary Studies*, trans. Linda M. Maloney (Collegeville, MN: Liturgical, 2000), 13–14, 158–98. From the third to the eleventh century CE deaconesses are attested in Syria, who renounced their worldly possessions in service of the church and assisted women in baptism and receiving communion in their homes. Vassa Kontouma, "Women in Orthodoxy," in *The Orthodox Christian World*, ed. Augustine Casiday (New York: Routledge, 2012), 432–41, at 437.

115. See also the punishments for kings, judges, and governors or princes in the Isaiah Fragment (Chron. Jer. 16.5); Eth. Apoc. Bar. 72–73; Eth. Apoc. Mary 105a; Apoc. Gorg. 86.

Chapter 3. Becoming Female and Deformed through Suffering in Hell

1. Jerome is not alone in his use of this approach to chastity and the body, but is here using a topos that is present in other early Christian literature. See, for instance, the *Life of Olympias* in Elizabeth Clark, *Jerome, Chrysostom, and Friends: Essays and Translations* (New York: Edwin Mellen Press, 1979), 127–44.

2. Ellen Muehlberger, *Moment of Reckoning: Imagined Death and Its Consequences in Late Ancient Christianity* (Oxford: Oxford University Press, 2019) 147–82, at 180–82, argues that Christians not only understood there to be corporal continuity between this life and the next, but as part of that embodied afterlife, those who were typically invulnerable to punishments in this life could become vulnerable in hell. On the capacious nature of the category of "heresy" for early Christians, see Todd S. Berzon, *Classifying Christians: Ethnography, Heresiology, and the Limits of Knowledge in Late Antiquity* (Berkeley: University of California Press, 2016).

3. Richard Bauckham, *The Fate of the Dead: Studies in Jewish and Christian Apocalypses* (Leiden: Brill, 1998), 160–258, has argued that the "false messiah" in the Apocalypse of Peter is Bar Kokhba. Michael J. Gilmour, "Delighting in the Suffering of Others: Early Christian *Schadenfreude* and the Function of the Apocalypse of Peter," *BBR* 16 (2006): 129–39, has suggested that the torments of hell are designed to make Christians feel vindicated because those who commit crimes against them will be punished. I have argued against both these positions in Meghan Henning, *Educating Early Christians through the Rhetoric of Hell: "Weeping and Gnashing of Teeth" as Paideia in Matthew and the Early Church*, Wissenschaftliche Untersuchungen zum Neuen Testament II. 382 (Tübingen: Mohr Siebeck, 2014), 176, 212; Henning, "Lacerated Lips and Lush Landscapes: Constructing This-Worldly Theological Identities in the Otherworld," in *The Other Side: Apocryphal Perspectives on Ancient Christian "Orthodoxies,"* ed. Candida R. Moss, Tobias Nicklas, Christopher Tuckett, and Joseph Verheyden (Göttingen: Vandenhoeck and Ruprecht, 2017), 99–116, 102–4.

4. Tertullian, *Val.* 32; Henning, "Lacerated Lips and Lush Landscapes," 102. I thank Ismo Dunderberg for this reference.

5. Bill Hughes, "What Can Foucauldian Analysis Contribute to Disability Theory?" in *Foucault and the Government of Disability*, ed. Shelley Tremain (Ann Arbor: University of Michigan Press, 2005), 78–92.

6. See the English translation of Foucault's March 1967 lecture "Of Other Spaces," trans. J. Miskowiec, *Diacritics* 16, no. 1 (1986): 22–27. For my initial (and more thorough) attempt to bring together Foucault's concept of heterotopias and the ancient notions of the afterlife, see Meghan Henning, "Hell as 'Heterotopia': Edification and Interpretation from Enoch to the Apocalypses of Peter and Paul," in *Between Canonical and Apocryphal Texts: Processes of Reception, Rewriting and Interpretation in Early Judaism and Early Christianity*, ed. Jörg Frey, Claire Clivaz, and Tobias Nicklas (Tübingen: Mohr Siebeck, 2019), 297–318.

7. On a superficial level one could see the overlap here between Foucault and Henri Lefebvre's concept of lived space and its relationship to conceived space and perceived space. In substance, however, Foucault's discussion of heterotopias is, like the rest of his thinking, antidialectical and resists phenomenology, whereas Lefebvre's epistemology of space is built upon the dialectics of Hegel and Nietzsche. For a thorough theoretical discussion of spatial theory and its application to biblical texts, see Christl Maier, *Daughter Zion, Mother Zion: Gender, Space, and the Sacred in Ancient Israel* (Minneapolis: Fortress, 2008).

8. Foucault, "Of Other Spaces," 26, gives the examples of the garden and the zoo, as "happy universalizing heterotopias," which bring together disparate things from around the world into one small space. As spaces that interpret lived spaces, heterotopias are able to have a flexible relationship to time, so that they are both dependent upon and outside of the flow of time. This aspect of Foucault's concept of heterotopias fits very well with the ancient apocalypse, which like a heterotopia is able to play with the flow of time, depicting future events, eternal spaces, and people and events in the present world all in the same narrative.

9. As Berzon, *Classifying Christians*, 218–46, argues compellingly, heresy and a concrete way to classify it were elusive, revealing the limits of knowledge and the vicissitudes of the ethnographic enterprise itself.

10. The Ascension of Isaiah reminds readers that righteousness and holding the correct beliefs are not enough on their own to merit a place in heaven; a person must also "be in the Holy Spirit" (Ascen. Isa. 11:40). The Apocalypse of Zephaniah urges that a person be sure that their Christian education is complete lest they end up like the catechumens who wander around Hades blind (Apoc. Zeph. 10).

11. Henning, "Lacerated Lips and Lush Landscapes," 109–16.

12. Michel Foucault, *Discipline and Punish: The Birth of the Prison* (New York: Vintage, 1995 [1975]), 196–200.

13. In his analysis of the modern criminal justice system, Foucault observes that punitive disciplinary structures often reverse the traditional "axis of individualization" of a society, so that those who have less power (in this case, the damned) are actually more individualized. Of course, the spaces of the ancient afterlife are not exactly like those of the modern prisons in Foucault's analysis, but the continuity between these spaces is the unseen power dynamic that is in play in both. Foucault, *Discipline and Punish*, 192–94.

14. Julia Hillner, *Prison, Punishment and Penance in Late Antiquity* (Cambridge: Cambridge University Press, 2015), 91.

15. Valerio Neri, "Chiesa e carcere in età tardoantica,'" in *Carcer II. Prison et privation de liberté dans l'Empire romain et l'Occident médiéval*, ed. Cécile Bertrand-Dagenbach (Paris: De Boccard, 2005), 243–56. Hillner, *Prison, Punishment, and Penance*, 267, argues, "The idea that suffering in prison was similar to what could be expected of hell was widespread in late antiquity."

16. In *Hom. Matt.* 30.6, Chrysostom encourages that one use the fear of hell to persuade women to eschew adornment, saying, "Well then, man works and thou addest not; but doth God work, and dost thou amend it? And dost thou not consider the fire of hell? Dost thou not consider the destitution of thy soul? For on this account it is neglected, because all thy care is wasted on the flesh." In *Hom. Matt.* 43, he directs listeners to imagine hell, observing "how great the condemnation, how great the mockery" in order to gain access to the "door of repentance." In *Hom. John* 60.4–60.6 (PG 59:331–35), Chrysostom uses the fear of hell to encourage hearers to heed Matthew 25 by visiting prisoners rather than spending time in the marketplace or going to the theater. And in *Hom. Act.* 42.2 (PG 60:301), he again compares prison and the theater, arguing that the experience of prison causes one to reflect on the final judgment, and as a result to treat others more kindly and gently: "For as it is with one here shut up in prison, so in that world also before the Judgment, before the Day that is to come. Towards wife, children, and servants, he will be more gentle." Augustine, *City of God* 21.11; Henning, *Educating Early Christians*, 218–20. Hillner, *Prison, Punishment, and Penance*, 268–74, argues that these traditions also became a metaphor for the demands of ascetic life. See in particular the sixth-century *Rule of the Master* 90.16–19 (SC 106:380–82), which compares torture and prison to the distress of the monk who is fasting and sexually abstinent, alluding to the Apocalypse of Paul. On the function of exile for early Christian thinkers, see the work of Jennifer Barry, *Bishops in Flight: Exile and Displacement in Late Antiquity* (Oakland: University of California Press, 2019). On the role of the divine courtroom in framing the apocalyptic tours of hell, see Meira Z. Kensky, *Trying Man, Trying God: The Divine Courtroom in Early Jewish and Christian Literature*, WUNT 289 (Tübingen: Mohr Siebeck, 2010), 255–92.

17. When discussing disability in the ancient world, we are careful to note that disability is not inextricably linked to bodily suffering, despite the fact that

this link is often made in ancient literature. See Julia Watts Belser, *Rabbinic Tales of Destruction: Gender, Sex, and Disability in the Ruins of Jerusalem* (Oxford: Oxford University Press, 2018), xxx, for discussion of the ways in which some disabled figures in antiquity are able to "flip the script." On the moral responsibility borne by real bodies after death, see Muehlberger, *Moment of Reckoning*, 180.

18. Meghan Henning, "Metaphorical, Punitive, and Pedagogical Blindness in Hell," *Studia Patristica* 81, no. 7 (2017): 139–52, at 140. Scholars have argued that the Greek and Roman worlds shared a "physiognomic consciousness" in which physical appearance and ethical behavior are correlated so that ethical behavior is emphasized. See Robert Garland, *The Eye of the Beholder: Deformity and Disability in the Graeco-Roman World* (Ithaca, NY: Cornell University Press, 1995), 87–104; Nicholas Vlahogiannis, "Disabling Bodies," in *Changing Bodies, Changing Meanings: Studies on the Human Body in Antiquity*, ed. Dominic Monsterrat (New York: Routledge, 1998), 13–36, especially 15–23; Mikeal Parsons, *Body and Character in Luke and Acts: The Subversion of Physiognomy in Early Christianity* (Grand Rapids, MI: Baker Academic, 2006); Chad Hartsock, *Sight and Blindness in Luke-Acts: The Use of Physical Features in Characterization* (Leiden: Brill, 2008), 146–55.

19. See, for instance, the blindness and deafness of the people in Isa 6:9–11, the spiritualized interpretation of the "man born blind" in John 9, or the vituperation against the Pharisees as "blind guides" in Matt 23:16–26.

20. There are countless examples of this theme in ancient literature. See *IG* IV², 1, no. 121:4, stele A4, in Lynn R. LiDonnici, *The Epidaurian Miracle Inscriptions: Text, Translation, and Commentary* (Atlanta: Scholars, 1995). For a succinct summary of other ancient texts that link blindness and ignorance, see Hartsock, *Sight and Blindness in Luke-Acts*, 73–81.

21. O. S. Wintermute, "Apocalypse of Zephaniah," in *The Old Testament Pseudepigrapha*, ed. James H. Charlesworth, 2 vols. (Garden City, NY: Doubleday, 1983), 1:500–515.

22. See especially Matt 6:1–4. For further discussion of how the ethics of the Sermon on the Mount are reinforced through the pedagogical message of the Apocalypse of Peter, see Henning, *Educating Early Christians*, 174–223. For discussion of the rhetoric of blindness in Matthew, see Candida R. Moss, "Blurred Vision and Ethical Confusion: The Rhetorical Function of Matthew 6:22–23," *CBQ* 73 (2011): 757–76. In antiquity being "dumb" can refer to an inability to speak, a mental disability, or both. See the tale of Kroisos's disabled son who was "deaf and dumb" (*kōphos* and *aphōnos*): Herodotus, *Hist.* 1.34.2 and 1.85.4. The Latin terms for deafness were *surditas* and *surdus*. See the discussion of Herodotean subversion in this story in Garland, *The Eye of the Beholder*, 96–97.

23. Martha Himmelfarb, *Tours of Hell: An Apocalyptic Form in Jewish and Christian Literature* (Philadelphia: University of Pennsylvania Press, 1983), 105, has evalu-

ated the link between "the lack of self-awareness" and the punishment of blindness here as "appropriate." For a discussion of how Himmelfarb's assessment assumes the popularity of metaphorical and punitive violence in pagan literature, and internalizes implicit ableism in the contemporary world, see Henning, "Metaphorical, Punitive, and Pedagogical Blindness in Hell."

24. See also Apoc. Paul 31 for another ocular punishment, in which those who give not to one another but secretly prepare evil are immersed in the river of fire up to their eyebrows. Here the immersion of the body past the eyes is used to punish the sin of false pretense.

25. Matt 8:12; 22:13; 25:30. The concept of outer darkness is unique to Matthew; although some scholars have argued it was taken over from Q, there is no definitive evidence for this, and we can only conclude that it was a significant phrase for Matthew. Henning, *Educating Early Christians*, 121, 154.

26. Tertullian, *Res.* 35, says, "Moreover, whence can come weeping and gnashing of teeth, if not from eyes and from teeth? In fact, even when the body has been slain in hell and thrust down into outer darkness—and this is a torture particularly attaching to eyes—any one who at the marriage-feast is clothed in works less than worthy will at once be bound hand and foot, which shows that he will have risen again with a body. So again that reclining at meat in the kingdom of God, and sitting on twelve thrones, and standing then at the right hand or the left, and eating of the tree of life, are most trustworthy evidence of attitude of body." Translation from Ernest Evans, *Tertullian's Treatise on the Resurrection* (London: S.P.C.K., 1960).

27. Margaret Tallmadge May, *Galen: On the Usefulness of the Parts of the Body* (Ithaca, NY: Cornell University Press, 1968), 472–73n19. As May notes, in addition to *Func. Part.* X 2.66, the clearest exposition of Galen's understanding of vision is in *Doct. Hipp. Plat.* VII 5. On darkness and the lamp of the eye, see Moss, "Blurred Vision and Ethical Confusion," 757–76.

28. In the case of Teiresias, the blind seer, blindness actually endows the seer with special powers, making him "superrational." Even though Teiresias may have been blinded as the result of divine punishment, there is no trace of that idea here. There are other examples of "blind seers" or prophets in ancient literature, including Phineus, Phormio, Ophioneus, and the story of Democritus, who blinds himself in order to gain spiritual insight. Eleftheria A. Bernidaki-Aldous, *Blindness in a Culture of Light: Especially the Case of Oedipus at Colonus of Sophocles* (New York: Peter Lang, 1990), 72–94; Hartsock, *Sight and Blindness in Luke-Acts*, 77; Richard Buxton, *Myths and Tragedies in Their Ancient Greek Contexts* (Oxford: Oxford University Press, 2013), 173–200.

29. See Plutarch, *Mor. Div. Veng.* 563F–67F, in which souls that see properly in Hades can return to earth, while those that don't are "metaphorically blind," and trapped in Hades because they do not understand. See also 591E–F, in which some of the souls that have seen the torments of Hades become bright

stars and are said to "possess understanding," while others are extinguished and "sink entirely into the body."

30. David Brakke, *Demons and the Making of the Monk: Spiritual Combat in Early Christianity* (Cambridge, MA: Harvard University Press, 2006), 201–2. Cf. Blake Leyerle, "John Chrysostom on the Gaze," *JECS* 1, no. 2 (1993): 160; Emily R. Cain, "Medically Modified Eyes: A Baptismal Cataract Surgery in Clement of Alexandria," *SLA* 2, no. 4 (Winter 2018): 491–511.

31. As Candida R. Moss, *Divine Bodies: Resurrecting Perfection in the New Testament and Early Christianity* (New Haven: Yale University Press, 2019), 41–65, has noted, amputation was not as anomalous in the ancient world as it is in our own.

32. For other instances of limb amputation or laceration, see Apoc. Pet. 9; 11; and Apoc. Paul 40.

33. John Chrysostom, *Hom. Matt.* 43.6, invites hearers to compare the torments of hell with the pain of gout, reflecting on how enduring eternal torment, like extreme pain of gout, does not afford one the solace of seeing that they have co-sufferers. Like the disabled, Chrysostom reflects, those damned in hell are utterly isolated. "Think, I pray you, of those that are seized with gout, how, when they are racked by sharp pain, though you show them ten thousand suffering worse, they do not so much as take it into their mind. For the intensity of their anguish allows not their reason any leisure for thinking of others, and so finding consolation. Let us not then feed ourselves with these cold hopes . . . Now if in that case it hath no strength, much less in the anguish and burden unspeakable, which 'the gnashing of teeth' indicates."

34. The different kinds of suffering bodies that we survey here are by no means exhaustive, for the most part leaving out the body of the tourist, the angelic bodies, or the heavenly bodies, due to the constraints of time and space.

35. Himmelfarb, *Tours of Hell*, 82. As she rightly cautions, each of these punishments "has its own history," and Himmelfarb's work tracing the history of each of these distinctive punishments is still foundational in that regard. What we hope to add here is an awareness of the way that those distinctive punishments were likely interpreted by early and late antique Christians once they were assembled together into the early Christian hellscapes of the apocalypses.

36. For places in which "weeping" is associated with the physical pain of eternal punishment, see 1 En. 108:3, 5; 2 En. 40:12; Apoc. Pet. 3; 5–6; Apoc. Paul 16; 17; 32; 36; 42–43; Lat. Vis. Ez. 27; 43; Gk. Apoc. Mary 3–4. For weeping as the response of the righteous, see both versions of 2 En. 41:1, in which Enoch weeps at the sight of punishment. Although in 2 En. 41:1, both versions have Enoch weeping at the sight of punishment, in 2 En. 40:12 it is only the longer version [J] that describes hell as "open and weeping." See also the longer version of 2 En. 38:3 [J], in which Enoch warns his sons with "weeping and great lamentation," while the shorter version [A] simply states that Enoch instructs his sons. See also Apoc. Zeph. 6:4–7, in which the seer cries out in distress

and beseeches the Lord to save him; Apoc. Zeph. 11, in which the righteous attempt to intercede for those in torment; and the weeping of the righteous at the sight of the damned in Apoc. Pet. 3; the propitious tears of Mary and Michael in Mary's Rep. 93; 100; Paul's repeated weeping in Apoc. Paul 9; 10; 14; 33; 36; 38–40; 42–43; 48. Ezra mentions his own cries in the citation of a Psalm in Lat. Vis. Ez. 108 and offers blessing upon those who weep for their sins in Gk. Apoc. Ez. 5.11. And in the Oxford manuscript of Gk. Apoc. Mary 4, Mary weeps at the sight of the damned.

37. Brent D. Shaw, "Judicial Nightmares and Christian Memory," *JECS* 11, no. 4 (2003): 533–63, at 544, argues that the body language of "blushing, sweating, shuffling, bowing, scraping, and weeping" was widely recognized as a behavioral symptom of guilt, elicited by judicial rituals.

38. Shaw, "Judicial Nightmares and Christian Memory," 539, notes that the judicial process was designed to "induce fear" so that those watching would become "mentally overwhelmed." See also Henning, *Educating Early Christians*, 186–88.

39. This is one way early Christian hell parallels the Greek and Roman depictions of Hades, in which we also find tearful scenes between loved ones (Odysseus weeps with compassion at the sight of his unburied friend Elpenor, *Od.*11.55, and Anchises is overcome with tears when he sees his son, Virgil, *Aen.* 6.688–89).

40. The translation by Emily Wilson, *The Odyssey* (New York: W. W. Norton, 2018), 237–38, captures this passage forcefully: "Odysseus was melting into tears; his cheeks were wet with weeping, as a woman weeps, as she falls to wrap her arms around her husband, fallen fighting for his home and children. She is watching as he gasps and dies. She shrieks, a clear high wail, collapsing upon his corpse. The men are right behind. They hit her shoulders with their spears and lead her to slavery, hard labor, and a life of pain. Her face is marked with her despair. In that same desperate way, Odysseus was crying. No one noticed that his eyes were wet with tears, except Alcinous, who sat right next to him and heard his sobs. Quickly he spoke to his seafaring people." *Od.* 8 is bookended by Odysseus weeping and throwing his cloak over his head; see also 8.85–95. I am grateful to Jonathan Zecher for this reference.

41. Stephanie L. Cobb, *Dying to Be Men: Gender and Language in Early Martyr Texts* (New York: Columbia University Press, 2008), 100–102. See also the performative aspect of tears in the ancient novel, as observed by Georgia Frank, *The Memory of the Eyes: Pilgrims to Living Saints in Christian Late Antiquity* (Berkeley: University of California Press, 2000), 21–23, in which the subtle tears of the true lover are contrasted with the crocodile tears of the villain (Achilles Tatius, *Clitophon and Leucippe* 6.7; 7.4). For overall treatments of tears in antiquity, see Thorsten Fögen, *Tears in the Graeco-Roman World* (Berlin: W. de Gruyter, 2009); and Margaret Alexiou and Douglas L. Cairns, *Greek Laughter and Tears: Antiquity and After* (Edinburgh: Edinburgh University Press, 2017).

42. Blake Leyerle, "The Etiology of Sorrow and Its Therapeutic Benefits in the Preaching of John Chrysostom," *JLA* 8, no. 2 (2015): 368–85, at 385.

43. Leyerle, "The Etiology of Sorrow," 382–85. John Chrysostom, *Stag.* 3.13–14 (PG 47:491–92), cautions against using grief in the wrong context because it could aggravate other illnesses, just like taking a medicine that is prescribed for someone else.

44. Chrysostom, *Stag.* 3.13–14 (PG 47:491–92), in Leyerle, "The Etiology of Sorrow," 384.

45. Leyerle, "The Etiology of Sorrow," 383, Ellen Muehlberger, "Simeon and Other Women in Theodoret's Religious History: Gender in the Representation of Late Ancient Christian Asceticism," *JECS* 23, no. 4 (2015): 585–606, at 593; Hannah Hunt, *Joy Bearing Grief: Tears of Contrition in the Writings of the Early Syrian and Byzantine Fathers* (Leiden: Brill, 2004), 6–8.

46. Hunt, *Joy Bearing Grief*, 15.

47. Muehlberger, "Simeon and Other Women," 592–93.

48. Hunt, *Joy Bearing Grief*, 108–12.

49. In many cases these tears are propitious, in a typical scene where the tears and pleas of the apostolic seer win a period of respite for the damned. Apoc. Pet. 13–14. Cf. Rainer Fragment; Mary's Rep. 100; Apoc. Paul 43–44; Lat. Vis. Ez. 90–91; Gk. Apoc. Ez. 5:10; Eth. Apoc. Vir., in M. Chaîne, *Apocrypha B. Maria Virgine*, CSCO: Scriptores Aethiopici: Ser I, 8 (Rome: De Luigi, 1909), 45–80, at 68; Gk. Apoc. Mary 29 (Oxford manuscript); Gk. Apoc. Mary 34 (Vatican manuscript). The period of rest granted to sinners is best preserved in H. Pernot, "Descente de la Vierge aux Enfers d'après les manuscrits grecs de Paris," *Revue des études grecques* 13 (1900): 233–57, at paragraph 25; Coptic Apoc. Paul in E. A. W. Budge, *Miscellaneous Coptic Texts in the Dialect of Upper Egypt* (London: British Museum, 1915), 534–74, 1022–29, at 1070; and the fourth recension of the Armenian Apoc. Paul, in L. Leloir, *Écrits Apocryphes sur les Apôtres. Traduction de l'Édition Arménienne de Venise*, vol. 1, CCSA 3 (Turnhout: Brepols, 1986), 87–172, paragraph 35. In the Armenian Apocalypse of Paul, hell's inhabitants are released and hell is destroyed.

50. Shaw, "Judicial Nightmares and Christian Memory," 533–63.

51. Himmelfarb, *Tours of Hell*, 108–10, describes the way that fire imagery made its way into visions of hell, largely because of fire's association with earthly places of punishment.

52. Henning, *Educating Early Christians*, 108–37, 153–56. Cf. Gen 19:24; Isa 1:7; 30:27, 30; Jer 11:16; Amos 1:4, 7, 10, 12, 14; 2:5; Joel 2:1–3; Lam 4:11.

53. Himmelfarb, *Tours of Hell*, 109, 118–19; Jdt 16:17; Sir 7:17; Mark 9:47–48; Joshua b. Levi Frag.; Ged. Mosh. 18; Apoc. Pet. 9; Apoc. Paul 42; Gk. Apoc. Mary 18 (Oxford and Vatican manuscripts), 23 (Oxford manuscript); Gk. Apoc. Ez. 4:20; Lat. Vis. Ez. 34; Eth. Apoc. Mary 64.

54. Himmelfarb, *Tours of Hell*, 110; Mark 9:42–48; Matt 5:22; 18:9; Jas 3:6. See also the lake of fire in Rev 19:20; 20:10, 14.

55. Homer, *Od.* 10.513; Lucian, *Men.* 14; *True Story* 2.31; *Funerals* 8; Himmelfarb, *Tours of Hell*, 110–11.

56. As duBois, *Torture and Truth*, 36, argues, "The *basanos* assumes first that the slave always lies, then that torture makes him or her always tell the truth, then that the truth produced through torture will always expose the truth or falsehood of the free man's evidence." Albert J. Harrill, "'Exegetical Torture' in Early Christian Biblical Interpretation: The Case of Origen of Alexandria," *Biblical Interpretation* 25 (2017): 39–57, at 55, argues that *basanos* works this way for Origen as well: "He located 'truth' in bodies figured as outsider and inferior—what he terms as servile 'flesh.'"

57. Augustine, for instance, condoned torture as a means to elicit confessions from Donatists in his letters to Marcellinus and Boniface. Augustine, *Let.* 133.2 (CSEL 44:32); *Let.* 185.21 (CSEL 57:19), cited in Hillner, *Prison, Punishment and Penance*, 81. Similarly, Origen applies the concept of *basanos* to both the "real" violence of martyrdom and the exegesis of Scripture. See Harrill, "Exegetical Torture," 43–49, 54–57.

58. Smoke, heat, and damp were common forms of torture, along with the rack, the wheel, and the whip. On the connection between fire and martyrdom, see Gerhard Thür, "Folter," "Folterwerkzeuge," *RAC*, vol. 8 (1972), 101–4; Hillner, *Prison, Punishment and Penance*, 250; and Origen, *Ex. Mart.* 15.

59. Hippocratic Corpus, *Aff.* 15, prescribes that the patient sit by the fire to induce vomiting, using fire as a purgative treatment. Galen, *Ther. Glau.* 1.15 (57K). Those who collapse due to extreme cold are prescribed to sit by the fire, drink wine, and get a massage.

60. Galen, *Hyg.* 5, describes fire as analogous to the female body, having "large pores," unlike earth and water which have small pores.

61. Galen, *Meth. Med.* 5 5.3 (515K–516K). And likewise, excessive uterine hemorrhaging is cured by cupping the breasts to draw the blood upward.

62. Hippocratic Corpus, *Aph.* 87. See also Hippocratic Corpus, *Art* 8, which calls fire the "most caustic of the caustics" and notes that if fire does not cure someone, it is the fault of the disease and not the doctor. Galen, *Ther. Glau.* 2.3 (89K): fire is compared to other caustic medications as treatment for ulcers (misu, chalcitis, yellow orpiment, gypsum, and realgar [red sulfate of arsenic]). Hippocratic Corpus, *Art* 12, mentions the use of fire on inoperable diseases, and Galen, *Ther. Glau.* 2.3 (89K), describes fire as a treatment to be used after other caustic medications are exhausted.

63. David Frankfurter, "Martyrology and the Prurient Gaze," *JECS* 17, no. 2 (2009): 215–45, at 224, observes that in female martyrdom narratives, the phallic imagery of the sword is commonplace, functioning as a sado-erotic image.

64. Himmelfarb, *Tours of Hell*, 116–21; István Czachesz, "Torture in Hell and Reality: The *Visio Pauli*," in *The Visio Pauli and the Gnostic Apocalypse of Paul*, ed. Jan N. Bremmer and István Czachesz (Leuven: Peeters, 2007), 142.

65. See, for instance, Aristophanes, *Frogs* 145 and following, for a detailed description of those who have "wronged a stranger" lying in "mud and ever-flowing shit" in Hades.

66. Worms reminiscent of Isaiah: Apoc. Pet. 9 (27); Apoc. Paul 42; Gk. Apoc. Mary 18 (Oxford and Vatican manuscripts), 23 (Oxford manuscript); Gk. Apoc. Ez. 4.20; Lat. Vis. Ez. 34–36; Elijah Fragment in R. Joshua b. Levi 7. Unspecified worms: Apoc. Pet. 7 (25); Acts Thom. (Gk.) 56; Apoc. Paul 36–37, 39, 42; Eth. Apoc. Mary 64; Ged. Moshe. 14; Coptic AP 210 (edited by Chaîne). I am grateful to Christine Luckritz Marquis for drawing my attention to the tour of hell in the Apophthegmata Patrum. In the Apoc. Pet. 7 the worm is listed among other venomous beasts. In a later text that is attributed to John of Damascus (but may be a later pseudonomous work), *Barlaam and Ioseph* 25, the worm of Gehenna is "venomous."

67. Hippocratic Corpus, *Aph.* 26; Hippocratic Corpus, *Pror.* 2.28; Celsus, *Med.* 4.24; Galen, *Aff. Part.* 1.4, 2.5, 6.2–4. See also Piers D. Mitchell, "Human Parasites in the Roman World: Health Consequences of Conquering and Empire," *Parasitology* 144 (2017): 48–58.

68. And as Celsus notes, vomiting worms is "nastier" than discharging them from the intestines. *Med.* 4.24.

69. See also the story of Eumenes's wife in *Epid.* 4.16.

70. Hippocratic Corpus, *Pror.* 2.28, "This disease occurs mainly in women, next in girls, but less in others."

71. I am extremely grateful to Kristi Upson-Saia for this reference.

72. *IG* IV², 1, no. 122:25, describes a woman, Sostrata of Pherai, who was pregnant and carried to the Asklepieion on a litter, and leaves the sanctuary healed after a "handsome man" cuts open her stomach and removes lots of creatures (two footbasins full). While Emma and Ludwig Edelstein, *Asclepius: A Collection and Interpretation of the Testimonies* (Baltimore: Johns Hopkins University Press, 1945), 234, translate this as "pregnancy with worms," the reader of the Greek text may have interpreted that the "creatures" were worms based upon the close proximity of this inscription to another that describes a woman with a worm in her belly who is "cured" via the removal of her head (*IG* IV², 1, no. 122:23). There is a well-known parallel between the latter inscription and a story about healing a tapeworm at the Asklepieion in Epidaurus, attributed to ancient historian Hippys of Rhegium, preserved in Aelian, *Char. An.* 9.33. Edelstein and Edelstein, *Asclepius*, 220–21 (#422); LiDonnici, *The Epidaurian Miracle Inscriptions*, 70–72.

73. Pliny the Elder, *Nat. Hist.* 29.27 (85). "There is also a third type of phalangium, a hairy spider with an enormous head. When this is cut open, there are said to be found inside two little worms, which tied in deer skin as an amulet on women before sunrise, act as a contraceptive, as Caecilius has told us in his Commentaries. They retain this property for a year. Of all such preventives this only would it be right for me to mention, to help those women who are so prolific that they stand in need of such respite." I am extremely grateful to Sarah Bond for drawing my attention to this reference.

74. I am grateful to Candida Moss for passing along this reference to worms, paralysis, and blood flow.

75. Athanasius, *Life Ant.* 58.

76. Meghan Henning, "Paralysis and Sexuality in Medical Literature and the *Acts of Peter*," *JLA* 8, no. 2 (2015): 306–21.

77. AP 210 contains a similar punishment, in which a young virgin sees her mother, who had committed adultery and drunkenness, with chattering teeth, ravaged by fire and worms.

78. For an incisive discussion of worms as retributive justice that was applied particularly to male tyrants and persecutors, see Candida R. Moss, "A Note on the Death of Judas," *NTS* 65, no. 3 (2019): 388–97. See especially 2 Chr 21:11–19; 2 Macc 9:9; Lactantius, *Death Pers.* 33.6–8; Pausanias, *Descr.* 9.7.2; David J. Ladouceur, "The Death of Herod the Great," *Classical Philology* 76, no. 1 (1981): 25–34; Thomas Africa, "Worms and the Death of Kings: A Cautionary Note on Disease and History," *Classical Antiquity* 1 (1982): 1–17. As Moss, "A Note on the Death of Judas," 390n6, observes, "In the majority of sources, retributive justice tends to have focused on men, the clear example is Pheretime, Queen of Cyrene, who utilized brutal strategies to harm her enemies (Herodotus, *Hist.*, 4.205)." Ellen Muehlberger, "The Legend of Arius's Death: Imagination, Space, and Filth in Late Ancient Historiography," *Past and Present* 77 (2015): 8–10; T. D. Barnes, "The Funerary Speech for John Chrysostom (BHG3 871 = CPG 6517)," *SP* 37 (2001): 332–34; and Jennifer Barry, "Diagnosing Heresy: Ps.-Martyrius's Funerary Speech for John Chrysostom," *JECS* 24, no. 3 (2016): 395–418. The inverse of this trope is found in the vision of heaven in Apoc. Paul 26, in which the infants that Herod had slain are seen bathing in a river of milk. In heaven, then, Apoc. Paul contains a clear antipode for the gendered consumption of the tyrants, whereas the babies who were victimized and powerless on earth are now forever fortified with nourishment.

79. Timotheus, *Frag.* 791.70 (cf. P. Berol. 9875); Oppian, *Cyn.* 4.134.

80. See Henning, *Educating Early Christians*, 162–73, 186–92.

81. Origen, in Methodius, *Res.* 3.7.1–7. I thank Candida Moss for bringing this reference to my attention.

82. Chron. Jer. XIV.4, in Michael E. Stone and John Strugnell, *The Books of Elijah, Parts 1 and 2* (Missoula, MT: Scholars, 1979), 20–23; AP 210.

83. Hillner, *Prison, Punishment, and Penance,* 242–78, 339.

84. Aristophanes, *Wasps* 775; Lucian, *Tyr.* 20; Plautus, *Capt.*, act 4, line 913.

85. Hippocratic Corpus, *Superf.* 20; *Barr.* 2.3; *Nat. Wom.* 378, 37 (380 and following); *Dis.* 2.46.

86. Clement of Alexandria, *Ex. Proph.* 41. Commenting on the protection by an angel of children who are exposed by their parents, Clement says, "Wherefore Peter also says in his Apocalypse 'and a flash of fire, coming from their children and smiting the eyes of the women.'"

87. Patrick Gray, "Abortion, Infanticide, and the Social Rhetoric of the Apocalypse of Peter," *JECS* 9 (2001): 313–37.

88. Clement of Alexandria, *Ex. Proph.* 48, interprets this as a reference to "children born abortively," but the text itself only states that the parents killed their children.

89. Himmelfarb, *Tours of Hell*, 97. Martha Himmelfarb, like Clement long before her, argues that the punishments for parents in the Apocalypse of Peter are "measure for measure" punishments that fit the crime in measure and intensity. She reasons that the breast-milk beasts are an "appropriate" punishment for rejection of nursing or infanticide. Here Himmelfarb uses "the logic of talion" to attribute blame for not nursing to the men and women in the second punishment.

90. Plutarch, *Cons. Wife* 609e. See also Plutarch, *Educ. Ch.* 3 (most likely not by Plutarch); Tacitus, *Germ.* 20; Aulus Gellius, *Attic* 12.1.17.

91. John David Penniman, *Raised on Christian Milk: Food and the Formation of the Soul in Early Christianity* (New Haven: Yale University Press, 2017), 23, 37–38.

92. Penniman, *Raised on Christian Milk*, 37–43, adduces traces of the centrality of breast milk and the nursing mother in Roman art, Augustus's description of the ideal wife (Dio Cassius, *Rom. Hist.* 56.3.4), Plato (*Rep.* 376e–77c), and Aristotle (*Soul* 415a) arguing that nourishment was essential to *paideia*, and in depictions of nursing and breast milk as the key to balance and the transfer of "elemental substances" of the parents to the child in the Hippocratic Corpus and Galen (Hippocratic Corpus, *Reg.* 28 and 35; Galen, *Cap. Soul* 1–2, 9). Likewise, a nurse could transmit disease (kidney stones specifically) to a child if her milk was "unclean" as a result of phlegmatic or unclean food and drink (Hippocratic Corpus, *Dis.* 4.24).

93. As Ann Ellis Hanson, "The Medical Writer's Woman," in *Before Sexuality: The Construction of Erotic Experience in the Ancient Greek World*, ed. David M. Halperin, John J. Winkler, and Froma I. Zeitlin (Princeton, NJ: Princeton University Press, 1990), has argued, the ancient gynecological literature is "protonatalistic," first and foremost concerned with producing heirs for the household.

94. Penniman, *Raised on Christian Milk*, 35 and 45; cf. Galen, *Prop. Food* (Kuhn 6:681–89).

95. As Bernadette J. Brooten has demonstrated, Christians mention wet nurses in passing and in metaphor, indicating that the nurses were commonplace and that the practice was not worthy of comment. Brooten, "Early Christian Enslaved Families (First to Fourth Century)," in *Children and Family in Late Antiquity: Life, Death and Interaction*, ed. Christian Laes, Katarina Mustakallio, and Ville Vuolanto (Leuven: Peeters, 2015), 111–34, at 121n32, citing Tertullian, *Soul* 19; Cyprian, *Laps.* 25; Gregory of Nyssa, *Life Macr.* 972M. Augustine says that he was fed by both his mother and wet nurses (*Conf.* 1, 6). And Arnobius of Sicca, *Ag. Pag.* 2.21, uses the image of a wet nurse metaphorically. See also Anna Rebecca Solevåg, *Birthing Salvation: Gender and Class in Early Christian*

Childbearing Discourse (Leiden: Brill, 2013), 168–73, who deftly traces the gender significance of the metaphor of wet nursing in Acts Andr. 7–9. On the social history of Christian motherhood, see also Gillian Clark, *Monica: An Ordinary Saint* (Oxford: Oxford University Press, 2016).

96. Rebecca Flemming, *Medicine and the Making of Roman Women: Gender, Nature, and Authority from Celsus to Galen* (New York: Oxford University Press, 2000), 239n165; Soranus, *Gyn.* 2.17–18.

97. Plutarch, *Educ. Ch.* 3e.

98. Solevåg, *Birthing Salvation*, 51–53, 60–62.

99. Brooten, "Early Christian Enslaved Families," 122. Brooten also provides an exhaustive review of the evidence for wet nursing in antiquity, which comes from epigraphic sources that record contracts for both free and enslaved wet nurses. See Keith R. Bradley, "Wet-Nursing at Rome: A Study in Social Relations," in *The Family in Ancient Rome: New Perspectives*, ed. Beryl Rawson (Ithaca, NY: Cornell University Press, 1987), 201–29; Bradley, *Discovering the Roman Family: Studies in Roman Social History* (Oxford: Oxford University Press, 1991), 13–36. For another excellent discussion of the "slave as nurse," see Chris L. de Wet, *Preaching Bondage: John Chrysostom and the Discourse of Slavery in Early Christianity* (Oakland: University of California Press, 2015), 127–69.

100. See Dawn LaValle, "Divine Breastfeeding: Milk, Blood, and *Pneuma* in Clement of Alexandria's *Paedagogus*," *JLA* 8, no. 2 (2015): 322–36, at 326, who points out an important exception in the Hippocratic Corpus, in which there is discussion of the fetus consuming both blood and milk in the womb late in pregnancy, seeing them as distinct nutritional substances (cf. *Nat. Boy* 21.4; 30.5). For a discussion of the connection between blood and breast milk, see Lesley Dean-Jones, *Women's Bodies in Classical Greek Science* (Oxford: Oxford University Press, 1994), 215–24.

101. Galen, *Func. Part.* 14.8 (Kühn 4:176–78; May 2:638) and Soranus, *Gyn.* 1.15, cited in Dawn Lavalle, "Divine Breastfeeding," 326–27. Galen, *Hyg.* 7 (36K), says in passing that milk is made from blood that has undergone a change in the breasts.

102. Fleming, *Medicine and the Making of Roman Women*, 316, observes that in Galen's text *Health. Cond.*, which is largely focused on the correct regimen for the male body, the rare mention of the female body is in the case of women who are acting as nurses (*Health. Cond.* 1.9.1–9; CMG v.4.2.21.34–23.3).

103. Fleming, *Medicine and the Making of Roman Women*, 316; Bradley, "Wet Nursing at Rome," 201–29.

104. Pure milk tastes and smells sweet, is white, and uniform in texture, neither too watery nor too thick. Curdled milk, Galen notes elsewhere, is "harmful to all." Galen, *Meth. Med.* 7.6 (475K).

105. Theodosian Code 9.24.1.1, cited in Penniman, *Raised on Christian Milk*, 30n27.

106. Theodosian Code 9.24.1.1, cited in Penniman, *Raised on Christian Milk*, 30n27. "Since milk continues to leave the uterus and flow out towards the upper

regions of the body as it did before, not having a proper receptacle, it lights upon the principal parts of the body such as the heart and lung, and the women suffocate." See also Galen, *Meth. Med.* 14.11 (983K), which describes the swelling of glands, including milk ducts along with the glands that produce sperm and saliva. When any of these glands becomes swollen, the affected area is to be treated with medicine or removed surgically via scalpel.

107. As Penniman, *Raised on Christian Milk*, 163, notes, the nursing infant is the one place where male receptivity was socially acceptable. This does not extend to adults consuming breast milk directly from the breast. Galen, *Meth. Med.* 7.6 (474K), recommends human breast milk taken directly from the breast (to keep it as warm as possible) as a treatment for something like tuberculosis ("wasting due to phthisis"), but observes that "most people cannot bear to do this." There seems to be a strong taboo against consuming breast milk directly from the breast, even if it is not spoiled or beastly, and even if it is perceived to be life-saving to do so.

108. As Himmelfarb, *Tours of Hell*, 98, has noted, Clement appears to have swapped the sins and punishments as they are written in the Ethiopic text, attributing the punishment for abortion to those who have committed infanticide and vice versa.

109. Gk. Apoc. Mary 7 (Oxford manuscript) reads "brought down their own children from the womb and cast them out as food for the dogs," which could simply be a reference to infant exposure, whereas Gk. Apoc. Mary 9 (Vatican manuscript) reads "threw off their own unborn children from their wombs and cast them out as food for the dogs."

110. Himmelfarb, *Tours of Hell*, 99.

111. As Himmelfarb, *Tours of Hell*, 99–100, has noted, beasts sucking at the breasts of women are a terrifying image that appears outside of the apocalyptic tours of hell as well. In both the Cop. Apoc. Eli. and the *Life of Shenoute* beasts nursing from women are one of the woes that will come upon Egypt in the last days.

112. Mary's Rep. 7: Mary, while nursing Jesus, expresses worry about where she and Joseph will find food, and the infant Jesus stops nursing and commands a date palm to bend its head for Mary and Joseph.

113. In the later Greek version of this text, the Akhmim Fragment, the text is even more explicit about the homoerotic behavior it wishes to isolate: "These are those who defiled their bodies, behaving like women. And the women with them, these were those who behaved with one another as men with a woman." As Bernadette Brooten, *Love between Women: Early Christian Responses to Female Homoeroticism* (Chicago: University of Chicago Press, 1996), 307, has argued, this is referring to passive male partners (the active male partner is not condemned here), as well as both active and passive female partners.

114. The pairing of idolatry and homoeroticism is likely drawn from Paul's discussion of idolatry in Romans. Several of the early Christian apocalypses feature

punishments for both female and male homoeroticism. Apoc. Pet. 10; Acts Thom. 55; Apoc. Paul 40. As Brooten, *Love between Women*, 308, has argued, the discussion of female and male homoeroticism together was not universal in the Roman world, and this, along with the close association between this sin and idolatry, was likely borrowed from Paul.

115. Brooten, *Love between Women*, 306.

116. See, for instance, Pomponius Bononiensis, *Pros.* fr. 148–49R: "I have buggered no citizen through deceit, only the kind who bent over, himself begging me." We take care to note that despite the visual discourse around bending over during sex, homoeroticism is not a zero-sum game of "winners and losers" in Greek and Roman antiquity. As James Davidson is careful to note, "buggery became a problem through the meaning it acquired in the context of other symbolic structures, in particular those of prostitution and commodification, excess and self-control." James Davidson, "Dover, Foucault, and Greek Homosexuality: Penetration and the Truth of Sex," in *Studies in Ancient Greek and Roman Society*, ed. Robin Osborne (Cambridge: Cambridge University Press, 2004), 78–118, at 98.

117. As Amy C. Smith, "Eurymedon and the Evolution of Political Personifications in the Early Classical Period," *Journal of Hellenic Studies* 119 (1999): 128–41, argues, this scene is unique in Greek vase paintings. However, as Craig A. Williams, *Roman Homosexuality*, 2d ed. (Oxford: Oxford University Press, 2009), 101, 261–62, notes, in Roman art the image of male penetration of another male was very common, occurring not only in expensive pieces like vases and mirrors, but also in frescoes in homes, bathhouses, and brothels and on inexpensive Arretine pottery.

118. For a thorough reception history of the vase, see Lloyd Llewellyn-Jones, "Reviewing Space, Context and Meaning: The Eurymedon Vase Again," in *Greek Art in Context: Archeological and Art Historical Perspectives*, ed. Diana Rodríguez Pérez (New York: Routledge, 2017), 97–115. In contrast to the "heroic nudity" of the Greek figure, the Persian archer is dressed in a tight cat-suit, a garment that is meant to humiliate the wearer. As Smith "Eurymedon," 136, has argued, the archer is further effeminized by his lack of undergarments, meant to contrast "Greek virility" and "Oriental effeminacy."

119. As Llewellyn-Jones, "Reviewing Space, Context and Meaning," 110, notes, this gesture was a perplexing one for the Greeks, who saw prostrating oneself before another man to be an abrogation of one's freedom. See Xenophon, *Hell.* 4.1.35.

120. Llewellyn-Jones, "Reviewing Space, Context and Meaning," 110.

121. For the argument that Christians collapsed all same-sex contact into one category, see Kyle Harper, *From Shame to Sin: The Christian Transformation of Sexual Morality in Late Antiquity* (Cambridge, MA: Harvard University Press, 2013), 99.

122. Harper, *From Shame to Sin*, 155.
123. The Ethiopic manuscript is corrupt at this point and makes it difficult to de-cipher exactly who is cannibalizing the deacon. Two other nutritive punish-ments are also described in two of the Elijah fragments, which are preserved in Hebrew. In one fragment (in the Chron. Jer. XIV.4) the men who stole food are made to eat fine sand until their teeth are broken by the sand in order to fulfill Psalm 3:8: "I have broken the teeth of the wicked." This punishment re-curs in the fragment found in *Reshith Ḥokmah*, but here Elijah also sees "men who are made to eat their own flesh," who are simply identified as those whose worm does not die (cf. Isa 66:24). See Stone and Strugnell, *The Books of Elijah*, 16–19, for text and translation.
124. This is especially the case for Plutarch and other moralists, but it is a well-worn trope. See, for instance, Plutarch, *Talk.* 502–19.
125. As Jeremy Hultin, *The Ethics of Obscene Speech in Early Christianity and Its En-vironment* (Leiden: Brill, 2008), 236, argues, "But the second-century Chris-tians evidently felt no need to deal with foul language directly. There was so clearly a sense of propriety about the matter that it did not often need to be addressed."
126. Maud W. Gleason, *Making Men: Sophists and Self-Presentation in Ancient Rome* (Princeton, NJ: Princeton University Press, 1995).
127. Marianne Bjelland Kartzow, *Gossip and Gender: Othering of Speech in the Pasto-ral Epistles* (Berlin: Walter de Gruyter, 2009), 180–82.
128. Gleason, *Making Men*, xxi–xxvi; Margaret Y. MacDonald, *Early Christian Women and Pagan Opinion: The Power of the Hysterical Woman* (Cambridge: Cambridge University Press, 1996); Jennifer A. Glancy, "Protocols of Mascu-linity in the Pastoral Epistles," in *New Testament Masculinities*, ed. Stephen D. Moore and Janice Capel Anderson (Atlanta: Society of Biblical Literature, 2003), 235–64; Kartzow, *Gossip and Gender*, 180–82.
129. As Hultin, *The Ethics of Obscene Speech*, 13–14, has noted, there were also a num-ber of ancient medical texts that connected obscene speech with mental ill-ness. Hippocractic Corpus, *Epid.* 3.17.11; 4.15. See also Seneca the Younger, *Wise Man* 13.1; and Plato, *Laws* 11 (934E).
130. Teresa M. Shaw, *The Burden of the Flesh: Fasting and Sexuality in Early Chris-tianity* (Minneapolis: Fortress, 1998), 53–64.
131. John David Penniman, "Blended with the Savior: Gregory of Nyssa's Eucha-ristic Pharmacology in the *Catechetical Oration*," *SLA* 4, no. 2 (2018): 512–41, at 524.
132. Penniman, "Blended with the Savior," 518. Penniman's argument here takes up a compelling line of thinking regarding medicine and theology in late antiquity: "I want to reconsider the ritual of Eucharistic eating as a medical regimen of dietetics—a mode of gastronomic therapy premised on the belief that health care was, in fact, a form of soul care, and that the transformation of the physi-

cal body into a spiritual one required the ingestion of an edible matter imbued with spiritual power."

133. The Acts Andr. Mth. also plays with the relationship between cannibalism and Eucharist, depicting cannibals who are transformed into Christians who celebrate the Eucharist. Lautaro Roig Lanzillotta, "Cannibals: Myrmidonians, Sinopeans or Jews? The Five Versions of the Acts of Andrew and Matthias (in the City of the Cannibals) and Their Sources," in *Wonders Never Cease: The Purpose of Narrating Miracle Stories in the New Testament and Its Religious Environment*, ed. Michael Labahn and Bert Jan Lietaert Peerbolte (New York: T. and T. Clark, 2006), 221–43.

134. Theophilus, *Autol.* 3.4; Tatian, *Gr.* 25; Justin Martyr, *1 Apol.* 26; 8; Origen, *Cels.* 6.27; Tertullian, *Apol.* 7.1; 8.3, 7; R. L. Wilken, *The Christians as the Romans Saw Them* (New Haven: Yale University Press, 1984), 18; Bart Wagemakers, "Incest, Infanticide, and Cannibalism: Anti-Christian Imputations in the Roman Empire," *Greece and Rome* 57, no. 2 (2010): 337–54, at 339–41.

135. For other references to black tongues as symptom of fever or disease, see Hippocratic Corpus, *Aff.* 11; *Aph.* 87; *Epid.* 7.74. These are just a sampling; the references to changes in the tongue as a diagnostic tool are too numerous to cite.

136. Contrast the horrifying hair of this passage with the heavenly hair of Elijah in Apoc. Pet. 15: "like the rainbow in the water was his hair." For an excellent discussion of ascetic views of hair as a sign of holiness or angelic countenance, see Kristi Upson-Saia, "Hairiness and Holiness in the Early Christian Desert," in *Dressing Judeans and Christians in Antiquity*, ed. Kristi Upson-Saia, Carly Daniel-Hughes, and Alicia J. Batten (Burlington, VT: Ashgate, 2014), 155–72.

137. Galen, *Art* 394K–95K; Galen, *Meth. Med.* 13.20–22; the "cure" for such an excess would be removing blood from the body to get rid of the excess.

138. See Polemo 1.1.158 F, quoted in Gleason, *Making Men*, 62, who describes the importance of straight eyelids and unmoving pupils for conveying masculinity. If these traits are absent, Polemo says, "you may be sure that this is the profile of someone who is really feminine, even though you might find him among real men." For a thorough discussion of the philosophical theories of vision in the ancient world, the prominence of the "extramission" theory of vision in which the eye was thought to emit light, and the influence of these theories upon Second Temple Jewish and early Christian literature, see Moss, "Blurred Vision and Ethical Confusion."

139. P. W. van der Horst, "Pseudo-Phocylides: A New Translation and Introduction," in *OTP* 2:581.

140. There are a plethora of ancient sources that describe long hair as a feminine, and thus undesirable, trait. On the nature of hair in 1 Corinthians and the medical literature, see Troy W. Martin, "Paul's Argument from Nature for the Veil in 1 Corinthians 11:13–15: A Testicle Instead of a Head Covering," *JBL* 123, no. 1 (2004): 75–84.

141. Maria Doerfler, "'Hair!' Remnants of Ascetic Exegesis in Augustine of Hippo's *De Opere Monacharum,*" *JECS* 22, no. 1 (2014): 79–111, at 101n72.

142. Galen, *Art* 7–16. See also Aristotle's argument that lions with curly hair are not as brave as those with "good hair"; Aristotle, *Hist. An.* 8 (9).35 (635a). As Helen King, *The One Sex Body on Trial: The Classical and Early Modern Evidence* (New York: Ashgate, 2013), 218, argues, the gendered valence of hair in the medical authors often has to do with whether men are being compared with women (men are very hairy) or animals (men are not as hairy).

143. Troy W. Martin, "Paul's Argument from Nature," 77.

144. Hippocratic Corpus, *Genit.* 1; Aristotle, *Probl.* 893b.10–17; *Gen. An.* 783b.38–784a.4; Martin, "Paul's Argument from Nature," 78.

145. Hippocratic Corpus, *Nat. Ch.* 20; Martin, "Paul's Argument from Nature," 78; Helen King, "Between Male and Female in Ancient Medicine," in *Bodies in Transition: Dissolving the Boundaries of Embodied Knowledge,* ed. Dietrich Boschung, Alan Shapiro, and Frank Waschek (Paderborn: Wilhelm Fink, 2015), 249–64, at 251.

146. Martin, "Paul's Argument from Nature," 79; Hippocratic Corpus, *Glands* 4; Aristotle, *Gen. An.* 739a.37–b.20.

147. King, "Between Male and Female," 259–61.

148. I am grateful to Adam Booth for these references.

149. This is a different view of angels than the one we find in Tertullian, *Veil Vir.* 10, who argues that the celibacy of male asceticism places one in an "angelic state."

150. Taylor Petrey, *Resurrecting Parts: Early Christians on Desire, Reproduction, and Sexual Difference* (New York: Routledge, 2016), 106.

151. Sexual immodesty was punished in a variety of ancient contexts via depilation. See Saul Lieberman, "Shaving of the Hair and Uncovering of the Face among Jewish Women," appendix to "On Sins and Their Punishments," in *Texts and Studies* (New York: KTAV, 1974), 52–54; Aristophanes, *Clouds* 1083.

152. For hanging adulterers by genitals, see Aelius Theon, *Exerc.* 99.2; Lucian, *True Story* 2.25–26; Himmelfarb, *Tours of Hell,* 84–92; István Czachesz, "The Grotesque Body in the Apocalypse of Peter," in *The Apocalypse of Peter,* ed. Jan N. Bremmer and Istvan Czachesz (Leuven: Peeters, 2003), 108–10.

153. Himmelfarb, *Tours of Hell,* 132n13.

154. Judith Lynn Sebesta, "Tunica Ralla, Tunica Spissa: The Colors and Textiles of Roman Costume," in *The World of Roman Costume,* ed. Judith Lynn Sebesta and Larissa Bonfante (Madison: University of Wisconsin Press, 1994), 65–100; Kelly Olson, *Dress and the Roman Woman: Self-Presentation and Society* (New York: Routledge, 2008), 41–42.

155. Within the rainbow women were expected to choose particular colors according to class, with yellow-green and cherry red being reserved as colors for low-class women. Olson, *Dress and the Roman Woman,* 12.

156. Martial, *Epig.* 2.39; 6.64.4; 10.52; Juvenal, *Sat.* 2.68–70; Nonius, 653L; Cicero, *Phil. Or.* 2.44. See also the scholia on Horace by Porphyrio and pseudo-

Acronis: Porph. schol. Horace, *Sat.* 1.2.63; Acro schol. Hor. 1.2.63. As Olson, *Dress and the Roman Woman*, 48–49, argues, the distinction between adulteress and whore is frequently elided in these passages, perhaps because they are the same in the minds of the authors.

157. Olson, *Dress and the Roman Woman*, 50. On the significance of the toga for signaling gender, status, and ethnicity, see Mary Harlow, "Clothes Maketh the Man: Power Dressing and Masculinity in the Later Roman World," in *Gender in the Early Medieval World: East and West 300–900*, ed. Leslie Brubaker and Julia M. H. Smith (Cambridge: Cambridge University Press, 2004), 44–69.

158. Olson, *Dress and the Roman Woman*, 50. See also Ernst Benz, "Color in Christian Visionary Experience," in *Color Symbolism: Six Excerpts from the Eranos Yearbook, 1972*, ed. Adolf Portmann et al. (Dallas: Spring, 1994), 81–127.

159. Judith Hauptman, *Rereading the Rabbis: A Woman's Voice* (Boulder, CO: Westview Press, 1998), 15–18; Ishay Rosen-Zvi, *The Mishnaic Sotah Ritual: Temple, Gender, and Midrash*, trans. Orr Scharf (Leiden: Brill, 2012; originally published in Hebrew as *The Rite That Was Not*, 2008); Naftali S. Cohn, "What to Wear: Women's Adornment and Judean Identity in the Third Century Mishnah," in Upson-Saia, Daniel-Hughes, and Batten, *Dressing Judeans and Christians in Antiquity*, 21–36.

160. Mishnah Sotah 1:6, trans. in Cohn, "What to Wear," 30. See also Tosefta Sotah 3:2–5.

161. This is contrasted in the Apoc. Pet. 12, where those who behave hypocritically are misleadingly dressed in white, a color that was used to signal moral purity. In hell they mislead with their appearance, just as they did on earth. For instance, in the *Digest* of M. Antistius Labeo, sartorial distinction appears to be the ideal that is not always achieved, leading to inappropriately dressed matrons being pestered by men. See Olson, *Dress and the Roman Woman*, 51; Kelly Olsen, "Matrona and Whore: Clothing and Definition in Roman Antiquity," in *Prostitutes and Courtesans in the Ancient World*, ed. Christopher A. Faraone and Laura K. McClure (Madison: University of Wisconsin Press, 2006), 186–204, at 198–99. For discussion of this "problem" among early Christian authors, see Tertullian, *Pall.* 4.9; *Shows* 25; *App. Wom.* 2.12.3; Clement of Alexandria, *Educ.* 2.11–13; 3.1–2; and an excellent discussion of this concern in Tertullian in Carly Daniel-Hughes, *The Salvation of the Flesh in Tertullian of Carthage: Dressing for the Resurrection* (New York: Palgrave Macmillan, 2011).

162. Hillner, *Prison, Punishment and Penance*, 338; Julia Hillner, "Monastic Imprisonment in Justinian's Novels," *JECS* 15, no. 2 (2007): 205–37. The Miaphysites rejected Justin II's Henotikon of 571, ending the peace between the Miaphysites and the Chalcedonians, and beginning a persecution that lasted until 577.

163. While the text does not specify, the faces of the adulterers could have become black from soot after dwelling in the fiery pit.

164. On the way that blackness in antiquity is an index for Roman ethnocentrism and boundary policing, see Lloyd A. Thompson, *Romans and Blacks*,

Oklahoma Series in Classical Culture 2 (Norman: University of Oklahoma Press, 1989).

165. Eric Barreto, *Ethnic Negotiations: The Function of Race and Ethnicity in Acts 16* (Tübingen: Mohr Siebeck, 2010), 23. See also Vincent Wimbush, "Ascetic Behavior and Color-ful Language: Stories about Ethiopian Moses," *Semeia* 58 (1992): 81–92; Gay Byron, *Symbolic Blackness and Ethnic Difference in Early Christian Literature* (New York: Routledge, 2002); Denise Kimber Buell, *Why This New Race? Ethnic Reasoning in Early Christianity* (New York: Columbia University Press, 2005). I use *race* as a term here, acknowledging that ancient thinkers did not think about race in the same way that we do in the contemporary world. As Buell, *Why This New Race*, 20–21, has cautioned, however, I also acknowledge that our contemporary understanding of race is indebted to history, and thus, I think it is imperative to think about race in antiquity.

166. Byron, *Symbolic Blackness*, 24–25, 77, argues that vituperative rhetoric about Ethiopians was "ethno-political" in nature, and had become a useful pedagogical tool for instructing monks in their cultivation of discipline and self-control. For previous discussions about Egyptians and Ethiopians in antiquity, see Alan Cameron, *Callimachus and His Critics* (Princeton, NJ: Princeton University Press, 1995), 233–36; Jan den Boeft et al., *Philological and Historical Commentary on Ammianus Marcellinus XXII* (Groningen: Egbert Forsten, 1995), 310; Susan Walker and Morris Bierbrier, *Ancient Faces: Mummy Portraits from Roman Egypt* (London: British Museum, 1997). On blackness and the demonic in early Christianity: Loyd A. Thompson, *Romans and Blacks* (London: University of Oklahoma Press, 1989), 110–13; Peter Frost, "Attitudes towards Blacks in the Early Christian Era," *Second Century* 8 (1991): 1–11; Jean-Jacques Aubert, "Du Noir et noir et blanc. Éloge de la dispersion," *Museum Helveticum* 56 (1999): 159–82; David Brakke, "Ethiopian Demons: Male Sexuality, the Black Skinned Other, and the Monastic Self," *Journal of the History of Sexuality* 10, nos. 3–4 (2001): 501–35; Peter Habermehl, *Perpetua und der Ägypter oder Bilder des Bösen im frühen afrikanischen Christentum* (Berlin: De Gruyter, 2004), 161–77; Paul André Jacob, "Le Noir, l'Éthiopien, l'Égyptien dans la littérature chrétienne des premièrs siècles, " *Studia Monastica* 49 (2007): 7–28; Jan N. Bremmer, *Maidens, Magic and Martyrs in Early Christianity* (Tübingen: Mohr Siebeck, 2017), 139, 230, 302, 382.

167. Brakke, "Ethiopian Demons," 503.

168. Frank, *The Memory of the Eyes*, 161.

169. AP Paul the Simple 1 (PG 65:381–84), trans. Benedicta Ward, *The Sayings of the Desert Fathers: The Alphabetical Collection*, rev. ed. (Kalamazoo, MI: Liturgical, 1984), 205–6, cited in Brakke, "Ethiopian Demons," 516.

170. Thompson, *Romans and Blacks*, 104–9; John Clarke, *Looking at Lovemaking: Constructions of Sexuality in Roman Art 100 B.C.–A.D. 250* (Berkeley: University of California Press, 1998), 119–42. These jokes persisted even though an-

cient medical theories allowed for the possibility that a woman could control the color of her child's skin with her thoughts at the time of conception. According to the ancient medical theory of ideoplasty, the physical appearance of a woman's offspring could be determined by what she thought about during conception, so black faces could also be the result of a mother who was thinking about another man during conception. See, for instance, Heliodorus, *Aeth.* 4.119, in which a dark-skinned Egyptian queen gives birth to a pale baby because she was looking at a picture of pale-skinned Andromeda during conception. See also Soranus, *Gyn.* 1.39; Galen, *Hist. Phil.* 116; *Ther.* (in vol. 14) 253–54; Dionysius Halicarnassensis, *Imit.* 17, 18; Pliny the Elder, *Nat. Hist.* 7.12; Aëtius, *Philos.* 5.12.3; James Wilberding, "Porphyry and Plotinus on the Seed," *Phronesis* 53 (2008): 406–32.

171. Brakke, "Ethiopian Demons," 513.
172. Brakke, "Ethiopian Demons," 533.
173. Athanasius, *Life Ant.* 6.1–3 (SC 400:146–48).
174. Matthew Kuefler, *The Manly Eunuch: Masculinity, Gender Ambiguity, and Christian Ideology in Late Antiquity* (Chicago: University of Chicago Press, 2001); De Wet, *Preaching Bondage.*
175. Candida R. Moss, "Mark and Matthew," in *The Bible and Disability: A Commentary*, ed. Sarah H. Melcher, Mikeal C. Parsons, and Amos Yong (Waco, TX: Baylor University Press, 2017), 275–76, 299–300.
176. Meghan Henning, "Metaphorical, Punitive, and Pedagogical Blindness in Hell," *Studia Patristica* 80, no. 3 (2017): 148–51.
177. Rosemarie Garland-Thomson, *Extraordinary Bodies: Figuring Physical Disability in American Culture and Literature* (New York: Columbia University Press, 1997), 41, has argued that "the disabled figure in cultural discourse assures the rest of the citizenry of who they are not while arousing their suspicions about who they could become."
178. As Garland-Thomson, *Extraordinary Bodies*, 66, has argued, "the freak's body mocked the boundaries and similarities that a well-ordered democratic society required to avoid anarchy and create national unity. By exoticizing and trivializing bodies that were physically nonconformist, the freak show symbolically contained the potential threat that difference among the polity might erupt as anarchy."
179. Michel Foucault talks about disability in antiquity as having a relatively positive connotation, pointing to the "heroization" of some prominent disabled figures. This enables Foucault, and those who follow him on this score, to depict bodily normativity as a thoroughly modern phenomenon. Foucault, *Madness and Civilization: A History of Insanity in the Age of Reason*, trans. Richard Howard (New York: Pantheon, 1965), 38, 48; Foucault, *Discipline and Punish: The Birth of the Prison*, trans. Alan Sheridan (New York: Vintage, 1979), 184, 192–93; Foucault, *Power/Knowledge: Selected Interviews and Other Writings, 1972–1977*, ed.

and trans. Colin Gordon (New York: Pantheon, 1980), 166; Garland-Thomson, *Extraordinary Bodies*, 39–41; Harlan Hahn, "Can Disability Be Beautiful?" *Social Policy* (1988): 26–31, at 31.

180. This is distinct from the role of the disabled body in modernity, as Garland-Thomson, *Extraordinary Bodies*, 44, demonstrates: the modern disabled body is "extraordinary," and "able to inspire with its irreverent individuality and to threaten with its violation of equality."

181. Moss, *Divine Bodies*, 59.

182. Moss, *Divine Bodies*, 61.

183. Peter Brown, "Bodies and Minds: Sexuality and Renunciation in Early Christianity," in Halperin et al., *Before Sexuality*, 479–94, has argued that by the end of the fourth century gender and sexuality had become "fixed" for early Christians. In the apocalyptic visions of hell, however, this does not hold true at all. Hell proves to be a space in which gender play was still possible, if only as a "strategy of containment," to terrify earthly bodies into more rigid conformity.

184. Theodosian Code 9.24.1.1, cited in Penniman, *Raised on Christian Milk*, 30n27; Hillner, *Prison, Punishment and Penance*, 338; Hillner, "Monastic Imprisonment," 205–37.

Chapter 4. From Passive to Active

1. Unless otherwise noted, citations from the Book of Mary's Repose are from the Ethiopic *Liber Requiei*, and English translations are from Stephen J. Shoemaker, *Ancient Traditions of the Virgin Mary's Dormition and Assumption*, Oxford Early Christian Studies (Oxford: Oxford University Press, 2002), 290–350. Ethiopic text in Victor Arras, ed., *De Transitu Mariae Aethiopice*, 2 vols., CSCO 342–43 (Louvain: Secrétariat du Corpus SCO, 1973). For a discussion of the later Ethiopic manuscript tradition as the more reliable witness to the Greek original, see Stephen J. Shoemaker, *Mary in Early Christian Faith and Devotion* (New Haven: Yale University Press, 2016), 101–3. Shoemaker's translation uses the word "master," which invokes the kyriarchy and discourse of ancient slavery. I reproduce his translations here without editing them, in order to reflect the host of images of domination that these texts drew upon. At the same time I wish to note that this language and imagery is part of the complex of punitive violence that these texts replicate when they are imported to our contemporary world.

2. Enrico Norelli, *Marie des apocryphes. Enquête sur la mère de Jésus dans le christianisme antique*, Christianismes antiques (Geneva: Labor et Fides, 2009), 132–36.

3. Richard Bauckham, *The Fate of the Dead: Studies on Jewish and Christian Apocalypses*, Supplements to Novum Testamentum 93 (Leiden: Brill, 1998), 332–62; Norelli, *Marie des apocryphes*, 115, 134; Shoemaker, *Mary in Early Christian Faith*, 133–34.

4. Hans von Campenhausen, *The Virgin Birth in the Theology of the Ancient Church*, trans. Frank Clark, Studies in Historical Theology 2 (London: SCM Press, 1964); Averil Cameron, "The Early Cult of the Virgin," in *Mother of God: Representations of the Virgin in Byzantine Art*, ed. Maria Vassilaki (Milan: Skira, 2000), 3–15; Averil Cameron, "The Cult of the Virgin in Late Antiquity," in *The Church and Mary*, ed. Robert N. Swanson, Studies in Church History 39 (Woodbridge, UK: Boydell and Brewer, 2004), 121. In contrast, Kate Cooper and Stephen Shoemaker argue that Marian devotion predates the Council of Ephesus: Kate Cooper, "Contesting the Nativity: Wives, Virgins, and Pulcheria's *Imitatio Mariae*," *Scottish Journal of Religious Studies* 19 (1998): 31–43; Cooper, "Empress and *Theotokos*: Gender and Patronage in the Christological Controversy," in Swanson, *The Church and Mary*, 39–51; Stephen J. Shoemaker, "The Ancient Dormition Apocrypha and the Origins of Marian Piety: Early Evidence of Marian Intercession from Late Ancient Palestine," in *Presbeia Theotokou: The Intercessory Role of Mary across Times and Places in Byzantium (4th–9th century)*, ed. Leena Mari Peltomaa, Pauline Allen, and Andreas Külzer (Vienna: Austrian Academy of Sciences, 2015), 25–44, at 40–41.

5. The Six Books Apocryphon was used liturgically as early as the middle of the fourth century, and the Book of Mary's Repose was revised to make it suitable for worship in the early Byzantine period (via translation but also by redacting heterodox elements of the story). The Book of Mary's Repose was edited into texts that still bore striking similarities to the Ethiopic and Greek texts that survive today, suggesting that these editors were attempting to be faithful to the text of the Book of Mary's Repose that they had received while also making it theologically acceptable for their contexts. See Stephen J. Shoemaker, "From Mother of Mysteries to Mother of the Church: The Institutionalization of the Dormition Apocrypha," *Apocrypha* 22 (2011): 11–47, at 28–39. The Six Books Apocryphon contains detailed liturgical instructions for three annual commemorations of Mary, commemorations that Stephen J. Shoemaker and Ally Kateusz argue are strikingly similar to those rituals of the Kollyridians that Epiphanius critiques in the 370s. For discussion of this evidence, as well as the homilies and liturgical manuals that document the feast of the Memory of Mary, see Stephen J. Shoemaker, "The Cult of the Virgin in the Fourth Century: A Fresh Look at Some Old and New Sources," in *Origins of the Cult of the Virgin Mary*, ed. Chris Maunder (London: Continuum, 2008), 74–79; Shoemaker, "Apocrypha and Liturgy in the Fourth Century: The Case of the 'Six Books' Dormition Apocryphon," in *Jewish and Christian Scriptures: The Function of "Canonical" and "Non-canonical" Religious Texts*, ed. James H. Charlesworth and Lee Martin McDonald (London: T. and T. Clark, 2010), 153–63; Ally Kateusz, "Collyridian Deja Vu: The Trajectory of Redaction of the Markers of Mary's Liturgical Leadership," *Journal of Feminist Studies in Religion* 29, no. 2 (Fall 2013): 75–92, 85–89. These texts are still incorporated in

today's Orthodox liturgy, and I thank Silviu Bunta for drawing my attention to this fact.

6. See the foundational discussion for understanding the textual diversity and its implications in Jane Ralls Baun, *Tales from Another Byzantium: Celestial Journey and Local Community in the Medieval Greek Apocrypha* (Cambridge: Cambridge University Press, 2007), 35–38, regarding the way in which modern philology's desire for a stable text has warped and marginalized the study of this text.

7. Gk. Apoc. Mary 3–4, 15–20. In the Greek Apocalypse of Mary, these punishments may reflect the way that holiness functions to counterbalance hierarchy, which is still a theme today in eastern Christian thought. See Alexander Golitzin, "Hierarchy versus Anarchy? Dionysius Areopagita, Symeon the New Theologian, Nicetas Stethatos, and Their Common Roots in the Ascetical Tradition," *St. Vladimir's Theological Quarterly* 38 (1994): 131–79; Golitzin, *St. Symeon the New Theologian on the Mystical Life: The Ethical Discourses*, vol. 3, *Life, Time and Theology* (Crestwood, NY: SVS, 1997), 38–53. I thank Silviu Bunta for directing me to this tension and these references.

8. Bauckham, *The Fate of the Dead*, 339, argues that it follows the Apocalypse of Paul so closely that "it could be regarded as in effect the Ethiopic version of that text [the Apocalypse of Paul]."

9. Himmelfarb, *Tours of Hell*, 19–24, 171.

10. While this medieval text represents one of the most elaborate retellings of the descent of the Redeemer tradition, it is not the earliest. The text itself was likely written in the fifth or sixth century, and the manuscripts themselves date from the fourteenth century and later. Although Bart D. Ehrman and Zlatko Pleše, *The Apocryphal Gospels: Texts and Translations* (Oxford: Oxford University Press, 2011), 466, state that the Gospel of Nicodemus B is "the earliest surviving record of these stories," it is probably more accurate to say that it is one of the most elaborate of these stories. Plenty of earlier *descensus* traditions exist, particularly if one abandons the old scholarly tendencies to keep conversations about the apocrypha separate from other types of literature or to distinguish sharply between different genres of source material (excluding the tours of hell, or separating them from other early traditions about the *descensus*).

11. Matthew 27 describes the resurrection of the dead saints, who emerge from their tombs after the death of Jesus. Although this text does not mention Hades at all, its imagery of the victory over death is often cited as a source for later reflections on the descent to hell. J. A. MacCulloch, *The Harrowing of Hell* (Edinburgh: T. and T. Clark, 1930), 65–66, 288–99; Ulrich Luz, *Matthew 21–28*, Hermeneia (Minneapolis: Fortress, 2005), 564. Luz cites several third- and fourth-century interpretations of this passage, but concludes that "only secondarily and occasionally was our text associated with the creedal article about Christ's descent into hell. Our passage never served as the exegetical limitation for it. That speaks decidedly against the idea that behind Matt 27:52–53 there is

already a Christian tradition of Jesus's descent into hell." As Adele Reinhartz, *Word in the World: The Cosmological Tale in the Fourth Gospel* (Atlanta: Scholars Press, 1992), 105–31, has argued, John 10 may allude to the descent tradition, a tradition that she contends was already well developed enough to be alluded to in these texts. While Eph 4 may speak of the descent of Jesus to hell "into the lower parts of the earth," others have read the passage as a reference to a descent from heaven to earth. W. Hall Harris III, *The Descent of Christ: Ephesians 4:7–11 and Traditional Hebrew Imagery* (Leiden: Brill, 1996), 192–97, argues that the descent in this passage is influenced by traditions about Moses's descent from Sinai, and thus refers to the descent of Christ to earth (in the form of the Spirit at Pentecost), to "distribute gifts (or gifted individuals) to his church" (197). In 1 Peter 3 and 4, the reader is left to wonder whether Christ descends before or after the resurrection, and to whom he preaches (who are these "spirits in prison" and "the dead"—angels? saints? those who heard the gospel and have already died?). See William J. Dalton, *Christ's Proclamation to the Spirits: A Study of 1 Peter 3:18–4:6*, 2d ed. (Rome: Editrice Pontificio Istituto Biblico, 1989); Paul J. Achtemeier, *1 Peter*, Hermeneia (Minneapolis: Fortress, 1996), 253–63. Scholars now widely accept that this passage does not refer to Christ preaching in Hades after his death, but to a postresurrection address that is delivered to the rebellious angels; cf. the Enochic literature. In this reading of the passage, the content of Christ's preaching is focused not upon the salvation of these "spirits in prison" but upon their condemnation. Additionally, Rom 10:6–8 is adduced as a possible antecedent, though the passage is much less frequently cited, and does not pertain directly to the "salvific activity of Jesus Christ." See Ella Laufer, *Hell's Destruction: An Exploration of Christ's Descent to the Dead* (Burlington, VT: Ashgate, 2013), 20. Other texts that have been tied to the descent of the Redeemer to hell include Matt 12:40; Acts 2:24, 27, 31; Rom 10:7; Col 1:18; Ign. *Magn.* 9.2; Polycarp, *Ep.* 1.2.

12. Bauckham, *The Fate of the Dead*, 1–48 (especially 38–44).

13. MacCulloch, *The Harrowing of Hell*. See also Bauckham, *The Fate of the Dead*, 38–44; Laufer, *Hell's Destruction*; Rémi Gounelle, *La descente du Christ aux enfers: Institutionnalisation d'une croyance*, Collection des Études Augustiniennes, Série Antiquité, 162 (Paris: Institut d'Études Augustiniennes, 2000). Gounelle's study focuses on texts from the fourth to the sixth centuries, reading data from the second and third centuries as a "theologomenon" to the institutionalization of the descent as doctrine.

14. See, for instance, Bauckham, *The Fate of the Dead*, 39–40; Martin F. Connell, "Descensus Christi ad Inferos: Christ's Descent to the Dead," *Theological Studies* 62 (2001): 262–82; Hieromonk Ilarion, *Christ the Conqueror of Hell: The Descent into Hades from an Orthodox Perspective* (Crestwood, NY: St. Vladimir's, 2009), 20–34, which summarizes the apocrypha, but does not reflect on their theological contributions.

15. See also Odes Sol. 42:15–26, in which the focus is on the Redeemer's preaching to the dead, who rush toward him and ask for mercy. Gos. Pet. 10 is another apocryphal text that refers to the *descensus*, though it also focuses on the preaching to the dead. When the cross is raised and walks out of the tomb, the elders and the centurion hear a voice from the heavens, saying, "Thou hast preached to them that sleep. And a response was heard from the cross, Yea."

16. Contra Bauckham, *The Fate of the Dead*, 38, who argues that the descent is a "natural corollary" of the death of Jesus because Hades was still understood as a neutral abode for all of the dead at the end of the first century and early second century, I contend that early Christians are already constructing a dichotomous understanding of the afterlife in the first century. Meghan Henning, *Educating Early Christians through the Rhetoric of Hell: "Weeping and Gnashing of Teeth" as Paideia in Matthew and the Early Church*, Wissenschaftliche Untersuchungen zum Neuen Testament II. 382 (Tübingen: Mohr Siebeck, 2014), 111.

17. For additional descent traditions in the apocrypha, see Gos. Pet. 40–42.

18. R. Joseph Hoffman, "Confluence in Early Christian and Gnostic Literature: The Descensus Christi ad Inferos (Acta Pilati XVII–XXVII)," *JSNT* 10 (1981): 42–60, discusses the ways in which form criticism influenced the study of the *descensus* in the twentieth century. Bauckham, *The Fate of the Dead*, 39–40, calls Ascen. Isa., Apoc. Pet., and Ode Sol. representatives of the "primitive view" that the dead left Hades with Christ at the resurrection and ascended to heaven at the ascension.

19. A. Wenger, "Foi et piété Mariales à Byzance," in *Maria. Études sur la Sainte Vierge*, ed. H. du Manoir, vol. 5 (Paris: Beauchesne, 1958), 956–63; S. Mimouni, "Les Apocalypses de la Vierge. État de la question," *Apocrypha* 4 (1993): 101–12, at 102, 109.

20. Bauckham, *The Fate of the Dead*, 338.

21. For overview and discussion, see Henning, *Educating Early Christians*, 83–107, 174–222.

22. Norbert Brox, *Der Hirt des Hermas*, Kommentar zu den apostolischen Vätern. Ergänzungreihe zum kritisch-exegetischen Kommentar über das Neue Testament, 7 (Göttingen: Vandenhoeck and Ruprecht, 1991–93), 412–35; Carolyn Osiek, *The Shepherd of Hermas*, Hermeneia (Minneapolis: Fortress Press, 1999), 237–38.

23. To be sure, the idea that something salvific or efficacious for the damned might occur in Hades has precedent in texts like Plato's *Republic* or Plutarch's *Moralia*. But this occurs as a result of the punishments themselves, not as a result of a third party's journey to the place of the dead. This is also one way the early Christian apocalypses develop the tradition of the descent—the saint or apostle descends, and not Jesus. See, for examples, Apoc. Pet., Apoc. Paul, Gk. Apoc. Ez.

24. Ign. *Magn.* 9.2. Ignatius is also drawing upon the tradition that the prophets had seen Christ in order to argue that his audience should long for Christ all the

more because they had not seen him yet. I thank Silviu Bunta for this insight into the text. English translations cited are from Bart D. Ehrman, *The Apostolic Fathers*, vol. 1 (Cambridge, MA: Harvard University Press, 2003). See also Ign. *Phld.* 5.2. MacCulloch, *Harrowing of Hell*, 132, wrongly assumes that Ignatius is citing Odes Sol. 17, based upon the assumption that parallel themes indicate literary dependence.

25. Justin Martyr, *Dial.* 72.4; Eric Francis Osborn, *Justin Martyr* (Tübingen: Mohr Siebeck, 1973), 104–6. For the critical edition of the *Dialogue with Trypho*, see Miroslav Marcovich, *Iustini Martyris: Dialogus cum Tryphone* (Berlin: De Gruyter, 1997). Translation mine. Justin's argument here is part of an overall attempt to distance himself from Trypho, as a representative of Christianity's roots in Judaism, and as such can be read as an anti-Jewish discourse. For the contours of this discourse, see Maren R. Niehoff, "A Jew for Roman Tastes: The Parting of the Ways in Justin Martyr's *Dialogue with Trypho* from a Post-Colonial Perspective," *JECS* 27, no. 4 (2019): 549–78.

26. For a discussion of the precise nature of this particular hermeneutical move in Justin, and the extent to which he believes that Christians replace Israel, see Oskar Skarsaune, *Proof from Prophecy: A Study of Justin Martyr's Proof-Text Tradition; Text-Type, Provenance, Theological Profile* (Leiden: Brill, 1987), 326–52; Denise Kimber Buell, *Why This New Race: Ethnic Reasoning in Early Christianity* (New York: Columbia University Press, 2005), 98–108; Susan Wendel, *Scriptural Interpretation and Community Self-Definition in Luke-Acts and the Writings of Justin Martyr* (Leiden: Brill, 2011), 212–14.

27. Oskar Skarsaune, "Justin and His Bible," in *Justin Martyr and His Worlds*, ed. Sara Paris and Paul Foster (Minneapolis: Fortress, 2007) 63–64, has interpreted this passage as evidence for Justin's understanding of Hebrew Bible texts as records of divine promises, explaining that "he can't imagine anything else than that these passages must have been part of the authentic text." In *Ag. Her.* 4.22.1 and 5.31.1, Irenaeus also cites passages from descent traditions that he attributes to Jeremiah and Isaiah, but that are not part of the extant text of those prophetic books.

28. In *Dial.* 138.2 Justin again cites a prophecy that does not appear in the Jewish Scriptures: "I saved thee in the deluge of Noah." Here Justin attributes the prophecy to the biblical Isaiah, and then interprets the citation through a figural reading of the Noah story. In his interpretation, Christ's postresurrection appearance to Noah is not at the center of his reading of the text, but rather the elements of the deluge, "water, faith, and wood." Thus, if Justin is reading 1 Peter 3:18–22 in *Dial.* 138.2, his interpretation "corrects" 1 Peter's understanding of the descent tradition, revising it to emphasize the salvific significance of his appearance to the righteous eight (not the "spirits in prison," as in 1 Peter), and removing any reference to the unrighteous dead. Justin, then, mentions the postresurrection appearance of Christ to Noah as a means of correcting his opponent's understanding of the deluge, but does not actually connect this appearance to any kind of "descent," or redemption of the wicked dead.

29. Irenaeus, *Ag. Her.* 4.27.2. In addition to this passage Irenaeus also briefly mentions the descent of the Redeemer in 3.20.4, 4.22.1, and 5.31.1. Critical edition in *Irénée de Lyon, Contre les hérésies*, ed. Adelin Rousseau, Livre IV. SC 100, 1–2 (Paris: Éditions du Cerf, 1965). Translation mine. MacCulloch, *Harrowing of Hell*, 288–91, and Bauckham, *The Fate of the Dead*, 41, both read this passage as an interpretation of Matt 27:52. While Irenaeus may have had this tradition in mind, there is no direct reference or allusion.

30. *Propter quos nondum Filius Dei passus erat.*

31. Irenaeus argues that Christians and the patriarchs follow the same God: "And it is for our instruction that their actions have been committed to writing, that we might know, in the first place, that our God and theirs is one, and that sins do not please Him although committed by men of renown; and in the second place that we should keep from wickedness" (*Ag. Her.* 4.27.2).

32. See *Ag. Her.* 4.27.1, where Irenaeus cites all of the sins and misdeeds of the "righteous" patriarchs. The hermeneutic here in chapter 27 is similar to the passing reference he makes to the Jeremiah apocryphon in *Ag. Her.* 4.22.1 as evidence for the universal applicability of Christ's ministry and message.

33. Here, Irenaeus may well have adapted his own understanding of the descent tradition around that of his opponents. In *Ag. Her.* 1.27.3, he reports that Marcion taught that Christ left the prophets and patriarchs in hell and saved the unrighteous of the Hebrew Bible.

34. Clement does not reflect at all on the unrighteousness that is attributed to these souls in 1 Peter 3:18–22, misreading the passage in a way that suits his theological aims. The critical edition of the Greek text is found in *Stromata I–VI: Clemens Alexandrinus II*, GCS 52, ed. Otto Stählin, Ludwig Früchtel, and U. Treu, 4th ed. (Berlin: Akademie Verlag, 1985). Translations are my own.

35. Earlier in this same chapter, Clement remarks that "it is not right that these should be condemned without a trial," also betraying a concern for justice (*Misc.* 6.6.48.4–6). Ilarion, *Christ the Conqueror*, 48, notes that in Clement's argument, hell is a place "not for retribution, but for reformation," arguing that Clement's teaching is the root of the later idea that torment has the ability to purify souls. As I have argued elsewhere, the idea that punishments could purify the soul was an element of Platonic rhetoric surrounding Hades, adapted by early Christians like Clement. See Henning, *Educating Early Christians*, 75–76, 214.

36. Clement also quotes this passage of Hermas in *Misc.* 2.357. Scholars have typically identified *Misc.* 6.6 as the first time that 1 Pet 3 is cited as a reference to the descent (Dalton, *Christ's Proclamation*, 16–17; Bauckham, *The Fate of the Dead*, 41). However, Clement does not actually "cite" 1 Pet 3 here, but rather generally refers to a scriptural tradition in which Jesus preaches to "those that perished in the flood, or rather had been chained and kept in ward and guard." While Clement may have had 1 Pet 3 in mind, he does not mention Peter and does not have the "disobedient spirits" of 1 Peter in mind as the object of Jesus's preach-

ing, but all of the "Hebrews." Instead, Clement does directly cite (giving the name of the book and a direct quotation) the Shepherd of Hermas, Matthew, and the *Kerygma Petrou*, and he quotes parts of Isaiah as "Scripture."

37. Where I have translated "by means of the peculiar nature of the soul," the Greek reads *dia tēn tēs psyxēs idiotēta*.

38. Clement reads these sources together as a harmony, a set of viable traditions about the descent, not seeing one or the other as more or less authoritative or valuable, but seeing them simply as discrete pieces of data that need to be collected and presented to tell a story about the inclusion of Gentiles.

39. Candida R. Moss, *The Other Christs: Imitating Jesus in Ancient Christian Ideologies of Martyrdom* (Oxford: Oxford University Press, 2010), 75–111.

40. Bauckham, *The Fate of the Dead*, 358–59, argues that as Christians shifted to thinking that the wicked suffered prior to the final judgment, "the intended paraenetic effect on the readers is thereby made much more vivid and effective."

41. George W. E. Nickelsburg, *1 Enoch 1: A Commentary on the Book of 1 Enoch, Chapters 1–36; 81–108* (Minneapolis: Fortress, 2001), 234–50.

42. Cf. Matt 26:24; see also Apoc. Pet. 3; Apoc. Paul 40, 42; Gk. Apoc. Ez. 1.6; 5.1–15; Gk. Apoc. Mary 11. Lat. Vis. Ez. 62 and Gk. Apoc. Ez. 1.22 also recall the idea that animals have it easier than humans when it comes to divine judgment (cf. 4 Ezra 7:65–69).

43. Cf. Rainer Fragment, which Bauckham, *The Fate of the Dead*, 145, has argued is to be preferred because the Ethiopic text appears to deliberately suppress the reference to the salvation of the damned (P.Oxy. XVII, 1924, 482 and following; M. R. James, "The Rainer Fragment of the Apocalypse of Peter," *JTS* 32 [1931]: 270–79). See also Sib. Or. II 330–39.

44. English translations are cited from O. S. Wintermute, "Apocalypse of Zephaniah," in *The Old Testament Pseudepigrapha*, ed. James H. Charlesworth, 2 vols. (Garden City, NY: Doubleday, 1983), 1:500–501. The Coptic texts and a German translation of the Apocalypse of Zephaniah are available in George Steindorff, *Die Apokalypse des Elias, eine unbekannte Apokalypse und Bruchstücke der Sophonias-Apokalypse* (Leipzig: J. C. Hinrichs, 1899), 34–65. Richard Bauckham, *The Fate of the Dead*, 132–48; 3 Bar. 16:7–8; Apoc. Pet. 3:3–4; Apoc. Paul 33, 40, 42–43; Gk. Apoc. Ez. 1:6, 21; 5:9, 14; Lat. Vis. Ez. 8a, 11, 18, 22, 33, 42, 47, 55, 57c, 61; Gk. Apoc. Mary 25–28; Eth. Apoc Vir.; and the Syriac Transitus Mariae. In the following texts the seer intercedes for the damned but does not see them in hell: Quest. Ezra A7; Apoc. Sedr. 5:7; 8:10; 16:2; Ques. Bar. 4:49.

45. MS A has "three days."

46. Eth. Apoc. Vir., in M. Chaîne, *Apocrypha de B. Maria Virgine*, CSCO: Scriptores Aethiopici: Ser I, 8 (Rome: de Luigi, 1909), 45–80, at 68; Lat. Vis. Ez. 90–91. In Gk. Apoc. Ez. 5:10 it is clear that the damned gain some respite because of Ezra's pleas, but it is unclear when or for how long. On the Sabbath rest for the damned, see I. Lévi, "Le repos sabbatique des âmes damnées," *REJ* 25 (1892): 1–13; 26 (1893): 131–35; T. Silverstein, *Visio Sancti Pauli*, Studies and Documents

4 (London: Christophers, 1935), 79–81; Jan N. Bremmer, "The Long Latin Version of the Vision of Ezra: Date, Place, and Tour of Hell," in *Figures of Ezra*, ed. Jan N. Bremmer, Veronika Hirschberger, and Tobias Nicklas (Leuven: Peeters, 2018), 162–84, at 179–80.

47. The period of rest granted to sinners is best preserved in H. Pernot, "Descente de la Vierge aux Enfers d'après les manuscrits grecs de Paris," *Revue des études grecques* 13 (1900): 233–57, at par. 25; and A. Vassiliev, *Anecdota Graeca-Byzantina* (Moscow: Imperial University Press, 1893), xxxii–xxxv, 125–34, at 132. The Coptic text of the Apocalypse of Paul, and a translation of this text, are available in E. A. W. Budge, *Miscellaneous Coptic Texts in the Dialect of Upper Egypt* (London: British Museum, 1915), 534–74, 1022–29, at 1070.

48. See the fourth recension of the Armenian Apocalypse of Paul in L. Leloir, *Écrits Apocryphes sur les Apôtres: Traduction de l'Édition Arménienne de Venise*, vol. 1, CCSA 3 (Turnhout: Brepols, 1986), 87–172, par. 35. Bauckham, *The Fate of the Dead*, 142, connects this passage to *apokatastasis*.

49. See Richard Bauckham, *The Fate of the Dead*, 147–59.

50. *Donabit enim eos, inquit, misericors Deus praecibus et intercessionibus sanctorum suorum.* For more on the tradition of the intercession for the dead, see Thomas J. Kraus, "Fürbitte für die Toten im frühen Christentum," in *Das Gebet im Neuen Testament*, ed. Hans Klein et al., WUNT 249 (Tübingen: Mohr Siebeck, 2009), 355–96. On the connection between this tradition and martyrdom literature, see Jan N. Bremmer, *Maidens, Magic and Martyrs in Early Christianity* (Tübingen: Mohr Siebeck, 2017), 161, 375. See Bauckham, *The Fate of the Dead*, 146–48; Meghan Henning, review of Peter Brown, *The Ransom of the Soul: Afterlife and Wealth in Early Western Christianity*, *JAAR* 84, no. 1 (2016): 266–68.

51. At the same time, intercession in proconsular North Africa had its own particular and fraught history that may have influenced Augustine's concerns. During the "Confessors controversy" of the mid-third century, Christians who had confessed and been imprisoned were believed to have the power to absolve apostate Christians of their sins. The practice of lay intercession created a crisis of authority in North Africa that contributed to the Donatist schism (a major concern for Augustine). We should compare Augustine's concerns about intercession in the tours of hell to the positive way he compares saintly intercession in heaven, which was uncorrupted, in discussion of the earthly administration of justice (*Enarrat. 1 Ps.* 103.19 CCL 40:1491).

52. In *City of God* 21.11 Augustine also argues that people must be punished for all eternity because for certain offenses *lex talionis* is not a severe enough punishment.

53. Bauckham, *The Fate of the Dead*, 138–39.

54. Bauckham, *The Fate of the Dead*, 139–40. The idea that God is good and merciful is also used in the Six Books Apocryphon in W. Wright, "The Departure of My Lady Mary from the World," *Journal of Sacred Literature* 6 (1865): 417–48; 7 (1865): 110–60 (Syriac text and translation), at 159, in addition to the other itera-

tions of this argument that Bauckham cites. In both of these texts, however, the damned themselves make this argument, not the interceding saint or apostle.

55. Bauckham, *The Fate of the Dead*, 140–41. In addition to the texts that Bauckham adduces for each of these tropes, Mary's Rep. 94 also includes the "you cannot be more loving than God" argument.

56. Apoc. Pet. 3:3–4; 14:1; Apoc. Paul 33, 40, 42–44; Gk. Apoc. Ez. 1:6, 10, 15, 21–22; 2:23; 5:9, 14, 16, 18, 26; Lat. Vis. Ez. 8a, 11, 18, 22, 33, 42, 47, 55, 57c, 61, 62, 63; Gk. Apoc. Mary 11, 26, 28–29 (Vatican manuscript 31). See discussion of this motif in the Ezra apocalypses in Meghan Henning, "Substitutes in Hell: Schemes of Atonement in the Ezra Apocalypses," in Bremmer, Hirschberger, and Nicklas, *Figures of Ezra*, 185–204.

57. For other iterations of the divine rebuttal that the saint is not more loving than God, see 4 Ezra 5:33; 8:47; Armenian 4 Ezra 7:19; Apoc. Pet 3:6; Apoc. Paul 33, 40; cf. 4 Ezra 7:19.

58. "Mary, our queen, beseech your son to give us a little rest."

59. Bauckham, *The Fate of the Dead*, 137–38; Shoemaker, "Ancient Dormition Apocrypha and the Origins of Marian Piety," 31. The text does not contain the apocalyptic tradition of "protest" that became conventional in many of the other tours of hell.

60. Shoemaker, *Ancient Traditions of the Virgin Mary's Dormition and Assumption*, 345n160, notes in his translation that "master" here is actually a feminine form in the Ethiopic, which traditionally gets translated as "mistress" or "lady." But since those terms are gendered in English, and the Ethiopic is not intending to convey that, the word "master" is more appropriate to convey the sense of the text in English.

61. Suzanne Dixon, *The Roman Mother* (Norman: University of Oklahoma Press, 1988).

62. Kathleen Gallagher Elkins, *Mary, Mother of Martyrs: How Motherhood Became Self-Sacrifice in Early Christianity* (Cambridge, MA: Feminist Studies in Religion Press, 2017), xv–xvi.

63. Helen King, "Sacrificial Blood: The Role of the *Amnion* in Ancient Gynecology," *Helios* 13 (1987): 117–26; Lesley Ann Dean-Jones, *Women's Bodies in Classical Greek Science* (Oxford: Oxford University Press, 1994), 101, 215.

64. Candida R. Moss and Joel S. Baden, *Reconceiving Infertility: Biblical Perspectives on Procreation and Childlessness* (Princeton, NJ: Princeton University Press, 2015), 160. For an excellent overview of the ancient medical understandings of the physiology of nursing, see Dawn LaValle, "Divine Breastfeeding: Milk, Blood, and *Pneuma* in Clement of Alexandria's Paedagogus," *JLA* 8, no. 2 (2015): 322–36, at 322–27. On the relationship between pure milk and the sexual continence of wet nurses, see Bernadette J. Brooten, "Enslaved Women in Basil of Caesarea's Canonical Letters: An Intersectional Analysis," in *Doing Gender, Doing Religion*, ed. Ute Eisen, Christine Gerber, and Angela Standhartinger (Tübingen: Mohr Siebeck, 2013).

65. According to Bruce J. Malina and Richard L. Rohrbaugh, *Social Science Commentary on the Gospel of John* (Minneapolis: Augsburg Fortress, 1998), 67, Mary is prevailing upon Jesus from within their intimate social relationship as mother and son, presuming that he will "act as patron on behalf of this family." Raymond E. Brown, *The Gospel according to John* (New Haven: Yale University Press, 1966), 102, argues that what is being rejected here in Jesus's response to Mary is "a role not a person. Jesus is placing himself beyond natural family relationships even as he demanded of his disciples." This passage has had a range of interpretations, owing to theological differences over the role of Mary. Raymond E. Brown, Karl P. Donfried, Joseph A. Fitzmyer, and John Reumann, eds., *Mary in the New Testament* (Philadelphia: Fortress, 1978), 193.

66. Moss and Baden, *Reconceiving Infertility*, 164–68, at 167: "In the waning hours of Jesus's life, John recasts motherhood as potentially, if not primarily, non-biological. The disciple enters into a family, but so too does Jesus's mother, who gains the social standing and benefits of motherhood without biological ties." In the later Syriac tradition, beginning with Tatian's *Diatessaron*, Jesus also appears to Mary his mother after his resurrection (and not to Mary Magdalene, cf. John 20). Robert Murray, *Symbols of Church and Kingdom: A Study in Early Syriac Tradition* (London: Cambridge University Press, 1975), 329–35; Stephen J. Shoemaker, "Re-thinking the Gnostic Mary: Mary of Nazareth and Mary of Magdala in Early Christian Tradition," *JECS* 9, no. 4 (2001): 555–95.

67. Heiki Räisänen, *Die Mutter Jesu im Neuen Testament* (Helsinki: Suomalainenen Tiedeakatemia, 1969), 104–6, argues that Mary is both mother of Jesus and a member of the eschatological family.

68. The text of the Protevangelium of James was also translated into nine different ancient languages. Ronald F. Hock, *The Infancy Gospels of James and Thomas: Introduction, Greek Text, English Translation, and Notes* (Santa Rosa, CA: Polebridge Press, 1995), 15, offers a discussion of the encomiastic function of this work, arguing against the scholarly tendency to read it as an apologetic text. See Lily C. Vuong, *The Protevangelium of James* (Eugene, OR: Cascade, 2019), 1–4, for a discussion of the text, its translations, and its influence. Unless otherwise noted, English translations of the Protevangelium are cited from this translation.

69. Beverly Roberts Gaventa, *Mary: Glimpses of the Mother of Jesus* (Columbia: University of South Carolina Press, 1995), 120–22; Mary F. Foskett, *A Virgin Conceived: Mary and Classical Representations of Virginity* (Bloomington: Indiana University Press, 2002), 147, 159; Lily C. Vuong, *Gender and Purity in the Protevangelium of James* (Tübingen: Mohr Siebeck, 2013), 119–36.

70. Regarding this element of the narrative, Foskett, *A Virgin Conceived*, 149, argues, "Thus the very narrative that praises Mary perpetuates an androcentric assessment of its heroine."

71. Foskett, *A Virgin Conceived*, 159, and Eric M. Vanden Eykel, *"But Their Faces Were All Looking Up": Author and Reader in the Protevangelium of James* (London:

Bloomsbury, 2016), 146–48, also contrast Anna and Mary nursing, and argue that the difference is primarily about projecting the image of Mary's purity as virgin, and not as an image of the bodily experience of motherhood. As Jennifer A. Glancy, *Corporeal Knowledge: Early Christian Bodies* (Oxford: Oxford University Press, 2010), 114, and Vuong, *Gender and Purity*, 187, have argued, Mary's purity is so exceptional that it is even retained through childbirth.

72. Foskett, *A Virgin Conceived*, 161: "As the narrative progresses, it becomes clear that Mary's purity is more often ascribed to her than achieved by her."

73. Vernon K. Robbins, *Who Do People Say I Am? Rewriting Gospel in Emerging Christianity* (Grand Rapids, MI: Eerdmans, 2013), 157–73, demonstrates that elements of Lukan and Johannine theology are woven together in the Protevangelium of James.

74. Shoemaker, *Mary in Early Christian Faith*, 179. See Athanasius of Alexandria, *Letter to Epictetus* 4 (PG 26:1056–57); and Athanasius of Alexandria, *Letter to Maximus* 3 (PG 26:1088). Virginia Burrus, *Saving Shame: Martyrs, Saints, and Other Abject Subjects* (Philadelphia: University of Pennsylvania Press, 2008), 55, has argued that this emphasis on Mary's womb as the critical juncture of the incarnation is present in Tertullian's thinking, in which Tertullian "has thus interjected into John's gospel the vivid presence of a maternal womb, to which John himself does not, of course, refer directly."

75. Prefiguring Mary's assumption, the date palm is assumed into paradise, and Jesus interprets his actions for Mary as prefiguring his resurrection of the dead (Mary's Rep. 10). This story is more widely known through a medieval text, the Gospel of Pseudo-Matthew (Ps. Matt. 20).

76. Candida R. Moss, "Blood Ties: Martyrdom, Motherhood, and Family in the Passion of Perpetua and Felicity," in *Women and Gender in Ancient Religions: Interdisciplinary Approaches*, ed. Stephen P. Ahearne-Kroll, Paul A. Holloway, and James A. Kellhoffer (Tübingen: Mohr-Siebeck, 2010), 189–205, at 197, 198–204, argues that the theme of "the female Christian's abandonment of her family" was an ancient literary topos that served to reconfigure ancient notions of family and "focus the Christian's gaze on their obligation to Christ."

77. On gnosticism in the Book of Mary's Repose, see Shoemaker, "Mother of Mysteries," 24, who notes that this early apocryphal picture of Mary represents "a worldview seemingly having much more in common with the *Gospel of Mary* than the *Protevangelium.*"

78. Arguing with Mary, John plays the part of the disciple and father who is torn between his competing familial responsibilities to spread the gospel and care for Mary, citing Matt 28:19.

79. Eth. Apoc. Mary; E. A. W. Budge, *Legends of Our Lady the Perpetual Virgin and Her Mother Hannâ* (Oxford: Oxford University Press, 1922), 251.

80. 6 Bks. Apoc. 6 (trans. Wright, "Departure of My Lady," 160).

81. This phrase is a form of the common expression "it is better not to be born/to be dead" that we find throughout the Hebrew Bible and apocalyptic literature.

1 Kgs 19:4; Jer 15:10; 20:14; 20:17–18; Job 3:11; 10:18; Jonah 4:3; Qoh 4:2–3; Mark 14:21 and parallels; 1 En. 38:2; 2 Bar. 10:6; 2 En. 41:2; Herm. Vis. 23:6; Apoc. Pet. 3; Apoc. Paul 40, 42; Gk. Apoc. Mary 11. In the Ezra apocalypses: 4 Ezra 4:12; 7:46; 7:62; 7:116, cf. 7:69; 13:13–20; Gk. Apoc. Ez. 1:6; 1:21; 5:9; 5:14; and Apoc. Sedr. 4:2. See also discussion of this expression in M. E. Stone, *Fourth Ezra* (Minneapolis: Fortress, 1990), 86; and Henning, *Educating Early Christians*, 104, 197.

82. See also 2 En. 41:2; Apoc. Pet. 3; Apoc. Paul 40, 42; Gk. Apoc. Ez. 1.6; 5.1–15; Lat. Vis. Ez. 62.

83. Eth. Apoc. Mary, in Budge, *Legends of Our Lady Mary*, 277. In this statement pregnant women are included among women who are menstruating and women who commit fornication, reflecting a set of purity concerns that are exclusive to women's bodies.

84. Proclus of Constantinople, *Homily I: On the Holy Virgin Theotokos*; Nicholas Constas, *Proclus of Constantinople and the Cult of the Virgin in Late Antiquity: Homilies 1–5, Texts and Translations*, Supplements to Vigiliae Christianae 66 (Leiden: Brill, 2003), 128. As Shoemaker, "The Cult of the Virgin in the Fourth Century," 83, has argued, "it is almost certain that popular devotion to the Virgin must have played a central role in the Nestorian controversy and was not merely its by-product."

85. The Vatican manuscript of the Gk. Apoc. Mary 34 reads, "But now because of the supplication of my mother"; Eth. Apoc. Mary, in Budge, *Legends of Our Lady Mary*, 251.

86. Eth. Apoc. Mary, in Budge, *Legends of Our Lady Mary*, 256.

87. Eth. Apoc. Mary, in Budge, *Legends of Our Lady Mary*, 276.

88. Eth. Apoc. Mary, in Budge, *Legends of Our Lady Mary*, 278.

89. Virginia Burrus, *Saving Shame*, 74, demonstrates that Athanasius's arguments about Mary always maintain that "the Logos remains, however, uncompromised by the flesh."

90. On the distinction between Western Christian notions of "original sin" and Eastern Christian ideas about "ancestral sin," see Peter Bouteneff, "Christ and Salvation," in *The Cambridge Companion to Orthodox Christian Theology*, ed. Mary B. Cunningham and Elizabeth Theokritoff (Cambridge: Cambridge University Press, 2008), 93–106; Andrew Louth, *Introducing Eastern Orthodox Theology* (Downers Grove, IL: InterVarsity, 2013), 72–78; Andreas Andreopoulos, "Eschatology in Maximus the Confessor," in *The Oxford Handbook of Maximus the Confessor*, ed. Pauline Allen and Bronwen Neil (Oxford: Oxford University Press, 2015), 322–34. As Mary B. Cunningham, "Mary the Theotokos," in *The Orthodox Christian World*, ed. Augustine Casiday (New York: Routledge, 2012), 189–200, at 196–98, summarizes, Eastern Orthodox Christians are "reluctant to separate the Mother of God from the rest of humanity." I am extremely grateful to Jonathan Zecher for directing me to these sources.

91. Bauckham, *The Fate of the Dead,* 137.

92. While Mary is the first female apocalyptic seer in hell, the Sibyl could be seen as another female apocalyptic seer, and one who becomes popular again in late antique Christianity via the Tiburtine Sibyl. I am grateful to Tobias Nicklas for this comparison. For an excellent discussion of gender and the role of the Sibyl in Jewish apocalyptic literature, see Annette Yoshiko Reed, "Gendering Revealed Knowledge? Prophesy, Positionality, and Perspective in Ancient Jewish Apocalyptic and Related Literatures," paper presented at the tenth annual Nangeroni Meeting in Rome, June 20, 2018: http://dx.doi.org/10.17613/M6W08WG08. For a discussion of the date and provenance and a translation of the Apocalypse of Anastasia, see Baun, *Tales from Another Byzantium,* 18, 401–24.

93. Beverly Roberts Gaventa, *Mary: Glimpses of the Mother of Jesus* (Columbia: University of South Carolina Press, 1995), 49–78, at 73; Raymond Brown, *An Introduction to the New Testament* (New York: Doubleday, 1997), 229–33.

94. Joseph A. Fitzmyer, *The Gospel according to Luke,* Anchor Bible 28 (Garden City, NY: Doubleday, 1981), 341.

95. Miri Rubin, *Mother of God: A History of the Virgin Mary* (New Haven: Yale University Press, 2009), 4–33. Ephrem, confused at the command that Mary not touch the risen Jesus, explains, "Why, therefore, did he prevent Mary from touching him? Perhaps it was because he had confided her to John in his place, Woman, behold your son." Ephrem, *Comm. Diat.* 21.27. Louis Leloir, *Saint Éphrem, Commentaire de l'Évangile concordant, Texte syriaque (Manuscrit Chester Beatty 709),* Chester Beatty Monographs 8 (Dublin: Hodges Figgis and Co., 1963), 228. Translation: Carmel McCarthy, *Ephrem's Commentary on Tatian's Diatessaron* (Oxford: Oxford University Press, 1994), 331. See Shoemaker, "Re-thinking the Gnostic Mary," 561–69.

96. Michael Peppard, *The World's Oldest Church: Bible, Art, and Ritual at Dura-Europos, Syria* (New Haven: Yale University Press, 2016), 193.

97. Ephrem, *Hymn Nat.* 16 and *Hymn Chu.* 36, in Sebastian P. Brock, *Bride of Light: Hymns on Mary from the Syriac Churches,* rev. ed. (Piscataway, NJ: Gorgias, 2010), 23–33. As Brock notes in his introduction, these Syriac hymns date to the fourth century.

98. Ephrem, *Hymn Nat.* 11, in Brock, *Bride of Light,* 21–23.

99. Peppard, *The World's Oldest Church,* 155–201.

100. Peppard, *The World's Oldest Church,* 192–201.

101. Ephrem, *Hymn Nat.* 11.2: "She was Your bride too, along with all chaste souls," in Brock, *Bride of Light,* 21. Rubin, *Mother of God,* 34–36.

102. Alexander of Alexandria, *Letter to Alexandria of Thessalonica* (PG 18:517B); Athanasius, *Let. Vir.* 1.35; 2.9; 11–12, 17; Basil of Caesarea, *Let. 260, 9* (PG 32:965C–968A); *No. 208* (PG 30:477B); *No. 201* (PG 30:465A); Gregory of Nazianzus, *Or.* 45.9 (PG 36:633D); Gregory of Nyssa, *Test. Jews* 3 (PG 46:208–9); *Bir.*

Chr. (PG 46:1140D–1141A); Ambrose, *Vir.* 1.2.63; 2.2.7, 6–16; Jerome, *Ag. Hel.* (PL 23:182–306); *Let.* (PL 22:483–92); V. E. F. Harrison, "Gender, Generation, and Virginity in Cappadocian Theology," *JTS* 47 (1996): 38–68; Averil Cameron, "The Virgin in Late Antiquity," *Studies in Church History* 39 (2004): 1–21; Hilda C. Graef, *Mary: A History of Doctrine and Devotion* (Notre Dame, IN: Christian Classics, 2009), 32–78.

103. Tina Beattie, "Mary in Patristic Theology," in *Mary: The Complete Guide*, ed. Sarah Jane Boss (London: Continuum, 2007), 75–105; David G. Hunter, "Helvidius, Jovinian, and the Virginity of Mary," in *Christianity and Society: The Social World of Early Christianity*, ed. Everett Ferguson (New York: Garland, 1999), 51–61. This section is based on the excellent summary of Shoemaker, *Mary in Early Christian Faith and Devotion*, 169–74.

104. David Brakke, *Athanasius and Asceticism* (Baltimore: Johns Hopkins University Press, 1995), 52–54, 70–73, 165, 169, 254, 268, 276–79.

105. Ambrose, *Vir.* 1.2.63; 2.2.7, 6–16; Jerome, *Ag. Hel.* (PL 23:182–306); *Let.* (PL 22:483–92); Kate Cooper, *The Virgin and the Bride: Idealized Womanhood in Late Antiquity* (Cambridge, MA: Harvard University Press, 1996), 96–97.

106. Shoemaker, *Mary in Early Christian Faith and Devotion*, 171–74.

107. This letter is published in G. Morin, "Pages inédites de deux Pseudo-Jérômes des environs de l'an 400," *RBén* 40 (1928): 289–318, at 297–301, and is also cited in Virginia Burrus, "Word and Flesh: The Bodies and Sexuality of Ascetic Women in Christian Antiquity," *Journal of Feminist Studies in Religion* 10 (1994): 27–51. *Huius ergo mysterii sacramentum in decimo mense, hoc est, trecentesimo dierum numero scimus esse conpletum; ubi nobis parturientis sanctae Mariae gemitus imitandi sunt, ut velut intra occultam vulvam uteri, sic intra secretam monasterii cellulam aliquid formetur in nobis, quod proficiat ad salutem, et in decimo mense novum opus ex fructibus nostris, quod mundus miretur, appareat. Si enim illa incorrupta et sancta Maria non sine gemitibus ac suspiriis spem suae salutis effudit, qualiter nobis aestimas laborandum, quos serpentis decepere consilia, ut aliquid tale valeamus imitari? Sed forsitan dicas: Qur [sic] me vanae spei pollicitatione frustraris? Solis Christum parere virginibus licet. Nolo enim gratiam dei intra unius personae angustias claudas. Aspice enim ubi apostolus peccatoribus et praevaricatoribus dicit, donec Christus formetur in vobis. Sed momento quia sancta Maria, cum hoc opus exercuit, valde secretum locum ac solitarium requisivit: nullus ei minister, nullus comes fuisse describitur; sed et si beatus Joseph contubernium praestaret officii, tamen inter parturientis gemitus quid nisi abfuisse credatur?*

108. Meghan R. Henning, "Contested Authority in Asia Minor: Thecla and Mary as Mediators of Divine Power," in *More Than Female Disciples: An Examination of Women's Authority in Ancient Christianity (1st–6th Centuries)*, ed. R. Franchi and A. Barnes (forthcoming, expected 2021).

109. Shoemaker, "Mother of Mysteries," 21. See also Shoemaker, "Rethinking the 'Gnostic Mary,'" 589–95. Shoemaker, *Mary in Early Christian Faith and Devo-*

tion, 97, argues that Tertullian's insistence that Mary was not a disciple of Jesus in his own lifetime is a direct response to the apocryphal traditions about Mary as disciple and teacher of the other apostles.

110. 6 Bks. Apoc. 2 (trans. Wright, "Departure of My Lady," 136–41).

111. 6 Bks. Apoc. 2 (trans. Wright, "Departure of My Lady," 135).

112. 6 Bks. Apoc. 2 (trans. Wright, "Departure of My Lady," 140). As Stephen J. Davis, *The Cult of Saint Thecla: A Tradition of Women's Piety in Late Antiquity* (Oxford: Oxford University Press, 2001), 117, has observed, the orans pose symbolized the "prayer and intercession of the deceased," and in particular Mary and Thecla are depicted in this pose throughout Asia Minor in late antiquity. Shoemaker, *Mary in Early Christian Faith and Devotion*, 196–98.

113. 6 Bks. Apoc. 4 (trans. Wright, "Departure of My Lady," 151). See Kateusz, "Collyridian Deja Vu," 76–81, for an excellent discussion of the way that the markers of Mary's ministry and liturgical leadership (the retinue of female followers, prayer leadership in orans pose) were redacted over time.

114. 6 Bks. Apoc. 3 (trans. Wright, "Departure of My Lady," 141–49, 151, 156, 160).

115. Eth. Apoc. Mary, in Budge, *Legends of Our Lady Mary*, 251; elsewhere in the Ethiopic Apocalypse, Mary is revered by all of the other holy women in heaven, and the women who are in the river of milk in heaven are those women who have not had children or had sex, depicting Mary as a leader of other women, and highlighting the importance of female asceticism for this text. Budge, *Legends of Our Lady Mary*, 256 and 258.

116. From the third to eleventh centuries, deaconesses are attested in Syria, who renounced their worldly possessions in service of the church and assisted women in baptism and receiving communion in their homes. Vassa Kontouma, "Women in Orthodoxy," in Casiday, *The Orthodox Christian World*, 432–41, at 437. For discussion of Mary's intercessory role as protectress of Constantinople for people of both genders, see Cunningham, "Mary the Theotokos," 192. Her intercessory role in these particular texts is tied specifically to the increased focus on her human and motherly qualities, as argued by Baun, *Tales from Another Byzantium*.

117. Gregory of Nazianzus, *Or.* 24.9–11; English translation in Martha Vinson, *St. Gregory of Nazianzus: Select Orations*, The Fathers of the Church 107 (Washington, DC: Catholic University of America Press, 2003), 147–49. Mary also makes an appearance in a number of fourth-century martyrdom accounts in which her intercessory role is presupposed; see Acts of Acacius ("The Acts of Acacius," *Analalecta Bollandiana* 33 [1914]: 346–47) and *Martyrdom of Paese and Thekla* (Pierpont Morgan Codex M 591 T. 28 FF 49–88R), in E. A. E. Reymond and J. W. B. Barns, *Four Martyrdoms from the Pierpont Morgan Coptic Codices* (Oxford: Clarendon Press, 1973), 31–79 (text) and 151–84 (translation).

118. Gregory of Nazianzus, *Or.* 24.11.

119. Gregory of Nyssa, *Gregorii Nysseni Opera*, ed. Günter Heil and Werner Jaeger (Leiden: Brill, 1990), 10.1:16–18; Sozomen, *Eccl. Hist.* 7.5.1–3. Much of this

section is drawn from Stephen Shoemaker's excellent summary of patristic evidence for Marian intercession and apparition in Shoemaker, *Mary in Early Christian Faith and Devotion*, 174–78. See also Constas, *Proclus of Constantinople and the Cult of the Virgin*, 246. For discussion of the evidence for Marian intercession in different geographic regions in Byzantium, see Peltomaa, Allen, and Külzer, *Presbeia Theotokou*.

120. Severian of Gabala, *Hom. 6 Creat.* 10 (PG 56:498).

121. Shoemaker, *Mary in Early Christian Faith and Devotion*, 176; Brian Reynolds, *Gateway to Heaven: Marian Doctrine and Devotion, Image and Typology in the Patristic and Medieval Periods* (Hyde Park, NY: New City Press, 2012), 162–63.

122. Severian of Gabala, *Hom. Leg.* 7 (PG 56:409–10); Shoemaker, *Mary in Early Christian Faith and Devotion*, 177; Gregory of Nyssa, *Grt. Cat.* 24–26. For a discussion of what he calls the "classic theory of atonement," see Gustaf Aulén, *Christus Victor: An Historical Study of the Three Main Types of the Idea of Atonement*, trans. A. G. Hebert (New York: Macmillan, 1969). For others who perform this role, see *Martyrdom of Agape, Irene and Chione at Thessalonica* 1.1: "the invisible substance of the demons has been handed over to the flames by pure and respectable women who were full of the Holy Spirit," and discussion in Moss, *Other Christs*, 75–111.

123. Rubin, *Mother of God*, 132. See, for instance, Severus of Antioch, *Cathedral Homily* 67, who implied that Mary has unrivalled powers of intercession. Maurice Brière, ed., *Les* Homiliae cathedrales *de Sévère d'Antioche: Homélies LVIII à LXIX*, PO 37 (8.2) (Paris: Firmin-Didot, 1912), 364–65.

124. Filial piety norms applied not only to mothers and sons, but to all parents and children, and were present across ancient Greek, Roman, and Jewish cultural contexts. See Dixon, *The Roman Mother*, 176; Teresa Morgan, *Popular Morality in the Early Roman Empire* (Cambridge: Cambridge University Press, 2007), 31; Adele Reinhartz, "A Rebellious Son? Jesus and His Mother in John 2:4," in *The Opening of John's Narrative*, ed. R. Alan Culpepper and Jörg Frey (Tübingen: Mohr Siebeck, 2017), 235–49, 241–47. By the medieval period these norms were tightly interwoven into Christian practices. In a Byzantine context, there is evidence of this filial piety in the eulogy that Leo VI gave for Basil I, despite his distant relationship with his biological father. Meredith L. D. Riedel, *Leo VI and the Transformation of a Byzantine Christian Identity: Writings of an Unexpected Emperor* (Cambridge: Cambridge University Press, 2018), 151. Or, more germane to the Marian apocalypses, this filial piety is evidenced in the way that the depictions of Anne, Mary, and Jesus mirrored the upper-class urban ideals of "raising your chidren properly" that entailed the devotion and obedience of Mary and Jesus to their respective Mothers. Jennifer Welsh, *The Cult of St. Anne in Medieval and Early Modern Europe* (New York: Routledge, 2017), 36, 68–74, 83.

125. The phrase "give us a little rest" plays upon the idea that heaven is a place of rest, or an eternal Sabbath, which is rooted in images of heaven as a new Eden, or lush garden, as well as imagery of the glorified earthly Jerusalem. Ephrem the Syrian, for instance, compares heaven to resting in the branches of a tree. See *Hymn Par.* 9.5–6. See Jeffrey Burton Russell, *A History of Heaven: The Singing Silence* (Princeton, NJ: Princeton University Press, 1997), 33, 85, 116; J. Edward Wright, *The Early History of Heaven* (Oxford: Oxford University Press, 2000), 188–89.

126. Manuscript A has "three days."

127. Cf. Rainer Fragment; Tobias Nicklas, "Petrusoffenbarung, Christusoffenbarung und ihre Funktion. Autoritätskonstruktion in der Petrusapokalypse," in *Autorschaft und Autorisierungsstrategien in apokalyptischen Texten*, ed. Jörg Frey, Michael R. Jost, and Franz Tóth (Tübingen: Mohr Siebeck, 2019), 347–63.

128. Mary's tour and intercession for the damned are through Jesus in Mary's Rep., the 6 Bks. Apoc., and the Eth. Apoc. Mary. In the Gk. Apoc. Mary, Mary is led around hell by the archangel Michael, whom she calls "the commander in chief." In Mary's Rep. and the 6 Bks. Apoc., as in the Dormition narratives, Mary's intercession is depicted after her Assumption, in contrast to the other apocalyptic tours of hell in which the apostolic seer tours hell during his lifetime.

129. 6 Bks. Apoc. 3 (trans. Wright, "Departure of My Lady," 142–43). In this text, Mary becomes sick and ministers to the apostles and other people who flock to her before her death. Shoemaker, "Ancient Dormition Apocrypha and the Origins of Marian Piety," 33–37.

130. 6 Bks. Apoc. 3 (trans. Wright, "Departure of My Lady," 146–47).

131. Translation of the Apocalypse of Paul is adapted from Hugo Duensing and Aurelio de Santos Otero, "Apocalypse of Paul," in *New Testament Apocrypha*, ed. Wilhelm Schneemelcher and Edgar Hennecke, trans. R. Wilson (Louisville, KY: Westminster John Knox, 1991), 2:712–47; translation of the Greek Apocalypse of Ezra is from M. E. Stone, "Greek Apocalypse of Ezra," in Charlesworth, *The Old Testament Pseudepigrapha*, 1:561–613; translation of the Oxford manuscript of the Greek Apocalypse of Mary is from Baun, *Tales from Another Byzantium*, 391–400; translation of the Vatican manuscript of the Greek Apocalypse of Mary is from Stephen Shoemaker, "The Apocalypse of the Virgin: A New Translation and Introduction," in *New Testament Apocrypha: More Noncanonical Scriptures*, ed. Tony Burke and Brent Landau (Grand Rapids, MI: Eerdmans, 2016), 492–509.

132. See Meira Z. Kensky, *Trying Man, Trying God: The Divine Courtroom in Early Jewish and Christian Literature*, WUNT 289 (Tübingen: Mohr Siebeck, 2010), 255–92, at 259, for an excellent discussion of how the vivid depictions of the divine courtroom would impact audiences.

133. The Greek of the Oxford manuscript reads as *kolizōmai egō me tous hamartōlous Christianous*, which has been rendered differently in translation (James reads

"for the Christians," and Baun reads "with the Christians"). Here Baun's translation seems more faithful to the Greek and its context. On use of Johannine language in the Ezra apocalypses, see Henning, "Substitutes in Hell," 185–204.

134. 6 Bks. Apoc. 4 and 6 (trans. Wright, "Departure of My Lady," 151–52, 160); Gk. Apoc. Mary 26; Eth. Apoc. Mary, in Budge, *Legends of Our Lady Mary*, 277.

135. 6 Bks. Apoc. 4 (trans. Wright, "Departure of My Lady," 55–56).

136. Eth. Apoc. Mary, in Budge, *Legends of Our Lady Mary*, 276.

137. Gk. Apoc. Mary 26 (Oxford manuscript); the Vatican manuscript of Gk. Apoc. Mary 26 (29) reads: "Then the Lord said to her, 'Listen, Holy of Holies, All-Holy Virgin, if anyone calls upon your name, I will not forsake him, either in heaven or on earth.'" Henning, "Substitutes in Hell," 194–98. In Gk. Apoc. Ez. 7 and Lat. Vis. Ez. 117, recalling the name of Ezra, preserving his memory, and celebrating his feast are also tied to blessing from heaven and, in the Latin Vision of Ezra, dwelling in heaven with "the blessed mother of God Mary."

138. In fact, after the Lord proclaims the efficacy of Mary's intercession, Mary goes on to gather up all of the apostles and saints so that they can all follow her leadership in praying for mercy for the Christian sinners, saying, "Where is Moses? Where are all the prophets and fathers who have never sinned? Where are you, O holy Paul of God?" (Gk. Apoc. Mary 27, Oxford manuscript). See similar language in Gk. Apoc. Mary 30, Vatican manuscript, followed by a direct command from the *Theotokos*: "Come and let us pray for the Christian sinners, that the Lord will hear them and have mercy on them."

139. Louth, *Introducing Eastern Orthodoxy*, 70, describes how the *descensus* is an ultimate victory over hell.

Conclusion

1. Theodosian Code 1.16.7; 6.1.3; 10.10.2.

2. Candida R. Moss, *Divine Bodies: Resurrecting Perfection in the New Testament and Early Christianity* (New Haven: Yale University Press, 2019), 116.

3. Contrast with Rosemarie Garland-Thomson, *Extraordinary Bodies: Figuring Disability in American Culture and Literature* (New York: Columbia University Press, 1997), 9, who reads nineteenth- and twentieth-century narratives of disability this way: "Disabled literary characters usually remain on the margins of fiction as uncomplicated figures or exotic aliens whose bodily configurations operate as spectacles, eliciting responses from other characters or producing rhetorical effects that depend on disability's cultural resonance."

Epilogue

1. Kelly J. Baker, "Hell House," *Sacred Matters*, October 29, 2015 (https://sacred mattersmagazine .com/ hell -house/); Jeff Sharlet, "Hell House," *Lapham's Quarterly* 11, no. 1 (2009), https://www.laphamsquarterly.org/eros/hell-house.

2. Ana Diez-Sampedro, Monica Flowers, Maria Olenick, Tatayana Maltseva, and Guillermo Valdes, "Women's Choice Regarding Breastfeeding and Its Effect on Well-Being," *Nursing for Women's Health*, August 2019 (https://doi.org/10.1016/j.nwh.2019.08.002).

3. Neomi De Anda, "Miscarriage Matters, Stillbirth's Significance, and the Tree of Many Breasts," in *Parenting as Spiritual Practice and Source for Theology*, ed. Claire Bischoff, Elizabeth O'Donnell Gandolfo, and Annie Hardison-Moody (New York: Palgrave Macmillan, 2017), 173–85; Danielle Tuminio-Hansen, *Conceiving Family: A Practical Theology of Surrogacy and the Self* (Waco, TX: Baylor University Press, 2019). See Jacqueline H. Watts, *Gender, Health and Healthcare: Women's and Men's Experience of Health and Working in Healthcare Roles* (London: Routledge, 2015), 71, and 84–85, on the higher instances of mental health conditions among women, and the medicalization of pregnancy, childbirth, premenstrual syndrome, and menopause as illnesses rather than normal stages of a woman's life.

4. In October 2000 the U.S. Supreme Court heard arguments in *Ferguson v. City of Charleston*, and ruled in favor of plaintiffs on March 21, 2001, that the state had indeed violated Fourth Amendment protections. At the time, South Carolina was the only state that had a child-abuse law that could be applied to fetuses, and McKnight was the first woman convicted of murder for cocaine use during a pregnancy. Randell G. Shelden, *Our Punitive Society: Race, Class, Gender, and Punishment in America* (Long Grove, IL: Waveland, 2010), 147; Linda C. Fentiman, *Blaming Mothers: American Law and the Risks to Children's Health* (New York: New York University Press, 2017), 111–45. In 2008, the South Carolina Supreme Court ruled that McKnight did not have a fair trial, and she was released from prison.

5. Sarah Artt and Anne Schwan, "Screening Women's Imprisonment," *Television and New Media* 17, no. 6 (2016): 467–72; Suzanne M. Enck and Megan E. Morrissey, "If Orange Is the New Black, I Must Be Color Blind: Comic Framings of Post Racism in the Prison-Industrial Complex," *Critical Studies in Media Communication* 32, no. 5 (2015): 303–17.

6. Lauren J. DeCarvalho and Nicole B. Cox, "Extended 'Visiting Hours,'" *Television and New Media* 17, no. 6 (2016): 504–19.

7. Christina Belcher, "There Is No Such Thing as a Post-racial Prison," *Television and New Media* 17, no. 6 (2016): 491–503, critiques the lack of narrative framing around the death of Vee at the end of season 2: "Vee is the black dragon, slain at the season's close with no remorse" (498). Similarly, the death of Poussey at the end of season four, though critiqued by the inmates in the form of riots, still attempts to tell the story through a postracial lens, chronicling the feelings of the white guard who murdered her more closely than those of her father, and generalizing her victimization as the plight of "all bodies" through the discourses of the prison riots that ensue in season five. Cate Young, "On 'Orange

Is the New Black' and the Destruction of Black Bodies," Bitchmedia, July 14, 2016 (https://www.bitchmedia.org/article/orange-new-black-and-destruction -black-bodies). For a critique of the "accidental death" trope in the show from an intersectional lens, see Ashley Ruderman-Looff, "Looking beyond the Lesbian: The Intersectionality of Death on Netflix's *Orange Is the New Black,*" *Journal of Lesbian Studies* (2019), https://doi.org/10.1080/10894160.2019.1652084.

8. By the same token, women murdering their husbands are also punished more than men murdering their wives. "The husband had rights over his wife that resembled in many ways the rights of masters over their slaves." Shelden, *Our Punitive Society*, 131.

9. Allison McKim, *Addicted to Rehab: Race, Gender, and Drugs in the Era of Mass Incarceration* (New Brunswick, NJ: Rutgers University Press, 2017), 51; Shelden, *Our Punitive Society*, 136.

10. M. Hallett, *Private Prisons in America: A Critical Race Perspective* (Champaign: University of Illinois Press, 2005); D. A. Blackmon, *Slavery by Another Name: The Re-enslavement of Black Americans from the Civil War to World War II* (New York: Anchor, 2008).

11. Jeffery Reiman, "And the Poor Get Prison," in *Rethinking the Color Line*, ed. Charles A. Ghallager, 4th ed. (McGraw Hill, 2009), 234–45; Michelle Alexander, *The New Jim Crow: Mass Incarceration in the Age of Colorblindness* (New York: New Press, 2012); Ruth Thompson-Miller, Joe R. Feagin, and Leslie H. Picca, *Jim Crow's Legacy: The Lasting Impact of Segregation* (New York: Rowman and Littlefield, 2015), 35–68. Shelden, *Our Punitive Society*, 57, argues that jails are the modern-day equivalent of eighteenth- and nineteenth-century "poor houses." A particularly salient example is found in the 1980s: incarceration of women who tested positive for cocaine during pregnancy, fixating on low-income black women with untreated drug addictions. See Shelden, *Our Punitive Society*, 145–46; Fentiman, *Blaming Mothers*, 109–54. I am extremely grateful for conversations with Leslie H. Picca on race and incarceration, which have led me into this literature.

12. Gillian Balfour and Elizabeth Comack, *Criminalizing Women: Gender and (In)justice in Neo-Liberal Times*, 2d ed. (Blackpoint, Nova Scotia: Fernwood, 2014), 15. "Atavistically, women offenders were considered to display fewer signs of degeneration than men." For examples, see Cesare Lombroso and William Ferrero, *The Female Offender* (New York: Appleton, 1885); Sheldon Glueck and Eleanor Glueck, *Five Hundred Delinquent Women* (New York: Alfred A. Knopf, 1934). The "monstrous bodies" of women were the explanation for women's crimes in the United Kingdom, using nebulous conditions like hysteria or premenstrual syndrome (for which there are no biomedical tests) to locate the source of criminality in the "unruly" female body. Balfour and Comack, *Criminalizing Women*, 17. As recently as 1985, premenstrual syndrome (PMS) was used in British courts as a factor in homicide cases, on the grounds that female bodies were by "nature" prone to monthly "madness."

13. Kate Seear, *The Makings of a Modern Epidemic: Endometriosis, Gender and Politics* (London: Routledge, 2014), 3.

14. Seear, *The Makings of a Modern Epidemic*, 49, 143, 147; Kant Patel and Mark E. Rushefsky, *Health Care in America: Separate and Unequal* (London: Routledge, 2008), 164–67. Seear, *The Makings of a Modern Epidemic*, 67, also tells of the way in which the female body, and, in particular, the womb, emerges as a battle zone, using military metaphors for the experience of endometrial pain.

15. Watts, *Gender, Health, and Healthcare*, 39.

16. Diane E. Hoffman and Anita J. Tarzian, "The Girl Who Cried Pain: A Bias against Women in the Treatment of Pain," *Journal of Law Medicine and Ethics* 29 (2001): 13–27; Esther H. Chen, Frances S. Shofer, Anthony J. Dean, Judd E. Hollander, William G. Baxt, Jennifer L. Robey, Keara L. Sease, and Angela M. Mills, "Gender Disparity in Analgesic Treatment of Emergency Department Patients with Acute Abdominal Pain," *Academic Emergency Medicine* 15, no. 5 (2008): 414–18; Judith H. Lichtman, Erica C. Leifheit-Limson, Emi Watanabe, Norrina B. Allen, Brian Garavalia, Linda S. Garavalia, John A. Spertus, Harlan M. Krumholz, and Leslie A. Curry, "Symptom Recognition and Healthcare Experiences of Young Women with Acute Myocardial Infarction," *Circulation: Cardiovascular Quality and Outcomes* 8, no. 2 (2015): S31—S38; Eva C. Igler, Ellen K. Defenderfer, Amy C. Lang, Kathleen Bauer, Julia Uihlein, and W. Hobart Davies, "Gender Differences in the Experience of Pain Dismissal in Adolescence," *Journal of Child Healthcare* 21, no. 4 (2017): 381–91.

17. Tressie McMillan Cottom, *Thick: And Other Essays* (New York: New Press, 2019), 77–97. Despite the perception that womanhood is equivalent to sickness, women and racial minorities were actually left out of most clinical trials and observational studies for the majority of the twentieth century, with Congress finally passing a law in 1993 that required NIH-funded clinical research to include women and racial minorities. Maya Dusenbury, *The Truth about How Bad Medicine and Lazy Science Leave Women Dismissed, Misdiagnosed, and Sick* (New York: Harper Collins, 2018), 109–36, 213–50.

18. Harrison Reed, "7 Medical Terms to Ditch in 2017," NEJM Journal Watch, January 8, 2017 (https://blogs.jwatch.org/frontlines-clinical-medicine/2017/01/08/7-medical-terms-ditch-2017/). The bias that women are weaker and more emotive in the face of pain begins with childhood—participants in a recent study viewing a video of a child in pain assessed the child's pain as greater if the child was described as a boy. Brian D. Earp, Joshua T. Monrad, Marianne LaFrance, John A. Bargh, Lindsey L. Cohen, and Jennifer A. Richeson, "Gender Bias in Pediatric Pain Assessment," *Journal of Pediatric Psychology* 44, no. 4 (2019): 403–14.

19. Watts, *Gender, Health, and Healthcare*, 143.

20. Rosemarie Garland-Thomson, *Extraordinary Bodies: Figuring Disability in American Culture and Literature* (New York: Columbia University Press, 1997), 9, remarks that she is focusing on female figures in her work because "the

non-normate status accorded disability feminizes all disabled figures," and again (19) states, "Indeed the discursive equation of femaleness with disability is common, sometimes to denigrate women and sometimes to defend them." Karen Bourrier, *The Measure of Manliness: Disability and Masculinity in the Mid-Victorian Novel* (Ann Arbor: University of Michigan, 2015). The idea that disability is a threat to masculinity is so well worn that it is axiomatic for some scholars, as in Russel J. Shuttleworth, Nikki Wedgewood, and Nathan J. Wilson, "The Dilemma of Disabled Masculinity," *Men and Masculinities* 15, no. 2 (2012): 174–94.

21. Garland-Thomson, *Extraordinary Bodies*, 79–80, argues that the disabled body in modern medicine plays a similar role to the bodies in the freak shows of the nineteenth and early twentieth centuries, appearing as the sign of the "pathological" but also "prodigious" as the promise of what the wonders of medicine could accomplish. Garland-Thomson, 43, further argues that "disability's indisputably random and unpredictable character translates as appalling disorder and persistent menace in a social order predicated on self-government."

22. Charis Hill, "'The Cripples Will Save You': A Critical Coronavirus Message from a Disability Activist," March 6, 2020 (https://creakyjoints.org/living-with -arthritis/ coronavirus/ patient -perspectives/ coronavirus -disability -activism). Julia Watts Belser, "Disability and the Politics of Vulnerability," Berkley Forum, April 15, 2020 (https://berkleycenter.georgetown.edu/responses/disability-and -the-politics-of-vulnerability). Doha Madani, "Dan Patrick on Coronavirus: 'More Important Things Than Living,'" NBC News, April 21, 2020 (https:// www .nbcnews .com/ news/ us -news/ texas -lt -gov -dan -patrick -reopening -economy-more-important-things-n1188911).

23. Jana Bennett, "Disabilities in Hiding, How the Pandemic Might Shape Justice for All of Us," Berkley Forum, April 16, 2020 (https://berkleycenter.georgetown .edu/responses/disabilities-in-hiding-how-the-pandemic-might-shape-justice -for-all-of-us).

24. N'dea Yancey Bragg, "Virginia Bishop Who Preached 'God Is Larger than This Dreaded Virus' Dies of Covid 19," *USA Today*, April 14, 2020 (https:// www .usatoday.com/story/news/nation/2020/04/14/coronavirus-bishop-who-defied -social-distancing-dies-covid-19/2987693001); A. James, L. Eagle, C. Phillips, et al., "High COVID-19 Attack Rate among Attendees at Events at a Church— Arkansas, March 2020," *Morbidity and Mortality Weekly Report*, CDC, May 22, 2020, 69:632–35 (http://dx.doi.org/10.15585/mmwr.mm6920e2external icon).

25. S. Kumar, K. Piper, D. D. Galloway, J. L. Hadler, and J. J. Grefenstette, "Is Population Structure Sufficient to Generate Area-Level Inequalities in Influenza Rates? An Examination Using Agent-Based Models," *BMC Public Health* 15 (2015): 947; Max Fisher and Emma Bubola, "As Coronavirus Deepens Inequality, Inequality Worsens its Spread," *New York Times*, March 15, 2020 (https:// www .nytimes .com/ 2020/ 03/ 15/ world/ europe/ coronavirus -inequality .html);

Karin Willison, "If I Get Covid 19 It Might Be Ableism—Not the Virus—That Kills Me," Yahoo Life, March 24, 2020 (https://www.yahoo.com/lifestyle/covid -19-might-ableism-not-002309991.html).

26. Garland-Thomson, *Extraordinary Bodies*, 112, theorizes that disabled bodies continue to be read this way in the modern world: "Depoliticized and aestheticized by the authoritative critical frame of the grotesque, the disabled body is perpetually read as a sign for a degenerate soul or bankrupt universe."

Index

Vision of Ezra (Latin), citations: *8–9,*
61; *12–17,* 62–63; *15–16,* 62; *16–17,*
58, 61; *19–23,* 67; *24–32,* 94; *27,* 91;
34–36, 97; *38,* 78; *43–44,* 74; *48–49,*
78; *50,* 73, 75; *52–53,* 69, 71–72;
53–54, 69, 104; *54,* 72; *58,* 72
Vitruvius, 181n60

wedding at Cana (biblical scene), 132
weeping, 91–94, 207n26, 208n36,
209n40; efficacious, 129; in hell,
117, 150
wet nurses, 102–4, 214n92, 214n95
wet nursing, 72–73, 101–3, 132, 197n72,
200n94–200n95
widows, and abortion, 199n86
Wimbush, Vincent, 114
womb: as battle zone, 245n14; as
beginning of suffering, 136;

Mary's, 235n74; and presence of
worms, 97
women: and adultery, 56–63, 190n24;
assigned to suffering, 23–25, 131,
148, 150; as church officeholders,
78, 203n114, 239n116; and sexual
agency, 194n48. *See also* bodies,
female; Mary, Virgin; mothers;
prostitutes/prostitution; young
women
worms, 94, 96–99; intestinal, 18
worm that never dies, 96, 99, 218n123
wounds, bodily, 17–18. *See also*
disability

young women, 73–75; and chastity,
81–82; no longer virgins, 14–15, 66,
74–75, 113